ART AND DECORATION
IN ELIZABETHAN AND
JACOBEAN ENGLAND

ART AND DECORATION IN ELIZABETHAN AND JACOBEAN ENGLAND

The Influence of Continental Prints, 1558–1625

ANTHONY WELLS-COLE

Published for
THE PAUL MELLON CENTRE
FOR STUDIES IN BRITISH ART
by
YALE UNIVERSITY PRESS
NEW HAVEN & LONDON

Designed by Gillian Malpass
Printed in Singapore

Library of Congress Cataloging-in-publication Data

Wells-Cole, Anthony.
    Art and decoration in Elizabethan and Jacobean England:
the influence of continental prints, 1558–1625 / Anthony
Wells-Cole.
        p.   cm.
    Includes bibliographical references and indexes.
    ISBN 0-300-06651-1 (cloth)
    1. Decoration and ornament – England – History – 16th
century.   2. Decoration and ornament, Architectural –
England – History – 16th century.   3. Decoration and
ornament – England – Tudor style.   4. Prints. Renaissance –
Influence. I. Title.
NK1443.W45   1997
745.4'4942'09031 – dc20   96-25132
                                                                CIP

A catalogue record for this book is available from
The British Library

Frontispiece: Hardwick Hall, Derbyshire, detail of the overmantel
depicting Apollo and the Muses, made for Elizabethan
Chatsworth, *c.*1570.

For
Simon, Rosie and David

PROCIDENTES ADORAVERVNT
EVM, ET APERTIS THESAV
RIS SVIS OBTVLERVNT EI
MVNERA AVRVM THVS
ET MYRRHAM MATH 5
VERSE II

Contents

(*facing page*)   Overmantel relief depicting the Adoration of the Magi, from Clervaux Castle, see Fig. 316. Private Collection.

Preface

Prints are, I am happy to say, coming back into fashion again. This book is not about prints as such, but attempts to investigate their use as sources of inspiration. The period it covers to some extent selects itself, although no historical period is self-contained in terms of style. Prints were comparatively little used in England – judging by surviving objects – before the reign of Elizabeth I, so that a start at her accession seems reasonable; much the same range of prints continued to be used through the reign of James I, which represented, architecturally speaking, a development of what had gone before, except in court circles. Real change began in the reign of Charles I, when the availability of potential source material was so extensive (whether it was actually used or not) as to suggest that a separate study should start at that point.

In the late fifteenth and early sixteenth centuries two developments transformed the arts all over Europe: the coming of the Renaissance and the onset of the Reformation. The first brought a renewed interest in all aspects of Italy's Classical past, particularly in Classical mythology as appropriate subject matter, the second banned particular kinds of devotional imagery, replacing them with more acceptable narrative biblical subjects. In England, the Gothic style was substantially – though neither completely nor universally – replaced by the Renaissance, initially under the stimulus of Henry VIII's contacts with the French court, itself in thrall to the arts of the Renaissance in Italy. It lingered on through the reigns of Elizabeth and James I, oddly juxtaposed with decoration based on newer continental models. Amongst the identified agents of this change are the work of foreign artists lured to Henry's court, the example of imported luxury goods and the products of European printing presses. The impact of foreign artists has been much studied, of imported goods only sporadically and of prints hardly at all. Their part in the process has, it is true, been recognised for many years but no concerted attempt has been made either to quantify their influence or to identify precise instances of dependence. This book, while concentrating unashamedly on the influence of prints, does not assume

that the shift from the Gothic to the Renaissance can be explained solely by the increasing availability of prints – prints (to adapt Elizabeth Eisenstein's words)[1] are *an* agent, not *the* agent, let alone *the only* agent of change.

There are very good reasons why no introduction to the use of continental prints in Elizabethan and Jacobean England has been attempted hitherto. In the first place, while political and religious, social and biographical studies proliferate, Elizabethan and Jacobean art and architecture have for nearly a generation been somewhat unfashionable, as though the 'barbarous and ungraceful ornaments' which upset Horace Walpole so much continued to offend those brought up to admire the architectural work of Inigo Jones and the Georgian elegance of the following century. However, a flurry of conferences and new books are welcome signs that the situation is changing for the better. In the second place, references to prints in literature of the period are so few and far between that contemporary pointers are all but non-existent. Finally, the amount of printed material that emerged from the presses of sixteenth-century Europe is so extensive that no one has been foolhardy enough to try to get to grips with it.

Where does the researcher start? Ornament prints, for instance, are illustrated in modern anthologies but invariably only one or two plates are reproduced from a set which may number two or three dozen. For subject prints, *The Illustrated Bartsch* has proved invaluable but is far from comprehensive, while the Hollstein surveys of Dutch, Flemish and German prints (which are nearing completion as I write) are only now appearing as fully-illustrated volumes, with two on Heemskerck and three on de Vos published in recent years. Even then, the editors have had to take the decision not to include all prints appearing in illustrated books. There are simply too many of them: the 1532 Antwerp edition of the Bible has over two hundred woodcuts, and this is only one of numerous illustrated Bibles printed during the period. Bernard Salomon designed a similar number of prints for de Tournes's edition of Ovid's *Metamorphoses*, which was again only one of many such editions. Individual

(*facing page*) Detail of Sheldon tapestry long cushion-cover, the Annunciation, *c.*1600. The Metropolitan Museum of Art, New York. Bequest of Mary Stillman Harkness, 1950.

artists were enormously prolific: Jan Vredeman de Vries and Jacques Androuet Ducerceau each produced over five hundred designs, Virgil Solis and Jost Amman several times that tally. The Wierix family engraved almost two thousand prints, Philips Galle published over four thousand. The total number of images available even today certainly runs into hundreds of thousands, possibly millions. Who can tell how much has been lost?

Ideally, then, the researcher in England would be based somewhere like the Prints and Drawings Department of the British Museum and would devote ten years' undivided attention to the task, with an unlimited photographic budget. Having a full-time job and a young family to help look after, I have only been able to devote part of my spare time to this project. So I have been obliged to restrict my material and my ambitions. I have − not altogether reluctantly − decided to leave the influence of emblem books to others more qualified or energetic than myself. The sheer quantity of additional material that would need virtually to be committed to memory is daunting: the earliest to be composed in French, Guillaume de la Perriere's *Le Theatre des Bons Engins* of 1539, has a hundred poems and woodcuts and is amongst the briefest of such books published before 1600. It has been estimated that 'over 1,000 were published in over 2,000 printings, and no one even knows how many manuscript collections still exist'.[2] While emblem books were indisputably influential, the extent of their impact on the visual arts seems to have been markedly less than that of other types of printed image, particularly figurative and ornament prints. I also decided not to attempt to trace the sources of the many portraits which appear in decoration of the period: once again, to have included the very many collections published during the sixteenth century would have magnified the task beyond my capabilities; the same is true for costume books, of which over two hundred were published before 1600,[3] and herbals. I have also chosen to ignore specific areas of the decorative arts, such as arms and armour, and some types of ornament, such as arabesques and moresques, because they responded disappointingly to my approach.

With these main provisos, I have, however, attempted a comprehensive survey, taking into account discoveries made by others (I hope with due acknowledgement) and adding ones of my own. I am painfully aware, nevertheless, that there will be many print sources known to others and not to me; and that, despite my best efforts, more have so far eluded my searches. If I have left every area which I have covered in need of further research − whether it be the influence of engravings after a particular artist or the extent to which work in a specific medium was affected by prints − it is because the task of identifying print sources for all the arts of a period truly exceeds what one individual can do.

I can only hope that others will take up the job. It is worthwhile because, at the most superficial level, a study of the prints used by artists and craftsmen in England throws light on the cultural relations between this country and her neighbours. But it can be much more positive than that: it can help historians build up a picture of networks of patronage, reveal similarities between objects or buildings where none was suspected, illuminate a craftsman's work, indeed go some way to explain the origins of the style of a period covering three-quarters of a century. Ultimately, a knowledge of print sources can afford an insight, perhaps impossible to obtain by any other means, into the minds of people of the time.

I could not have made this start without the support of several grant bodies and the encouragement of numerous individuals. I am delighted to be able to record my gratitude to The British Academy, the Baring Foundation (for a bursary at the Victoria and Albert Museum) and to the Brigadier Hargreaves Trust for enabling me to study in libraries and print rooms in many European and Scandinavian countries; also to the Mark Fitch Fund and the Paul Mellon Foundation for generous grants towards the cost of the illustrations.

If there is one individual to whom I owe a particular debt of thanks it is to Mark Girouard: his *Robert Smythson and the Architecture of the Elizabethan Era*, which appeared in 1966 − a thrilling book about thrilling buildings − first awakened my interest in the period, and his continual encouragement has been invaluable. I have not hesitated to seek his opinion on problems of all sorts, and he has not hesitated to help. Moreover, he has kindly read the text and made numerous suggestions for its improvement. I am also most grateful to John Cornforth, Christopher Gilbert, Simon Jervis, Michael Snodin and Peter Thornton for their support and encouragement over the years.

For access to collections of prints and illustrations of buildings I am indebted to past and present staff of numerous institutions both in England and abroad: Dr (now Professor) Michael Kauffman, Susan Lambert, Anne Buddle and Moira Thunder of the Victoria and Albert Museum; Antony Griffiths, Hilary Williams and colleagues in the Print Room of the British Museum; the Librarian and staff of the Brotherton Library, University of Leeds; Dr Elizabeth McGrath and Paul Taylor at the Warburg Institute. Anna Eavis at the National Monuments Record, has been outstandingly helpful.

I have received great kindness and courtesy whilst working in continental libraries and print rooms, and special thanks are due to the following: Dr Dolk in

Leeuwarden, Dr Ger Luijten and Mrs Drs Irene de Groot and the staff in the Rijksprentenkabinet in Amsterdam; Dr Francine de Nave, Carl Depauw and Monique Morbé at the Stedelijk Prentenkabinet in Antwerp; Dr Marianne Fischer at the Kunstbibliothek and the late Dr Hans Mielke, at the Preussicher Kulturbesitz in Berlin; Dr Ingrid Molander at the Kungliga Biblioteket in Stockholm. Elisabet and Ove Hidemark made it possible for me to work in the beautiful library at Skokloster Slott, between Stockholm and Uppsala, and provided idyllic accommodation as well; and all the staff of the Nationalmuseum there were both welcoming and helpful. More recently, Manfred Sellink in Rotterdam has helped with information about Philips Galle.

Continental prints of the second half of the sixteenth century are now being studied more energetically than ever before, partly as a result of the renewed interest in religious and ethical subject-matter aroused by the Rijksmuseum exhibitions devoted to *Art before the Iconoclasm* (1986) and the *Dawn of the Golden Age* (1993). One of the pioneers in this field is Professor Ilja Veldman, now of the Vrij Universiteit in Amsterdam, and I am most grateful to her for reading parts of the manuscript and making numerous helpful comments. I have benefited greatly from discussions with Christiaan Schuckman (who has also given me much practical assistance) and with Margaret Aston: I have relied heavily on her many publications and have found her book *The King's Bedpost* an irresistible *tour de force*. Had I met these three scholars at the outset of my investigations, this book would have been very different and significantly better.

I have also consulted leading experts in subjects other than prints, including Nicolas Barker, who kindly read the whole text at galley stage, David Bostwick, Tom Campbell (whilst at the Tapestry Research Archive established and maintained by S. Franses in London), Claire Gapper, Wendy Hefford, Santina Levey and Margaret Swain; I have not always followed their advice, and the responsibility for any errors is naturally entirely mine. In these days, when Britons are learning to become good Europeans, it is embarrassing to have had to rely on translations from German and Dutch by Gisela Lazar in Munich and Leslie Hamel in Stuttgart. I also owe an immense debt of gratitude to Chita Clarke and Elliot Hutton-Wilson in London who have treated me like a member of the family over many years; and to numerous individuals for access to buildings, practical assistance, encouragement or hospitality including Geoffrey Beard, Helen Bower, Jane Clark, Susan Cunliffe-Lister, Alice Dugdale, Brian Kingham, Sarah Medlam, Simon Murray, Rebecca Palmer, Anneke Tjan-Bakker, Professor and Mrs John Wilson (who,

alas, did not live to see the book in print) and, not least, my parents.

I would like to express warm thanks to Celia Jones, who had the unenviable task of copy-editing my typescript; to John Nicoll of Yale University Press; to Gillian Malpass who has converted my text and illustrations into a design of great elegance, and to Laura Church for invaluable help.

My greatest debt, however, is to my wife, Priscilla. Although she has enjoyed some of the research fieldwork, she has also had to endure many lonely hours while I was occupied in another part of the hive. My children unknowingly have spurred me on to write this for them.

A note about authorship of prints and the structure of this book

Every print involves at least three stages, which may or may not be the responsibility of the same individual: the design, the engraving or etching, and the printing, publication and distribution. In deciding to arrange my material by designer, I cater for what is of most interest to English readers — that such and such derives from a design by Michelangelo, Bruegel or Rubens. But in terms of the availability of prints it was the publisher who was of prime importance, for it was he who researched the potential market outlets and exploited them; the fact that the publisher was often the engraver as well means that I have tried, wherever possible, to give the engraver and publisher.

As this book is concerned with sources and destinations it is divided into two parts. After an introductory chapter on continental prints and their use in England before the reign of Elizabeth I, artists and designers are discussed by nationality, beginning with Italian, German and French, before moving on to Netherlandish and concluding with English. As Netherlandish prints provided overwhelmingly the greatest influence, this section is correspondingly the longest.

Part II of the book deals with destinations — where the prints ended up — in masonry, plasterwork, woodwork and so on. This allows the range of source material, often used in combination, to register with proper force. Then follows detailed examination of the prints used in the decorative work executed for (and occasionally by) Elizabeth, Countess of Shrewsbury, at Hardwick and elsewhere.

A brief note on method may be necessary. Time and again during my research I found that writers have leapt to optimistic conclusions about the relationship between a print and a piece of decoration, so much so that sometimes I have been able to discern only the slightest resemblance between the two. I have therefore tried to confine myself to remarking on what has been described as a 'sibling relationship' between source print and destination. Occasionally it takes a while to see that the one derives from the other for certain, but details always provide the proof. This is especially true of the rare occasions in this country when an artist had the ability to select from numerous sources and re-compose them in a new arrangement. Those who have tried will know that it is always easier to appreciate the relationship between source and destination once it is pointed out than it is to discover it in the first place.

My task would have been made easier had the fully illustrated volumes in the Hollstein *Dutch and Flemish Etchings, Engravings and Woodcuts* series appeared before I started researching: the two devoted to Heemskerck appeared in 1993–4, the three on Maarten de Vos in 1995–6, just as this book was about to go to press, and two on Jan Vredeman de Vries will be published in 1997. Much to-ing and fro-ing between Yorkshire and print rooms in this country and abroad would have been obviated; but actually these volumes have so far enabled me to add just two instances of dependence on prints, though to be sure they are extremely interesting (pp.208–9).

Biblical quotations have been taken from the Geneva Bible of 1560 because this was the Bible that people would have read at home; it remained so until well after the publication in 1611 of the Authorised Version, 'appointed to be read in churches'.[4]

Finally, I have retained – some would say perversely – the historic names for English counties, in the hope that readers will more easily find their way to the relevant descriptions in Pevsner's *Buildings of England*.

Part I

SOURCES

Chapter 1

INTRODUCTION: CONTINENTAL PRINTS AND THEIR USE IN ENGLAND BEFORE THE REIGN OF ELIZABETH I

> We ought to favor the Strangers from whom we learned so great benefits . . . because we are not so good devisers as followers of others.[1]

This remark (made in 1577) aptly describes English art and architecture during the reigns of Elizabeth and James I, although the subject of the comment was actually the cloth industry. By that date England had been absorbing influences from Renaissance Europe for at least a century and, like most of northern Europe, had undergone traumatic religious change and fundamental artistic transformations. In keeping abreast of artistic developments that originated in Italy but came via Germany, France and the Netherlands, patrons in England were indeed generally obliged to follow rather than to devise. Various means were open to them: they acquired foreign works of art, though rarely; they employed continental craftsmen; and they used continental prints. Existing histories of sixteenth- and early seventeenth-century English art have rightly focused on the work of continental craftsmen in England. They were mostly far more accomplished than their native-born contemporaries, and had trained or worked with some of the greatest artists in Italy and France: Pietro Torrigiano, for example, had personal contact with no less an artist than Michelangelo, reputedly breaking the nose of the irascible genius in a brawl. The contribution of the printed page, on the other hand, though acknowledged has never begun to be properly assessed. And yet, as early as 1512 Johannes Cochlaeus, in his edition of the *Cosmographia* of Pomponius Mela published in Nuremberg, noted that 'the merchants of Italy, France and Spain are purchasing Dürer's engravings as models for the painters of their homelands'.

Printing revolutionised the spread of knowledge of all kinds. Since Elizabeth Eisenstein explored, in her remarkable book, *The Printing Press as an Agent of Change*,[2] the impact of printing on early-modern Europe no one can be unaware of the importance of this invention, whose modern equivalent is the computer. Francis Bacon was well aware of it at the time: 'We should note the force, effect, and consequences of inventions which are nowhere more conspicuous than in those three which were unknown to the ancients, namely, printing, gunpowder, and the compass. For these three have changed the appearance and state of the whole world . . .'[3]

Just one of Eisenstein's illustrations of the difference between the product of the scribal and the print cultures sufficiently highlights the vast chasm in their potential influence: 'In 1483, the Ripoli Press charged three florins per quinterno for setting up and printing Ficino's translation of Plato's *Dialogues*. A scribe might have charged one florin per quinterno for duplicating the same work. The Ripoli Press produced 1,025 copies; the scribe would have turned out one.'[4]

Frances Yates commented on the impact of printing in the following terms:

> Elizabeth Eisenstein argues that printing should not be listed with gunpowder and the compass as one of several inventions that came into use in the Renaissance. It was the one invention that made possible the whole subsequent astonishingly rapid evolution of European culture, which spread the scientific advance which fostered the rapid interchange of ideas. The print culture released the scribe from the bondage of copying. It also released memory from the heavy artificial burdens upon it. A culture which the needs for memorization renders static is replaced by a culture liberated by print to put all its powers into original thinking and advance.[5]

The power of the print medium was quickly demonstrated during the course of the greatest historical event of the sixteenth century, as A.G. Dickens has written:

> Altogether in relation to the spread of religious ideas it seems difficult to exaggerate the significance of the Press, without which a revolution of this

magnitude could scarcely have been consummated . . . for the first time in human history a great reading public judged the validity of revolutionary ideas [promoted by Martin Luther] through a mass-medium which used the vernacular languages together with the arts of the journalist and the cartoonist . . .[6]

In the same way that printing revolutionised the spread of learning and – to use a metaphor from photography – fixed the Reformation, it had the capacity for transforming style in the arts. The influence of Mediterranean countries on England of course pre-dated the invention of printing by many centuries, as Saxl and Wittkower showed.[7] Perceptible from the prehistoric period onwards, it was particularly strong during the four centuries in which Britain was dominated by Rome, diminishing naturally when the legions were recalled from Britain in AD 412. Anglo-Saxon art was influenced by the appearance of the human figure, which arrived as part of Christian art from the Mediterranean, and there was a revival of Classical learning during the reign of Alfred the Great (reigned 871–99); this was strengthened when England became a Mediterranean power in the mid-twelfth century through the marriage of Henry II to Eleanor of Aquitaine in 1152, which brought him an empire stretching from Northumbria to Toulouse. Echoes of Byzantine paintings and mosaics can be found in contemporary English art and there was, at around the same date, a short period in architecture, 'almost amounting to a classical interlude', which accounts for the antique-looking columns and capitals in Canterbury Cathedral. Direct Italian influence came during the late thirteenth century with the cosmati mosaic workers employed by Henry III in Westminster Abbey, but although there were contacts between England and Italy in the literary and scholastic fields during the following century, Italian influence was not so apparent in the visual arts. It was in the fifteenth century that humanistic script began to influence handwriting in England, but the pace and extent of continental influence in general was transformed from the mid-century by the change from a scribal culture to a print culture; a hundred years later, when Elizabeth I came to the throne of England, prints had become 'the standard medium for passing visual information and artistic themes across geographical distances'.[8]

How had they achieved such a stature? It is not necessary to delve too deeply into the early history of printmaking, for the subject has been covered exhaustively in the recent study by David Landau and Peter Parshall,[9] but a brief survey might be useful. The relief technique of woodcut and wood-engraving had been used in Europe from the late fourteenth century, while the intaglio techniques of engraving and etching date from no later than the mid-fifteenth century. Both, therefore, were in existence long before the beginning of the period covered here, and were employed primarily for the production of inexpensive devotional images. Woodcut, however, was the natural medium for book illustration for, like movable type, it was a surface technique: the ground having been cut away leaving the image to take ink on the surface, the woodblock was then combined with type in the same form, or chase, and printed. Nevertheless, the greater definition and tonal sophistication possible using the intaglio techniques of engraving and etching (in which the ink was wiped off the surface leaving only the engraved or etched lines to print) ensured that, despite the need for separate printings for the type and illustrations, woodcut was ultimately relegated to less expensive illustrated books. All three techniques will, to some extent, be relevant to this study, as will book illustration, independent prints, prints bound up into 'suites', and suites combined to form larger publications or picture books, such as the print Bibles of the later sixteenth century.

The invention of craftsmen, printmaking was, during the last quarter of the fifteenth century, taken up by artists, some entering into collaborative ventures with block-cutters, others teaching themselves the skills of engraving and etching. Either way, they stimulated a market for prints and ensured that more and more artists felt obliged to become involved in printmaking. During the first three decades of the sixteenth century, designs by one artist began to be engraved by another, leading at best to a collaboration 'in which both artist and printmaker contributed their skills to the creation of an independent work of art . . . The real birth of the "reproductive" print did not come about, however, until the relationship between painter and printmaker became so tenuous that the printmaker felt entitled to copy a work of art that the painter had made for an entirely different purpose'.[10]

By the middle of the century it was comparatively rare for an artist who was principally a painter to be an engraver as well – Pieter Bruegel, for instance, produced only one engraving – whereas sometimes a printmaker who began by collaborating with other artists subsequently began to design prints himself – as in the case of Philips Galle or the Wierix brothers. Whether the prints were the unaided product of the painter-engraver or the result of collaboration between artist and printmaker, in this exploration of the transmission of style it is the artist responsible for the original design, rather than the block-cutter or engraver, who is of prime importance.

A significant contribution was also made by the publisher. Once the woodblock or engraved plate had been printed, it had to be distributed. Until the middle of the sixteenth century, an artist generally designed the image to be printed, engraved the copper plate himself, printed it and distributed the resulting prints, acting effectively as designer, engraver and publisher. This method is clearly inefficient from many points of view: the artist was obliged to undertake the time-consuming business of engraving the copper plate himself, which limited his output, and had also to distribute the finished product, a task that was much better performed by a specialist. One of the pioneers of printing and distributing other artists' work was Willem Liefrinck – one of the block-cutters who had worked on one of the Emperor Maximilian's heroic publications, *The Triumphal Procession* (an enormous composition made up of 136 separate blocks). Returning from Augsburg, Liefrinck had settled in Antwerp by 1528, when he was admitted to the Guild of St Luke, and established a thriving business. Its connections included several printmakers whose names will figure in this book, Willem's son Hans, who specialised in woodcut portraits of the aristocracy but also printed suites of ornament, maps and a book of architecture;[11] and his son-in-law Frans Huys who engraved designs by such prominent artists as Frans Floris and Pieter Bruegel for the publisher Hieronymus Cock. By the end of the period, print production could involve not only artist, engraver, printer and publisher, but often poet and calligrapher as well. Any one of these individuals may have had the potential to tip the balance when someone came to decide whether to purchase a print or not, whether by their abilities or their philosophies.

The well-nigh industrial scale of print (and book) publication was matched by means of distribution which, by 1600, had become increasingly sophisticated, although even in the early sixteenth century the means of distribution were such that it was possible for John Yonge, a Fellow of New College, Oxford, to obtain works by Savanorola published in Paris only a month before.[12] The annual Frankfurt Fair (which continues to this day) was the major market for the book trade, enabling dealers to buy paper and sell their finished products, and dealers to buy and sell prints. As late as the second half of the seventeenth century Bishop John Cosin's London bookseller, Robert Scott, who is known to have purchased stock abroad, probably bought at the Frankfurt Fair.[13] London booksellers, trading particularly in the streets around St Paul's Churchyard and Blackfriars, had dealt in prints as well since the reign of Elizabeth and perhaps earlier, although Lord Burghley sent to Sir Thomas Smith in Paris for a copy of Philibert de L'Orme. Yet other books and prints must have been brought to this country and sold here by immigrants, like the religious prints pasted into a prayerbook at St

George's Chapel in Windsor for the use of the queen (see p.296). Still others were brought in by English and continental craftsmen for use in their workshops, where they eventually became worn out or outmoded and were discarded. A different system of distribution existed for the inexpensive single-leaf woodcuts, which reached a popular market via itinerant ballad-singers and other vagrants. The influence of these prints on the decoration of humbler homes is incalculable today when so much has been lost.

It would be virtually impossible to list all the types of prints being produced by the middle of the sixteenth century. The range was vast, from illustrations to the Bible, Classical and modern literature, scientific discoveries, through titlepages and page borders, printers' devices and emblems, to a whole range of popular printed ballads and broadsheets. There were also ornament prints, and as this book is concerned with these as well as with subject prints, a few words are needed on them here.

Ornament prints arose as a genre in response to the spread of wealth from the Church and to some extent the court to the merchant class as a result both of the Reformation and of the expansion of trade during the early sixteenth century. They were originally aimed at professional tradesmen, to assist them in the design and decoration of needlework and lace, jewellery, armour, furniture and wood-carving, ceramics and metalwork, and for what Peter Ward-Jackson called 'almost every appurtenance of civilised life'.[14] By the 1520s they were being issued as pattern-books, and in this form are very familiar during this period. They were collected by wealthy patrons – Philip II of Spain gathered more than 5,000 ornament prints and drawings for the craftsmen building and decorating the Escorial[15] – but were also used by amateurs, particularly by ladies for their embroidery.

The durability of woodblocks, and to a lesser extent of engraved or etched plates, enabled numerous impressions to be printed. Precise numbers of editions are hard to arrive at as there is so little contemporary evidence, but are likely to have been greater than has sometimes been suggested. One popular work, Clemens Perret's copy-book *Exercitatio Alphabetica* (Antwerp, 1569), achieved at least five hundred copies – and probably more – in several separate editions,[16] while a mid-sixteenth-century Fontainebleau printer is supposed to have pulled two thousand impressions from his copper plate; as late as 1754 the Antwerp publisher J.J. Moretus's printer achieved more than four thousand copies before the plates had to be retouched.[17] The geographical distribution – and consequent influence – of each design was potentially enormous.

Because pattern-books and ornament prints tended to be destroyed in use or discarded when out of fashion, their survival rate from the late sixteenth and early seventeenth centuries is not high. To take Clemens Perret's *Exercitatio Alphabetica* again, Ton van Uchelen discovered twenty-six copies in existence – six in England – from a conservative estimate of around five hundred printed, a survival rate of around five per cent. For popular woodcut illustrations the survival rate is much poorer: for broadside ballads it may be as low as one in ten thousand, that is three hundred examples out of perhaps three thousand titles, representing as many as three million copies.[18]

The size of an edition might be expected to affect the price, and price was a significant factor in determining patterns of print distribution. The wholesale price of Perret's book, which contained thirty-four calligraphic examples in strapwork frames designed by Vredeman de Vries, is known precisely, for in 1570 Plantin bought eighty copies of *Exercitatio* for 100 guilders, and in 1575 a further hundred for 75 guilders. At 20 stuivers to the guilder, the copy-book therefore cost between 15 and 25 stuivers each. Prices, currencies and coinage are a complex subject,[19] and it is impossible to translate these sums into contemporary values, although some equivalent costs are given below. The price of individual prints must anyway have varied substantially according to their nature. It has been estimated that Titian's ten-block woodcut of *The Triumph of Christ*, impressions of which were dispersed in the sale of Cornelis Bos's Antwerp workshop in 1544, might have retailed at a price equivalent only to between a third and half a day's work for a skilled workman (a mason or a carpenter) in Antwerp. Karel van Mander stated that during his lifetime folio engravings by Lucas van Leyden brought him a gold guilder apiece, while it is possible that a large and finely worked print such as Dürer's *Adam and Eve* of 1504 could have been bought for significantly less than a pair of shoes.[20] But this was a print of exceptional quality, not the kind – as will be seen – that had much influence in England. At the other end of the scale, it has been suggested that the cheapest engraved prints in Jacobean England cost around sixpence, the more expensive as much as a shilling, perhaps equivalent to £12.50 and £25 at today's prices.[21] Fine-quality continental prints of the later sixteenth century must have cost considerably more. Medium and size also affected price, woodcuts probably costing less than elaborate engravings and etchings, smaller prints fetching much less than half-sheets, which were themselves little less costly than whole sheets. Age and wear detracted from value. Suites were less expensive per print than individual prints. What is certain is that only single-sheet woodcuts of devotional subjects, which sold for a penny in Elizabethan England (perhaps £2 today), fell within the reach of the vast majority of the population:[22] the rest were undoubtedly accessible only to a wealthy minority.

Some information about the distribution of continental prints – at any rate when bound in book form – in Elizabethan and Jacobean England can be gleaned from library lists. Much useful work has been done on this subject by Lucy Gent, who searched for books on art, architecture and perspective in book lists dating between 1580 and 1630.[23] All were libraries belonging to members of the social or intellectual élite and she found references to thirty-seven different treatises, often in several different editions. In aristocratic circles at least, books were sometimes lent out, which increased their potential for influence. But book lists give only a very partial picture: many book collections existed but few lists survive, and virtually no actual books that can be identified in them; descriptions of books are terse or ambiguous; composite volumes, especially of books of prints, are common but makers of inventories gave only the titlepage of the first work: the Longleat copy of Vredeman's *Architectura* comprises no fewer than eight different publications, not all of them by Vredeman.[24] Most serious is the obvious fact that far more books and prints came into England than ever found their way into lists: no list mentions van Mander's *Schilder-Boeck*, for instance, but the volume was used by Henry Peacham. Some books that may have been used by their owners for building purposes still survive, though not necessarily in their original locations – these include Sir Thomas Tresham's (at Deene in Northamptonshire) and Sir Robert Cecil's at Hatfield – but ideally there should be contemporary lists of books at Longleat, or Wollaton or Hardwick (all houses where prints were unquestionably used) in the sixteenth century, with the volumes still standing on the shelves, as at Skokloster in Sweden.[25]

Continental prints may survive in libraries in England but very little is known about how they got there, particularly about the extent to which sixteenth-century booksellers anticipated their seventeenth-century successors in stocking and selling prints. Some prints were undoubtedly brought into England by such continental scholars as Hadrianus Junius, and by craftsmen. We know, of course, that William Cecil had to write to a friend in Paris asking him to send a copy of a recently published architectural treatise (p.38) presumably for his team of workmen to use at Burghley. But it is also clear that the leading Antwerp printer, the Touraine-born Christopher Plantin, contemplated setting up an agency in London to sell books and prints; in the event, he was content to draw up a contract in 1567 with Jean Desserans, a Huguenot refugee, offering to supply him with 'toutes sortes de livres communs et permis' from his own or any other European printing house. Plantin also dealt with Thomas Vautrollier and many more London booksellers, especially Ascanius de Renialme.[26]

The situation in the 1560s was probably not at all unlike that of the half-century from July 1660 when Samuel Pepys began to purchase prints, recording when and where he did so. 'To the Change, where I bought fine prints . . .' is the first relevant diary entry; 'and so to a picture-seller by the Half Moon in the Strand . . .' (22 February 1664). Though stimulated by collectors such as John Evelyn and Lord Peterborough, Pepys bought mainly from Thomas Jenner (engraver and bookseller), Roger Daniel (printer and bookseller), William Faithorne (limner, engraver and printseller) and John Cade (stationer), whose names recur in the diary and in correspondence.[27] Later in life Pepys deliberately cultivated learned friends, and from 1689 financed his nephew on his foreign travels, when he bought prints for his uncle. In the almost universal absence of such specific information for the 1560s, deductions will have to be made about who owned the prints used for inspiration in England, and how they acquired them.

The fact is that people rarely referred to the availability or use of continental prints in Elizabethan and Jacobean England. Henry Peacham is an exception, commenting that engravings by Dürer were hard to obtain but those by Hubert Goltzius (did he mean Hendrick?) were to be had in Popeshead Alley.[28] As to their use, here is an unknown Englishman instructing a painter: 'behynde must be a panther and a crocodyll standynge ryghte up, trewly drawn in theyre coloures as gesner descreibeth them.'[29] He is referring, of course, to Conrad Gesner (1516–65) the encyclopaedic writer on all aspects of knowledge. Archbishop Laud was accused of using 'the great Roman Missall, or Masse Book' in the restoration of glass in the chapel at Lambeth Palace.[30] Lucy Gent has said, 'There is little evidence [from literary sources] that good prints were available in England', and she added: 'This is a difficult field which has not been systematically researched; it is extremely hard to assess the circulation of engravings.'[31] Of course, it is possible that the use of prints was seldom referred to because it was so common a practice as to need no special emphasis. But it means that other methods are needed to assess their influence.

Fortunately, works of art, architecture and decoration themselves can enable us to discover something of the range of printed material circulating and in use in Elizabethan and Jacobean England, even though the actual prints that inspired them have long since disappeared (possibly in the very act of their creation). Before glancing briefly at the use of continental prints in England before the reign of Elizabeth, it may be useful to summarise the factors – many of them interrelated – that must have affected the influence of prints of one country on the arts of another. Amongst these factors are political and dynastic ties, trade relations, similarities or differences in religion, size of print production, subject matter, cost, availability.

★　　★　　★

The earliest printed publications from which borrowings were made were probably block-books in which the text and illustrations were cut in the block. These were produced mainly in the Netherlands and reached the peak of their popularity and artistic quality in the 1460s. They included the *Apocalypse*, the *Canticum canticorum* (the *Song of Songs*) and the *Ars Moriendi*; but particular favourites were the fifteenth-century picture Bible, popularly known as the *Biblia Pauperum*, and *Speculum Humanae Salvationis*, which depict the life of Christ with Old Testament prefigurations. These were aimed not, as the abbreviated title *Biblia Pauperum* seems to suggest, at illiterate lay people but, as the full title *Biblia Pauperum Praedicatorum* indicates, 'at poor preachers who had a mere smattering of Latin and found scriptural exposition easier when given picture books as guides'.[32] Their drawings have tentatively been ascribed to the atelier of Rogier van der Weyden in Brussels[33] and the woodcuts are still entirely medieval in style. The carver William Bromflet and his assistants were responsible for the choir-stalls in Ripon Cathedral between 1489 and 1494. At least four misericords, illustrating Samson Carrying off the Gates of Gaza, Jonah Cast into the Sea, Jonah Cast up by the Whale, and The Spies with the Grapes from the Promised Land, were copied from this source, the *Biblia Pauperum*, as well as from a woodcut by the monogrammist B.S.; at Manchester before 1508, the same carvers copied an engraving of the *Rabbits' Revenge* by Israhel van Meckenem, and doubtless others which have still to be identified.[34] The practice of using prints was not confined to this northern school of carvers: the chantry chapel to Thomas West, Lord La Warr, in Boxgrove Priory, Sussex, has panels copied from woodcuts in books of hours published in Paris by Simon Vostre, Thielman Kerver and others, while in Henry VII's chapel at Westminster, three misericords were copied from prints by Dürer and at least two from Israhel van Meckenen.[35]

Contemporary decorative painting displays considerable continental influence, too, mostly following the style of Flemish painters, occasionally that of the more Italianate artists, van der Weyden, Memling and David. Sometime between 1510 and 1520, an unknown painter copied two prints by Lucas van Leyden, one an undated Annunciation of *c*.1490, the other issued in 1509 depicting the Temptation of St Anthony, on the screen at Tacolneston in Norfolk.[36] In 1512 or shortly after, a group of painters copied the same artist's series of *The Twelve Apostles*, of *c*.1511, on the panels of the screen of St Mary, Worstead, in the same county, along with two designed by Martin Schongauer, probably from the versions by Israhel van Meckenem.[37]

Less than ten years later the King's Printer, Richard Pynson (who had been appointed in 1504), produced the first English titlepages in the antique – that is, the early Renaissance – style, copying them from designs by Urs Graf and Hans Holbein no more than two years after the originals had appeared: as Simon Thurley commented, 'Clearer evidence of the influence of imported foreign woodcuts on English design would be hard to find'.[38] Their influence on English titlepages continued into the reign of Elizabeth and beyond:

> It was, of course, natural enough that the earlier English border designs should be based on foreign originals, for the use of such ornamentation was already fully established on the continent at the time when the earliest English borders were attempted. Even so, it is perhaps remarkable how large a proportion of the early wood-cut borders and other ornaments were directly imitated from foreign work. The amount of borrowing is indeed so large that up to 1550 or even later one comes to expect a foreign original for every design save the very simplest, while even after that date and almost to the close of the century foreign influence is still very considerable.[39]

Artistically speaking, these titlepages are insignificant when compared with the finest work executed by Italian and French artists and sculptors who enjoyed the patronage of Henry VIII – Torrigiano, da Maiano, da Treviso and others – and yet such was the potential of printing that they might have exercised an influence in England at least comparable to that of these distinguished foreigners.

Like the printed page, stained glass is a medium readily suited to the use of continental prints, and Hilary Wayment has shown that the most prestigious glass of the early sixteenth century, in the windows of King's College Chapel in Cambridge, derives from several sources.[40] One window, depicting the Golden Table offered in the Temple of the Sun, bears a close correspondence with the plate in the *Speculum Humanae Salvationis*, and others are less closely related. Many more windows are related to the *Biblia Pauperum*: of the forty-eight that are, eleven are close to their source and nine of these are types from the Old Testament, for which alternative sources would have been hard to find. Illustrations from these two block-books were augmented by more recent engrav-

ings, chiefly by Lucas van Leyden, Albrecht Dürer and the school of Raphael, in the windows of the second phase (1526–31).[41] Dirck Vellert, to whom these later windows are attributed, tended to use individual features rather than transfer an entire composition, as less-accomplished, probably native-born, artists were inclined to do. As far as the glass in King's College Chapel is concerned, it should not be assumed

> that engravings were necessarily the most important, much less the only sources of the designs; but it may be useful to point out how the designers used their most convenient and portable sources before going on to study the more suggestive and often less tangible influences – from painting, tapestry design, drawings, illuminated manuscripts, and from other painted glass – fields in which the gaps in our knowledge are no doubt much greater.[42]

Whereas in France important classical work was under way for François I at the châteaux of Blois (1515–24) and Chambord (from 1519), and for private patrons at Bury (1511–24), Chenonceau (from 1515) and Azay-le-Rideau (1518–27), in England few major building works survive from the decade following the completion of the fabric of King's College Chapel in 1515 and of Torrigiano's tomb of Henry VII in 1518. It was probably a French carver who was responsible for the two classical capitals in Chelsea Old Church, dated 1528, which so closely resemble contemporary capitals at Chambord, and a foreigner must have made the several terracotta tombs in East Anglian churches, their concentration in Norfolk and Suffolk suggesting a Flemish origin, despite the fact that no known tombs of this kind survive in the Netherlands.[43]

As distinguished a foreign artist as Hans Holbein, who spent two periods in England totalling several years, relied on prints for his decorative paintings in the Privy Chamber in the Palace of Whitehall (which were destroyed in a fire in January 1698), taking one idea from an engraving of an architectural fantasy by Bernardo Preverdi after Bramante, and adapting Andrea Mantegna's engraving *The Battle of the Sea Gods* for a piece of architectural detail. It seems likely that Holbein's inclusion of an Italianate pilaster and capital in his portrait of Erasmus dated 1523 (now at Longford Castle) was a direct response to the publication of Cesare Cesariano's edition of Vitruvius two years earlier.[44] Someone in Holbein's circle was evidently aware of Raphael's decoration of the Vatican *loggie* via a print by Agostino Veneziano.[45] Holbein's own designs for an illustrated Bible, the *Icones Biblicae* (Lyons, 1539), on the other hand, display an encouraging independence of the standardised iconography of much early sixteenth-century biblical illustration. They may themselves have exerted some influence in this country: his illustration of the Sacrifice of Isaac, which unusually places Isaac in a prone position on the altar, was demonstrably used as the basis of a magnificent English jewel, an *enseigne* made between 1530 and 1550.[46]

Continental prints after designs by leading Italian and German Renaissance artists also inspired decorative paintings at Hampton Court, now surviving in the Wolsey Closet but possibly executed for Henry's study (where, in 1529, joiners were working on five 'tables to be painted').[47] They form an incomplete series of the Passion, in which *The Last Supper* was derived from Dürer's woodcut in *The Great Passion* suite, the *Flagellation* from Sebastiano del Piombo's wall painting in San Paolo in Montorio in Rome, the *Journey to Calvary* from Raphael's *Spasimo di Sicilia* and the *Resurrection* from one of the Scuola Nuova tapestries designed by Raphael's followers.[48] On a much smaller scale, the painted decoration of a remarkable table-desk made for Henry VIII, and bearing his badge with that of Catherine of Aragon, depends on German prints: the figures of Mars and Venus were copied from woodcuts by Hans Burgkmair, while the profile heads, together with much of the other decoration, may likewise derive from prints as yet unidentified.[49] The painter is more likely to have been a German working in this country than an Englishman.

These commissions were all either royal or courtly, and there is plenty of evidence that the patrons as well as their artists owned pattern-books of one kind or another: a small collection of patterns and pattern-books was kept in the King's study at Whitehall where it was inventoried in 1547.[50] At a lower social level wall paintings were much more rudimentary, often consisting only of repeated patterns, perhaps copied from contemporary textiles, and it would be surprising if the sources used by the painters could now be identified. Renaissance grotesques of the kind found on the titlepages and ornamental page borders of continental books had become popular in decorative painting during the first two decades of the sixteenth century, and remained popular throughout England during the reign of Elizabeth. Recent discoveries include three fine quality painted panels in the east wing of Acton Court near Iron Acton, north-east of Bristol, a building that seems to have been hurriedly thrown up for a progress of Henry VIII to the south-west in 1535.[51] However, efforts to pinpoint precise printed sources for these or indeed any decoration of this kind have so far proved fruitless, so it may be that the actual prints, whether Italian, French, German or Flemish in origin, have since disappeared, or that artists managed to devise satisfactory 'antickwork' compositions for themselves. Much research remains to done on the subject.

Despite the occasional use of engravings after Raphael and his contemporaries, it is notable that the prints available and employed for decoration in England up to the 1530s tended to be either Flemish or German. Even in Italy the relatively sophisticated prints of Martin Schongauer and Albrecht Dürer were quarried for the decoration of *istoriato* maiolica until 1520 or 1525, when the influence of Raphael became all-pervasive.[52] In England, Henry's break with Rome over the crucial issue of his divorce from his Spanish queen in the 1530s resulted in Italian artists and craftsmen beginning to return home, so that by 1545 Lord Cobham in Rome had been instructed to 'send over no more strangers, and move the rest there to send none, for the King is not content'.[53] Although Italian prints were, with a few notable exceptions, henceforward seldom copied in England, Italian influence in architecture and the arts did not plunge into terminal decline but was maintained by the publication in Venice in 1537 of an immensely significant work, the fourth book of Serlio's architectural treatise, the *Regole Generali di Architettura*.

Sebastiano Serlio was born in Bologna in 1475 and trained as a painter, but from 1514 he became an assistant to Baldassare Peruzzi who, with Antonio Sangallo, took over as architect of St Peter's in Rome after the death of Raphael in 1520. Serlio remained in Rome until the city was sacked in 1527, when he moved to Venice, applying for a copyright to publish illustrations of the orders cut by Agostino Veneziano. This ambition was realised in the publication of Book IV in 1537, with the help of a grant from François I.

Serlio's *Architettura* was essentially practical in character. W.B. Dinsmoor has said: 'The emphasis on illustration . . . was the ideal which guided Serlio in the preparation of his published works. It was a new conception in architectural writing, though it has since become so general that we tend to forget that it was an innovation that we owe to him.'[54] Anthony Blunt reinforced these remarks, commenting that 'the value of the book was to depend more on its plates than on its text. It was to be a pattern-book in which the architect could find solutions for all sorts of problems'. In the eight books that make up the treatise, together with the unpublished manuscript that survives in copies in Munich and New York, Serlio achieved a flexibility of style that enabled almost any architect, or indeed craftsman, to find something of use to him. Robert Peake accurately gauged the universal serviceability of Serlio's *Architettura* in the first English edition of 1611, when he wrote that 'it not onely tendeth to the great profit of the Architect or Workeman, but also generally to all other Artificers of our Nation'.

Book IV of the *Architettura* is devoted to the five orders of architecture and it is entirely Italian in

9

1 King's College, Cambridge,
choir screen from the west,
traditionally dated 1533–6.

*Serlio
(cont'd)*

character. In Book III, which followed in 1540, Serlio described and illustrated the finest buildings of Classical times together with some modern paragons of architecture. These two were the books that were most copied in England, and the dedication of the latter to François I indicates that, far from aiming just at Italians, Serlio already had his eye set on France, whither he moved in 1541 and where, four years later, the next two parts appeared. These were Books I and II, dealing with geometry and perspective. Book V, depicting twelve designs for churches, appeared in 1547, but Serlio's intended Book VI, devoted to houses and villas, was never published and is only known from manuscripts in Munich and at Columbia University in New York. In its place is put the *Libro*

Estraordinario (1551), containing fifty designs for doors and gates, while Books VII and VIII were published posthumously by Jacopo da Strada in Frankfurt in 1575 and deal respectively with houses and buildings planned on asymmetrical sites and with military architecture.

Meanwhile, long before his death in 1554, Serlio's influence had begun to be extended considerably by the publication of reprints and unauthorised foreign-language editions.[55] So, although Robert Peake's translation in 1611 was the first and only English edition, Serlio's designs were widely available in England during the sixteenth century (and remained so throughout the seventeenth and eighteenth).

The appearance of Serlio's *Architettura* did not

change the course of architecture in England overnight – such was the general conservatism of English patrons that it was almost another century before Inigo Jones was able to design buildings in the Italian manner, from the inside out – but it had an irreversible impact on architectural decoration. So speedy was the uptake in England of Serlian detail, that the influence of the book seems even to have preceded its publication: the precise nature of the relationship between the Serlio patterns and analogous work in Henrician England is debatable.

By far the most obvious analogies are those between Serlio's woodcuts of coffered ceilings[56] and ceilings in Henry's palaces and elsewhere. Matching Serlio's pattern of overlapping octagons (folios 68v and 69r) is the ceiling of the so-called Wolsey Closet at Hampton Court, decorated with the Prince of Wales feathers and executed after the birth of Edward VI in 1537. The same pattern was used for three other almost exactly contemporary ceilings surviving in the gallery in the Warden's Lodgings at New College, Oxford, constructed in 1541, the late-medieval chapel of The Vyne in Hampshire, complete before the death of Lord Sandys in 1540,[57] and in the church of St John the Evangelist, Digswell, Hertfordshire.[58] Serlio's pattern of greek crosses, hexagons and octagons (folio 68v, top left), is matched by the ceiling of St James's Chapel, Westminster, which bears the mottoes and badges of Anne of Cleves with the date 1540, and must therefore have been painted during the four months' of her marriage to Henry VIII, between January and April that year.[59]

So far so good: all these ceilings probably postdate Serlio's publication. Two further ceilings at Hampton Court – in Wolsey's south range (c.1526) and in the King's Holyday Closet (1536) – are more problematical. Their elaborate patterns of ribwork (embellished with Renaissance grotesques cast from the same moulds) were seemingly manipulated from patterns published by Serlio as much as a decade later.

The most enigmatic analogy between a Serlian pattern and decorative work in England occurs on the most celebrated monument of the early Renaissance in England, where it has unaccountably gone unrecognised until now. This is the screen of King's College Chapel, Cambridge (Fig. 1).

Most readers will be familiar with the main architectural character of the screen which spans the chapel from north to south. The lower part consists of three bays either side of a central opening that gives access to the choir and occupies the width of two normal bays. Above the level of the cornice of the main arcade rises a coved soffit which supports the upper part of the screen (Fig. 2). When Christopher Hussey published the screen in a superbly illustrated article in *Country Life* in 1926 he was of the opinion

2 (*above*) King's College, Cambridge, choir screen, detail of coved soffit. underside concaved cross section

3 Sebastiano Serlio, one of four designs for ceilings, 1537 (from the London edition of Book IV, 1611, folio 69r).

that the 'only trace – if a trace it is – of Gothic influence in the screen is the ribbing of the cove, which might be said to be a derivation from lierne vaulting, and thus exclusively English'. This rare error of judgement is ironical, for this pattern of ribbing derives precisely from folio 69r, lower right, of Serlio's Book IV and is unarguably Italian in origin (Fig. 3). The same pattern appears on the coved soffit to the lower stalls in the choir itself. Its appearance in these two positions tends to suggest that these portions of the work postdate the publication in 1537.

However, there is the difficulty that the badge and cipher of Anne Boleyn appear under the soffit, pointing to a date of completion before her execution in 1536 and a year before the publication of Serlio's Book IV.

How is this to be explained? There are several possibilities. The ceiling designs might conceivably have appeared in separate impressions of the woodcuts during the 1520s, as some of Serlio's illustrations did. Or the designer of the screen may have used a pattern-sheet of some other kind,[60] or known at first hand the Renaissance ceiling on which the pattern was based: the ceiling of the Wolsey Closet at Hampton Court is of the same pattern as that of the Camera dei Venti at the Palazzo del Tè in Mantua, which was executed by Girolamo da Treviso, who later came to England in 1542. A third possibility is that the carver executed the cove after the death of Anne but before the news had reached him, although for this to have happened he must have been working at a considerable distance from Cambridge.

Serlio may well have provided inspiration for the decoration of Nonsuch, the 'privy palace' whose construction occupied the last ten years of Henry's life and which was intended only for his own use and that of his closest courtiers and favourites. Little of its decoration survives, but there is sufficient evidence from one source or another to suggest that it was a mixture of Italian and French styles in character – not surprisingly, for the artists Henry employed were mostly Italians and Frenchmen. Nicholas Bellin, for instance, came from Modena but had worked for twenty years for François I in France, collaborating with Primaticcio and Rosso on the decoration of Fontainebleau, before arriving in England in 1537. Involved in a wide range of royal building projects, he was supported by a team of French, Netherlandish and German craftsmen. The well-known drawing of a decorative scheme for one of Henry's palaces together with the fireplace from Bletchingley (now in Reigate Priory)[61] provides clear evidence of the influence of Fontainebleau, but there is no surviving decoration from this period that displays precise debts to French prints.

Eng – 1552

However, something of the Franco-Italianate character of late-Henrician decoration is demonstrated by a remarkable architectural drawing for a triumphal arch (Fig. 5), possibly for a state entry, by Robert Pytt, Graver to the Mint, who died in 1552. Its overall character is perhaps more French than Italian, having many points of resemblance with French classical-style arches and church monuments, in particular with Ducerceau's *Arcs* (Orleans, 1549) and tomb designs with their characteristic *pleurons*. But some of the details were copied – indeed probably traced – direct from Serlio's Book IV, folio 62v (Fig.

4), accounting for the frieze of the second storey and the panelled attic above.

The publication of Serlio's *Architettura* encouraged Venetian and Netherlandish painters during the mid-sixteenth century to introduce Serlian architecture into the backgrounds of their paintings – Tintoretto and Pieter Aertsen and his pupil Joachim Beuckelaer are notable examples.[62] Artists working in England seem to have matched their continental contemporaries to a lesser extent, classical columns perhaps suggested by Serlio's woodcuts making quite frequent appearances in portraits; in the French or Flemish painter Guillim Scrots's portrait of *Edward VI*, in the Royal Collection, a Serlian ceiling pattern (folio 68v, upper right) was reincarnated for the paving of the floor on which the King stands.[63] If recent theories about architecture during the protectorate of the Duke of Somerset are correct, and classical forms were deliberately espoused by advanced Protestant reformers in order to mark a complete break with the

5   Robert Pytt, *Triumphal Arch*, drawing and wash, before 1552. Victoria and Albert Museum, London.

past, Serlio would have been a major source of direct influence.[64]

Even from the evidence that survives, prints are likely to emerge as having been considerably more influential in pre-Elizabethan England than this brief survey suggests. The scarcity of examples from the first half of the century – compared with the second half – can partly be explained by the fact that, the Church having been the principal artistic patron, two waves of iconoclasm – in 1549 and again in 1559 – did much to destroy religious images in England, precisely the ones likely to have been based on continental prints.

Nevertheless, the impact of prints seems to have been transformed during the reign of Elizabeth. Increased contact with the Continent, particularly as a result of the movement of religious refugees, and more sophisticated methods of print distribution were contributory factors. The accession of the new queen in 1558 – though no-one knew it then – heralded for England a period of nearly half a century of unrivalled prosperity. Stability was precarious, however, and

Protestantism though confirmed in the Settlement of 1559 was still something to be fought for, using the print medium for propaganda.

Elizabeth, though highly educated and intelligent, never gathered about herself the kind of Renaissance court embracing artists and architects, writers and musicians favoured by other crowned heads in Europe around the end of the century, the Emperor Rudolf II in Prague or Christian IV in Denmark; during the reign of his father, James I (Elizabeth's successor), Henry Prince of Wales came close to it during the brief flowering of his life. Instead, Elizabeth left building to her courtiers rather than indulging in it herself (she husbanded her resources for building and equipping the navy). These courtiers, anxious to divert attention from their new-made fortunes, built extravagantly in order to impress, reinforcing the spurious age of their lineage with displays of heraldry and demonstrating their awareness of continental fashions in a riot of architectural ornament. For the latter, the stream of prints now emerging from European presses proved ideal.

Chapter 2

THE INFLUENCE OF ITALIAN PRINTS

Italy, though not united under a single crown, was from the beginning of the fifteenth century through to the end of the period considered here the cultural centre of Europe. The country boasted the largest concentration of printing presses in the western world, and from the 1460s Italian books were imported directly into England. During the early sixteenth century the influence of Italian art had been disseminated principally by the migration of artists to the courts of kings and princes north of the Alps, a process hastened by the Sack of Rome in 1527 by Spanish and unpaid German mercenaries of the Emperor. However, by the accession of Elizabeth in 1558, none of the Italian artists and craftsmen who had braved the hazards of employment in an England now effectively Protestant – Nicholas Bellin of Modena, John of Padua and Toto del Nunziata – remained in this country. Italian influence remained strong in music and in literature (the Queen was not alone in speaking the language with ease), philosophical and emblematic works being particularly popular. Since Henry VIII's break with Rome, the association of Italy with papism minimised the impact of the growing output of reproductive prints after the work of such artists as Raphael and Michelangelo. Nevertheless, prints and printed books sustained her influence on the visual arts, which was also transmitted, as will be seen, through French and Flemish channels. Amongst the Italian material that was demonstrably circulating in England during the reign of Elizabeth were the architectural pattern-books of Serlio (since 1541 an honorary Frenchman) in reprinted editions, Vignola (1562) and Palladio (1570); the architectural ornament of Agostino Veneziano (*c*.1490–*c*.1536), Enea Vico (1523–67) and Benedetto Battini (working 1550s); and subject prints after the Flemish painter Michiel Coxie, engraved by the Master of the Die and Agostino Veneziano.

The biggest influence was undoubtedly that of Sebastiano Serlio, as it had been since his *Regole generale* first began to appear in 1537. It continued throughout the period, although nowhere in England is there the exceptional, almost obsessive dependence on his plates displayed by the designer of the Stuebchen of the Fuggerhaus at Donauworth in Germany. Virtually every feature of this room was taken without alteration from the *Architettura* – ceiling pattern, doorway, niches, oeil-de-boeuf, bracket and overdoor combined with guilloche ornament – to make an interior that was as Italian as was conceivably possible around 1555.[1] No Elizabethan interior even remotely measured up to this, although the so-called Haynes Grange Room now belonging to the Victoria and Albert Museum, with quotations from Serlio and Palladio, is the nearest. Nevertheless, the appetite in this country for Serlian detail became apparent from the 1560s onwards and was perhaps whetted afresh by the publication of a convenient collected quarto edition in Venice in 1566.

From that decade, for example, dates the first of a series of five identical funerary monuments in the church at Burford in Oxfordshire (in the chapel of St Mary and St Anne), commemorating Edmund Sylvester who died in 1568. Made of the local stone and surely by a native mason rather than a foreigner, the monuments consist of a tomb-chest with a boldly scrolled backplate, the design of which recalls a scrolled overmantel included by Serlio as folio 44r in his Book IV. Edmund Harmon, Henry VIII's barber-surgeon,[2] who commissioned a now-famous monument to himself in the same church in 1569 (see Fig. 54), must have known Sylvester, and probably employed the same mason: for although the inscription cartouche derives from a Flemish source, the frieze was taken from Serlio's folio 61r.

Serlio's chimneypiece designs were demonstrably influential in this country from the 1560s or 1570s onwards. Examples at Burghley, Wollaton and Hardwick, dating from the 1570s to the 1590s, are well known and need no further comment, but there are others whose derivation from Serlio has not hitherto been recognised. One element from folio 58r in Book IV was used on a remarkable chimneypiece at Wiston in Sussex (discussed in more detail on pp.140–42). Elsewhere there are several that depend on an element in the composite chimneypiece illustrated in folio 61r (Fig. 6). The design is instantly recognisable from the jambs, which are in the form

6 Serlio, chimneypiece, 1537 (from the London edition of Book IV, 1611, folio 61r).

7 (*far right*) Wentworth Woodhouse, Yorkshire, entrance to the Bear Pit, *c.*1630.

N. bowl end.

of paired scrolls surmounted by a capital with a mask. Serlio derived the motif – as Raphael had done before him – from the colossal statue of Jupiter seated on a throne decorated with mirrored lyres,[3] commenting (in the words of the English translation of 1611): 'I have made this Pilaster very much differing from the rest . . . taking a part of this invention from an ancient stoole, which is at S. Iohn de Lateranes in Rome.'[4]

Serlio's chimneypieces in Midlands!

This Serlian design provided the source for five chimneypieces in Midlands houses. The chimneypiece in the hall at Baddesley Clinton in Warwickshire may have been installed around 1580 in the Great Chamber of the gatehouse by Henry Ferrers, who died in 1633:[5] it was only brought into the hall in 1737, where it was set up incorrectly with the upper scroll inverted. The example in the gallery at Arbury Hall, no more than fifteen miles from Baddesley Clinton as the crow flies, is probably contemporary, a survival of about 1580, before the house was sold to John Newdegate in 1586.[6] The chimneypiece at Hardwick in Derbyshire is in what was in 1601 'My Ladys Withdrawing Chamber', and was presumably made by the masons John and Christopher Rodes. Despite the thirty-year time-lag, a Hardwick mason is likely to have transmitted the design to Lower Old Hall, Norland,[7] a house of 1634 near Halifax in the old West Riding of Yorkshire.

Fig 6!

One further piece of work shows a debt to the same plate in Serlio, and may therefore also be related to this North Midlands group. This is the little-known entrance to the Bear Pit at Wentworth Woodhouse in Yorkshire (Fig. 7), described by Pevsner as an 'odd garden ornament on two levels. Spiral stair inside. Domical vault. Exit below by a vaulted, grotto-like passage. The outer doorway is part of the architecture of about 1630. Wildly ornamental pilasters and open segmental pediment'. The architecture of about 1630 at Wentworth Woodhouse is of very great interest: a gateway into the court between the two houses that make up the whole derives from a design by Wendel Dietterlin (see p.28), and must represent the influence, if not the actual hand, of John or Huntingdon Smythson.

A small architectural feature that English masons probably derived from Serlio (although it was certainly available through other prints) was the shell-headed niche that appears prominently in folio 48r in Book III, an illustration of the gate known in ancient times as the Temple of Janus. It has triplets of them and may have inspired the gatehouse of Clifton Maybank in Dorset. This intriguing little building sported four circular roof-turrets and possessed a sophisticated contrapuntal rhythm of projection and recession. Its designer may have been William Arnold. Used as early as the 1560s at Longleat, the

16

shell-headed niche became something of a leitmotif of West-Country houses, as described later (pp.147–9).

Another, more idiosyncratic motif (in Book IV, folio 54r) was a bipartite window of which the upper part has a scrolled frame. This might have spawned a bevy of such windows on Sir William Cecil's lodge at Wothorpe, near Stamford in Lincolnshire, which is now an evocative ruin.

By far the most popular plates in Serlio, however, were the ceiling designs in Book IV, which, almost immediately after their publication in 1537, were used for ceilings that replicated both pattern and ornament quite closely. Satisfying the quintessentially English love of pattern-making as well as the demand for fashionable continental design, their influence continued unabated during the second half of the century, although Serlio's early-Renaissance ornament was either omitted or modified. The result was a distinctively English ceiling type, in which the ribwork patterns were often combined with dramatic pendants. Examples are so numerous that only a small selection can be mentioned here.

The coffered pattern of Book IV, folio 70v, lower left (deriving from the Basilica of Maxentius in Rome which dates from AD 304, and found in Renaissance buildings such as the ceilings of San Giovanni degli Spagnuoli and the Palazzo Farnese), was copied on the Continent[8] but rarely in England before the early eighteenth century – the wooden-ribbed ceiling of the chantry at Bishop's Stortford, however, is one example.[9]

Far more widely used were the four patterns on folio 68v (Fig. 8). The system of overlapping octagons, lower left, had remained popular in northern Europe from its first appearance,[10] and in England was employed for ceilings in many parts of the country: the Star Chamber at Broughton Castle in Oxfordshire has one of the earliest Elizabethan examples, possibly dating from the 1560s; Yorkshire has perhaps the greatest concentration and the widest timespan – from the Great Chamber at Gilling Castle or a room in the Elizabethan range at Helmsley Castle (between 1563 and 1587) to East Riddlesden Hall of about 1648 (Fig. 9);[11] the northernmost instance may be the ceiling of the King Charles Room at Pinkie Castle, Musselburgh, Midlothian. The pattern was also used for paving, in the Pillar Parlour at Bolsover Castle in Derbyshire during the second decade of the seventeenth century.

The ceiling design, upper left, consisting of greek crosses, hexagons and octagons – widely employed throughout northern Europe[12] and in Henrician England – was also popular in northern England for ceilings during this period: examples occur in the Queen's Room at Sizergh Castle in Westmorland (1569) and at Low Hall, Little Strickland, in the same

county (Fig. 10).[13] The pattern was also used for panelling at Burton Agnes and at St John's College, Oxford,[14] and (way beyond the period) for a quilt dated 1709 at Levens Hall in Westmorland.

The hexagons and triangles of Serlio's folio 68v upper right – copied for the ceiling of the Kunstkammer of the castle at Ambras in the Austrian Tyrol – seem only to have been used in sixteenth-century England for the paving on which Edward VI stands in his portrait by Guillim Scrots, mentioned earlier.[15]

On the other hand, the design on folio 68v lower right – which can be read as a pattern of repeated greek crosses with pointed arms – was widely popular in England, sometimes unmodified (as in a room at Cotehele)[16] though mostly modified by overlapping the points of the crosses or by adding ribs, as at Avebury Manor and Longford Castle in Wiltshire, in the chapel in the Upper Ward at Windsor Castle in Berkshire and in the room over the Common Gate at New College, Oxford: all may date from the 1570s. Northern uses must be contemporary or even slightly earlier, in the Inlaid Room, dining room (dated 1564) and Tapestry Room at Sizergh Castle.[17] The pattern also found its way on to the walls at Pittleworth Manor in Hampshire, in a wall painting dated 1580.

The design of intersecting circles (Book IV, folio 70v, lower right, Fig. 11) – that of a room in the Villa Medici at Poggio a Caiano, designed by Giulio da Sangallo in the early 1480s – inspired the ironwork on the north and south transept doors of the cathedral in Toledo, perhaps around 1545, and the vault of the almost contemporary porch of the church at Gisors near Beauvais in France. The only sixteenth-century borrowing in England is the ceiling of the Tapestry Room at Deene Park in Northamptonshire (Fig. 12), which, from the ornamental details, must date from the very last years of the century.

Equally rare to find is one of the patterns of vaulting of the Temple of Bacchus in Rome, that given by Serlio in Book III, folio 8v, lower right. It was, nonetheless, used in England in the 1570s at Kirby Hall in Northamptonshire for the soffit of the central arch of the loggia in the courtyard,[18] and may have inspired that of ceilings in the Blue Bedroom at Levens Hall in Westmorland. The chapel of Charterhouse in London has ceilings of this and two other Serlian patterns, although almost certainly these date from alterations of 1824 or 1841 rather than from the early seventeenth century.

These patterns, in short, were highly adaptable and they continued to be popular into the eighteenth and nineteenth centuries.[19] In one instance, even a garden design (Book IV, folio 69v, top right) was adapted by a plasterer, for the ceiling of the staircase at Blickling Hall in Norfolk.

By the late sixteenth century, motifs derived from

Serlio's patterns

Fig 10, lower r.

From Poggio
↓
Serlio; Deene Pk.

From Ro: Bacchus
↓
Kirby

Gdns
↓
Blickling ceily stairs

plates in Serlio had begun to filter down from architectural decoration to that of fittings and furniture. To take one county only, Norfolk can show several instances of this phenomenon: the friezes of some benches dated 1590 in the church at Brisley are carved with fluting and a distinctive double-guilloche, motifs that appear on folio 71r in Book IV.[20]

Although Andrea Palladio's *I quattri libri dell'architettura* had been published in Venice in 1570, Elizabethans clearly were not ready for it, and there is little evidence that it exerted much influence until what Wittkower called England's 'radical conversion to continental and specifically Italian standards of taste' in the 1610s and 1620s:[21] Sir Thomas Tresham

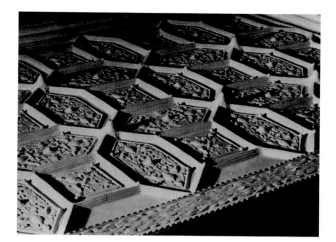

plates seem to have been employed in the design of that remarkable early Elizabethan interior generally known as the Haynes Grange Room,[23] and a frieze he illustrated served to decorate a chimneypiece at Wiston Park in Sussex (p.141).

Vignola had to wait even longer for acceptance in England: Tresham had a copy of the 1582 Venice edition of the *Regole delli cinque ordini d'architettura* which had first appeared twenty years earlier, and

9 (*far left*) East Riddlesden, Yorkshire, ceiling, *c.*1648.

10 (*far left below*) Low Hall, Little Strickland, Westmorland, *c.*1600.

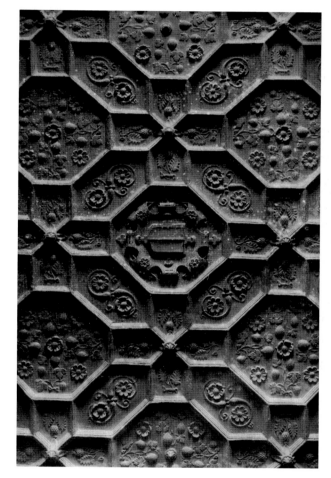

11 (*left*) Serlio, one of four designs for mazes or knots, 1537 (from the London edition of Book IV, 1611, folio 70v).

12 (*below*) Deene Park, Northamptonshire, ceiling of the Tapestry Room, 1590s.

(*c.*1543–1605) certainly owned a copy of the first edition and so did Sir Thomas Knyvett (*c.*1539–1609);[22] William Cecil, Lord Cranborne (1591–1668), was amongst the first Englishmen to be aware of Palladio's architecture, for in 1610 he wrote, of the Teatro Olimpico, 'Remarquez y bien le theatre fait depuis 25 ans par ce grand Architecte Palladius d'une rare inventionn qu'autre qui puisse estre.'

The surveyor and mason-architect John Thorpe was also aware of Palladio. Two or three of Palladio's

13 Ampney Crucis, Gloucestershire, monument to George Lloyd and wife (died 1584).

14 Benedetto Battini, *Vigilate quia nescitis diem neque horam* (Antwerp, 1553), pl.6, 'Judex damnatur . . .' and 'Plerique famam'. The Royal Library – National Library of Sweden, Stockholm, Maps and Prints Department, De la Gardie Collection.

there was a 1596 edition in the Bodleian.[24] But it was not until the work of Jones that features derived from Vignola became common, while it was as late as the 1650s that a gateway at Staunton Harold in Leicestershire was copied complete from one of the plates. Palladio and Vignola simply did not have the decorative potential that sixteenth-century English masons, plasterers and others craved. This goes some way towards explaining the relative popularity of a suite of strapwork cartouches – a type of ornament in which northern European artists held the field – designed by an Italian, Benedetto Battini, a Florentine painter of whom nothing else is known. The fact that his vigorous cartouches were published in Antwerp (by Hieronymus Cock in 1553 under the title *Vigilate quia nescitis diem neque horam*) doubtless also contributed to their success.[25]

These cartouches are of many and varied forms, but all are angular and have some architectural elements, unlike those of Flemish designers such as Jan Vredeman de Vries or Jacob Floris. In fact, Battini's set seems to depend more on Fontainebleau than on Antwerp, although some of what came to be characteristically Antwerp features appear in them – masks, putti, baskets and swags of fruit, and so on – perhaps as a result of Cock's intervention. Battini used the interesting and unusual device whereby his cartouches appear to stand on a white surface against a cross-hatched background, which gives them even greater three-dimensionality. One particularly attractive (if incomplete) set in the Victoria and Albert Museum is printed in black on a green paper and washed with red.

Battini's plates were, like those of his Netherlandish contemporaries Cornelis Bos and Jacob Floris, avidly plundered for other publications,[26] but in Britain there is only a handful of borrowings from his designs. By some years the earliest instance occurs at Sizergh Castle in Westmorland where cartouches derived from Battini's set are the only identifiable print-based features amongst a riot of Italianate decoration on two overmantels dated 1564 and 1575. The possible location of their accomplished carver's workshop is discussed later (pp.199–200). Approximately contemporary with the later of these overmantels, but very different in character, is the screen in the hall of Middle Temple (see Fig. 276). Two of the five designs of cartouches in the upper register were derived from Battini's *Vigilate*, those on the extreme left and right, together with their immediate neighbours (see p.170).

Next in date may be the monument commemorating George Lloyd and his wife (d.1584) at Ampney Crucis in Gloucestershire (Fig. 13). This is of elaborate pedimented design, with life-size figures, and it has on the back two strapwork cartouches enclosing heraldic achievements. These are of different design and come from a single plate in Battini's *Vigilate* (Fig. 14). This amusingly literal rendering of a print no doubt intended to present alternative designs makes it pretty certain that the anonymous carver was responsible fifteen years later for a chimneypiece (see Fig. 222) at South Wraxall Manor, near Bradford-on-Avon in Wiltshire, a fourteenth-century or earlier house altered and enlarged at the end of the sixteenth by Sir Walter Long. He used another plate from Battini's *Vigilate* for the lower cartouches on the overmantel in the Great Chamber (see Fig. 221).

No more than twelve miles from South Wraxall as the crow flies is another building with a cartouche derived from the Battini set. This is Syston (or Siston) Court in Gloucestershire (Fig. 15),[27] a house built by the Dennys family in the late-sixteenth century but sold by them in 1598. In the hall is a chimneypiece with a cartouche over the fire-arch copied from the plate inscribed 'O dij bonj' (Fig. 16). Paired caryatids flank the chimneypiece and the overmantel, and there is an imposing cartouche enclosing an armorial achievement, but none of these derives from obvious sources. The whole ensemble has very much the appearance of Bristol-made chimneypieces of the period.

Another context in which a cartouche by Battini

15 Syston Court, Gloucestershire, chimneypiece and overmantel, 1590s.

was copied in England is the sketchbook of the Abbott family of plasterers from north Devon (see pp.159–62). It occurs on the lower left of folio 113

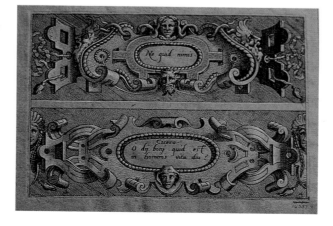

16 Benedetto Battini, *Vigilate . . .* (Antwerp, 1553), pl.4, two cartouches inscribed 'Ne quid nimis' and 'O dij bonj quid est in hominis vita diu?' Victoria and Albert Museum, London.

and the source is the cartouche inscribed 'Utendum est divitiis'. Stylistic evidence suggests that this usage dates from the late sixteenth or early seventeenth century, although the book was compiled over a period of several generations; the copyist might well have been John Abbott the elder (1565–1635) with whom the underrated West-Country mason-architect William Arnold seems to have collaborated so frequently throughout his career.

An early and apparently isolated instance of the use of cartouches designed by Benedetto Battini occurs in Cheshire, on the frontispiece of the eccentrically designed Brereton Hall. The house was built around 1586 and depends for much of its decoration on prints by a better-known Antwerp contemporary of Battini's, Vredeman de Vries (see pp.64–8). Three of the cartouches over the front door, however, were copied from plates in the *Vigilate*, those enclosing the inscriptions 'Iudex damnatur . . .', 'Plerique famam . . .' and 'Cicero. O dij bonj . . .' It seems likely that the owner, Sir William Brereton, designed the frontispiece of his house himself and chose the prints for his masons to copy.

If the influence of Italian architectural and decorative plates was limited in the sixteenth century, how much more so was that of biblical or historical illustrations. Amongst the rare instances known today are the Cupid and Psyche wall paintings from Hill Hall in Essex, adapted from prints by the Master of the Die and Marcantonio Raimondi after Michiel Coxie. Nevertheless, Italian paintings or prints seem to lie behind the decoration of the Elysium Room at Bolsover Castle in Derbyshire, whose ceiling depends on a print by Cornelis Cort after a design by Primaticcio for a ceiling at Fontainebleau. It would be satisfying to say that the woodcuts illustrating Francesco Colonna's celebrated romantic antiquarian novel, the *Hypnerotomachia Poliphili*, made an impact on the visual arts in England, but their influence seems to be restricted to the copying of a triumphal arch for the titlepage of Samuel Daniel's *Complaynt of Rosamund* (1592).[28]

Chapter 3

THE INFLUENCE OF GERMAN PRINTS

Southern Germany had participated in the spread of printing from Italy, the increase of trade across the Alps and the exchange of scholars. She had also witnessed revolts of the peasantry and the emergence of Martin Luther. Used to disseminate propaganda in support of the Reformation, in the visual arts the print medium had been applied during the first half of the sixteenth century to the production of a wide range of material, from innumerable coarsely illustrated broadsheets to woodcuts and other prints of the utmost refinement, designed by such masters as Albrecht Dürer and Lucas Cranach the elder, Hans Burgkmair and Albrecht Altdorfer. Alongside these appeared pattern-books largely designed for goldsmiths and jewellers – minutely executed engravings produced by the so-called *Kleinmeister* to satisfy demands for up-to-date ornament. Native-born designers such as Peter Flötner (some of whose designs were circulated in the form of plaquettes), Matthias Zündt and Virgil Solis were joined by foreigners such as the Netherlander Erasmus Hornick and the Frenchman Etienne Delaune, who lived in southern Germany briefly. The main centres of print production were Nuremberg and Augsburg, cities which 'became the most important sources of style and fashion throughout the German-speaking world'.[1] At Nuremberg two rival entrepreneurs, Hans Guldenmund and Nicolaus Meldemann, published the work of the leading draughtsmen of the mid-century.

During the second half of the sixteenth century the traditional German print medium of woodcut gave way to engraving, and the relationship between engraving on copper for reproduction and engraving on silver became very close. It was around this time that English trade with Germany intensified. As a result of the rupturing of trade relations with Antwerp in 1563 and alarming reports of serious political troubles there following the outbust of iconoclasm in 1566, the Merchant Adventurers established their mart not at Emden – threatened as it might have been by the Duke of Alba's professional forces – but at Hamburg in 1567.[2] Although the longer sea-journey meant that Hamburg was never as convenient a port

for English merchants as Antwerp, their contacts with towns such as Frankfurt and Leipzig were enhanced; Nuremberg developed the skills of dyeing and finishing English cloth whilst retaining its importance as one of the prime centres of printing in Germany. Could these improved trade connections have contributed to the influence of German prints in Elizabethan and Jacobean England?

Somewhat surprisingly perhaps, Albrecht Dürer, whose prints had occasionally been used in England during the first half of the sixteenth century, continued to provide inspiration for artists in England during the second: both Nicholas Hilliard and Isaac Oliver apparently adapted his woodcuts and engravings and his *Prodigal Son* suite may have been known to the maker of a leather-covered chest traditionally associated with Lady Catherine Grey, sister of Lady Jane Grey.[3]

German prints – along with Flemish – featured in the decoration of the fairly numerous pieces of silver, some hallmarked in London in 1567–8, decorated by the unidentified engraver with the monogram P over M. These are special instances, for it seems that he was a foreigner who only came to England irregularly.[4] Although he often made use of the biblical woodcuts of Bernard Salomon, on one occasion he adapted those of Virgil Solis. Additionally, he copied the twelve Labours of Hercules for a set of parcel-gilt plates from a suite dated 1550 by Heinrich Aldegrever,[5] and either owned himself or had access to prints by Hans Sebald Beham (see p.202).

Like Hans Sebald and Barthel Beham, Georg Pencz (*c*.1500–50) was a pupil of Dürer and became quite a prolific designer of ornament and subject prints. He came under the influence of Giulio Romano and Polidoro da Caravaggio while in Italy, which he visited in about 1529 and 1539.[6] Two or three instances of the use of his prints have been noticed in the West Country and another in Scotland: all will be discussed later (see pp.162 and 153–4).

No German print designer was more prolific than Virgil Solis (1514–62), who spent his working career in Nuremberg. He employed numerous assistants in his workshop which was in business from about 1540

and continued until about ten years after his death in 1562. Approaching twelve hundred intaglio prints have been attributed to Solis and his workshop, together with just under a thousand woodcuts. Amongst his most celebrated woodcuts are illustrations for Walter Rivius's edition of Vitruvius (1548), for the *Biblische Figuren*, a German Bible published in 1565, where they are contained within thirty-one different strapwork borders, and for an edition of Aesop's *Fables* the same year. His illustrations for the *Metamorphoses Ovidii* which appeared in 1563 are sometimes no more than reversed copies of Bernard Salomon's woodcuts published in Lyons six years earlier, and the copying of designs by Thiry, Ducerceau, Cornelis Floris, Benedetto Battini and others was what enabled Solis and his workshop to satisfy the enormous demand for ornament prints.

Apart from the silver ewer decorated by the engraver P over M already mentioned, direct quotations from his designs in England are, for such a prolific artist, surprisingly uncommon: the only well-known examples are the wall paintings at Stodmarsh Court in Kent which were copied from his suite of the planets,[7] while Solis (albeit in a reversed copy after Bernard Salomon) was the source for an embroidered cushion-cover at Hardwick depicting Europa and the Bull (see p.271). To these, a few further instances can now be added.

The celebrated overmantel in the drawing room at Loseley in Surrey (Fig. 17), which Sir William More built near the site of an existing house between 1560 and 1569, depends on no fewer than three separate suites of prints designed by Virgil Solis, besides at least one French set (see pp.35–8). It is carved with six heraldic achievements in strapwork cartouches, the latter adapted with great skill from the originals. In fact it is pretty certain that these were collected not for their decorative frames but for the figures and portraits they enclosed, the Nine Worthies, the Nine Female Worthies and an odd pair of portraits of the Emperors Charles V and Philip II dated 1549.[8] Considerable ingenuity was employed by the mason in transferring into actual relief these two-dimensional cartouches, for it is not always easy to decide on the planes occupied by the various strands of strapwork. In the overmantel the central cartouche of the upper row derives from the print depicting King Arthur, from *The Nine Worthies* (Figs 18, 19), and from here clockwise follow those framing Virginia, Veturia, Jahel and Judith from *The Nine Female Worthies*, and Philip of Spain. What personal whim lies behind the choice of these cartouches, from prints used nowhere else in England? They must have been among Sir William's books at Loseley, but the surviving list does not appear to mention them, either because they were bound in with another publication, or because they

17 (*facing page*) Loseley Hall, Surrey, overmantel, 1560s.

18 (*left*) Loseley Hall, Surrey, detail of overmantel.

19 Virgil Solis, King Arthur, from *The Nine Worthies*. Victoria and Albert Museum, London.

were acquired after the list was drawn up in 1556,[9] four years before he began the new house.

Another isolated instance of the use of a print by Virgil Solis occurred during the late 1580s in the design of the celebrated tapestry maps commissioned by Sir Ralph Sheldon from the Sheldon tapestry works for the dining room of his house at Weston Park, Warwickshire. Helping to populate the complex borders of these tapestries (which are discussed in detail on pp.223–6) is the figure of Mercury drawn from a frieze depicting the seven planetary deities.[10] A similar horizontal frieze features eight Virtues, two of which – Iusticia and Temperantia – were apparently used on the plaster lunette of a ceiling at Emrall Hall, Worthenbury in Flintshire.[11]

From Solis's illustrations for Ovid's *Metamorphoses* derives the plaster overmantel in the so-called Orpheus Chamber (originally the State Bedchamber) at Haddon Hall in Derbyshire (Fig. 20) which was expanded from the woodcut depicting Orpheus Charming the Beasts (Fig. 21): this was itself a reversed copy of Bernard Salomon's woodcut. The same scene was amongst several adapted by the carver of panels in the drawing room of The Grange, Broadhembury near Honiton in Devon.[12]

If Virgil Solis's biblical illustrations for the *Biblische Figuren dess Alten Testaments* . . . and *Biblische Figuren dess Newen Testaments* . . . published in Frankfurt in 1565 were widely known in England during this period, the evidence has all but disappeared . . . with one remarkable exception. During the Tudor and Stuart periods, special wooden trenchers, either circular or more rarely rectangular, were made for serving sweetmeats, jellied fruits and so on. These small,

20 (right) Haddon Hall, Derbyshire, State Bedchamber, c.1600.

21 (far right) Virgil Solis, Orpheus Charming the Beasts, from *Metamorphoses Ovidii* (Frankfurt, 1563). British Library, London (1068.g.4).

flat boards were often painted one on side with abstract patterns or with single figures. One set now consisting of three trenchers, however, has meticulously painted biblical scenes, Jonah Cast up by the Whale (Fig. 22), Dives and Lazarus, and Angels Swinging Sickles and Pressing Wine (Fig. 23), each one contained within elaborate strapwork borders,

his workshop and, though this is generally discounted, Amman inherited much of Solis's work, reputation and working methods from the 1560s onwards. His first substantial project for Solis's publisher Sigmund Feyerabend was a series of 134 woodcuts for the *Biblia Sacra* published in Frankfurt in 1564; they also appeared the same year in a picture Bible, the

22 (right) Banqueting trencher depicting Jonah Cast up by the Whale. Strangers Hall, Norwich.

23 (far right) Banqueting trencher depicting Angels Swinging Sickles and Pressing Wine. Strangers Hall, Norwich.

titled above and captioned below. All derive from Solis's illustrations, the first copied with only minor alteration the last reproduced feature by feature (Fig. 24). Dives and Lazarus for some reason derives not from the equivalent scene in the *Biblische Figuren* but from Solis's print of the *Marriage at Cana*. Did the painter possess a defective copy of the book or was there another reason why he adapted a different woodcut? We shall never know.[13]

Jost Amman (1539–91) was a Swiss artist, from a Protestant and humanist family, who moved to Nuremberg from Zurich and perhaps met Virgil Solis in the last year or two of the latter's life. There has even been the suggestion that Amman was a pupil in

24 Virgil Solis, 'Angels Swinging Sickles and Pressing Wine', from *Biblische Figuren* (Frankfurt, 1565). Victoria and Albert Museum, London.

26

Neuwe Biblische Figuren.[14] Amman's second illustrated Bible contained 198 woodcuts. These biblical illustrations have an international – ultimately Italianate – personality, which derives from the fact that many were adaptations in reverse of designs originally by that arch-Romanist, Maarten van Heemskerck.[15]

Amman was almost as prolific as Virgil Solis, producing well over a thousand woodcuts alone. Other important publications included plates for Wenzel Jamnitzer's *Perspectiva* and for Hans Sach's book illustrating contemporary professions and trades, the so-called *Ständebuch*, both published in Nuremberg in 1568; a drawing manual entitled *Kunst und Lehrbüchlein* (Zurich, 1578) and his celebrated *Kunstbüchlein*, which was published posthumously in Frankfurt in 1599. These later works are valuable today for the light they shed on life and society in sixteenth-century Germany. Prints from the *Kunstbüchlein* were used in the stained-glass windows made for Gorhambury Hall, Hertfordshire, between 1615 and 1626, as shown by Michael Archer.[16]

Amman's woodcuts were also copied in needlework. Two English embroidered bookbindings in the British Library, for instance, derive either from the *Biblia Sacra* (or its picture-book equivalent, the *Neuwe Biblische Figuren*) or the *Opera Josephi*:[17] Esther before Ahasuerus and Jacob Wrestling with the Angel appear on the binding of a Bible dated 1612, and Jacob's Dream and his Struggle with the Angel (reversed) on a book of Psalms of 1643. Further needlework pictures follow Amman's illustrations of Jacob's Dream and the Death of Jezebel.[18]

To these textiles can now be added other decorative work inspired by Amman's illustrations. Two interesting instances, at Chatsworth in Derbyshire in the 1570s and at Wiston in Sussex during the following decade, will be discussed in Part II (pp.250–52 and 141–2). Otherwise, there is the family pew in the church at Holcombe Rogus in Devon (Fig. 25), whose screen has decorative panels above the frieze, carved with Old Testament subjects. Among them is the scene in which the walls of Jerico fall down before the Ark of the Covenant which (unlike most of the other scenes on the screen) derives from the *Neuwe Biblische Figuren* (Fig. 26).[19]

Of the many designers working in Germany during the later sixteenth century, none has today quite such a reputation as Wendel Dietterlin. This reputation rests entirely on his one architectural pattern-book published in instalments during the 1590s: the plates are admired today presumably for their nightmarish qualities and for the scarcely concealed eroticism of many of the constituent figures.

Wendel Gapp – or Dietterlin, as he was later named – was born in 1550 or 1551 in Pullendorf on Lake Constance. By 1570 he had moved to Stras-

25 Holcombe Rogus, Devon, family pew, *c.*1600.

bourg and married, becoming a citizen the following year. He entered the guild of artists, decorators and painters, specialising in the painting of house façades and in architectural painting in general. None of his work in this field has survived, not even the huge ceiling painting in the Lusthaus of the Duke of Württemburg in Stuttgart. Most of his energies in the latter part of his short life – he died at the age of forty-eight in Strasbourg in 1599 – were devoted to the work for which he is famous, his *Architectura*.

The *Architectura und Ausztheilung der V Seülen* was issued in instalments, beginning with forty plates published in Stuttgart and Strasbourg in 1593, a further

26 Jost Amman, The Walls of Jerico, from *Neuwe Biblische Figuren* (Frankfurt, 1564). British Library, London (680.a.9).

IOSVAE VI.

Circumeunt duris muros Ierichontidos armis,
Et resonant graciles classica dira tubæ.

Iámque ruunt turres, uastantur & omnia ferro,
Et de tot Rachab sola relicta manet.

Vmb Jericho sie drey mal tretten/
Blasen mit freuden jr Trommeten.

Die Statt fellt/ wirt alls gschlagen tod/
Rahab allein kompt auß der not.

fifty in Strasbourg in 1594 and the definitive edition of 194 plates published in Nuremberg in 1598. Like comparable enterprises by earlier designers, including the Swiss architect Hans Blum and Jan Vredeman de Vries, by whom Dietterlin must have been influenced to some extent, the work is divided into five sections corresponding to the five orders of architecture; it contains designs for doors, windows, chimneypieces, monuments and fountains, all in the extravagantly three-dimensional strapwork grotesque style ultimately derived from Antwerp via, no doubt, the *tours-de-force* of titlepage and commemorative stained-glass design of German-speaking designers. The work combines a sinister suggestion of impending doom with attractively comical elements.

The *Architectura* must have been very influential on the Continent,[20] but very few examples of direct derivation from Dietterlin's designs have so far been traced in England. For a long time, Charlton House in Greenwich remained virtually the only undeniable instance of copying from his plates.

Charlton House was built by Adam Newton, one-time schoolmaster to Prince Henry, between 1607 and 1612. It has been suggested that — his own personal means being very limited — Newton built the house to receive the Prince.[21] Inside, the decorative detail shows dependence on several suites of Antwerp-published ornament (see pp.92, 98–9); outside there is little decoration. It is confined to the frontispiece where the term figure on its elaborate Mannerist support, at first-floor level, is derived from the right-hand element of plate 183 of Dietterlin's *Architectura*. This was for England a remarkably speedy borrowing from a continental source and, as usual, the architectural ornament was simply applied to the surface of the building rather than being an integral part of it: any other term figure would have served equally well and the Dietterlin figure is indeed somewhat out of place in the company of the Antwerp-style ornament inside the house.

Another almost precisely contemporary building apparently demonstrated a debt to Dietterlin. This was the old Northumberland House, Charing Cross, London, built by the Earl of Northampton from about 1608, probably to the designs of the sculptor and tomb-maker Bernard Janssen. Little more than a century after it was built, Nicholas Hawksmoor noted, in a letter to the Dean of Westminster in 1734–5: 'There is yet another manner of Building which was the invention of John Ditterlyn, at Strasbourg (a fantasticall painter) about the year 1500, where he put the whole disposition of Antient building into Masquarade . . . see some of this Taste in the West front of Northumberland house. This Burlesque Style of Building, is still called Ditterlyn, but not imitated.'[22]

Neither the famous view by Canaletto nor the poignant photographs taken of the great house before its demolition in 1870, stranded like a dinosaur from a forgotten age, show the detail quite clearly enough to be sure that Dietterlin was actually copied for the architectural ornament, but Hawksmoor's description confirms that it was indeed Dietterlin whom this façade most suggested. Dietterlin's *Architectura* has also been suggested as the inspiration for a piece of decoration on the frontispiece of Bramshill House in Hampshire, a house built by Edward, 11th Baron Zouche, between 1605 and 1625: here a pair of grotesque heads flanking the central oriel window bear some resemblance to Dietterlin's plate 192.[23] Perhaps closest to him in spirit — without, however, exactly reproducing any of his designs exactly — are the highly distinctive fittings of the churches in County Durham that were built or furnished under the aegis of John Cosin both before and after the Civil War: the stalls at Brancepeth, with their segmental broken pediments and applied Mannerist ornament, are characteristic examples dating from the 1630s.

Some new discoveries have been made in recent years which show that Dietterlin's influence in England was somewhat greater than had been suspected. John Smythson has emerged beyond any possibility of doubt as one of those who had access to a copy of *Architectura*. The gallery façade at Bolsover Castle in Derbyshire displays what Sir John Summerson felicitously described as 'shattered pediments' over the windows and central door, which were considered to have been based on plates in Dietterlin's *Architectura*. Smythson certainly knew this work, for he copied one of the plates, plate 62, in a drawing that was the basis for the chimneypiece in the Great Chamber at Clifton Hall in Nottingham.[24]

It was conceivably John Smythson, or his son Huntingdon, who was responsible for the early seventeenth-century gate to the western courtyard at Wentworth Woodhouse (Fig. 27), hardly more than thirty miles from Clifton Hall; this depends precisely on Dietterlin's plate 67 (Fig. 28).[25]

Interest in this eccentric designer's work must have been rekindled during the Commonwealth by a second edition of the *Architectura*, which appeared in 1655. Dietterlin's influence has been detected in several impressive doorcases on the first-floor landing at Tyttenhanger in Hertfordshire, while at Forde Abbey in Dorset the central niche in the hall seems to have been adapted from another plate.[26] It has not hitherto been noticed, however, that the artist Wenceslas Hollar, when designing the titlepage for the *Golden Remains of the ever Memorable Mr John Hales of Eton College &c*, published in London in 1659 (Fig. 29), ingeniously used elements from two separate plates in Dietterlin's *Architectura*. His niches, in

which the figures of Reason and Revelation stand, were taken from a design for a window surround, on plate 14 (Fig. 30), while the grotesque mask that separates these niches and surmounts the title itself

was borrowed from an immensely elaborate doorcase on plate 76.

Something of Dietterlin's manic quality survived in the pattern-books designed or published by Gerhard

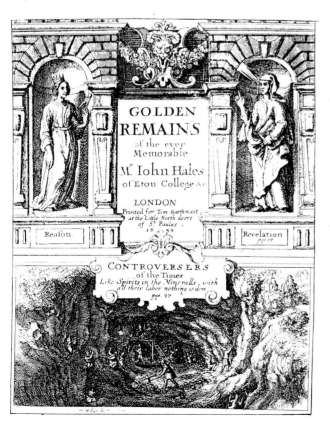

31 J.J. Ebelmann, *Thresur Buch* (Strasbourg, 1598), pl.6. Victoria and Albert Museum, London.

Altzenbach, Gabriel Krammer, Rutger Kasemann and Johann Jacob Ebelmann (active 1598–1609).[27] The latter was born in Speir and may have worked as a cabinetmaker in Strasbourg. He produced a set of six designs for cabinets in 1598, a suite of twelve architectural plates bearing his own monogram, and contributed to three further sets of designs with Jakob Guckheisen.[28] A solitary unquestionable instance of Ebelmann's influence on furniture made – presumably – in England has come to light, a cabinet on a stand (formerly in the collection of Ronald Lee) made in the 1630s, whose doors are decorated with cartouches clearly derived from plate 6 of his *Thresur Buch* of 1598 (Figs 31, 32).[29] This cabinet has a near-companion at Arbury Hall in Warwickshire, made for William Laud while Bishop of London between 1628 and 1633, and is also associated stylistically with a whole group of work dating from the late 1620s and early 1630s: at St John's and other Oxford colleges, and in London, for example at Westminster Abbey, where the overmantel of the Jerusalem Chamber was made by the joiner Adam Browne in 1629.[30]

It would be good to be able to record the direct influence in England of the *Neues Zieratenbuch* by another German cabinetmaker and designer, Friedrich Unteutsch (*c*.1600–1670), for his style is very apparent in northern European and Scandinavian countries, most obviously in church monuments, furniture and

32 Cabinet on stand, 1630s. Ronald Lee.

33 (*far right*) Lucas Kilian, *Newes Gradesca Büchlein* (Augsburg, 1607). Victoria and Albert Museum, London.

34 (*facing page*) Chamber organ by 'John Haan' (Hahn), detail of painted decoration by Rowland Buckett, 1611–12. The Marquess of Salisbury.

35 Chamber organ by 'John Haan' (Hahn), 1609. The Marquess of Salisbury.

woodwork.[31] However, there is only the slightest evidence that the highly mannered style was known in England. Two instances only come to mind, a stall of mid-seventeenth-century date in Gloucester Cathedral and the monument commemorating Sir William Bourchier, 3rd Earl of Bath (d.1623), at Tawstock in Devon: here the inscription plate is framed by ornament in a very subdued version of Unteutsch's manner.

In fact, there is some evidence – not yet adding up to very much – that German prints published in the years around 1600 *were* being used in England during the first half of the seventeenth century. One occurs at Hatfield House in Hertfordshire, where the joiner and painter Rowland Buckett (or Bucket) was employed by Robert Cecil, 1st Earl of Salisbury, in supplying furniture and decorating the house. In

1611–12 Buckett painted the case of the celebrated Hatfield chamber organ (Fig. 35) identifiable with the 'great wind instrument bought of a Dutchman, £1,084 6s. 8d.' in 1609; its maker was probably John Haan.[32] For one of the painted panels on the case Buckett adapted a plate from *Newes Gradesca Büchlein*, a suite of grotesques designed by the engraver Lucas Kilian (1579–1637) and published in Augsburg in 1607 (Figs 34, 33). Rowland Buckett's father Michael was a German refugee described as being 'of London, Cordwainer', when denizened in 1571/2,[33] and Rowland's use of a print by Kilian suggests that he maintained contacts with the German community in London and with his countrymen at home. Kilian's suite of auricular cartouches, *Newes Schildtbyhlin* (Augsburg, 1610), was also known in England, see p.161.[34]

Theodor Bang (before 1600–after 1617) was another designer who catered principally for goldsmiths. He had himself become a master goldsmith in Nuremberg in 1609 and published around forty ornament designs, mostly friezes of scrolling foliage and flowers sometimes incorporating mythical creatures and strapwork suitable for use as bands or borders on metalwork. The only derivation from his designs I have come across in England occurs in the improbable medium of plasterwork (see p.197).

These early seventeenth-century examples may indeed be evidence, as suggested earlier, of the somewhat closer links between England and Germany that followed the worsening of England's relations with Antwerp from the 1560s. That the influence of German prints was not greater may partly be attributable to the fact that, with the decline of the Hanse, they did not reach England in very great quantities. But it is also noticeable that, with the exception of moralities and religious subjects, the most popular subject-matter – contemporary battles, Germanic costume figures and portraits – was largely irrelevant to an English audience. This was certainly not the case with Flemish prints, but before discussing their extraordinarily pervasive influence we need to look at that of prints issuing from France.

Chapter 4

THE INFLUENCE OF FRENCH PRINTS

Political and religious circumstances did not favour artistic contacts between England and France at the beginning of Elizabeth's reign. Her father's foreign policy was chiefly directed to the containment and isolation of the potentially expansionist France, and his retention of a gateway to the French mainland in the form of Calais had been a permanent irritant to relations between the two countries. Although her sister Mary had succeeded in losing this toe-hold with the surrender of Calais in January 1558, shortly before her death, the confirmation of Protestantism in England during the second year of Elizabeth's reign ensured that France remained, as she had traditionally been, the natural cross-channel enemy. Years of civil war in France during the 1560s and 1570s prevented the Catholic Valois and Protestant Tudors from achieving true amity, and English confidence in the French Catholics was shattered by the infamous massacre of Huguenots in Paris on the Eve of St Bartholomew's Day 1572. This was (mistakenly) seen as the first step in a concerted Catholic action against all Protestant countries. Catholic intrigue, much of it centred around the person of Mary Queen of Scots, was fomented at the English College seminary at Rheims:[1] there were many abortive or suspected plots to overthrow Elizabeth. Eventually, with the traditional alliance with Spain under increasing pressure (which eventually led to open war), the old enmity with France 'was replaced by a partial though uneasy reconciliation secure enough in France's distracted state to prevent at all times the dreaded Catholic alliance against England'.[2] But by then, paradoxically, French influence on the visual arts in England had been almost entirely superseded by Netherlandish.

During the ten years before the accession of Elizabeth, the influence of France had been evidenced by the remarkable drawing for a triumphal arch by Robert Pytt (though its details were drawn from Serlio, see p.12), by the façade of the original Somerset House in the Strand, built for the Protector Somerset between 1547 and 1552, and by the pure classical monument erected to commemorate Sir Robert Dormer at Wing in Buckinghamshire, apparently in 1552. In the hands of French craftsmen

this French classical style continued at Lacock in Wiltshire, where John Chapman carved the remarkable stone tables in Sharington's Tower in the manner of Ducerceau; at Winchester Cathedral, in the equally remarkable Gardiner Chantry Chapel and tomb to Robert Mason; and at Longleat in the work done by the mason Allen Maynard and the joiner Adrian Gaunt.

The most influential French graphic work of the period immediately before the middle of the century were the prints etched and engraved after drawings by Fontainebleau artists, particularly those of Francesco Primaticcio (b.1504/5) and Antonio Rosso (called Fiorentino, b.1494); their production seems to have been limited to the years 1542–8.[3] The essence of the Fontainebleau style of decoration which these artists invented was the combination of paintings (having a distinctively artificial quality) and elaborately moulded, three-dimensional stucco frames. It is epitomised by the overmantel of the Chambre de la Reine (c.1533–7), the decoration of the Galerie François I (c.1533–40) and the Chambre de la Duchesse d'Estampes (c.1541–5).[4] The other artists whose work was reproduced were the Italians Giulio Romano – Primaticcio's master – and Parmigianino. Luca Penni was a rather special case: he was a prolific designer in the Fontainebleau manner and, after the Fontainebleau etchers ceased production, his drawings continued to be engraved in Paris. The etchers included Antonio Fantuzzi, Léon Davent, Jean Mignon, the engravers Pierre Milan, Domenico del Barbiere and René Boyvin.

Amongst the most celebrated images is the collection of plates illustrating the *Livre de la Conquête de la Toison d'Or*, published by Jean de Mauregard and Jacques Gohory in Paris in 1563, with twenty-six plates derived from designs for tapestries by Leonard Thiry, probably engraved by René Boyvin.[5] Another famous print is the *Nymph of Fontainebleau*, which was started by Pierre Milan in the mid-1540s and finished by René Boyvin in 1553–4. It reproduces the ornamental frame designed by Francesco Primaticcio for the figure of Danaë in the Galerie. The arrangement of three caryatid nymphs supporting baskets either

↗

36 (*top*) Broughton Castle, Oxfordshire, overmantel in the Star Chamber, after 1554.

37 Pierre Milan after Rosso Fiorentino, *The Dance of the Dryads*. Bibliothèque Nationale de France, Paris, Cabinet des Estampes.

side seems to have struck a particular chord with Antwerp designers: they reappear in facsimile on a pair of amphora-shaped ewers made in Antwerp,[6] and, greatly modified, in a print by Jacob Floris, whence they find their way into England (see p.147). Antwerp fell heavily under the influence of Fontainebleau: geographically, the distance between the two was not great and one of the artists working at Fontainebleau, Leonard Thiry, was Flemish, and returned to Antwerp where he died in 1550.[7]

In England there is scant surviving evidence that Fontainebleau-school prints were copied outright. One instance is the overmantel in the Star Chamber at Broughton Castle in Oxfordshire (Fig. 36), which belongs to the work executed for Sir Richard Fiennes

in the years after 1554, the date on the central chimney on the north front.[8] The chimneypiece and overmantel are impressively classical and may derive from a plate in Serlio. The stucco panel in the overmantel depicts dryads dancing around an oak tree and, as Martin Biddle demonstrated some years ago, derives from the engraving, *The Dance of the Dryads* by Pierre Milan after a design by Rosso Fiorentino (Fig. 37).[9] He commented that the surrounding cartouche is very close in style to plasterwork in the Galerie François I at Fontainebleau: in fact it is a literal copy of another engraving by an unidentified Fontainebleau-school artist (Fig. 38).

This ensemble represents an impressively speedy take-up of published continental material and is noticeably more sophisticated than the other work of the period at Broughton, a fact that perhaps lends credence to the suggestion that it was in fact intended for Dudley Castle instead.[10] The same cartouche, incidentally, may also have inspired the design of the overmantel in the gallery at Lyme Park in Cheshire.

French influence was discerned many years ago by Saxl and Wittkower in the portrait of Sir John Luttrell at Dunster Castle in Somerset, and reiterated by Frances Yates in her brilliant comparison of the picture with the original version, painted in 1550, which now belongs to the Courtauld Institute of Art, London.[11] She suggested that the allegorical scene in the upper left-hand corner, which has such a strong whiff of Fontainebleau, was actually painted by a Fontainebleau artist; this suggestion has not met with universal acceptance.[12] If prints were used in the composition of this picture they have not been identified.

Identifiable Fontainebleau-school prints were, however, employed by Gerlach Flicke in his portrait of Thomas Cranmer dated 1546 (Fig. 41).[13] Flicke was not at all an inspired artist, indeed he has been characterised as 'a painter of meticulous dreariness, memorable only for his painstaking image of Cranmer. The gulf between Flicke's *Cranmer* and Holbein's *Warham*, by which it was inspired and next to which it must have hung, epitomises Flicke's depressing talents'.[14] Quite so. Nevertheless, Flicke's use of French prints for incidental elements is both interesting and instructive. Cranmer is shown seated before a window which is framed on one side by some bizarre, up-to-date ornament. This consists of a grotesque mask set against a piece of metallic-looking strapwork, superimposed above a female term figure whose accentuated nudity forms a striking contrast with the image of the sober archbishop, who was, incidentally, godfather to the Princess Elizabeth. These French features actually derive from two separate prints by Jean Mignon after designs by Luca Penni. The mask comes from the frame of his *Metamorphosis of Actaeon* (Fig. 39)[15] and the term figure from the right-hand side of that

from his *Creation of Eve* (Fig. 40).[16] Could it possibly have been Cranmer himself who asked for these elements to be included in his portrait? It seems most improbable. More likely the artist himself owned the prints: Flicke was a German from Osnabruck and is known to have been in England from about 1545 until his death in 1558.[17] Whether he acquired them before he left Germany or after his arrival in England is another matter; they were published in France perhaps between 1543 and 1545, and therefore predate the portrait by at most three years.

In 1551–2, five years after Flicke painted his portrait of Cranmer, Guillim Scrots was paid for several versions of a posthumous portrait of Henry Howard, Earl of Surrey (Fig. 44), who had been a loyal supporter of the King against the Yorkshire rebels in 1536; he was also a humanist, translating the *Aeneid* and contributing to the introduction of the sonnet from Italy, but he made himself unpopular and was executed on a trumped-up charge of treason in 1547. Scrots had been appointed court painter to Queen Mary, Regent of the Netherlands, in 1537 and had arrived in England before autumn 1545.[18] In the simpler versions he depicts the Earl standing with one elbow on a broken column (probably alluding to the principal attribute of Fortitude), with a putto in the top left-hand corner, holding a heraldic shield.[19] These details have been taken as evidence of the influence on Scrots of Italian Renaissance impulses in general, and his inclusion of draperies and classical architecture in his portrait of Edward VI as implying a knowledge of the Florentine court portraiture of Bronzino. In the elaborate version, however,[20] the artist has placed the subject within a frame consisting of an arched niche flanked by a male and female figure (with putti and ram's-head masks), each supporting a heraldic shield and standing on a ledge supported by grotesque masks and *boukrania*, the whole edifice surmounted by six putti, grouped in three pairs. The vocabulary is that of Fontainebleau, and it turns out that Scrots copied this composition from another print by an anonymous Fontainebleau-school artist, perhaps after a design by Luca Penni (Fig. 42).[21] If the available evidence suggests that actual Fontainebleau-school prints were rarely copied outright in England, the style was nevertheless promoted in two collections of plates published by the designer and architect Ducerceau, and thereby achieved a limited popularity in this country during the 1560s and 1570s.

Jacques Androuet Ducerceau (*c.*1520–86) was an extremely prolific designer whose output appears to start in 1549 with a suite of triumphal arches published in Orléans. Over the next twenty-five years, a stream of publications followed:[22] suites of imaginary views of Rome after Leonard Thiry, *Fragmenta*

Structurae Veteris, and grotesques in 1550,[23] and two suites of plates based on the decoration of Fontainebleau, *Grands cartouches de Fontainebleau* and *Petits cartouches de Fontainebleau*,[24] which include copies after Fantuzzi. His most influential architectural works were published in Paris, the *Livre d'Architecture* (1559), with a second and third in 1561 and 1572; *Leçons de perspective pratique* appeared in 1576, and two volumes illustrating many of the great Renaissance palaces appeared under the title *Les Plus Excellents Bastiments de France* in 1576 and 1579. Two suites of grotesques were published in 1562 and 1566,[25] and a collection of furniture designs in the later 1560s.[26]

English buildings influenced by Ducerceau's architectural plates include – modified almost beyond recognition – the elevation of the west front of Burghley, from the Château de Madrid (built 1528–70),[27] the layout of Wollaton Hall and its formal surroundings in the 1580s, and the elevation of the sides of the court at Audley End. Sir John Summerson has identified the influence of the French architect on the English mason-architect John Thorpe, particularly the *Leçons de perspective pratique* and *Le Premier Volume des Plus Excellents Bastiments de France*.[28] The possible derivation from designs by Ducerceau of a Doric chimney-stack at Lacock and the semicircular gable on the frontispiece of Corsham Court have also been pointed out.[29]

Some borrowings from Ducerceau, however, have been overlooked. The chimneypiece and overmantel in the drawing room at Loseley, near Guildford in

38 Anonymous Fontainebleau-school artist, cartouche, 1540s. Bibliothèque Nationale de France, Paris, Cabinet des Estampes.

39 Jean Mignon after Luca Penni, *Metamorphosis of Actaeon*, perhaps datable to 1543–5. British Museum, London.

DOMINVM
COGNOSCITE
VESTRVM

40 Jean Mignon after Luca Penni, *Creation of Eve* perhaps datable to 1543–5. British Museum, London.

41 (*facing page*) Gerlach Flicke, *Thomas Cranmer*, dated 1546. National Portrait Gallery, London.

42 Unidentified Fontainebleau-school artist, cartouche, 1540s. Warburg Institute, London.

vinci turpe', published in the *Second Livre d'Architecture* in 1561 (Fig. 46).

For such a prolific designer this is a miserly haul of borrowings. The two architectural treatises of his contemporary Philibert de L'Orme made even less impact In England. These were the *Nouvelles inventions pour bien bâtir* published in Paris in 1561 and the *Premier Tome de L'architecture* of 1567.[32] The following year Lord Burghley wrote to the Queen's ambassador in Paris, Sir Thomas Smith, saying: 'The book I most desire is made by the same author, and is entitled "Novels insitutions per bien baster et a petits frais, par Philibert de Lorme", Paris, 1567.'[33]

Sir Thomas himself added a copy of the *Nouvelles Inventions* to his library sometime between 1566 and 1570.[34] There is little that is purely decorative in either book, but a favourite basket arch may have inspired those found on several West-Country funerary monuments, such as Sir William Sharington's at Lacock in Wiltshire or Sir Thomas Phelips's at Montacute in Somerset. Mark Girouard has pointed out that the columnar chimneys at Longleat with their domical caps may have been suggested by de L'Orme.[35] It is generally accepted that the extraordinary obelisk that tops the clock-tower at Burghley was derived from de L'Orme's illustration of Anet,[36] but was John Smythson inspired by de L'Orme when designing vaulting for the Marble Closet in the Little Castle at Bolsover?[37] There is no way of knowing

Surrey (see Fig. 17) – the house built by Sir William More[30] between 1560 and 1569 – have been endlessly (and somewhat fruitlessly) pondered. It has already been noted that cartouches in the overmantel were copied from prints after Virgil Solis (p.25). The fireplace itself is flanked by Corinthian columns paired-up on pedestals decorated with rams' heads and swags of fruit like the tomb-chest of the Dormer monument at Wing in Buckinghamshire.[31] The term figures flanking the overmantel come straight from prints, three of them from a single plate by Ducerceau (Fig. 43). There is also clear evidence of derivation from Ducerceau in a design, perhaps for Longleat, by the Frenchman Allan Maynard (see pp.136–7).

Ducerceau's influence can be seen at The Hall, Bradford-on-Avon, built about 1610 for John Hall, a clothier, perhaps by the West-Country mason-architect William Arnold to a design by Robert Smythson. The chimneypiece and overmantel in the parlour are Flemish in their details but the chimneypiece in the hall strongly recalls a design in the *Second Livre d'Architecture*: coupled columns, Ionic above Doric, and an enormous guilloche frieze; in the overmantel, two sunk panels – a circle within a square – enclose a heraldic achievement framed by egg-and-dart moulding. There is a precise quotation from Ducerceau in the Reynolds Room at Knole in Kent (Fig. 45). Here the chimneypiece and overmantel are taken, with only slight modifications to the proportions, from a plate inscribed 'Senes a pueris virtute

43 Jacques Androuet Ducerceau, term figures. Victoria and Albert Museum, London.

ANNO·DNI·1546·ÆTATIS·SVE·29

SAT SVPER EST

44   Guillim Scrots, *Henry Howard, Earl of Surrey*, c.1546. National Portrait Gallery, London.

45 Knole, Kent, overmantel in the Reynolds Room, c.1607–8.

46 Jacques Androuet Ducerceau, chimneypiece and overmantel from the *Second Livre d'Architecture* (Paris, 1561). Victoria and Albert Museum, London.

for certain, but de L'Orme's influence may have been greater than now appears: around 1610 Inigo Jones seems to have taken features from de L'Orme's engraving of his own house in Paris for his drawing for a stable-block, probably for Robert Cecil, 1st Earl of Salisbury;[38] and Howard Colvin has shown that de

L'Orme was still being quarried a hundred years later for capitals at Calke Abbey in Derbyshire.

Etienne Delaune was not an architect but a designer of ornament *par excellence*. He was born in Milan in 1518 or 1519, was living in France by 1536 and died in Paris in 1583.[39] A Protestant, he was employed as engraver to the Paris mint and medallist to Henri II from 1552, and from 1553 to 1570 he executed numerous designs for metalwork. In some of his elaborate armours for the king the French decorative style and the Netherlandish converge so closely that their authorship – even their country of origin – is disputed (see note 66 on p.306). Delaune's career as a medallist undoubtedly affected his output of engravings, to which he turned after the death of Henri II and his own flight as a Protestant refugee to Strasbourg where he lived on and off between 1573 and 1580. In all he published around four hundred and fifty, the earliest being dated 1561. Almost all are on a miniature scale and do not stray far from ornament associated with medals, jewellery or metalwork in general. Exceptions are a suite of thirty-six illustrations of the Book of Genesis, and other old Testament subjects, and the twelve Labours of the Months whose ornamental frames owe much to the School of Fontainebleau.

Delaune's designs were extremely influential amongst French jewellers and continental goldsmiths in general: John Hayward noted eight instances either of the general influence of Delaune or of direct borrowing from his designs – the Old Testament scenes on a gilt basin of French or Flemish manufacture, the Months, together with the Planets, the Elements and Hercules and Atlas on a basin perhaps made in Paris during the 1570s.[40] Delaune's influence in England, however, was extremely limited. One would expect, given his background as engraver to the mint, to find it in metalwork, and two of the very rare instances of direct derivation which can be identified are indeed on contemporary silver (see p.202). In other materials in England I have noticed only the adaptation of at least two separate prints for the design of textiles now at Hardwick Hall (see p.260). However, an important instance of direct copying from prints by Delaune (albeit somewhat beyond the period covered here) occurs north of the border in Scotland, a country with stronger links with France. In 1638, Sir Robert Montgomerie added an aisle of late-Gothic character to the church at Largs (Fig. 47), to serve both as a family pew and a memorial chapel to himself and his wife: it contains a spectacular canopied tomb. The boarded ceiling is painted with an imitation stone vault decorated with the Seasons and biblical scenes. Directly overhead are various grotesques, and two of these were copied from Delaune's grotesques with subjects from Genesis which he published around

1570 (Fig. 48), whilst the remainder appear to be clever adaptations of other prints of his. The painter signed his name – J. Stalker – with the date 1638.

Delaune was by far the most prolific ornament designer in sixteenth-century France. When biblical subjects were required for decoration in England, the small-scale woodcuts of the Protestant artist Bernard Salomon (1506/10–1561) were more likely to be chosen than Delaune's. These appeared in the *Quadrins Historiques de la Bible* published by Jean de Tournes in Lyons in 1553, a book which was quickly translated into English (under the title *The true and lyuely historyke pvrtreatvres of the vvoll Bible*), Spanish, German and Latin in 1554, and Flemish in 1557. Salomon's lucid compositions and elongated Mannerist figures were clearly popular in northern-European countries: borrowings have been recorded in embroideries of French and Swiss origin, in one case juxtaposed with scenes derived from Holbein,[41] whilst his woodcut of the *Sacrifice of Isaac* was copied for a tapestry woven in Bruges.[42]

In England, Salomon's biblical woodcuts were adapted by embroiderers, by the painters of the Hezekiah wall paintings at Hill Hall, Essex, and of the cloth hangings depicting scenes from the life of St Paul in the chapel at Hardwick,[43] as well as by the mysterious continental engraver who decorated some spectacular pieces of London-made plate. This engraver, known by the initials P over M which appear in some of his work though otherwise unidentified, may have been active in London for a short period or perhaps worked on the Continent decorating silver exported from England. His work is discussed more fully on pages 201–5 but it should be noted here that three groups of silver have scenes derived from Salomon's woodcuts, a set of plates probably made in London between 1565 and 1570, a ewer and basin in the Toledo Museum of Art and a ewer and basin of 1567–8 in Boston.[44] The last, incidentally, provide the only identified instance of derivation from the woodcuts of the French immigrant Gyles Godet, their royal portraits now accepted as based on Godet's *Genealogie of Kynges* published in London in 1562/3, see pp.201–2. Godet was potentially significant, as Tessa Watt has pointed out, for he not only published a number of carefully edited biblical woodcuts at his Blackfriars shop but also maintained contacts with publishers in the rue Montorgueil in Paris.[45]

Bernard Salomon also produced a popular suite

48 Etienne Delaune, grotesque, *c.*1570. Victoria and Albert Museum, London.

of illustrations to Ovid's *Metamorphoses*, published by Jean de Tournes under the title *Metamorphose d'Ovide figurée* in Lyons in 1557. Similar to his biblical illustrations in general character, these proved almost as popular for decoration: pirated versions soon appeared and the woodcuts were adapted for embroideries.[46] Salomon's woodcut of Europa and the Bull was copied for the elaborate titlepage of John Dee's *General and rare memorials pertaining to the Perfect Art of Navigation*, printed in London by John Day in 1577.[47]

Jean de Tournes also published in Lyons the work of another French artist active in the middle of the sixteenth century, although his chosen genre does not fall within the limits of this study. This was Claude Paradin, whose emblems, published under the title *Devises Héroïques*, appeared in 1557. Mary Queen of Scots adopted the device of a marigold turning towards the sun, substituting for his motto 'Non inferiora sequutus' her own, 'Sa Virtu m'Atire' (its strength draws me), an anagram on her name 'Marie Stvart'.[48] It is not surprising, therefore, that Paradin's emblems were sometimes used in embroidery done by Mary and Bess of Hardwick, in plasterwork executed at Sheffield Manor, one of the Shrewsburys'

houses, and perhaps at Hardwick itself (see p.256). They were also copied for a celebrated coverlet known as the Shepheard Buss and for a silver salt with the arms of Vyvyan, both in the Victoria and Albert Museum,[49] and adapted for some of the emblems painted on the walls of Lady Drury's Oratory at Hawstead Hall in Suffolk; they were also used in Scotland.[50]

This limited tally of borrowings from French prints – noticeably those designed by the Protestants, Ducerceau, Delaune, Salomon and Paradin – surely cannot be explained wholly by the rivalry and suspicion that existed between England and France during the first three-quarters of the sixteenth century, although these must have contributed. French prints may have been relatively difficult to come by in England, or they simply may not have appealed to English tastes. Perhaps French print-publishers lacked the business-like methods of print distribution that were such a prominent feature of their equivalents in Antwerp. Perhaps the true cause of France's dwindling influence on England transcended politics, religion or trade. French art was *passé*. In place of classical elegance, English patrons craved the Mannerist excess of Antwerp.

Chapter 5

THE INFLUENCE OF NETHERLANDISH PRINTS
I ORNAMENT PRINTS

Introduction

During the sixteenth century, twofold ties bound England to the Netherlands, countries which, though of dissimilar size, had roughly equal populations.[1] One was dynastic. From 1509, when Henry VIII married Katherine of Aragon, widow of his elder brother Prince Arthur, there was a Spanish queen in England. Her parents, Ferdinand and Isabella, no more than a decade later, bequeathed Aragon and Castile to Charles V, who also inherited Austria and Burgundy from Maximilian and Mary. By 1519, therefore, the Habsburg emperor – born in Ghent in 1500 to Philip of Burgundy and Joanna of Castile – ruled over Austria and parts of southern Germany, Franche-Comté, the Netherlands and Spain. Ties between England and Spain (and hence the Netherlands) survived Henry VIII's rejection of Katherine of Aragon and dynastic links were emphatically strengthened in 1554 when Queen Mary I married Philip II. England was thereby virtually absorbed into the Habsburg empire.

The other tie was trade, trade which had flourished since the Middle Ages, based at first on exports from England of raw wool, later replaced by 'white' undyed cloth which was finished in the Netherlands for resale. For England, as for the major trading countries of northern Europe – the Baltic, Germany, Italy and the Iberian peninsular – the most important town in the Netherlands was Antwerp.[2]

Designated by the English monarchy the 'staple' or town with an exclusive right of trading in woollen cloth during the fifteenth century, Antwerp enjoyed a meteoric rise achieved at the expense of Bruges, which was hampered by a combination of the silting of the river Zwijn and the outdated medieval protectionism there which discouraged merchants. Final ascendancy over Bruges had come in 1503 when the Portuguese chose Antwerp as their staple for the newly established East India trade, in which south-German copper and silver were bought to barter for Madeiran sugar, and ivory and spices from West Africa and India.

From the beginning of the sixteenth century, therefore, ~~Antwerp~~ was the commercial and financial hub of northern Europe.[3] The city boasted spacious quays on the Scheldt (which Dürer drew on his visit in 1520–21), an enlarged Exchange built in 1531, and broad streets punctuated at regular intervals by streams and canals with bridges. New city walls were built in 1543–53 with modern Italian-style ramparts,[4] and the northern part of the town was laid out on a plan of parallel canals by the property developer Gilbert van Schoonbeke.[5] The new Town Hall – by far the largest in Europe – was built in 1561–5 to the designs of Cornelis Floris.

Antwerp was also a major centre of printing. Printing was the most important of the secondary industries attracted to Antwerp as a direct result of her commercial success and consequent expansion in population.[6] In Antwerp, editions of the complete works of Erasmus were printed, together with editions of classical authors, textbooks, dictionaries, geographical, medical, botanical and other scientific treatises. Thomas More's *Utopia* (which he conceived while staying in the house of the town clerk, Pieter Gillis) was published in Antwerp in 1516, and the revised edition of William Tyndale's translation of the New Testament (which had first appeared in 1526) was published there in 1534.[7] The effect of the latter was that 'Europe's greatest commercial city became in a very real sense the cradle of the English Reformation'.[8]

The first half of the century was not without its troubles. The Netherlands (like England) began to feel the rise of Protestantism during the first two decades. Lutheranism was banned by government edict in 1520, two years later Charles V set up a state-run inquisition and the first Protestant martyr was burnt in Brussels in 1523. During his reign at least two thousand Netherlanders were executed for their heterodox beliefs and more were penalised by confiscations, fines or banishment. During the years 1536–8 and 1544–5 persecution was particularly severe (amongst those who fled for their life from Antwerp in 1544 was the artist and engraver, Cornelis Bos, who was a member of the fanatical sect of Loists, see pp.49–52).

The 1550s were a watershed for Antwerp. Thereafter her prosperity began to decline as a result of political and religious upheavals in the Netherlands. In 1555–6 Charles V felt confident enough of his ascendancy over the heretics to abdicate in favour of his son Philip II; but the latter remained in the Netherlands only until 1559, when he left for Spain, entrusting government to his half-sister Margaret, Duchess of Parma. Cardinal Granvelle, a career civil servant from Franche-Comté, was designated her principal adviser and later primate of the Netherlands. His dismissal in 1564 weakened the government and made it vulnerable to a series of revolts by militant Calvinists. The first followed a poor harvest in 1565. Near-starvation combined with high unemployment led to outbreaks of mob violence. These culminated in the infamous *Beeldenstorm* or iconoclasm of 20–23 August 1566, which in Antwerp left the cathedral, the parish churches and other religious foundations bereft of images – altars, crosses, statues, paintings, organs. Order was only restored when Philip sent money to enable Margaret to raise troops and in April 1567 they garrisoned Antwerp. Later that year the able and ruthless Duke of Alba arrived in the Netherlands and set up a new court which tried and condemned twelve thousand heretics. Huge numbers of refugees fled Antwerp during these years for the safety of the Protestant countries of northern Europe. Many arrived in England.[9]

Hand in hand with the religious and political strife of the 1560s went a worsening of relations between Antwerp and England. In 1563, irritated by English piracy in the Channel and by the steady flow of Protestants to England where they pursued heretical religious practices, Margaret of Parma placed an embargo on the import of English cloth; parliament in London retaliated with an embargo on all imports from the Netherlands. The Merchant Adventurers further damaged the dwindling prosperity of Antwerp by securing a market for their cloth at Emden. Trouble erupted again during the winter of 1568–9 with the reciprocal imprisonment of English merchants in Antwerp and of Netherlandish merchants in London. Antwerp was effectively closed to trade with England. The Merchant Adventurers had meanwhile succeeded in establishing an alternative market in the Baltic in July 1567, entering into a ten-year agreement with Hamburg.

Despite his success in suppressing heresy – not one town rose to support the Prince of Orange when he invaded the Netherlands from Germany in 1568 – the Duke of Alba never managed to put his government on a secure financial footing. In 1572 the second revolt of the Netherlands began, again triggered partly by an exceptionally severe winter which occasioned extreme poverty and high unemployment. Zeeland and Holland fell to the rebels and Alba was unable to recapture them, having had to concentrate on Louis of Nassau's invasion from France. In 1573 he was recalled to Spain; two years later the Spanish government was bankrupt once more and Philip was unable to pay his soldiers. In 1576 mercenaries sacked Antwerp in the so-called 'Spanish Fury', and shortly afterwards all the provinces signed the Pacification of Ghent to protect themselves against the marauding troops. However, after the withdrawal of these troops from Antwerp in 1577 extreme Calvinists took control both there and in Ghent, so incensing the Catholic nobility that in 1579 the latter joined in the Union of Arras under which they regained all their traditional privileges in return for renewing their allegiance to Spain and the re-establishment of the Catholic religion. In the same year the northern provinces formed the Union of Utrecht, renouncing in 1581 their allegiance to Philip II. By contrast, the southern Netherlands were eventually reconquered and Spanish rule – and Catholicism – re-established.

Eight years of increasingly Protestant government in Antwerp came to an end with a fourteen-month siege and the eventual capture of the city on 27 August 1585. Heretics were given four years' grace in which to settle their affairs and leave, those remaining being obliged to convert to Catholicism. By the end of this term, fewer than half Antwerp's population remained – no more than 42,000. The rest had fled to the Protestant countries of the North, to the Dutch Republic, Germany, Scandinavia and England. Antwerp's economic and cultural dominance passed to Amsterdam. The commercial *coup-de-grâce* was finally delivered by the blocking of the Scheldt in the late sixteenth century and the recognition of this fact by the treaty of Munster in 1648.

★　　★　　★

This picture both of dwindling trade between England and Antwerp during the reign of Elizabeth, and of the final ascendancy of Catholicism in Antwerp, is not matched by a decline in the influence of the products of her printing industry. Indeed, as Summerson remarked, 'What Englishmen got from Italy and France was, in literature and the arts, considerable; but in the visual arts it was nothing to what flowed in upon them, uninvited, from the Low Countries and especially from Antwerp'.[10] Although books and prints were traded in the same way as other commodities, other reasons have to be sought to explain their apparently paradoxical impact here.

One likely reason is that personal contacts between individuals – artists and patrons and merchants – in England and the Netherlands were maintained, indeed perhaps strengthened, by differences in religion at critical times. During the 1540s, when the Inquisition in the Netherlands was at its height, Protestantism was in the ascendancy in England. Seemingly unconnected instances of image-breaking during the 1520s and 1530s had been followed by Henry's break with Rome over his divorce from Katherine of Aragon, the dissolution of the monasteries in 1537–8 (when iconoclasm rose to a furious climax), the destruction of images in parish churches and, in 1541, the purging of Cathedral shrines. 'The full significance of these events was not lost on contemporaries. The shock of Catholic Europe – specially aroused by the king's treatment of the Canterbury shrine [of Thomas Becket, destroyed in 1538] – was matched by the unbounded delight of hopeful Protestants.'[11]

The reign of Edward VI, who succeeded his father in 1547 at the age of nine, was a brief period of extreme Protestantism, in which 'religious images of any kind were viewed as potential idols in any location.'[12] Hadrianus Junius, the celebrated Dutch humanist, and Emmanuel van Meteren, a leading merchant-scholar, were among the many aliens who visited, settled or simply remained in England 'for religion', whilst keeping their contacts with their compatriots at home in good order.[13]

During the reign of the Catholic Mary, many Protestants stayed in England, leading a precarious, semi-nomadic existence and forming an underworld that kept closely in touch with the exiles on the Continent. Around eight hundred English men and women fled the Marian persecutions, according to John Foxe, most going to Germany and Switzerland, some lingering in France; Antwerp under Charles V and Philip II was unsympathetic to Protestants. Amongst the mainly 'noble, gentle, moneyed and clerical refugees' were at least seven printers, 'who helped to send back a steady stream of anti-Marian propaganda and who exemplified the tendency of English printers to embrace the Reformation as eagerly as continental printers had embraced humanism'. One was the London printer, John Day.[14]

With the accession of Elizabeth in 1558 the majority of the Marian exiles returned, and they were joined during the later 1560s by Protestant refugees from Germany, France and the Netherlands. Marc Geerarts, the artist, was typical. He came to London in 1568, the year after the Duke of Alba's arrival in the Netherlands, and remained until 1577, when the withdrawal of foreign mercenaries from Antwerp made it safe to return. After the final capitulation of Antwerp to the Spanish in 1585, Geerarts retreated again to London, along with many of his compatriots.[15] Personal contacts of this kind must have ensured a steady flow of continental books and prints into England at times when trade in other commodities had dwindled almost to nothing.

Printing in Antwerp

The number of people associated with the book trade in Antwerp is recorded in the ledgers (*liggeren*) of masters and apprentices of the Guild of St Luke – membership of which was open to four main groups, painters, sculptors, engravers and printers. Of the 271 names in the last group, 224 were printers and publishers and 47 were exclusively booksellers. With reproductive prints becoming an important medium for the distribution of an artist's work, Antwerp's success in the field of book publication encouraged artists and craftsmen to move from Bruges, the principal artistic centre in the Netherlands during the fifteenth century. Altogether, a total of 1,925 masters were registered in the Guild between 1500 and 1600, and the occupations of 1,607 were noted: besides those engaged in the book trade there were 694 painters and 127 sculptors.[16] As Karel van Mander wrote in 1604, 'Antwerp in our Netherlands seems like a mother of artists, as Florence used to be in Italy'.[17]

Part of Antwerp's success must be attributed to the way in which, by the end of the 1540s, print production had begun to undergo a process of semi-industrialisation. Instead of the artist being his own engraver, printer and distributor as hitherto, a new breed of entrepreneur had emerged to take some of this burden off the artist's shoulders. Reproductive prints after artists' designs began to be produced by Cornelis Bos and Dirck Coornhert. Cornelis Bos had been received into the Guild of St Luke in 1540 but had already reproduced a work of Maarten van Heemskerck in 1537; besides engraving and printing his own work he also dealt in prints and books.[18] Coornhert may have been Bos's pupil. Unlike Bos, he remained in one town, Haarlem, for fifteen years and engraved many of the designs of his fellow-townsman, Maarten van Heemskerck.

The appearance of specialised print-publishing houses dates from around 1550 or just before. There were several. Hans Liefrinck ran one: he was born in Augsburg or Antwerp around 1518, had entered the Guild of St Luke as a printer in 1538 and proceeded to publish a sizeable number of prints, some of them engraved by his brother-in-law, Frans Huys; he issued an early set of woodcut cartouches designed by Jacob Floris and suites of ornament prints by Hans Collaert.

Gerard de Iode (1509/17–1591) ran another, having become a citizen of Antwerp in 1549 and received an admission privilege for printing in 1551. His output certainly exceeded five hundred individual prints[19] and among the artists whose work he published was Jan Vredeman de Vries, first in 1551 and again from 1565 to 1572.[20]

Vredeman's publisher during the interim, from 1560 to 1565, was Hieronymus Cock, the proprietor of the third publishing house – the celebrated In de Vier Winden (or Quatre Vents) which was situated on the corner of Korte Nieuwestraat and Katelijnevest in Antwerp. Cock's first dated publication came in 1548: it was an isolated and untitled suite of ornament prints depicting Mannerist vases and other metalwork designed by Cornelis Floris. Three publications appeared in 1550 and from that year until his death in 1571 his output was so prodigious that Cock established himself as the pre-eminent print publisher in Antwerp. Between 1552 and 1556 he concentrated mainly on engravings by the Italian, Giorgio Ghisi, after various Italian masters, Raphael, Bronzino and others, and works after such Netherlandish Romanists as Maarten van Heemskerck, Frans Floris and Lambert Lombard. However, when Ghisi returned to Italy in 1555, Cock was obliged to turn to landscape and genre prints after Pieter Bruegel, Hans Bol and Matthijs Cock, and ornament prints after Vredeman de Vries (from 1560)[21] and Jacob Floris (from 1566).[22]

These ten years were the most productive for Cock's print-publishing house, and the engravers with whom he was associated included Hans Collaert, Dirck Coornhert, Cornelis Cort, Jan and Lucas van Duetecum, Philips Galle (from c.1557), Pieter van der Heyden, Frans Huys and Herman Muller. Additionally, he himself practised etching and so did Frans Floris, Hans Bol and Pieter Bruegel, all three probably at Cock's suggestion.[23] After 1565, however, his output declined markedly, partly as a result of the religious and political situation in Antwerp and partly because several of the leading engravers stopped working for him.

Cock's significance lies not just in the sheer quantity of prints he published and their widespread distribution – they were reportedly sent to Frankfurt, Paris and to Spain – but also in their quality and their appeal to an educated public: his clientele included humanist scholars, rhetoricians and artists.[24] Although Cock's wife continued to issue prints from his plates after his death in 1571 until she herself died in 1600, his mantle as an international printseller catering particularly for the intellectual élite was assumed by one of his engravers, Philips Galle.

Galle was born in Haarlem in 1537, ran an unlicensed print shop there and took over from Coornhert the production of prints after Maarten van Heemskerck, which he executed for Hieronymus Cock in Antwerp.[25] After 1563 he began to publish his own engravings in Haarlem but by 1570 had left for Antwerp, becoming master in the Guild of St Luke and establishing his publishing house In de Witte Lelie (In the White Lily) in the Huidevetterstraat. He published many of the early prints of Hendrick Goltzius until the latter began to publish his own in 1582.[26] Besides satisfying the demand for humanist prints, Galle also published more popular prints, maps, portraits, ornament prints and pattern-books, establishing himself as the leading print publisher.[27] He employed amongst his artists his sons Theodoor (d.1633) and Cornelis, and his sons-in-law Adriaen Collaert and Karel de Mallery.

As far as the artistic life of Antwerp was concerned, the effect of its capture by the Spanish in 1585 was to drive abroad artists who could not bring themselves to embrace Catholicism, and to impose restrictive regulations on the publications of those who remained. The Sadeler and de Passe families were among those who left, setting up successful businesses in Italy and Germany. How individuals who stayed reconciled their inner consciences with the necessity of appearing to be good Catholics will emerge. The Wierix brothers devoted most (though not all) of their energies to producing prints for Catholic devotion. Galle's output until his death in 1612 apparently made concessions to Catholicism. But, as Cock had done, he maintained contacts with Christopher Plantin, the greatest book printer of the age, who was unusually adept at steering a course that kept him on the right side of the Spanish, whilst secretly sympathising with the underground community called the Family of Love which had a network of quietest adherents, among them humanists and members of the nobility.[28] Plantin was entirely at home in the cosmopolitan, scholarly and artistic world of Antwerp, but also travelled widely in the course of his publishing and bookselling business, attending the Lent and September fairs at Frankfurt and visiting Cologne, Paris, Rouen and other cities.[29] One of his sons-in-law was Jan Moretus who, with his own son Balthasar, established a business in scholarly and liturgical printing that lasted three hundred years. The success of the Antwerp print industry overall was such that their products reached almost every part of the civilised world, influencing the art of many countries including – besides England – Russia and Mogul India.[30]

Although print production continued actively in Antwerp throughout the period of Elizabeth's reign in England, the drain of artists from the city after 1585 contributed to shift the centre of the print-publishing business by the end of the sixteenth century to the northern provinces, which had secured their independence in 1581. Haarlem, as already noted, had been a centre of printmaking before the religious troubles; printmakers had also been working in Amsterdam, particularly Cornelis Anthonisz. and Jan Ewoutsz., although it seems that designs cut and printed in Amsterdam were sometimes sent on to Antwerp to be coloured and distributed. The main print publisher in Amsterdam during the second half of the sixteenth century was one who had worked extensively for Hieronymus Cock and others in Antwerp: Herman Muller published his own prints and those by his son Jan Muller who had been trained by Hendrick Goltzius.

Just how far did the prints disseminated by all these Netherlandish publishers influence the arts in England during the reigns of Elizabeth and James I? Even within the self-imposed limits of this book there are so many different kinds of prints that it is impossible to pigeon-hole them neatly. Nevertheless, we shall begin with prints whose main purpose was the straightforward transmission of style.

ORNAMENT PRINTS

The principal contribution of Antwerp artists to the development of the decorative arts was the highly distinctive combination of grotesques and strapwork. Grotesques had been derived by Raphael and his contemporaries from the wall paintings discovered in the Golden House of Nero and other palaces in Rome, while the system of metallic or leathery strapwork had been pioneered by Rosso and Primaticcio at Fontainebleau during the early 1530s. The process was felicitously described by Peter Ward-Jackson: 'It is clear that at this point the classical grotesque was joined by an underground tributary from the north, a tributary that had its source in the perennial love of the northern peoples for weird and comic distortion, that impulse which found expression in the capricci of the medieval stone mason and in the paintings of artists like Bosch and Brueghel.'[31] A number of artists including Pieter Coecke and Cornelis Bos worked in this distinctive style but its originator during the early 1540s is generally accepted to have been Cornelis Floris.

CORNELIS FLORIS

Cornelis Floris was born in Antwerp in 1514 into an artistic family. His father was Cornelis de Vriendt, his uncle Claudius was a sculptor and his brothers, Frans and Jacob, were painter and stained-glass-artist-cum-ornament-designer respectively. Cornelis may have been trained by Pieter Coecke van Alost (1502–50), a leading Antwerp painter, designer and publisher who had probably travelled in Italy and had the distinction of, amongst other things, publishing a Flemish translation of Serlio's influential Book IV in Antwerp in 1539. Floris travelled to Rome himself in the late 1530s, but when his father died in 1538 he returned to Antwerp, becoming a master in the Guild of St Luke the following year as a sculptor.

Cornelis Floris is perhaps the best example of the stylistic difference between an artist's major commissions in architecture or sculpture and his ornament drawings and prints. The former include the towering sepulchre at Zoutleeuw (1550–52), the Town Hall (1560–65) and the house of the Hanseatic Merchants (1564–8) in Antwerp, and the rood-screen in the Cathedral at Tournai (1571–4); of his funerary monuments perhaps the most important was that of the Danish king, Christian III, in Roskilde Cathedral (1568–after 1576), but he continued to carve funerary monuments and architectural decoration until the end of his life.[32] He died in 1575. Excepting only his decorations for the entry of Philip II into Antwerp (see below) which, being temporary, do hint at his original spirit, Floris's architectural and sculptural ornament is relatively conventional. His ornament drawings and prints, on the other hand, were often bizarre to the point of eccentricity, even perversity.

Floris's highly idiosyncratic ornament style was first expressed in the series of thirty-two decorated initial letters he drew for the *liggeren* (ledgers) recording the names of members of the Guild of St Luke in Antwerp. From 1541 to 1560 these initial letters took the form of strapwork enclosing human figures and, together with some drawings of the early 1540s, they are evidence that Floris rather than Cornelis Bos was the originator of this highly mannered style.[33]

Probably owing to his major architectural and sculptural commissions, Floris was not a prolific designer of ornament prints, and his output may also have been restricted because he was not himself an engraver – his prints were published by Hans Liefrinck and Hieronymus Cock. This may explain why an untitled suite of four fantastic cars, similar to drawings Floris had made in 1543, had to wait until 1552 before being published in Antwerp. They seem anyway to have had no direct influence in England. Similarly, Floris's earliest designs, a suite of extravagantly mannered cups and ewers issued in 1548,[34] do not appear to have inspired the design of actual objects in England, although given the convertible nature of objects of precious metal it may be that the evidence has simply not survived.[35]

The following year, Floris worked – under the direction of Pieter Coecke van Alost – on the structures erected for the triumphal entry into Antwerp of the future Philip II in 1549. These decorations took the form of arches, tableaux and other structures and they were publicised in an illustrated souvenir by Cornelius Graphaeus under the title *Le triumphe d'Anvers, faict en la susception du Prince Philips, Prince d'Espagne* in 1550. This work presented the most advanced Flemish strapwork ornament and showed how it could be applied to buildings, particularly if these were ephemeral structures of timber, canvas and painted plaster. Incidentally, among the 1,716 artists and tradesmen who collaborated with him on this project was Jan Vredeman de Vries, who became Floris's main disciple and apologist. Like other illustrated souvenirs of such temporary festival decorations of the sixteenth century, *Le triumphe d'Anvers* disappointingly failed to do more than ripple the surface of the Elizabethan architectural pool: the Spanish arch may have provided the source for Dr Caius's design for the Gate of Honour (1573–5) at his college in Cambridge.[36]

The most usable of Floris's ornament designs appeared between 1550 and 1555. This was a suite of masks, *Pourtraicture ingenieuxe de plusiers Façons de Masques*, engraved by Frans Huys and published by Hans Liefrinck.[37] These were so successful that they were pirated by an unknown Italian engraver who added some of his own designs and issued the enlarged set with a new title *Libro Di variate Mascare . . .* in 1560.[38]

Masks were as integral a feature of Mannerist art as they had been of Gothic, and they were clearly a continuation of the earlier tradition. Floris's designs were early in the field and evidently achieved a considerable circulation. Examples occur in England at Wiston Park in Sussex (built by Sir Thomas Shirley after 1575), on a doorcase in the east wing, in a plaster frieze at Lyme Park in Cheshire, built during the same decade, and on an appliqué wall hanging which was part of the furnishings of one of the Earl and Countess of Shrewsbury's houses (see p.258). The mask plays only a very insignificant part in the whole composition, but provides valuable evidence that the suite was known amongst avant-garde circles in England during the 1570s. It must have been a carver or plasterer employed by the Shrewsburys who introduced Floris into the decoration of numerous plaster ceilings in yeoman farmhouses in north Derbyshire and south Yorkshire – the list is considerable and includes Cartledge Hall, the Bishop's House in Sheffield, Attercliffe Hall, Greenhill Hall, Unthank Hall, Renishaw Hall, Old Hall Farm, Hagg Farm, Mansion House Farm, Norton, and Barlborough Old Hall.[39] All date from the first or second quarter of the seventeenth century and it is quite clear that the same moulds were used in every instance.[40]

Carvers of commemorative monuments also occasionally copied masks from Floris's designs, although the immigrant sculptors who settled in Southwark, south of the Thames in London, seem to have been so thoroughly versed in the Antwerp style of decoration that they hardly needed prints for inspiration,[41] while provincial carvers seldom came across them. Floris masks do, however, appear on the highly unusual triple-decker timber monument commemorating Sir Charles Grylls (d.1623) and his wife at Lanreath in Cornwall, and in the grander context of the overmantel in the Spangle Bedroom at Knole. The painted chimneypiece of about 1631 in the Kederminster Library in the church of Langley Marish, Buckinghamshire, incorporates at least one of Floris's masks, albeit from a pirated set.[42]

Grotesques and cartouches seem to have occupied his energies next, and three sets were published by Hieronymus Cock in Antwerp, beginning in 1554 with six cartouches enclosing Maxims of the Wise Men of Greece: these are lightly constructed, rather elegant cartouches set in grotesque ornament. Then followed in 1556 a set of twelve sinister designs with much reference to sea monsters and marine ornament, *Veelderleij Veränderinghe van grotissen ende compartimenten . . .*, with a second equally nightmarish suite the next year, *Veelderleij niewe inventien . . .* Amongst these designs are eight for tombs,[43] some, though probably not all, reproducing actual monuments that Floris designed and carved, mostly in the 1540s. They therefore summarise contemporary Flemish tomb-design by one of its principal exponents. A notable feature of three of the wall-monument designs is the way in which they are separated from the surrounding wall surface by a simplified silhouette reserved against the hatched ground representing the plaster of the wall: this parallels the darker silhouette to be found, for instance, on the wall-hung monuments at Breda.

The cartouches enclosing the Maxims of the Wise Men of Greece were, judging by survivals, very little used in England. One may have been adapted for a tapestry woven for the Earl of Leicester during the 1580s (see note 9 on p.316), and was indubitably copied for the decoration of the painted staircase at Knole around 1605 (Figs 369, 370). The distinctive addorsed figures of this plate are identifiable in the carved frieze of a panelled room from a house near Exeter:[44] the carver was probably a member of the Garrett/Hermon family whose workshop dominated Exeter around 1600 (p.172), and he may well have carved the block used to make the mould from which a plaster frieze at Dunsland House in Devon was cast.

The grotesques in the last of Floris's suites, *Veelderleij niewe inventien . . .*, published in 1557 seem never to have been used in England – indeed it is difficult to see in what context they might have been – but the eight designs for church monuments that form part of the set must (with Vredeman de Vries's *Pictores, Statuarii, Architecti* of 1563) have been the most readily available source of information for patrons in England about the style of funerary monument fashionable in Antwerp. They were certainly used by at least two out-of-London masons' shops.

One was that of an unknown mason formerly thought, erroneously, to be 'Thomas' Kirby.[45] Nine stylistically related tombs have been identified by Jon Bayliss,[46] two at Turvey (Bedfordshire) commemorating the 1st and 2nd Lords Mordaunt (d.1562 and 1571 respectively), the overall design of the latter closely resembling a plate in Vredeman's *Pictores, Statuarii, Architecti* of 1563; also in Bedfordshire, at Marston Mortaine (Thomas Snagge, d.1593), Husborne Crawley (John Thomson, d.1597), and Bromham (Sir Lewis Dyve, d.1603); in Buckinghamshire, at Hillesden (Alexander Denton, d.1576), and at Chicheley (Antony Cave, d.1558, monument erected 1576); the ninth monument is in Northamptonshire, at Fawsley (Knightley family, the latest – Sir Valentine – dying in 1619). To these can be added a tenth, at Hornby in Yorkshire (1578, commemorating Elizabeth Darcy who died in 1572). It is also worth noting stylistic links between these tombs and contemporary work at Burghley, as pointed out by Mark Girouard.[47]

Several of these display strong hints of Cornelis Floris, most obviously the winged eagles in relief,

with swags of foliage, usually carved on the sides of the sarcophagi, as at Turvey and on the Darcy tomb at Hornby in Yorkshire. In overall form the latter has similarities with two of Floris's designs, although if the mason had these on the bench in front of him he deliberately made significant alterations in scale and proportion (Figs. 49, 50).

The second workshop was that of Garrett Hollemans the elder,[48] who was responsible for a number of Flemish-style monuments in the Midlands, particularly the six at Chesterfield erected by Godfrey Foljambe to commemorate members of his family. Some combine a wall monument with a tomb-chest and conform to a type illustrated by Vredeman de Vries in 1563 (see p.86), others, both at Chesterfield and elsewhere, feature a distinctive pendant which is conspicuous (framing either an oval or a heart-shaped panel) in Cornelis Floris's designs.

These few suites make up Cornelis Floris's entire output of ornament prints. It seems likely that the sheer complexity of his most imaginative and innovative designs prevented them from exerting more direct influence in England.

CORNELIS BOS

Cornelis Bos was not, it now seems, the original spirit he once appeared to be. Born Cornelis Wellem Claussone in 's-Hertogenbosch about 1510, he may have travelled in France during the 1530s before settling in Antwerp where he was admitted to the Guild of St Luke in 1540/41. However, as a member of a fanatical Protestant sect (the Loists) he was obliged to leave Antwerp in 1544, fleeing to Paris and

50 Lucas or Johannes Duetecum after Cornelis Floris, tomb design from *Veelderleij niewe inventien* . . . (Antwerp, 1557). Museum Boijmans Van Beuningen, Rotterdam.

49 Hornby, Yorkshire, monument to Elizabeth Darcy, 1578.

52 Billesley Manor, Warwickshire, detail of the overmantel in the hall, c.1610.

Nuremberg (1546–8). In 1548 Bos went to live in the relative obscurity of Groningen in Friesland where he issued numerous suites of ornament prints. He died in 1555.[49]

Bos was primarily an engraver and his output was large and varied. He reproduced works by artists including Leonardo, Michelangelo and Raphael, Holbein, Heemskerck and Frans Floris, but he also issued ornament prints. He published his own interpretations of the Raphael–Udine decorations of the Vatican *loggie*. Some individual prints showing Italian influence were based on engravings by Agostino Veneziano. In 1544 he published a book of moresques mainly copied from Pellegrino, with a titlepage that is an early example of Antwerp strapwork grotesque in the manner of Cornelis Floris,[50] whose highly mannered style Bos imitated very successfully. Far from being the originator of the so-called Antwerp Mannerist syle of ornament, Bos seems to have followed current trends: engraving his own designs rather depending on others to do so, he was able to rush them into print before his competitors. For this reason they have seemed innovative.

Bos's subject prints were certainly used by craftsmen on the Continent,[51] but there seems no evidence

that they were known in England. What are principally of interest here are his ornament prints, and these were influential on both sides of the North Sea. One example, which surprisingly seems hitherto to have gone unnoticed, is the pulpit in Sint-Janskerck in Bos's home town of 's-Hertogenbosch.[52]

In England, most of Bos's suites of ornament prints exerted little or no influence. A single drawing in the Smythson collection in the Royal Institute of British Architects proves that Bos's set of caryatids and terms – or the Agostino Veneziano originals dated 1536 from which some were copied – existed in England during the period (see p.133).[53] Similarly, his set of strapwork grotesques published in 1540[54] was used in this country in what seems to be a solitary late-sixteenth-century instance. This is a wall painting in the Marble Hall at North Mymms Park, Hertfordshire, a late-Elizabethan house considered by Pevsner to be 'inferior perhaps to none [in the county] but Hatfield'. In the upper register of one wall, recently revealed by the removal of later panelling, the painter repeated a Bos grotesque no fewer than six times,[55] much as a plasterer had done a few years earlier – using a different print source – in an Oxford college, p.72.

There are no more than two instances in England of the use of a suite of five ornamental cartouches enclosing German translations of quotations from Seneca, which Bos designed in the mid-1550s (Fig.

51 Cornelis Bos, cartouche from the series inscribed with German translations from Seneca, 1554. The Royal Library – National Library of Sweden, Stockholm, Maps and Prints Department, De la Gardie Collection.

50

51).[56] Both occur in the Midlands and involve the same print. The earlier is a tapestry panel woven for Walter and Eleanor Jones (who built Chastleton House in Oxfordshire) in the Sheldon workshop at Barcheston in Warwickshire (see Fig. 388, p.229). The later is a panel in an overmantel at Billesley Manor (Fig. 52), fifteen miles north-west in the same county. This house was built around 1610 by Sir Robert Lee, the son of a London merchant. These occurrences are surely related and the possible agency in both of Richard Hickes, the director of the Sheldon workshops, cannot be discounted and will be discussed later (p.289).

Cornelis Bos's influence in England depends to a large extent on a single suite of plates dating from somewhat earlier in his career, perhaps even while he was still living in Antwerp (close to established trade networks) rather than while in semi-exile in remote Groningen.[57] This suite consists of strapwork cartouches enclosing French proverbs (Fig. 53). There is, indeed, some doubt whether he designed them himself: one plate bears Bos's regular monogram in reverse, but he may have copied them from an anonymous set enclosing landscapes.[58] The cartouches with French proverbs had been popular on the Continent – three reappearing on Hanns Lautensack's 1552 panorama of Nuremberg,[59] another as the printer's mark of Martin Vermeeren[60] and one borrowed by the Italian engraver, Giovanni Battista Pittoni, for his *Imprese di diversi principi* of 1562[61] – before they were taken up in England. Besides the adaptation of one for the titlepage of Stephen Harrison's book *The Triumphal Archs . . .*, which appeared in 1603, the instances fall into several fairly self-contained geographical groups, not necessarily unrelated.

Earliest is perhaps the tomb of Edmund Harmon (Fig. 54), the erection of which in Burford Church, Oxfordshire, he supervised in 1569, seven years before his death. Born around 1509, Harmon rose to become Master of the Barber-surgeons' Company in 1540, appearing in Holbein's painting of the handing over of the charter to Harmon's successor as Master, Thomas Vicary (the painting is still in the possession of the Worshipful Company of Barbers, London). No very plausible explanation for Harmon's choice for the inscription cartouche of this particular plate, featuring North-American Indians, has been advanced, although Harmon may have had many contacts with trade and Burford had historically traded with Italy and France, through the port of Southampton. A near twin is the monument Thomas Tipping erected, a quarter of a century later, for himself, his wife and nine children, at Ickford in Buckinghamshire. It was either by the same mason as Harmon's, or was as close a copy as possible. It, too, features the same Bos

53 Cornelis Bos, cartouche from the series inscribed with French proverbs, pl.8, perhaps early 1540s. Victoria and Albert Museum, London.

54 Burford, Oxfordshire, monument to Sir Edmund Harmon, 1569.

cartouche, and this fact tends to reinforce the impression that this plate was selected not so much for its symbolic content as for its ornamental character.

Almost contemporary with Harmon's tomb is the use of four of the plates at Wiston near Steyning in Sussex, Sir Thomas Shirley's house dating from the later 1570s, on a composite fragment of architectural decoration that is discussed in detail in part II (pp.141–2). It cannot be a coincidence that a plate from Bos's French proverbs was also used at Henry Bowyer's exactly contemporary house, Cuckfield Park, near Haywards Heath in Sussex. The engraving was copied twice for the decoration of the hall screen, dated 1581 (see Fig. 184).

The use of plates from Bos's French proverbs also reveals otherwise unsuspected links between three houses in counties further west. One is Wolfeton near Charminster in Dorset, owned and altered in the sixteenth century by the Trenchard family, who employed the Longleat mason, Allen Maynard, to execute the stone staircase and landing to the gallery. The gallery overmantel has the Bos cartouche (Fig. 55) and, being of a kind found in other houses within

55 Wolfeton Manor, Dorset, overmantel in the Gallery, c.1600

striking distance of Wolfeton – Montacute and Wayford in Somerset, and Stockton in Wiltshire – is attributable on stylistic grounds to another man with Longleat connections, William Arnold (see below, pp.146–53). There are also reasons for believing that William Arnold was responsible for alterations in the gallery at Beckington Abbey, a scarcely known house in north Somerset, built perhaps as the hospital of the Augustinian canons around 1502: here a different Bos cartouche was chosen for the decoration of the overmantel (which does not survive, see Fig. 70). Clearly related to this is another, also lost, at Claverton Old Manor, the early seventeenth-century house that was demolished when the present house was built in 1819–20. Fortunately some of its interiors had been recorded in drawings by C.J. Richardson and survive in the Victoria and Albert Museum. These show that one of its overmantels derives from the same Bos suite and make it likely that Arnold was again involved here, particularly as the two houses are no more than ten miles apart.[62]

From this brief survey it can be seen that Cornelis Bos had some impact on architectural decoration in England during the period, mainly through his suites of cartouches.

JACOB FLORIS

Cartouches were the speciality of Bos's slightly younger contemporary Jacob Floris (1524–81), whose older brothers were Frans Floris the painter and Cornelis Floris, architect, sculptor and ornament designer, whose influence has already been examined.

Jacob Floris was trained as a glass painter, becoming a member of the Guild of St Luke in 1551, and executed a Last Judgement window over the west door of St Gudule in Brussels and an Adoration of the Shepherds (now lost) for the Cathedral in Antwerp. A shadowy figure today, there is ample evidence that in his role as a designer of ornament he was well known in his own time, even in this country. Floris's output was apparently limited to, at most, sixty-six plates of cartouches. His authorship of twenty-four of these, early cartouches executed in woodcut and published by Hans Liefrinck in Antwerp in 1560 under the title *Varii generis partitionum . . . ,*[63] has been doubted. The woodcut technique makes them seem substantially different from those of the other undoubted Floris sets which are all intaglio prints, while some of the cartouches also have an atypical bi-axial symmetry. The area occupied by the inscriptions is in many instances very small in relation to the whole: this gives the cartouches a 'muscle-bound' appearance similar to the ornament of the triumphal arches erected for the entry of the Duke of Anjou into Antwerp in 1549, perhaps to designs by Jacob's brother, Cornelis.[64]

One of these cartouches (Fig. 57) was used on Christopher Saxton's map of Wiltshire first published in 1576 and reissued in the complete *Atlas* in 1579 (Fig. 56). This should, therefore, be the single piece of evidence needed to prove that this enigmatic set was known in England, were it not for the fact that most of Saxton's maps were engraved by Flemish artists in Antwerp: Wiltshire was engraved by Remigius Hogenberg. So, unless other instances of dependence on the set come to light, it may well be that these unusual woodcut cartouches never reached England in their original form during the sixteenth century.

A few years later, Jacob Floris designed a set that was engraved by Herman Jansz. Muller under the title *Veelderhande cierlijke Compertimenten* and published in Antwerp in 1564.[65] They immediately proved popular on the Continent, the earliest use apparently being the decoration of sumptuous parade armours. These are the helmet belonging to the parade armour of Erik XIV of Sweden apparently made by Elisais Libaerts of Antwerp between 1560 and 1563, which is in the Stockholm State Armoury, and the breastplate of a parade armour now in Dresden.[66] Both have cartouches closely resembling Floris's. One possibility is that the cartouches on the armours were actually

designed by Jacob Floris himself, which – given the versatility of Antwerp designers at the time – is eminently feasible: his drawing for them might later have been engraved for the *Veelderhande cierlijke Compertementen*. Cartouches from the same set were copied by an unknown Flemish carver of outstanding technical ability, only a few years later, in the decoration of a spinet dated 1568, in the Victoria and Albert Museum.[67]

It seems to have taken twelve years from their date of publication for the cartouches of *Veelderhande cierlijke Compertementen* to make themselves felt in England. As with Floris's early set *Varii generis partitionum . . .*, the first appearances are in the medium of print, <u>continental engravers</u> taking their

56 Remigius Hogenberg after Christopher Saxton, *Wiltshire*, 1576. Devonshire Collection, Chatsworth.

57 (*left*) Jacob Floris, *Varii generis partitionum . . .* (Antwerp, 1560), cartouche inscribed 'Camelus desiderans cornua etiam aures perdidit'. The Royal Library – National Library of Sweden, Stockholm, Maps and Prints Department, De la Gardie Collection.

53

cue from maps by Mercator and Ortelius by including no fewer than three Floris cartouches on Saxton's map of Cornwall (1576) and another on Lancaster (1577, both reissued in the *Atlas* in 1579).[68] Theoretically these map cartouches might subsequently have been used as models for ornament as easily as the originals themselves.

With one exception, the geographical distribution of uses of Floris's *Veelderhande cierlijke Compertementen* – as of derivations from Cornelis Bos – sees a concentration in West-Country contexts, perhaps to be explained by the possible involvement of the important local mason-architect William Arnold. The exception occurs at Knole in Kent (Fig. 58). Here, a carved relief of a sea monster entwining a putto, copied precisely from one of the Floris plates (Fig. 59) but without the strapwork frame, is to be found incorporated into the masonry of the east wall of the Bourchier courtyard, on the outside wall of the Great Hall. No explanation can yet be offered for its isolated appearance in this context.

Otherwise, there are three houses where prints from the suite were used, Buckland Abbey in Devon, on a plaster overmantel in the hall, where a frieze is dated 1576; Stockton House near Salisbury in Wiltshire, on the overmantel in the gallery; and Ford House, near Newton Abbot in Devon, in the plasterwork decoration of the end wall in the hall about 1610.

58   Knole, Kent, alabaster relief reset in the loggia of the Stone Court.

59   Herman Jansz. Muller after Jacob Floris, cartouche from *Veelderhande cierlijke Compertementen* (Antwerp, 1564). Rijksmuseum-Stichting, Amsterdam.

Similar West-Country concentration is also observable in instances of dependence on Floris's next suite, published two years later under the title *Compertimentorum quod vocant multiplex genus lepidissimis historiolis poetarumque fabellis ornatum 1566.*[69] As with the previous set, the plates are varied, Floris's sources including prints that must have been freely available in the cosmopolitan ambience of mid-sixteenth-century Antwerp. Most of the subjects are drawn from Ovid, the Europa story and the Judgement of Paris deriving from Marcantonio Raimondi's prints after Raphael. Floris framed the latter in a cartouche that is a very free adaptation of the celebrated frame to the *Nymph of Fontainebleau* by Pierre Milan,[70] and Fontainebleau was clearly the principal influence, even informing the design of a Raphael-type grotesque appropriate for a ceiling (see below p.55).

I have so far identified three-dozen instances of borrowings from this suite, which makes it overwhelmingly the most influential of Floris's limited output. The plates were evidently known not only in the Netherlands but also in Germany, Denmark, Spain and even Italy.[71]

In England the response to *Compertimentorum* was almost immediate, indeed, if Henry Shaw were to be believed, it happened even before the issue of the designs. In *Specimens of Ancient Furniture* published in 1836 Shaw illustrated a most improbable-looking mirror at Goodrich Court in Herefordshire: the looking-glass depends on a cartouche in this 1566 suite, but the object itself is dated 1559. Nonetheless, no more than a handful of years elapsed before the Floris cartouches were used in this country. The instances occur in two different geographical areas at almost precisely the same time, with another discrete geographical group only slightly later in date. All may be related, but for the time being we must be content here to note the instances, whose significance will be discussed more fully later on (see p.170).

The earliest surviving object in England whose decoration was based on this suite is the Eglantine Table, made to celebrate the marriage of the Earl and Countess of Shrewsbury in 1567. The prints were used again for the Judgement of Paris table-carpet dated 1574 and, twenty years later, for the overmantel cartouche in the Countess's bedchamber at Hardwick. A much more modest house in the area, Carbrook Hall on the outskirts of Sheffield, has an overmantel based on another design in the same suite, and may well be the work of the same plasterer. It was in this way that the decorative influence of a great house was disseminated in its locality.

Three cartouches from the *Compertimentorum* were adapted for the screen in the hall of Middle Temple in London (see Fig. 276), dating from the 1570s, one so radically that it is almost unrecognisable. Perhaps related to this, though apparently executed nearly two decades later, are two timber chimneypieces and overmantels from Canonbury House, Islington, built in the late sixteenth century by Sir John Spencer, Lord Mayor of London (Fig. 65). Dated 1599 and 1601, these have cartouches from this Floris suite (Fig. 62) and are now in the hall and King William's Room at Castle Ashby, Northamptonshire. The tomb of Sir Thomas Gresham (d.1579) in Great St Helen, Bishopsgate, London, may have been carved within a decade of the Middle Temple screen. It could hardly be more different, consisting of a chaste, fluted chest with applied Mannerist cartouches. With the exception of these, the tomb is so classical and accomplished that it might have been made in Antwerp and shipped over for setting up in the church. Whatever the truth, one of the armorial cartouches, on the west end of the chest, was based on a plate in Floris's *Compertimentorum* of 1566 (Figs 60, 61).

From what has gone before, it is not surprising to find that another geographically distinct group of work dependent on Floris's *Compertimentorum* and having associations with William Arnold is to be found in the West Country. Amongst the earliest instances is the monument commemorating Sir Thomas Phelips (d.1588) at Montacute in Somerset, which has an elaborate cresting based closely on the strapwork cartouche with which Jacob Floris framed the Judgement of Paris (see p.147 and Figs 227, 435). The backplate of the monument has a cartouche copied from an anonymous Flemish set and this combination of sources (with the addition of prints after Vredeman de Vries) also occurs in the house, which Arnold designed and built for Sir Edward Phelips after 1588. No fewer than three overmantel cartouches at Montacute derive from the *Compertimentorum*. Two plates from Floris's *Compertimentorum* were also used in the important early seventeenth-century alterations at Wolfeton in Dorset, where, as already seen, Arnold copied a Bos engraving. Particularly exciting is the derivation of the plaster ceiling in the east drawing room from the one ceiling design in the suite (Figs 63, 64).

Dunster Castle in north Somerset – another building where Arnold worked, remodelling the exterior and many interiors around 1617 for Sir George Luttrell – also has a plaster overmantel in the King Charles Room, whose cartouche is a direct copy of one in Floris's *Compertimentorum* (see Fig. 419). Another plaster overmantel from Dunster Castle appeared on the art market in 1988, and this too was based on a Floris cartouche (Figs 66, 67).[72] Flemish-style chimneypieces and overmantels survive at the Luttrell Arms at Dunster, but their engraved sources have so far proved impossible to identify.

Further west, in north Devon, is Barnstaple which

was a significant port during the period. Here too the *Compertimentorum* was used in plasterwork, particularly in the cartouches that form part of the elaborate decoration of ceilings: a superb example is that of an upper room at 69 High Street (see Fig. 158). This was undoubtedly executed by the Abbott family of plasterers and their use of a wide range of printed material is discussed later (see pp.159–64).[73]

Unlike the *Compertimentorum* of 1566, Floris's next suite, *Compertimenta pictoriis flosculis manubiisq bellicis variegata*, which appeared in 1567,[74] does not appear to have been much known on the Continent,[75] and exerted only minimal influence on the arts in England. One plate was adapted for the frame of the

60 (*top*) Great St Helen, Bishopsgate, London, detail of the monument to Sir Thomas Gresham (died 1579).

61 Pieter van der Heyden after Jacob Floris, cartouches from *Compertimentorum quod vocant multiplex genus* (Antwerp, 1566). The Royal Library – National Library of Sweden, Stockholm, Maps and Prints Department, De la Gardie Collection. The right-hand cartouche was used for the Gresham monument, see Fig. 60.

62 Pieter van der Heyden after Jacob Floris, cartouches from *Compertimentorum quod vocant multiplex genus* (Antwerp, 1566). The Royal Library – National Library of Sweden, Stockholm, Maps and Prints Department, De la Gardie Collection.

63 (*right*) Wolfeton Manor, Dorset, detail of the east drawing room ceiling, *c.*1600.

64 (*far right*) Pieter van der Heyden after Jacob Floris, grotesque from *Compertimentorum quod vocant multiplex genus* (Antwerp, 1566). The Royal Library – National Library of Sweden, Stockholm, Maps and Prints Department, De la Gardie Collection.

65 (*facing page*) Castle Ashby, Northamptonshire, overmantel dated 1599 from Canonbury House, Islington.

royal arms on the Apollo and the Muses overmantel made for Elizabethan Chatsworth in the 1570s (see Fig. 427) and another was modified for use in the painted decoration of the Kederminster Library in the church at Langley Marish, near Slough in Buckinghamshire: Floris's is the only identifiable cartouche among all the different designs in the library.

The success of Jacob Floris in appealing to masons, plasterers and other craftsmen in England was the result of his specialising in a type of ornament that seemed to embody the essence of the Antwerp Mannerist style without being impossibly difficult to adapt to their own purposes.

★　　★　　★

66 (top) Plaster overmantel formerly at Dunster Castle, Somerset, c.1617.

67 Pieter van der Heyden after Jacob Floris, cartouche from *Compertimentorum quod vocant multiplex genus* (Antwerp, 1566). The Royal Library – National Library of Sweden, Stockholm, Maps and Prints Department, De la Gardie Collection.

JAN VREDEMAN DE VRIES

Important though their prints undoubtedly were for decoration in Elizabethan and Jacobean England, the influence of these designers pales into insignificance beside that of Jan Vredeman de Vries, whose name has become synonymous with any decoration displaying a vestige of Antwerp Mannerism. He was an extremely prolific designer and the ready availability of his prints, coupled with their adaptability, ensured that his style affected most countries of northern Europe.[76]

Jan, Johannes or Hans Vredeman de Vries was born in Leeuwarden in Friesland in 1527 and was apprenticed to a glass painter. In his early life he led the somewhat itinerant existence of a young artist, but two events must have shaped his later career. At Kollum he worked for a cabinetmaker who introduced him to Pieter Coecke's edition of Serlio, published from 1539 onwards: from this experience may have developed his interest in idealised perspective views of cities[77] and in the classical orders themselves. The second event was his employment on the triumphal arches and floats erected to celebrate the entry into Antwerp of Charles V and the Infante Philip in 1549; the scheme was perhaps masterminded by Pieter Coecke and was recorded in an influential illustrated publication, Cornelis Graphaeus's *Le triumphe d'Anvers* of 1550. This commission must have brought Vredeman into direct contact with a number of fellow artists, including Cornelis Floris, and with the emerging Antwerp Mannerist style of decoration which Vredeman subsequently did so much to popularise. It is likely that he retained links with both Antwerp and Cornelis Floris during the next decade, for his first two publications – suites of ornamental cartouches – were published in that city by Gerard de Iode in 1555 and 1557, and at some time, like Floris, he became associated with Hieronymus Cock, the man who was to publish all his work from 1560 to 1565.

Vredeman remained in Antwerp, but being a Protestant was obliged to leave the city in 1570, going first to Aachen and then to Liège. He returned to Antwerp in 1575, overseeing two years later the design of new fortifications. The Spanish had garrisoned the city with foreign mercenaries in a new Renaissance-style citadel built by the Duke of Alba in 1567 and dominated by a statue of himself. After the withdrawal of the troops in 1577, the populace had wasted no time in demolishing it (and the statue), leaving only the outward-facing walls; Vredeman now incorporated these into the city's defences against Alessandro Farnese, Duke of Parma, by joining them to the Scheldt.[78] In 1581 Vredeman decorated the most important interior in the celebrated Town Hall to frame the Lamentation altarpiece from the chapel of the carpenters' guild, the masterpiece of the painter Quentin Matsys (the altarpiece now hangs in the Koninklijk Museum voor Schone Kunsten, Antwerp). In 1584–5 Vredeman registered as a Catholic,[79] painted the surrender of Antwerp to the Duke of Parma and designed the decorations for the latter's triumphal entry. However, he left Antwerp for ever in 1586, subsequently working for Duke Julius of Wolfenbüttel as architect, painter, designer and gardener. After the Duke's death in 1589, Vredeman moved to Hamburg, Danzig and Prague, where he entered the service of the Emperor Rudolf II. Later he returned to Hamburg, but apparently died in The Hague in 1604 having failed to win appointment as professor in Leiden.

Vredeman's designs for prints span more than half a century, number more than five hundred separate examples and range far and wide in subject-matter, from cartouches and caryatids to fountains and furniture. Cartouches were his first concern, and between 1555 and 1560/3 there appeared no fewer than five separate sets.[80] During the 1560s Vredeman designed three sets of perspective plates, following these in the mid-1560s with designs for monuments, vases, caryatids, grotesques and fountains. His first two suites of architectural ornament were published in 1565.[81] From the end of this decade into the 1570s he designed some of his most elaborate cartouches for publications devoted to coins and to calligraphy. Although he left Antwerp in 1570, he continued to send his publisher designs, for more cartouches, trophies and fountains.[82] Returning to Antwerp in 1575, Vredeman concentrated on the architectural orders and on garden designs, but after his departure in 1586 he had a suite of furniture designs published and a set of perspective plates.

Vredeman's significance will be more intelligible if it is examined thematically rather than chronologically by date of publication, even if some suites span more than one category.

Architectural Ornament

The classical orders of architecture were the most potent force in Vredeman de Vries's career as a designer of ornament, informing the suites of designs for gardens, his perspective plates, even the suite of views illustrating the Ages of Man.

There has been so much confusion among writers concerning Vredeman's architectural pattern-books – so much so that one can seldom be certain to which publication the writers are referring[83] – that what he did have published must be spelled out precisely. His earliest essays in the genre were, as it happens, also the most popular. They did not appear until Vredeman had been designing ornaments for publication for ten years, when his personal style had begun to reveal itself. The suites in question were *Das erst Büch, Gemacht avff de Zvvey Colomnen Dorica vnd Ionica*, and *Das ander Buech, Gemacht avff die Zvvay Colonnen, Corinthia vnd Composita*, both published by Hieronymus Cock in Antwerp in 1565.[84] Unquestionably the generic title *Architectura* should be prefaced to these suites.

Between them, these suites illustrate the ornament Vredeman designed for four of the classical orders, the fifth – the Tuscan – surprisingly not being treated

until these two sets went into their second edition thirteen years later, in 1578. It is probable that this third part, *Architectura 3e stuck. De Oorden Tvschana*,[85] was intended to complete Vredeman's treatment of the orders and was bound up with them, and possibly with his *Architectura* of 1577.

These suites are concerned not with the proportion of the columns or with the design of buildings from plan to façade, but with the decoration of the classical orders; this emphasis corresponded precisely with what English patrons and their masons required during the sixteenth century and ensured Vredeman's success. Additionally, appearing in their second edition in 1578, the year after the withdrawal of the Spanish from Antwerp and at a time when the city was re-establishing itself as a centre of Calvinism, it is possible – though at present unprovable – that the joint publication was seen as a statement of Protestant architecture, and enjoyed greater popularity in this country as a result.

The plates begin with pedestals, the Doric and Ionic side by side; next, the decorated lower columns, again side by side; then, in two plates, the capitals and entablatures of the two orders; finally (before the process is repeated for another set of designs) two alternative ideas for scrolled gables for each order, on another two plates. *Das Ander Buech* finishes with highly elaborate designs for scrolled brackets or crestings. Vredeman endowed these designs with almost every device and artifice of which he was capable: ribbonwork, angular strapwork, geometrical blocks, cartouches, masks and term figures are somehow contrived on pedestals, on lower columns, friezes and in scrolled gables. Designs for pendants and brackets add to the serviceability of the sets, which offer an unrivalled thesaurus of contemporary Mannerist architectural ornament.

There is ample evidence that these three suites of plates illustrating the classical orders were influential throughout continental Europe. Not surprisingly, this influence was almost exclusively confined to the realm of architectural decoration, although the plates were a potential quarry for the decorative artist in general. The earliest borrowing so far recorded occurs in the decoration of the Oosterpoort, dated 1571, at Hoorn, the important Zuider Zee port in the Dutch province of Noord Holland;[86] but they were demonstrably influential throughout the countries where Flemish or Dutch architects were employed. In Leiden, Lieven de Key's project drawing for the Gemeenlandhuis displays scrolled gables taken directly from *Das Erst Büch* and *Das Ander Buech*, as does the Raadhuis itself built in 1594. In Denmark, Frederick II's fairytale castle of Fredericksborg, at Hillerød in Zeeland, which was designed by the Antwerp architect Hans Ivan Steenwinckel, displays several features derived from one or another of these suites.[87] Their influence can also be seen in Germany and – more unexpectedly – in France.[88]

In England the monument commemorating Sir John Chichester, who died 1569, in the church at Pilton in north Devon has a scrolled gable clearly inspired by one of the designs in *Das Ander Buech*, but it is not a reliable guide to the immediacy with which these suites were taken up by masons, as the commission may have been delayed by several years after Sir John's death. The same may be true of two monuments in Shropshire, a county where Vredeman's architectural ornament had a short-lived vogue. These commemorate Sir Richard Lee (d.1581) at Acton Burnell and Thomas Scriven (d.1587) at Condover. Two elements on Sir Richard's monument were derived from *Das Erst Büch*, the lower strapwork of the cresting and the strapwork frieze, while a third – the pedestals of the side elements of the tomb and the flanking decoration – was copied from Vredeman's *Architectura 3e stuck. De Oorden Tvschana*. This suite may therefore have been bound up with the first two in the edition of 1578, which would make this monument (if erected around 1581) an unusually speedy response to a continental publication.

Thomas Scriven's tomb has a strapwork achievement based on a design in *Das Erst Büch*. The name of the mason is unknown but he was presumably involved with the building of Condover Hall between 1586/9 and 1595, for its scrolled gables are simplified from the same suite. The owner and builder of Condover Hall was Thomas Owen, who bought the estate in 1586. Three masons are known to have been employed on the house: John Richmond, a freemason of Acton Reynold, Walter Hancock of Much Wenlock and Lawrence Shipway, who is now thought to have designed the house. He may have been responsible for the monument too.[89]

Perhaps one of these masons had earlier been employed in building the advanced Elizabethan wing of Moreton Corbet, which now survives as a romantic ruin. The work done for Sir Andrew Corbet is dated 1579; its overall character is French, with attached Tuscan columns, but the detail is inclined to the Flemish and two metopes seem to have been derived from Vredeman's designs.

There is evidence for the use of Vredeman's *[Architectura] Das Erst Büch* and *Das Ander Buech* in a rather larger group of houses in the West Country. Most prominent of them is Montacute in Somerset, a house built for Edward Phelips after 1588 by the mason-architect William Arnold.

Montacute is a veritable pattern-book house (see pp.147–9), but all the identifiable details derive from no more than a few suites of plates designed by Jacob Floris, by an unknown deviser of cartouches and by Vredeman. Vredeman's influence is apparent as soon as the house is entered, for the hall screen is entirely dependent on details garnered from his *Architectura*; the capitals of the Ionic columns and the strapwork crestings which surmount it all derive from *Das Ander Buech*. The pierced taffril in the centre demonstrates how the plates could be adapted for use in architectural ornament, the design simply being mirror-imaged, or 'handed', to create this symmetrical feature.[90] Upstairs in the Great Chamber, the frieze of the chimneypiece displays strapwork derived from *Das Erst Büch*, whilst the handsome wind-porch, originally with polychrome decoration,[91] which served to reduce the draughts in the house has an elaborately scrolled gable that is copied directly from one of several variant designs in the same suite. This direct copy of one of Vredeman's scrolled gables is rare, and the more charming for being executed on an exquisite scale.

Adaptations from these suites confirm the relationship of Montacute with a number of other houses in the south-west. At Wolfeton in Dorset a system of arabesque bandwork from Plate D in Vredeman's *Das Erst Büch* was copied for the frieze of the chimneypiece in the first-floor gallery. Another plate was copied for the frieze of a chimneypiece at Wayford Manor in Somerset, built for Giles Daubeney around 1602, while at Stockton House in Wiltshire, built for John Toppe, a composition of panelling in what is now the Green Parlour was based on a design in the same publication.[92]

The Hall at Bradford-on-Avon in Wiltshire – a house built around 1610 for John Hall on the compact plan and with the powerfully articulated façade of a Smythson design – also has a classical chimneypiece with rams' head capitals copied (like those on the hall screen at Montacute) from *Das Erst Büch*; this proves that the interior, which Girouard firmly attributed to Arnold, was indeed designed by him.[93]

Besides confirming attributions already made, identifying uses of the three component suites making up Vredeman's *Architectura* (*Das Erst Büch*, *Das Ander Buech* and *Architectura 3e stuck. De Oorden Tvschana*) can also reveal links which have not hitherto been apparent. Claverton Old Manor, for instance, had a chimneypiece with a taffril derived from Vredeman's *Das Erst Büch*, while South Wraxall Manor, the ancestral home of the Long family not far from Bradford-on-Avon in Wiltshire, retains a fragment of carved wooden frieze in the Raleigh Room which derives from *Das Ander Buech*.[94]

Charlton Park in Wiltshire is a Jacobean prodigy house in miniature. It was built by the Countess of Suffolk, wife of the 1st Earl of Suffolk, the builder of what later became known as Northampton (and later still Northumberland) House, at Charing Cross in

68 Charlton Park, Wiltshire, gallery chimneypiece, early seventeenth century.

London. Outside, the metopes in the frieze on the south façade derive from *Das Erst Büch* while the gallery chimneypiece (Fig. 68) is carved with a literal interpretation of another design in the same suite (Fig. 70). The same mason (whether Arnold or not) was evidently also responsible for a very similar piece in a house in Enfield, in Middlesex.[95]

Plasterers also used Vredeman's *[Architectura] Das Erst Büch* for the low-relief strapwork decoration of ceilings. One demonstrates the ingenuity with which the plasterer adapted a print to another medium and

a completely different scale. Beckington Abbey in north Somerset was substantially altered during the early seventeenth century, gaining a sumptuously decorated gallery (Fig. 71), formerly with a plaster overmantel cartouche derived from a plate by Cornelis Bos (see p.52). Its barrel-vaulted ceiling has a pattern of low-relief strapwork and five pendants adapted from the decorated lower part of a Doric column in *Das Erst Büch* (Fig. 72). It was a masterly stroke of the imagination on the part of the ceiling's designer to choose a pattern intended for use on a

69 (*far left*) Charlton Park, Wiltshire, detail of gallery chimneypiece.

70 (*left*) Jan Vredeman de Vries, *[Architectura] Das Erst Büch* (Antwerp, 1565), pl.Q. Victoria and Albert Museum, London.

71 (*following page*) Beckington Abbey, Somerset, ceiling in the gallery, early seventeenth century.

convex field and to enlarge and invert it for use on a concave. This designer – judging by the combination of Vredeman and Bos – must again have been William Arnold, the architect of Montacute. The gallery at Montacute, too, originally had a decorated barrel-vaulted ceiling: how thrilling it would be to confirm that it once had the same pattern of broad-banded strapwork as at Beckington. Alas, we shall never know.[96]

Vredeman's [Architectura] Das Ander Buech also found its way into the hands of the plasterers working at the Court House, East Quantoxhead, in Somerset: one of its overmantel reliefs (see Fig. 152) is framed in a cartouche deriving from the left-hand design in Vredeman's plate 22 (Fig. 73).[97] Das Erst Büch also penetrated to the workshop of the Exeter-based mason John Deymond, who used it for his monuments at Whitchurch Canonicorum in Dorset (Figs 74, 77), commemorating Sir John Jefferey (d.1611), and at Bovey Tracey Sir Nicholas Evelegh (d.1618, monument 1620). Both sport ornamented lower columns copied direct from one of Vredeman's designs for the Doric order. Deymond also made doorcases for the Guildhall in Exeter and may have executed a group of chimneypieces whose character corresponds closely to the monuments. One was in the parlour of Bampfylde House in Exeter, built by a wealthy merchant at the end of the sixteenth century (and destroyed in 1940). Here Deymond would have come into contact with or even employed the carvers who made the panelling. These carvers were probably members of the Garrett or Hermon families who dominated this trade in Exeter around 1600 and may have carved the panelling of a house near Exeter, copying – amongst plates by several different Antwerp designers – two plates (K and Q) from Das Erst Büch.[98]

No other comparably self-contained and consistent group of work based on Vredeman's 1565 Architectura seems to exist in this country, although there are one or two much more limited groups. The use of a plate from Das Erst Büch on a chimneypiece from a house at Enfield in Middlesex has already been mentioned. Another was adapted for the frieze of a chimneypiece thought to be from Oatlands Palace; the piece must therefore date from sometime after 1565.[99] Of much the same date must be an overmantel in the Queen Elizabeth Gallery at Windsor Castle. This is a comparatively sophisticated composition of three bays articulated by pilasters and columns whose decorated lower parts and elaborate pedestals are identical in spirit to Das Ander Buech, and close in detail.

Vredeman's Architectura of 1565 was also used in the Midlands at Wollaton, the unforgettable house that Sir Francis Willoughby built for himself near Nottingham during the 1580s. His mason-architect was Robert Smythson. The plan was derived from

Ducerceau, the elevations from Vredeman's 1577 Architectura (see p.68), the hall chimneypiece was adapted from Serlio, but some of the architectural decoration was copied from Vredeman's 1565 publication: the scrolled gables of the corner towers, the main frieze with its metopes of circular paterae and boukrania, and the capitals at first-floor level which come from plate 4 of Das Ander Buech. The same plate

72 Jan Vredeman de Vries, [Architectura] Das Erst Büch (Antwerp, 1565), pl.o. Victoria and Albert Museum, London.

73 Jan Vredeman de Vries, [Architectura] Das Ander Buech (Antwerp, 1565), pl.22. Victoria and Albert Museum, London.

for this panel, but the change was made, perhaps by the mason who baulked at carving the figures. *Das Erst Büch* was later used at Hardwick by William Griffin, who adapted one of Vredeman's friezes for the decoration of the chimneypiece in the hall.

A plate from the third section of Vredeman's *Architectura*, showing details of his Tuscan order, was adapted for the design of the remarkable hall-screen at Burton Agnes, a house for which (like Hardwick) Smythson supplied a plan. Perhaps he also advised on the design of the screen, for this suite must have been amongst his belongings – at any rate, his grandson Huntingdon copied a print for a frieze in two rooms in the Riding School range at Bolsover Castle (Fig. 76), combining Vredeman's alternative ideas for a Tuscan frieze (Fig. 75) into one composition.[101]

There is evidence that Vredeman's 1565 *Architectura* may have been known in East Anglia[102] and it was certainly adapted for decoration at Knole, near Sevenoaks in Kent. Here the relationship between the taffrils of the hall-screen with a design in *Das Ander Buech* is pretty close, although the designer softened Vredeman's angular strapwork to accord better with the remainder of the decoration on the screen. The same kind of modification is also apparent in the ballroom, where the pilasters (Fig. 80) have low-relief strapwork adapted from a further design in the same publication (Fig. 78). Elsewhere in the house an overmantel frieze has a pattern taken from another plate in the same suite. The master carpenter at Knole was William Portington, a man who enjoyed royal patronage: he lived in the parish of St Martin-in-the-

74 Jan Vredeman de Vries, *[Architectura] Das Erst Büch* (Antwerp, 1565), pl.н. Victoria and Albert Museum, London.

supplied a bracket with human head which appears on the hall screen, while between the paired columns is a pattern of low-relief strapwork originally designed by Vredeman for the lower part of a Doric column; here Smythson flattened it to suit its new location.[100] Smythson had originally proposed a cartouche – derived from a set designed by Vredeman, see p.77 –

Fields in London and may therefore have been introduced to Vredeman's works by his fellow-parishioner John Thorpe, who was employed in the Queen's Works from 1582/3 to 1600/1.[103]

It only remains to mention two instances of derivation from these suites in Cheshire, a frieze at Crewe Hall around 1615, and various cartouches at Brereton Hall. Built by Sir William Brereton (d.1618) and

Within the monument inscription:

HERE LYETH THE BODY
OF S. IOHN IEFFEREY OF
CATHERSTONE KNIGHT
WHO DYED THE 7 OF
MAY AN DNI 1611

75 (*facing page bottom left*) Jan Vredeman de Vries, *[Architectura] 3e Stuck: Tuschana*. Victoria and Albert Museum, London.

76 (*facing page bottom right*) Bolsover Castle, Derbyshire, Riding School, frieze, 1630s.

77 Whitchurch Canonicorum, Dorset, monument to Sir John Jefferey (died 1611).

78 (*right*) Vredeman de Vries, *[Architectura] Das Ander Buech*, pl.7. Victoria and Albert Museum, London.

80 (*far right*) Knole, Kent, ballroom pilasters, *c.*1607.

81 (*facing page*) Brereton Hall, Cheshire, frontispiece, 1586.

79 Jan Vredeman de Vries, *[Architectura] Das Ander Buech* (Antwerp, 1565), pl.5. Victoria and Albert Museum, London.

dated 1586, Brereton is notable for its highly idiosyncratic façade: 'The front is not easily forgotten. It is of brick, symmetrical, and with in the middle a frontispiece with two towers once yet higher than they are now and crowned by ogee caps . . . The frontispiece has . . . a highly decorated sill zone of the first floor, with tapering pilasters, more decoration above the first-floor windows, and finally a bridge across from tower to tower.'[104]

Much of the decoration on this eccentric frontispiece (Fig. 81) derives from continental prints: three of the cartouches – the relief and the cartouches over the main entrance – were copied from the suite *Vigilate quia nescitis diem neque horam* designed by the Italian Benedetto Battini and published by Hieronymus Cock in Antwerp in 1553. The rest of the decoration depends on Vredeman's *[Architectura] Das Erst Büch* and *Das Ander Buech*. These account for the frieze on the upper arch on the façade, a panel copied from a metope in the second suite, a term figure and the central gable beneath the arch with

the rectangular cartouche below.[105] There is nothing particularly remarkable about these derivations in themselves. No: the astonishing thing about this façade is that the arched frontispiece itself was based on part of Vredeman's plate 5. This print (Fig. 79) presents four alternative designs for shaped gables, of which the upper right-hand design was selected for the central gable with decorative cartouche at Brereton. But Vredeman also offers two spandrels, and the way in which these arch above the gables in the print clearly caught the designer's fancy, for he reproduced these on the façade, forming the arched bridge spanning the void between the two towers. This uniquely dotty composition was probably a whim of the owner, William Brereton, himself, and there could be no better illustration of the versatile nature of Vredeman's 1565 and 1578 *Architectura*; his designs were used in many different media, and reproduced on a wide variety of scales. There is no doubt that further borrowings from the treatise will come to light.

★   ★   ★

For those who wanted an architectural publication that illustrated the proportions of the orders, provided plans and specimen elevations, even some interior details, Vredeman devised his *Architectura, Oder bavvng der Antiquen auss dem Vitruuius, vvoelches sein funff Columnen Orden, . . .*, which was published by Gerard de Iode in Antwerp in 1577. Its popularity is confirmed by the fact that it went into at least seven further editions,[106] but, lacking as it did detailed architectural decoration, it seems to have had far less overt influence in England than the suites just examined. Nevertheless, almost every feature of the elevation of Wollaton Hall, which was built in the 1580s, can be accounted for in the pages of Vredeman's *Architectura* of 1577 – the one-block rustication of the pilasters on each of the three storeys, the niches between them and the curious fenestration of the Prospect Room (Figs 82, 83).

The suite remained popular well into the seventeenth century. Vredeman's rusticated Tuscan order, illustrated on folio 1, seems to have been especially attractive, being used (to give a few examples) for the porch at Holland House, Kensington, at Bramshill in Hampshire for the reset arches on the terrace and on the entrance gate of the Abbot's Hospital in Guildford of about 1619.[107] The 1577 *Architectura* also seems to have inspired Robert Lyminge in his work at Hatfield and Blickling: the Hatfield frontispiece dated 1611 has three tiers of pilasters and columns with highly-decorated lower drums on elaborately-ornamented pedestals – absolutely in the spirit of Vredeman – while the cupola at Blickling was closely based on the publication.

The last of Vredeman's architectural pattern-books, which appeared (posthumously) in 1606, was also devoted to the orders, but was very different in character. His co-author was his son Paul, whose designs are much more conventionally correct. Their *Architectura Henric. Hondius Sculps. et Exc . . .*, was published by Henricus Hondius in The Hague in 1606 and achieved such popularity that it went into ten further editions, the last in 1662.[108] I have so far failed to discover more than generic similarities with any subsequent work, although it does seem possible that artists, in particular, were influenced by Vredeman's perspective plates.

Cartouches

More than a quarter of Vredeman's output of ornament designs was devoted to cartouches. The eight suites span a period of eighteen years from the mid-1550s and total nearly a hundred and fifty individual plates. In addition, cartouches play a significant part in many of his other suites, for example those nominally devoted to the classical orders, to perspective or to tombs. Little wonder, therefore, that almost any Antwerp-style cartouche found in architectural decoration in this country has tended to be attributed to Vredeman de Vries, regardless of whether he actually designed it or not.

Cartouches are the subject of Vredeman's two earliest accredited suites, both published in Antwerp in 1555, the year after Cornelis Floris's first printed cartouches, but nearly a decade after some of Cornelis Bos's designs in the same manner. This confirms that Vredeman de Vries was far from being a pioneer in the genre, even in his early work. The two early sets are *Multarum variarum'que protractionum (Compartimenta vulgus pictorum vocat)* and *Variarum protractionum (vulgo Compartimenta vocant)*, both published by Gerard de Iode in Antwerp.[109]

It is hardly surprising that these cartouches are somewhat tentative and awkward compared with those of Bos and Cornelis Floris: in 1555 Vredeman was still in his twenties, while they were respectively forty-nine and forty-one. Panels, mostly of regular form, are framed by cartouches which, by contrast, take on extremely complicated forms and are cut and pierced by metallic-looking elements which protrude and recede giving the appearance of considerable three-dimensionality. In *Variarum protractionum* short lengths of festooned ribbons hint at subsequent developments but there is no suggestion of Vredeman's later linkage of the cartouches to the image-edge – they stand isolated against a plain or hatched ground.

These two early suites provided inspiration mainly for continental engravers providing title-frames for

maps,[110] but were also known and used in England. A cartouche on the tomb of the Countess of Suffolk (d.1568) in Westminster Abbey, seems to have been adapted from one in the second set,[111] although it is rare to find a print source for any fashionable sixteenth-century tomb in London. In the country, on the other hand, unquestionable uses of *Multarum variarum'que* and *Variarum protractionum* occur in south-western counties of England.

A handsome canopied monument in the church at Bruton in Somerset (Fig. 84) commemorates Sir Maurice Berkeley who died in 1581, and his two wives (d.1559 and 1585): made of the local stone, its tomb-chest has pilasters and ribbonwork frieze in the Mannerist style with ribbon-like strapwork, while the back of the canopied upper stage carries two inscription plates framed in cartouches which are copied straight from *Multarum variarum'que* (Fig. 85). The same mason must have been responsible for the use of another cartouche from the suite on the overmantel in the first-floor Great Chamber of the Red Lodge in Bristol, built about 1585–95 by the wealthy merchant, Sir John Yonge (Figs 86, 87). From the second suite, *Variarum protractionum*, this mason copied at least one design for a decorative cartouche now fixed to the

84 Bruton, Somerset, detail of the monument to Sir Maurice Berkeley (died 1581).

85 Frans Huys after Jan Vredeman de Vries, *Multarum variarum'que . . .* (Antwerp, 1555), 'Ut pater miseretur liberorum . . .'. Stedelijk Bibliotheek, Leeuwarden.

82 (*facing page top*) Wollaton Hall, Nottinghamshire, built 1580s.

83 (*facing page bottom*) Jan Vredeman de Vries, *Architectura* (Antwerp, 1577), pl.B.1. Stedelijk Bibliotheek, Leeuwarden.

86 Frans Huys after Jan Vredeman de Vries, *Multarum variarum'que . . .* (Antwerp, 1555), 'Sic amavit . . .'. Stedelijk Bibliotheek, Leeuwarden.

Elizabethan eastern gate-tower of Wilton, near Salisbury in Wiltshire (Figs 88, 89).

A decorative cartouche corresponding to another plate in Vredeman's suite appears on a manuscript map of estates at Brailes in Warwickshire (Figs 90, 91). This map, which has recently come to light,[112] bears the Sheldon arms in the bottom right-hand corner and a collared Talbot crest surmounting the scale of perches on the left. The Brailes estates adjoin those of the manor of Barcheston, where William Sheldon established his successful tapestry weaving workshop during the 1560s, and also belonged to the Sheldon family at this date. The style of the cartography and the drawing is that of Christopher Saxton, on whose printed *Atlas* the celebrated Sheldon tapestry maps of Midland counties were based (see pp.223–6), and the present map may be the first hard and fast evidence that Sheldon and Saxton were personally acquainted. Indeed, it has been suggested that the map is actually a cartoon for a tapestry. The decorative title-cartouche might equally well have been copied from the Vredeman original or from the identical cartouche on Ortelius's map of Westphalia. Another instance in the West Midlands of the use of the same cartouche must, therefore, be related to this. This is an overmantel at Grafton Manor in Worcestershire, a house extended between 1567 and 1569 by Sir John Talbot, son-in-law of Sir William Petre who was Secretary of State under Henry VIII, Edward, Mary and Elizabeth.[113] Presumably it was his crest that was included on the manuscript map. Grafton Manor, which is less than ten miles as the

87 (*facing page*) The Red Lodge, Bristol, overmantel in the Great Chamber, 1585–95.

crow flies from Beoley where William and Ralph Sheldon owned the manor, is linked stylistically via its early classical porch with Longleat, whose hall-screen also has a cartouche derived from this suite.

An almost contemporary use of a plate from *Multarum variarum'que* occurs on an alabaster monument at Wirksworth in Derbyshire, commemorating Anthony Gell who died in 1583; the cartouches on the long sides were simplified by the sculptor from the plate inscribed 'qui in vobis sapiens est . . .'[114] Jon Bayliss attributes the tomb to an anonymous Nottingham workshop which may have been carving decoration at Wollaton.[115] Perhaps that house once had similar cartouches from these first two suites of cartouches by Vredeman.

★　　★　　★

These two suites issued in 1555 were followed, either in the same year or shortly afterwards, by an untitled set of three large cartouches which were published by Hieronymus Cock.[116] They are by far the most elaborate of Vredeman's cartouches and show a great advance on the earlier designs in the confident manner in which he filled the large (47.3 × 36 cm) format of the paper. Masterly from a decorative point of view, they were probably too complex to have been used as models for decoration: none was, to my knowledge, copied in any English or continental context. His next published cartouches were a different matter. These were two untitled sets of cartouches published by Hieronymus Cock about 1560–63.[117]

These cartouches show considerable similarities with plates in other suites by Vredeman around this date, notably with the two books devoted to architectural decoration (*Das Erst Büch* and *Das Ander Buech*) and the designs for tombs. The cartouches are distinctly metallic, and for the first time Vredeman integrated them into the overall picture area by introducing a system of subordinate strapwork, some aligned with the edge of the image area and offering the possibility of lateral, or indeed vertical duplication. In the second of these sets, the subsidiary strapwork takes the form of thin bands or ribbons. Both sets make much greater use of plant ornament, grotesque figures and masks, birds and animals. In not much more than five years, Vredeman had clearly developed his decorative ideas into a highly personal and successful style.

Their earliest use (as so often) was in the decoration of the printed page, both on the Continent[118] and in England: one of Christopher Saxton's engravers, Remigius Hogenberg, borrowed a solitary cartouche for the map of Lincoln and Nottingham, published in the *Atlas* in 1579. The suites were also the models for a number of anonymous cartouches, probably ori-

appearances of these cartouches in architectural decoration are infrequent but suggestive. Those of the set numbered with Roman numerals (Fig. 92) are found in four contexts, in the plaster frieze dating from around 1571 in a room formerly part of the former Lodging of the President over the gate at Corpus Christi College, Oxford (Fig. 93);[120] on the overmantel of the parlour at Levens Hall in Westmorland, in oak, and on another truncated overmantel from Lanercost Priory, now in the Bowes Museum; and in the sketchbook compiled by the Abbott family of plasterers in Devon.[121] Despite their wide geographical spread, it is not impossible, at least on technical grounds, that these instances are related. The plasterwork at Corpus Christi consists of repeated elements made by pressing plaster into moulds probably cast from a block carved in the round. It is conceivable that this block was carved by the craftsman responsible for the Levens and Lanercost panels, and it is by no means impossible that the Abbott family of plasterers knew of the Vredeman cartouches from this workman. The plates paginated with capital letters were only, I believe, adapted for the cartouches on the corner towers at Wollaton Hall.

Vredeman also seems to have designed the cartouches for a set of prints combining portrait medallions with strapwork cartouches, published under the title *Icones Duodecim Caesarum* by Gerard de Iode in Antwerp between 1565 and 1569.[122] With their dark background these show the influence

88 Frans Huys after Jan Vredeman de Vries, *Variarum protractionum* . . . (Antwerp 1555), 'Quo se fortuna . . .'. Stedelijk Bibliotheek, Leeuwarden.

ginating on maps, which survive in several bound volumes in the Victoria and Albert Museum.[119] In addition, one was borrowed for a cartouche on Molyneux's terrestial globe, printed by Jodocus Hondius in Amsterdam, an example of which survives at Petworth in Sussex.

Compared with this tally of printed examples, the

89 Wilton House, Wiltshire, cartouche on east façade of eastern gate-tower.

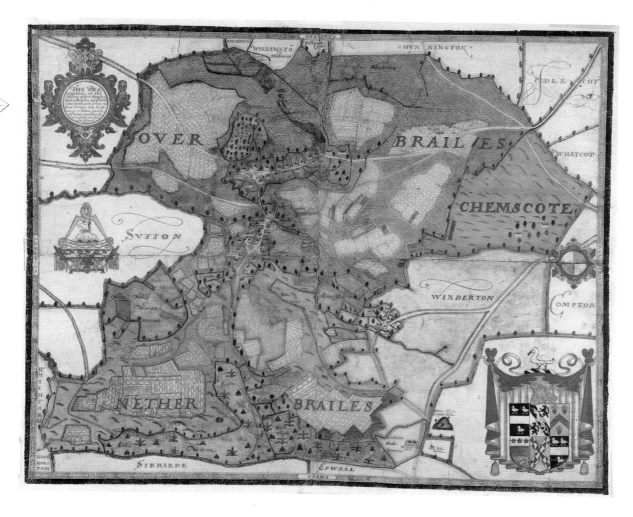

90 Christopher Saxton
(attributed), manuscript map of
the Brailes estate in
Warwickshire.

of Etienne Delaune.[123] Only one instance of their appearance in England has been recorded so far: part of one cartouche was borrowed for the decoration of Saxton's map of Hampshire, engraved by Leonardus Terwoort, probably in Antwerp. It is possible that the suite was never used in England for decoration.

There can be little argument that the cartouches for the next published set are Vredeman's masterpieces in the genre – if they are indeed accepted as being of Vredeman's design, as they have been almost universally since 1913.[124] The suite in question is *Exercitatio Alphabetica Nova et Utilissima, . . . Clementis Perreti Bruxellani . . .*, published by Christopher Plantin in Antwerp in 1569.[125]

In these large-format cartouches Vredeman achieved a remarkable variety within the restrictions of the type. There is a satisfying assortment of compartment shapes and the artist paid particular attention to the apparent fall of light, the two sides of the frame being brilliantly contrasted – one brightly lit, the other in deep shadow – to give a convincing illusion of three-dimensionality. Despite the wealth of detail, these cartouches never seem to be in danger of incoherence. In view of their complexity, the cartouches

91 Frans Huys after Jan
Vredeman de Vries, *Variarum
protractionum . . .* (Antwerp
1555), 'Non habemus hic
durabilem urbem . . .'. Stedelijk
Bibliotheek, Leeuwarden.

92 Jan Vredeman de Vries, cartouche from a series issued 1560–3. Bibliothèque Royale Albert 1er, Brussels.

93 Corpus Christi College, Oxford, frieze of the room over the gateway, *c*.1571.

Vredeman

were copied or adapted with remarkable frequency, both in the Netherlands and elsewhere in Europe.[126] This must reflect the status of the *Exercitatio Alphabetica* as the most popular of all Mannerist copy-books, the print-run possibly numbering as many as five hundred copies before the quality became unacceptably poor.[127]

In England, Queen Elizabeth owned a copy of the book (which still survives) and there are more extant in this country than in any other, perhaps an indica-tion that the reported employment of Clemens Perret as writing-master to the Queen's secretary has some foundation in fact.[128] Perret would have been in an position to promote and sell the book himself. The first identified instance of derivation from this writing-book occurs in 1573, only four years after its publication, when one cartouche was neatly adapted for the frame of a printed portrait of Archbishop Parker, and this was followed closely by the use of another on Christopher Saxton's map of Suffolk of 1575 (reprinted in the *Atlas* four years later) although the unknown engraver of this map may have been a Fleming working in Antwerp. The prime example of the influence of Vredeman's cartouches for *Exercitatio Alphabetica* on the printed page in this country is a large series of at least fourteen woodcut page borders used in many books from 1582 until well into the seventeenth century. 1582 is the publication date of Thomas Bentley's *The Monument of Matrones*, printed by Henry Denham: the book is divided into seven 'Lampes of Virginitie', the first five of which contain compartments of this kind. They consist of head, tail and sidepieces which could be, and were, assembled in many different combinations. None of the side or tailpieces was derived from Vredeman's designs, but ten of the fourteen recorded headpieces were copied from as many separate Vredeman cartouches in the *Exercitatio Alphabetica*. *The Monument of Matrones* and one or other of the folio editions of Spenser's *Fairie Queene* printed by H. Lownes for M. Lownes in 1609 and 1611–13 were certainly well known in their day and readers must have become familiar with the con-tinental style of their page borders. Headpieces based on these Vredeman cartouches were also used in *The Common Places of Peter Martyr*, published in 1574, a book which was on at least one occasion itself plun-dered for its decorative potential (see pp.222, 226).

Another publication that drew heavily on Vredeman de Vries's cartouches for Perret's *Exercitatio Alphabetica* was John Speed's *Theatrum Imperii Magnae Britanniae* which, although published in 1611 or 1612, brought together maps compiled between 1596 and 1610. Ten maps display cartouches borrowed from only four of the originals. All were engraved for Speed by Jodocus Hondius of Amsterdam (who was himself responsible for a popular writing-book) and it may thus have been he who was responsible for the use of the Vredeman cartouches rather than Speed himself. So, on the evidence of these maps, there is no absolute necessity for *Exercitatio Alphabetica* to have been in England at that date. Before leaving maps altogether, it is worth noting that Thomas Clerke's manuscript map of Borrowhall in Holkham, Norfolk, dated 1590, derives its cartouche from plate XXVII.[129] Perret's publication with its Vredeman cartouches certainly achieved a wide circulation amongst cartographic engravers.

The considerable complexity of the cartouches may have acted as a challenge to masons and carvers in this country, for many three-dimensional objects owe their appearance to this book. The instances of borrowing from the plates divide into several reasonably coherent geographical groups. Earliest in date are two instances in Kent. At Godington Park near Maidstone one of the panels of the overmantel, dated 1574, is carved with an adaptation of one of the Vredeman cartouches, only five years after their publication. This is a rather quicker uptake than was usual in England and may be explained by the fact that Kent was often the first haven for refugees fleeing religious persecution in the Netherlands. Not much later is a decorative cartouche, unfortunately without heraldry, traditionally said to have come from a house in Canterbury.[130] To the first decade of the seventeenth century probably belongs a handsome chimneypiece, carved in contrasting colours of marble, in a downstairs room at Knole, near Sevenoaks (Fig. 94). Its decoration, consisting of scrollwork and hunting dogs, was very deftly adapted from the top rail of Vredeman's design (Fig. 95), isolated from the remainder to form a perfectly satisfactory Mannerist frieze in its own right. These instances may have a simple link besides mere geographical proximity, though it is not known who any of the craftsmen were.

94 (*top*) Knole, Kent, detail of a chimneypiece, *c.*1610.

95 Lucas or Johannes Duetecum after Jan Vredeman de Vries, pl.XXII from Clemens Perret, *Exercitatio Alphabetica . . .* (Antwerp, 1569). The Royal Library – National Library of Sweden, Stockholm, Maps and Prints Department, De la Gardie Collection.

96 (*right*) Nettlecombe Court, Somerset, overmantel in the hall, *c.*1599.

These were copied or more extensively altered for armorial cartouches on the tapestry maps woven for Ralph Sheldon for his house at Weston in Warwickshire, probably in 1588, and for the cartouches framing scenes from the Life of Judah and the Judgement of Paris which were woven in 1595 for Walter Jones and his wife, Eleanor Pope, who some years later built their house at Chastleton in Oxfordshire.

There are two more instances of the use of *Exercitatio Alphabetica* in the Midlands which may or may not be related in some way. One is a decorative cartouche of oak with polychrome decoration, bearing the arms of Moule impaling Hawkings of Shropshire, and Rushall of Staffordshire,[131] which is based on Vredeman's original. The other is the only surviving fragment of a funerary monument commemorating Sir Herbert Westfaling (d.1601) in Hereford Cathedral (Fig. 97). The whole monument was illustrated in 1867 before it was dismembered[132] but there is still enough extant to show that the most likely source of the cartouche is plate IX from *Exercitatio Alphabetica* (Fig. 98). There are two slate monuments in the extreme south-west of England which also depend on cartouches in this copy-book. The earlier of these commemorates W. Hitchens (d.1592) with his wife and ten children, and stands in the church of St Stephen-by-Saltash, just on the Cornish side of the Tamar. The inscription cartouche is clearly based on plate XXX of *Exercitatio Alphabetica*. The later tomb was originally set up in the church at St Ive near Callington in Cornwall[133] and commemorates Sir John Wray who died in 1597. The backplate has the cartouche which depends on plate III (Figs 99, 100). It seems likely that the masons's workshop was in Plymouth, where the most notable exponent of this attractive provincial art, Peter Crocker, was based.[134]

A similarly precise copy of a design from *Exercitatio Alphabetica* (see Fig. 95) occurs at Nettlecombe Court in Somerset, on the plaster overmantel of *c.*1599 in the hall (Fig. 96), while at the opposite end of the British Isles another cartouche was copied for the plaster frieze in the hall of Glamis Castle at Forfar. This plasterwork dates from the 1620s and on the basis of stylistic comparison has been attributed to English plasterers working in Scotland. All these instances of the use of *Exercitatio Alphabetica* demonstrate how well these complex cartouche designs translated into other media.

Vredeman presumably designed the solitary compartment for the titlepage of Clemens Perret's second copy-book, the rarely surviving *Eximiae Peritiae Alphabetum complura graphica exemplaria continens . . . Clemens perret brabantius scribebat, aetatis suae. xx. Anno. 1571.*[135] No instances of derivation from this second copy-book have been identified. Vredeman

97 (*top*) Hereford Cathedral, fragment of the monument to Sir Herbert Westfaling (died 1601).

98 Lucas or Johannes Duetecum after Jan Vredeman de Vries, pl.IX from Clemens Perret, *Exercitatio Alphabetica . . .* (Antwerp, 1569). The Royal Library – National Library of Sweden, Stockholm, Maps and Prints Department, De la Gardie Collection.

During the 1580s work was in progress on some of the most significant decorative products of Elizabethan England, the tapestries woven on the looms set up by William Sheldon in the Midlands, as a means of providing worthwhile employment for the poor of the region. Their designers' familiarity with a wide variety of continental or continental-inspired ornament is discussed in a separate chapter, but they must be mentioned here as they make such prolific use of Vredeman's cartouches for *Exercitatio Alphabetica*.

may also have designed at about the same date the four decorative cartouches that frame engravings illustrating scenes from the parable of the Unmerciful Servant, after designs once attributed to Maarten van Heemskerck.[136] One of these cartouches was used in the decoration of another tapestry woven at William Sheldon's Barcheston works for Walter and Eleanor Jones, later of Chastleton House, Oxfordshire (see Figs 386, 387).

★   ★   ★

Vredeman's final set of independent cartouches was published under the title *Deorum Dearumque Capita Ex vetustis numismatibus . . . Ex museo Abrahami Ortelii . . .* by Philips Galle in Antwerp in 1573. Of the fifty-four plates, twenty-four are thought to be by Gerard Groenning and the remaining thirty by Vredeman.[137] These cartouches were commissioned by the distinguished humanist Abraham Ortelius to frame images of Classical gods and goddesses taken from antique coins in his own collection. The drawings themselves survive in the Library of Pembroke College, Cambridge: after they had served the engraver, Ortelius had them bound into a volume which served as his *album amicorum*, in which he had his humanist friends write laudatory words of greeting. The drawings comprise the largest single collection of Vredeman designs for ornament, and are still too little known.[138]

Compared with the Perret cartouches, Vredeman's frames for Ortelius's coins are more limited in variety, perhaps as a result of the severely restricted scale on which he was forced to work. The fact that the main field is always circular, with a rectangular inscription panel above and below, may have restricted the usefulness as models for decoration in other media. Although not unknown, instances of their use are rare except in the decoration of printed maps. It is hardly surprising to find that Ortelius himself had four reused on three maps in his *Additamentum* in the very year that the *Deorum Dearumque Capita* appeared. Christopher Saxton followed his example, using five cartouches on four maps in his *Atlas:* Essex was the earliest to be printed separately, in 1576, only three years after the original cartouches appeared. Gerard Mercator also copied three of the cartouches for maps in his own *Atlas* in 1595.[139]

Although there were several copies of the work in England by the early seventeenth century,[140] I have found no instance of the actual use of Vredeman's cartouches in architectural decoration in this country. But it was a close-run thing, for one of the Vredeman cartouches, framing the profile of Victoria, was copied by Robert Smythson in a project drawing for the hall-screen at Wollaton (Figs 101, 103), where the

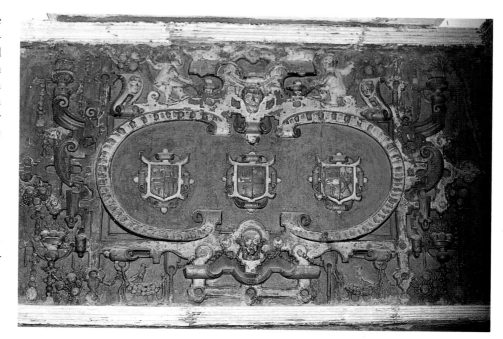

cartouche appears unmistakably in the upper panel between the paired columns; Smythson also derived the head of a bearded king in the cartouche from another plate in the same suite, labelled 'SARAPIDIS' (Fig. 102; Serapis was a god of the Greeks in Egypt and is identified with Apis and Osiris).[141] In the end, Smythson's proposal was not executed in this form: instead, another design by Vredeman was adapted for this position, as seen earlier (p.64).

Before leaving the subject of cartouches, mention should be made of a solitary borrowing from a suite not of cartouches but of plates illustrating the Ages

99 (*top*) Tawstock, Devon, monument to Sir John Wray (died 1597), originally set up at St Ive, Cornwall.

100 Lucas or Johannes Duetecum after Jan Vredeman de Vries, pl.III from Clemens Perret, *Exercitatio Alphabetica . . .* (Antwerp, 1569). The Royal Library – National Library of Sweden, Stockholm, Maps and Prints Department, De la Gardie Collection.

101 (*right*) Jan Vredeman de Vries, *Deorum dearumque capita* (Antwerp, 1573), 'Victoriae'. Stedelijk Prentenkabinet, Antwerp.

102 (*far right*) Jan Vredeman de Vries, *Deorum dearumque capita* (Antwerp, 1573), 'Sarapidis'. Stedelijk Prentenkabinet, Antwerp.

of Man, *Theatrum Vitae Humanae . . .*, published in Antwerp in 1577.[142] However, it was the cartouche that forms the titlepage border that was copied by William Arnold for the pendant feature on the chimneypiece in the parlour at Montacute (see Figs 232, 239).

This brief survey of the use made by engravers, masons, plasterers, decorative painters and others shows the extraordinary versatility of Vredeman's cartouche designs. They work equally well in tapestry, plasterwork, on the printed page or carved in stone or slate.

Perspective Plates

The study of perspective occupied almost as much of Vredeman's time as did the classical orders of architecture, and suites of perspective plates are amongst his earliest designs. They are very much Vredeman's speciality. Three suites are explicitly concerned with the art of perspective while at least five others which purport to be designs for gardens or fountains, for instance, are really lightly disguised exercises in perspective. Our concern here is with the decorative impact of the plates rather than Vredeman's influence on the development of perspective studies.

First come two suites related in their subject matter, both published in Antwerp by Hieronymus Cock in the 1560s: first, *Scenographiae, sive Perspectivae . . .*, 1560,[143] whose plates depict idealised cityscapes or interiors of buildings, without the intrusion of any human bystander or passer-by. Related to these plates are those of an untitled suite of twenty-eight architectural plates which appeared in 1562.[144] Many adopt a bird's-eye viewpoint; others introduce canals passing through urban scenes. Human figures appear in most but do little to dispel the other-worldly atmosphere of the plates. With a third set, consisting of designs in printed oval frames which should be considered separately, these are generally known as *Variae Architecturae Formae*, the title given first to the 1601 combined edition published by Theodore Galle.[145] All three suites owe a debt to Serlio, Vredeman's earliest inspiration, while other influences include J.A. Ducerceau and Hieronymus Cock's own views of Rome during rebuilding in 1532 after the Sack.

There is evidence that the first of the three, *Scenographiae, sive Perspectivae*, was used in the Netherlands as a source of ornament.[146] In England, the well-known portrait of Henry, Lord Darnley, with his younger brother Charles Stuart (Fig. 105) provides proof enough that *Scenographiae* was known in this country almost as soon as it appeared in print. The

103 Robert Smythson, design for the hall screen of Wollaton Hall, Nottinghamshire, 1580s. British Architectural Library, RIBA, London.

brothers are depicted standing within, or before, a room which has optimistically been taken for the sixteenth-century Great Chamber at Temple Newsam in Yorkshire, where Darnley was born in 1545. The truth is rather more prosaic: the background architecture was copied precisely from plate 10 of *Scenographiae* (Fig. 104), and this explains the unconvincing manner in which the figures are related to the architecture. The date of the portrait is 1563, only three years after the publication of the source, and the artist was Hans Eworth, a Fleming who would have been familiar with the Antwerp designers of the period.

Around 1574 an unidentified, probably German craftsman employed on the decoration of Elizabethan Chatsworth copied another of the prints for an intarsia panel that survives at Hardwick (see p.252). Fifteen years later, the suite was also used at the Sheldon tapestry works at Barcheston in Warwickshire (see p.226).

There appears to be no surviving instance of the use in England of the second, untitled, suite of bird's–eye perspective plates that followed *Scenographiae, sive Perspectivae*, but the architect and surveyor John Thorpe had at least one of the prints.[147] The third component suite consists of very distinctive perspective views of buildings in uncompleted form enclosed within oval frames, published (again untitled) by

Hieronymus Cock in Antwerp between 1560 and 1562. They were described by Karel van Mander as designs for intarsia work[148] and probably exercised a general influence on furniture made by continental craftsmen working in the Danzig area of Germany, and by their compatriots in Southwark, but I have been unable to discover instances of precise copying.

Next in time comes a suite of designs ostensibly for fountains, entitled *Artis Perspectivae plurium generum elegantissimae Formulae, multigenis Fontibus, nonnullisq[ue] Hortulis . . . Liber primus*, and published by Gerard de Iode in Antwerp in 1568.[149] Although somewhat smaller in format, the plates of another suite, this time untitled and published in Antwerp by Philips Galle in 1573, were probably intended to form the *liber secundus* to *Artis Perspectivae*.[150] Both sets are similar in character to the architectural views in the three suites already mentioned, but with an obvious emphasis on designs for fountains. They are mostly placed in idealised street scenes or in gardens typical of the period, but in two plates of *Artis Perspectivae* and seven of the later suite fountains are illustrated on their own, without any architectural setting.

The earlier suite, *Artis Perspectivae*, appears to have been used only rarely in England, but the instances are all noteworthy. Earliest of them is a tapestry from a set woven perhaps in England in 1584–5 for Robert

Still Vredeman

Dudleys tapes.

79

104 Lucas or Johannes Duetecum after Jan Vredeman de Vries, *Scenographiae, sive Perspectivae* (Antwerp, 1560), pl.10. Stedelijk Bibliotheek, Leeuwarden.

during his long life – architecture, street scenes, interiors, gardens, fountains and funerary monuments, even the orders themselves. The books were extraordinarily popular, even by Vredeman's standards, going into twelve further editions in less than half a century, but again seem to have had no direct influence on works of art in England.

Caryatids, Atlantes and Terms

After the columns of the classical orders, caryatids and atlantes – generally called terms – were the most fundamental elements of Renaissance and Mannerist architectural decoration. All have an impeccable Classical ancestry: caryatids originated in the figures supporting the south porch of the Erechtheum on the Acropolis in Athens and were depicted in illustrated editions of Vitruvius; atlantes – the male equivalent – were derived from Atlas in his mythological role as supporter of the heavens; terms were originally ancient Greek boundary stones topped with a carved head of Hermes. Terms in particular were exceptionally common elements in printed designs during the sixteenth century, although suites dedicated exclusively to them are relatively few. Agostino Veneziano, Jean Mignon, Jacques Androuet Ducerceau, Hugues Sambin, Crispijn de Passe the younger and Gabriel Krammer were amongst those who either put together sets of caryatids or included designs in more general publications.

Vredeman's own suite of designs was entitled *Caryatidum (Vvlgvs Termas Vocat) Sive Athlantidum . . .*, and was published by Gerard de Iode in Antwerp in 1565.[156] The titlepage (on which a pair of figures caught in a strapwork cage, and a pair of brackets with human heads and arms, support the entablature) announces in Latin and Flemish that the designs are appropriate for the five orders of architecture, and were useful for masons, cabinetmakers, glass painters and all craftsmen. The plates that follow present either six designs for single figures or, in the case of three plates, a mixture of single and paired caryatids: a total of eighty-two single-figure terms and seven pairs.

As already seen, caryatids or terms played a significant part in Vredeman's *[Architectura] Das Erst Büch* and *Das Ander Buech* of 1565; many of his other suites also featured them, but it was the *Caryatidum* that must have been most influential in transmitting designs for terms. It was clearly well known in northern Europe and in the Iberian peninsular.[157] In England, the instances of the use of Vredeman's caryatid designs fall into various geographical patterns. The earliest occurrence is a panel on a celebrated set of wall hangings made around 1570 – that is to say, no more than four or five years after the publication

Dudley, Earl of Leicester, and bearing his arms (see pp.222–3). Not more than a few years later, the miniaturist Isaac Oliver used another plate from the suite for his *Unknown Melancholy Man* (Fig. 108) in the Royal Collection. The fashonable Mannerist garden in the background has, even comparatively recently, been taken to represent some actual English garden, since lost. However, it was actually taken from a design in *Artis Perspectivae* (Fig. 106) and it demonstrates that Oliver was quite prepared to use a printed source for his background, if it suited him to do so.[151]

Two further sets of designs for gardens are also exercises in perspective; in the first, *Hortorum Viridariorumque elegantes et multiplicis formae . . .*, published by Philip Galle in Antwerp in 1583, the designs are again linked to the orders.[152] The same publisher issued a second untitled suite of eight plates of garden designs in 1587.[153] These garden designs – particularly the intricate mazes – were borrowed for other publications and were influential on garden design throughout Europe, but there is no evidence as yet that they were copied for architectural decoration or the applied arts in this country.[154] Vredeman's final thoughts on the subject of perspective are contained in a substantial two-volume work which was published by Henricus Hondius in Leyden in 1604 and 1605 under the title *Perspective*.[155] These plates summarise everything Vredeman knew about perspective in plates that are a model of clarity. They also touch on almost all the other subjects that concerned him

THES BE THE SONES OF ﬀ RIGHT HONERABLES ﬀERLLE OF LENOXE AD
ﬀE LADY MARGAPETZ GRACE COVNTYES OF LENOXE AD ANGWYSE.

1563

CHARLLES STEWARDE   HENRY STEWARDE LORD DAR̄
HIS BROTHER, ÆTATIS, 6,   LEY AND DOWGLAS, ÆTATIS, 17.

See p. 79

105 Hans Eworth, *Henry, Lord Darnley, and his Brother Charles Stuart*, 1563. The Royal Collection © 1996 Her Majesty The Queen.

106 Lucas or Johannes Duetecum after Jan Vredeman de Vries, *Artis Perspectivae* (Antwerp, 1568). Kunstbibliothek, Berlin.

107 Lucas or Johannes Duetecum after Jan Vredeman de Vries, *Caryatidum* (Antwerp, *c*.1565), pl.11. Victoria and Albert Museum, London.

of the suite from which its makers borrowed – by Mary Queen of Scots and Elizabeth, Countess of Shrewsbury (Bess of Hardwick), whose monograms appear on some of the constituent panels, together with the date 1570 (see p.257).

In the West Country, particularly in an area centring on Bristol, figures derived from Vredeman's *Caryatidum* were popular on the extremely elaborate chimneypieces for which the region is noted. The most distinguished is the one surviving in the Great Chamber of the Red Lodge in Bristol, built by Sir

John Yonge in about 1585–95 (see Fig. 87): for the cartouche, as already noted (p.69), the mason copied a Vredeman design, drawing on his *Caryatidum* for the term figures (Fig. 107). It was probably he who also carved another Bristol chimneypiece and overmantel which has term figures derived from another print in the same suite.[158] Again, the impressive overmantel in the Great Chamber of South Wraxall Manor, near Bradford-on-Avon, which was part of the substantial alterations made by Sir Walter Long in the late sixteenth century, derives its term figures from a plate in this book; there are other indications that this, too, is by the same mason – for instance, the distinctive frieze of the overmantel (see Fig. 221) is matched on another contemporary Bristol overmantel, from a house in St Nicholas Street but since removed to Red Maids' School. A further sumptuous, even barbaric, Bristol chimneypiece has recently come to light, with caryatids derived from the *Caryatidum*: they follow the left-hand design on plate 13 with only minor alterations.[159] The term figures supporting the frieze of the chimneypiece itself are more classical, even French, in character and were not copied from the Vredeman suite. Raglan Castle was another building where Bristol craftsmen were certainly employed: it boasted two timber chimneypieces and overmantels (now both at Badminton), one of which is similar to carving at the Red Lodge, and a handsome stone overmantel in the chapel which could have featured a Vredeman cartouche but only survives in a fragmentary state.[160] Bristol was clearly a provincial centre of great importance.

In the West Midlands a plate from Vredeman's *Caryatidum* was used in the design of the tomb of Sir Richard Lee (d.1591) in the Shropshire village of Acton Burnell, where the mason responsible employed two further suites of plates designed by Vredeman de Vries (see p.60). Although this appears to be an isolated example in this county, Norgrove Court in Worcestershire displays a truly remarkable dependence on the set. Built during the 1620s, this house has several overmantels based on Vredeman's designs, one of them reproducing the titlepage design almost unchanged. In this it recalls a drawing by Robert Smythson where elements from the titlepage are meticulously copied (Girouard 1962, I/25 (5 and 6)). Smythson's younger contemporary John Thorpe was also aware of the *Caryatidum*, for he copied one of the designs in his drawing (Summerson 1966, T60).

Other instances of borrowing from the *Caryatidum* indicate that the suite achieved a countrywide circulation. In London, the left-hand design in Vredeman's plate 3 was copied for the term figures of a woodblock titlepage border first printed by John Wolfe in 1583 and used for several books thereafter,

108 Isaac Oliver, *Unknown Melancholy Man*. The Royal Collection © 1996 Her Majesty The Queen.

upper floor of the Jacobean wing of Otley Hall, Suffolk (Figs 109, 110): here the date must be before 1616 when John Gosnold, whose arms appear in a cartouche framed by the terms, died.[162] Also in East Anglia, the panelling of the oak room at Holywell in Ipswich is articulated by term figures copied from the *Caryatidum*.[163] In Oxfordshire, the overall design of the tomb of John Baldeston at Burford is based on one of Vredeman's designs for monuments (see p.86) while the term figures are copied from his *Caryatidum*. In Cheshire, the term figures of the dining room overmantel at Crewe Hall derive from Vredeman's plate 6 (see Fig.169).

Grotesques

Vredeman was not a natural designer of grotesques. The fact that he had not travelled to Italy, unlike his compatriot Cornelis Floris, or the Frenchman, Jacques Androuet Ducerceau, may have had something to do with this. Nevertheless, Vredeman did make one attempt in the 1560s to design grotesques, and they also play a part in a set of four trapezium-shaped plates published by Hieronymus Cock in Antwerp in 1564 or 1565.[164] From their unusual format, these may have been intended mainly for the decoration of ceilings, or perhaps metalwork or ceramics. They have not always been attributed to Vredeman, and one closely resembles an almost exactly contemporary cartouche by Jacob Floris, who was also working in Antwerp.[165] There is no evidence that Vredeman's set was known in England.

Far more substantial is the specialised set of engravings which was published under the title *Grottesco: in diversche manieren . . . , ghemackt by Iohans vredeman vriese . . .* , by Gerard de Iode in Antwerp, probably in 1565.[166] These plates are derivative in nature, following the style of French grotesques of Etienne Delaune and Jacques Androuet Ducerceau (the latter's suite *Grotesque* itself including close copies of Enea Vico's 1541 set), and reproducing the kind of grotesques already familiar in Flemish tapestries before the middle of the century.

The only evidence that Vredeman's *Grottesco* was known in England, if the resemblance between one of the plates and the tapestry with the arms of Herbert (see below) is discounted, is the celebrated Shrewsbury Hanging worked by Mary Queen of Scots and Bess of Hardwick during the early years of Mary's imprisonment in England (see p.257).[167] But should the Herbert Tapestry (Fig. 111) be discounted? It is now thought to have been made in the Netherlands between 1548, when Sir William Herbert received the Order of the Garter, and 1551, when he was elevated to the peerage, for there is no coronet; the

109 (*top*) Lucas or Johannes Duetecum after Jan Vredeman de Vries, *Caryatidum* (Antwerp, *c*.1565), pl.7. Victoria and Albert Museum, London.

110 Otley Hall, Suffolk, painted decoration, before 1616.

including the 1588 edition of Sir Thomas Hoby's translation of Castiglione's *The Courtier*;[161] the figures flanking one of the overmantels from Northampton (Canonbury) House in Islington derive from another (see Fig. 65). In Cambridge, two of the terms on the highly-decorated hall screen at Trinity College depend on Vredeman, and one of the same figures reappears in painted decoration in a room on the

initials W and H in small cartouches beneath the medallions confirm that the tapestry was made for him rather than for his son Henry.[168] But this date would put the tapestry towards the beginning of the vogue for grotesques in the Netherlands and a later date seems preferable: the tapestry resembles Vredeman's grotesques both in general design and in one specific feature: the central compartment is framed by elongated brackets with human masks, precisely as one of Vredeman's plates (Fig. 112). It is possible that there was some common source, but if the tapestry was indeed based on the print it would have to be dated between the mid-1560s and 1570, when the bearer of the arms, Sir William Herbert, died. Might it then have been woven not in the Netherlands but at the Sheldon tapestry works, as was once thought?[169]

Designs for Monuments

Vredeman produced one complete suite of designs for funerary monuments, following the example of the suite designed by his contemporary Cornelis Floris

111 (*above*) Tapestry with the arms of Herbert, possibly woven *c*.1565–70. Victoria and Albert Museum, London.

112 Lucas or Johannes Duetecum after Jan Vredeman de Vries, plate from *Grottesco: in diversche manieren* (Antwerp, 1565). Victoria and Albert Museum, London.

(pp.48–9). Vredeman's was published under the title *Pictores, Statuarii, Architecti . . . varias Coenotaphiorum . . . formas*, by Hieronymus Cock in Antwerp in 1563.[170] The titlepage has a handsome strapwork cartouche decorated with symbols of mortality. The plates themselves summarise the types of tombs that were becoming popular in the Low Countries and, in the hands of Netherlandish masons, were spreading to London around this time.[171] There are free-standing sarcophagi, with and without columniated canopies, tomb-chests attached to walls, standing and hanging wall monuments. An isolated design for a tomb also occurs in Vredeman's *Perspective* of 1604, but there is no evidence that it was ever copied or adapted by a mason.

Commemorative monuments were naturally of interest to those wealthy enough to afford one, so that, considering that Cornelis Floris's were the only other printed designs for tombs in the fashionable Antwerp style, it is surprising that more use was not made in England of Vredeman's plates. Indeed, there are no more than a handful of instances of close similarity.

The earliest of these occurs at Turvey in Bedfordshire, where there are two remarkable sixteenth-century monuments in the church, both dependent to some extent on (different) continental sources. The tomb of the second Lord Mordaunt (d.1571) and his two wives consists of a tomb-chest under a canopy supported by Tuscan columns and in overall design closely follows that of Vredeman's plate 19. Several of

the Foljambe monuments in St Mary and All Saints, Chesterfield, appear to reflect the influence of Vredeman's *Pictores* in the manner in which the wall-hung tablet is related to the tomb-chest. Further south is an isolated instance at Burford in Oxfordshire, where a small wall monument commemorates John Baldeston, who died in 1624. Carved in the local freestone, presumably by an English mason, it follows the scheme, if not the precise details, of one of Vredeman's designs, having an inscription plate flanked by a caryatid figure and a column either side. In Bristol Cathedral, the tomb of Sir John Yonge attributed to Thomas Baldwin of Stroud or Gloucester is one of several (including the Westfaling monument in Hereford Cathedral, mentioned earlier) that have supporting creatures placed at an angle of forty-five degrees from the main axes. This feature could easily have been copied from one of three designs in the Vredeman suite.

Patterns derived from Vredeman's *Pictores, Statuarii, Architecti* also appear amongst the Smythson designs (Girouard 1962, II/24) for the hall screen at Wollaton Hall in the 1580s. Some distinctive strapwork was adapted for the lower of the upright panels between the paired columns. This was executed as drawn and more was copied for the horizontal panels of the balustrade (Figs 113, 114). Additionally, John Smythson simplified another Vredeman design in a drawing (Girouard 1962, III/27), which was further adapted for the tomb of the first Countess of Devonshire in the small church of Ault Hucknall in Derbyshire, on the edge of the park at Hardwick. The tomb is dated 1627.

Furniture Designs

During the 1580s, perhaps even as late as 1586 when Vredeman had already fled to Wolfenbüttel, Philips Galle published an important suite of furniture designs by Vredeman entitled *Differents pourtraicts de menuiserie asçauoir Portaux, Bancs, Escabelles, Tables, buffets, frises, ou corniches, licts-de camp, ornaments a pendre l'essuoir a mains, fontaines a lauer les mains. . . .*[172] It is the earliest Flemish furniture pattern-book: in France, Jacques Androuet Ducerceau had seen his published a quarter of a century earlier. Vredeman's failed to go into subsequent editions so its popularity and circulation may have been limited. As the title suggests, there is great variety amongst the designs. Vredeman opens with five (on four plates) for wind-porches of a kind very familiar in churches and, to a lesser extent, in English and continental country houses. Then follow three plates of tables, stools and a solitary triangular-shaped chair, and two plates of sideboards or buffets. Eight elaborate friezes on a single plate are succeeded

113 Lucas or Johannes Duetecum after Jan Vredeman de Vries, *Pictores Statuarii* (Antwerp, 1563), pl.14. Stedelijk Bibliotheek, Leeuwarden.

114 Wollaton Hall, Nottinghamshire, screen, 1580s.

by four designs for beds, seven canopies and four fountains (on two plates).

The plates illustrating movable furniture probably do little more than summarise contemporary Flemish furniture design, for Vredeman was not a specialist in this field. Moreover, they gave him comparatively little scope for a display of the Mannerist ornament he enjoyed so much. Consequently, it is difficult to demonstrate more than a generic similarity between any surviving pieces of furniture in this country and Vredeman's designs.[173] The designs for wind-porches and fountains, on the other hand, allowed him to incorporate personal elements such as strapwork cartouches and grotesque terms, and some of the many surviving wind-porches in sixteenth-century country houses may have been inspired by Vredeman's designs – there are notable examples at Broughton Castle in Oxfordshire, Sherborne Castle in Dorset, the Red Lodge in Bristol, Bradninch and Bradfield in Devon. The wind-porch in the Great

Chamber at Montacute derives from a different Vredeman source (see p.60), while the others resemble Vredeman's designs only loosely. There is, however, such a strong resemblance between the form and decoration of a tapered baluster support on the chancel screen in St John's, Briggate, Leeds (consecrated in 1634), and that of a buffet or sideboard in Vredeman's suite that it seems likely that this was the source.[174] The screen is a fine if late example of the Antwerp Mannerist style with which Vredeman's name is popularly associated: the elaborate strapwork frames to the armorials were clearly inspired by Vredeman's 1565 [*Architectura*] *Das Erst Büch*, which supplied the pattern for a carved panel in the church.

In the medium of sculpture, Vredeman's *Differents pourtraicts de menuiserie* provided the inspiration for one feature of the hanging wall monument at Nether Heyford in Northamptonshire, which commemorates Sir Richard Morgan (d.1557) and his wife (Fig. 115); it was carved by Garrett Hollemans the elder, a Dutch

and above the columns supporting the landing of the painted staircase, both dating from the first decade of the seventeenth century.[177]

Trophies

Following the example set earlier in the century by Enea Vico and Rosso Fiorentino or Leonard Thiry, Cornelis Bos and others, Vredeman designed a suite of trophies, *Panoplia seu armamentarium ac ornamenta*, which was published in 1572 by Gerard de Iode in Antwerp. They take the form of trophies of arms and armour, or of musical instruments or the tools of various trades; whether composed in a vertical or horizontal format, these objects are hung either from masks or from vestigial strapwork attached to the top of the image by means of ribbons with bows, ornamented with subsidiary ribbons. In four designs (on two prints) the trophies are arranged in a curved format as if intended for use on the rims of dishes or bowls. In view of the vast appetite in England for trophies of just this kind it has been surprisingly difficult to find examples copied precisely from these designs. One (Fig. 117) was perhaps used for the trophies on the overmantel in the Reynolds Room at Knole in Kent (see Fig. 45), where the mason wished to flesh-out a Ducerceau design, and trophies related to the Vredeman plates occur in woodwork on the Jacobean staircase from Slaugham Place in Sussex (see pp.196–7).

115 (*above left*) Nether Heyford, Northamptonshire, monument to Sir Richard Morgan (died 1557).

116 (*above right*) Pieter van der Borcht after Jan Vredeman de Vries, *Differents pourtraicts de menuiserie* (Antwerp, 1580s), pl.15.

carver of obscure origins who had his workshop at Burton-on-Trent.[175] The design features the kneeling figures of the deceased with children on either side, flanked by allegorical figures in niches enclosed by Corinthian columns. The figures themselves – only Spes now survives – stand on low plinths supported on elaborate brackets or corbels, the nearest parallel to which are those of one of Vredeman's fountain designs (Fig. 116).[176] They are not absolutely identical, but this suite was certainly in Hollemans's stock-in-trade because another plate was adapted for his wall monument at Thorpe Mandeville, also in Northamptonshire. This commemorates Thomas Kirton (d.1601) and his wife Mary (d.1597) and was probably commissioned by him after her death. Here the flanking features are Egyptian-looking terms on tapered supports and these derive not from Vredeman's *Caryatidum* published in 1565 (see pp.80–84), but from his *Differents pourtraicts de menuiserie*, plate 3. Hollemans's terms have arms, it is true, whereas Vredeman's finish below the breasts, but the distinctive form of the headdress, resembling a bicorne hat with a badge in the centre, is unmistakable. The same term design also occurs in a country house context at Knole in Kent, on the hall screen

Marc Geerarts had a more than usually close relationship with England as a direct result of having spent several years in enforced exile here during the 1560s and 1570s. Geerarts was a designer, painter, illustrator and draughtsman whose ornament suites were engraved, etched and published in Antwerp by Gerard de Iode, Jan Sadeler, Philips Galle and others. Born in Bruges around 1520, the son of a painter, he was admitted in his late thirties to the Guild of St Luke there in July 1558, a month after he and Johanna Struve had announced their intention to marry according to the laws of the Roman Catholic Church.[178] During the next ten years he supplied cartoons for stained glass, devised a suite of small cartouches (see below) and designed the illustrations for a celebrated edition of Aesop's Fables first published in Bruges in 1567. He may have formed his friendships with Lucas de Heere and Philips Galle during this period, and joined the Protestant community in Bruges. Following the arrival in the Netherlands of the brutal Duke of Alba, Geerarts fled to London in March 1568 accompanied by his son but leaving behind his wife, who adhered to the traditional faith. He arrived at an opportune moment: the great London printer John Day, noted for the publication of Bibles and other Protestant literature, was on the lookout for experienced continental illustrators to help with the expanded edition of John Foxe's monumental ecclesiastical history *The Actes and Monuments*, which had first appeared in English in 1563. It has been suggested that Geerarts may have been one of the artists who contributed to the second edition which appeared in 1570.[179] Geerarts's religious loyalties whilst in London are uncertain. He may have worshipped at the French church and appears not to have been a member of the congregation of the Dutch church in 1570; however, he married Susanna de Critz of Antwerp in the Dutch Reformed church in 1571, his first wife having died, perhaps earlier that year. It has been suggested that outwardly supporting Calvinism before fleeing the Netherlands but leaving behind a Catholic wife was symptomatic of sympathy with the underground religious community known as the Family of Love (see pp.299–300).[180] Certainly Geerarts had many Familist friends and relations, both in England and later in Antwerp.

During his nine years in London, Geerarts worked as an illustrator, exclusively for publications by the printer John Day: besides illustrations for *The Actes and Monuments*, he completed twenty for Jan van der Noot's *Het theatre* (1568) and designed thirty-seven woodcuts for Stephen Bateman's *A Christall Glasse* (1569). His celebrated etching *Allegory of Iconoclasm* was issued around 1566 and the *Procession of the*

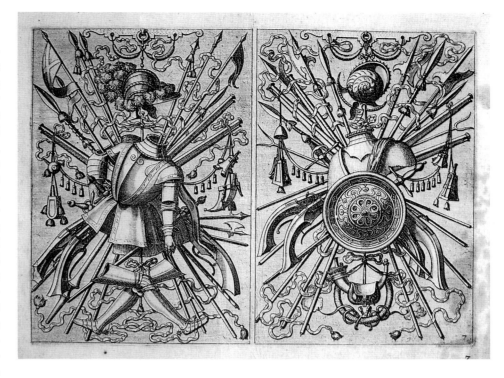

Knights of the Garter in 1576. He must also have painted portraits but only one survives, *Queen Elizabeth* at Welbeck Abbey.[181]

Geerarts returned to his native country in 1577, settling in Antwerp which had been vacated by the Spanish soldiery and almost immediately seeing the publication of his illustrations for Holinshed's *Chronicles.* There followed suites of prints that combine narrative illustrations or allegorical figures with strapwork grotesques: *The Labours of Hercules* and *The Passion* (both in an oval format), *The Continents* and *The Elements* (in a rectangular format), together with prints of birds, butterflies and animals. There is also a series of straightforward ornament without the subject content (in various shaped frames). Geerarts could certainly have promoted these suites in England, for he returned to London in 1586 where he died perhaps around 1590, but anyway by the publication of van Mander's *Schilder-Boeck* in 1604.[182]

Geerarts's suite of small cartouches, published under the title *Diversarum protractationum quas Vulgo Compartimenta vocat . . .* by Gerard de Iode in Antwerp in 1565, was certainly known in England. It consists of the title cartouche and thirteen plates, but the incomplete set of seven Geerarts cartouches in the Victoria and Albert Museum is there extended by no fewer than forty-four more (of thirty-six different designs) apparently by another hand, which also bear the same sort of titles as those undoubtedly by Geerarts. It is almost as if these cartouches were conceived of as individual titlepages, or advertisement sheets, for small sets of illustrations by other artists.

117 Lucas or Johannes Duetecum after Jan Vredeman de Vries, *Panoplia seu armamentarium ac ornamenta* (Antwerp, 1572, 2nd edn, c.1600), pl.7. Kunstbibliothek, Berlin.

These are not random sets, however: they add up to something more, for they are all components of a celebrated book of biblical illustrations, the *Thesaurus veteris et novi Testamenti* published by Gerard de Iode in Antwerp in 1579 with a second edition in 1585.[183] This will be discussed in due course (pp.103–6), but it is worth noting here that these title cartouches perform the function of a contents page, giving not only the title of each suite but also the name of the artist responsible for the design of the illustrations. In most instances these confirm the findings of modern scholarship. Where the use of these title cartouches and of the constituent illustrations from the *Thesaurus* occurs in the same part of England, it is surely safe to suggest a link between the instances. For the sake of convenience the cartouches will be considered together, as if Geerarts were responsible for all of them.

In 1593, John Norden published his *Speculum Britanniae*, including on his map of Middlesex two cartouches derived from those of the anonymous designer. In doing so he probably followed the example of Mercator (who made use of three of these ornamental cartouches on his maps of Catalonia and Tartaria), and Emery Molyneux whose terrestrial and celestial globes, engraved by Jodocus Hondius, include at least one decorative cartouche copied from the unknown designer.

Instances of the use of plates from this suite in architectural decoration seem to date from the late 1580s onwards. With the exception of one Midlands example,[184] instances are concentrated in the West Country and most can be connected either with William Arnold – again – or with the Exeter mason and statuary John Deymond, with whom Arnold may have had some association. For the time being it is only necessary to note that unquestionable derivations from this extended suite occur at Montacute in Somerset after 1588 (see pp.147, 149) and, from the Geerarts cartouches, in several church monuments which I have attributed to John Deymond.[185] The tombs are those of Sir Thomas Fulford (d.1610) at Dunsford in Devon, of Sir John Jefferey at Whitchurch Canonicorum in Dorset (d.1611) and of Sir John Acland at Broadclyst (he died in 1620 but the dates 1613 and 1614 appear on the monument). For Sir John Jefferey's (see Fig. 77), Deymond borrowed the plate inscribed 'Historia Davidis et Absalon . . .' (Fig. 118).

It is not easy, at this distance in time, to explain how these Geerarts cartouches found their way into the workshop of John Deymond, unless it was through William Arnold or even a member of the Garrett family of joiners in Exeter with whom Deymond shared some decorative motifs.[186]

The two other suites that were certainly used in England are *The Continents* and *The Elements*, each

consisting of four plates depicting female figures in strapwork grotesques published by Philips Galle in Antwerp sometime after 1577.[187] Features derived from both sets appear in painted glass apparently made for Verulam House, a small building erected by Sir Francis Bacon around 1608 in the corner of the park at Gorhambury, and probably intended only for occasional use, perhaps in the summer.[188] Five of the eight prints in the two suites have been recognised in the glass, suggesting that originally all eight were reproduced. The artist is thought to have been Lewys Dolphin, a Frenchman who was employed in painting glass for the chapel at Hatfield in about 1610 by Robert Cecil, Earl of Salisbury, who was Sir Francis Bacon's first cousin.

The Elements were used again even later at Boston Manor, Brentford, Middlesex. This medium-sized house, built about 1623, has a splendid gallery on the first floor which has one of the most spectacular of English plasterwork ceilings. Some of the many figures in the compartments are derived from Geerarts's suite (Figs 119, 120), others derive from prints after Frans Floris (see p.102).

Living in England for many years and enjoying aristocratic patronage (though not on the scale enjoyed by his son), Marc Geerarts may have been able to promote his ornamental designs himself rather than having to rely on the book trade to do it for him. If so, somewhat wider dependence on his prints might have been expected than has actually been discovered.

THEODOR DE BRY

Another artist who was obliged to leave the Netherlands as a result of the religious persecution was Theodor de Bry (1528–98). A native of Liège, he fled in 1570 not to London like Geerarts but to Frankfurt. There he specialised in the production of engraved ornament, most of it still in the style of his native

119 (*far left*) Boston Manor, Middlesex, figure of Aqua on the ceiling of the gallery, *c*.1623.

120 (*left*) Marc Geerarts, Aqua, from *The Elements* (Antwerp, after 1577). Victoria and Albert Museum, London.

country, starting in 1578 with a suite of circular grotesques surrounding portrait medallions that are overtly anti-Catholic, one depicting William of Orange as 'Capitaine prudent', another the Duke of Alba as 'Capitaine des Follie'.[189] This set was followed by several others concentrating on borders and frames of strapwork or grotesque ornament for use by goldsmiths and artists of all kinds. Perhaps his best-known suite is an alphabet published under the title *Nova Alphati Effictio* in 1595 which is in a *retardataire* manner reminiscent of his countryman Cornelis Floris.

The influence of his ornament prints may have been substantial on the Continent – particularly in the medium of metalwork[190] – but instances in Britain are rare. They occur exclusively in plasterwork. Friezes at Charlton House, Greenwich, and decorative ceiling panels in the church of St John's Briggate in Leeds (by the joiner and plasterer Francis Cunby or Gunby) are intriguingly similar to prints by de Bry. The only surviving instance of actual derivation, however, appears to be a plasterwork frieze in the hall at Craigievar Castle in Aberdeenshire (see p.168).

★   ★   ★

ABRAHAM AND NICOLAES DE BRUYN

The hybrid character noted in some of Geerarts's prints – part illustration, part ornament – is also found in the graphic work of Abraham de Bruyn. Born in Antwerp in 1540, de Bruyn was somewhat younger than any of the artists so far discussed. In his mid-twenties he started to produce suites of ornament, consisting of friezes with hunting scenes. In 1570 he settled in Breda but by 1577 was in Cologne. He was in Antwerp again in 1580 but probably died in Cologne in 1587, presumably as a refugee.[191] He was a prolific engraver, Hollstein listing as many as 536 prints, including suites of biblical illustrations, figures of the Five Senses, the Planets and the Twelve Caesars as well as engravings for costume books and nearly fifty engraved portraits. His output of ornament prints included friezes with hunting scenes (1565–6), the titlepage to his *Equitum Descriptio* (1576) and some grotesques for jewellery. But the suite that seems to have caught the imagination of designers in England during the first twenty years of the seventeenth century was an untitled series of six scenes from the life of Perseus in oval frames, set in elaborate grotesque

121 (*right*) Boston House, Middlesex, overmantel in the gallery, *c.*1623.

124 (*facing page top right*) Abraham de Bruyn, Andromeda, from a set of cartouches with the story of Perseus (Antwerp, 1584). Victoria and Albert Museum, London.

123 (*facing page left*) London, ceiling of the chapel in Sir Paul Pindar's house, *c.*1624, from C.J. Richardson, *Architectural Remains of . . . Elizabeth and James I* (London, 1840). Victoria and Albert Museum, London.

borders which he designed, engraved and published himself in 1584.

Since 1924 at the latest, when Margaret Jourdain published her *English Decoration and Furniture of the Early Renaissance*, this suite has been identified as the source of overmantels at Charlton House in Greenwich (*c.*1607) and Boston Manor in Brentford (*c.*1623). At Charlton, four plates were used: the scene in which Danaë is visited by Zeus in the form of a shower of gold has been combined with elements from the frames of Atlas, Andromeda and Medusa for one overmantel, while the scene in which Perseus decapitates the Gorgon Medusa appears framed by a cartouche from another, unidentified, source in a second. These transformations of the original prints seem to be inexplicable, except as a result of personal whim, and differentiate the Charlton overmantels from that of the gallery at Boston Manor (Fig. 121).

The designer of the Boston overmantel reproduced de Bruyn's frame from Andromeda virtually unchanged (Fig. 124), but replaced the scene, selecting instead the Sacrifice of Isaac, probably for its moral message. (It will be shown later that this derives from a little-known Flemish print – by Egbert van Panderen after a design by Pieter de Iode – see p.121.)

To these published instances of the use of prints by de Bruyn can be added a number of others. An almost

122 Boston House, Middlesex, detail of overmantel in the Gallery.

exactly contemporaneous use of the same de Bruyn plate occurred in the Bishopsgate house of Sir Paul Pindar of about 1624 (Fig. 123), where the central part of the strapwork frame was adapted for the pattern of plaster ribs of the chapel ceiling, visible in an illustration by C.J. Richardson; at Blickling in Norfolk there is another ceiling, in the former closet to the gallery in the north-east turret (Fig. 125),[192] which depends on this de Bruyn print. It was executed by the plasterer Edward Stanyon who was paid 4s. 6d. per yard. It seems highly likely he was also responsible

for the ceiling in Sir Paul Pindar's chapel, particularly in view of the close correspondence in dates.

A further use of de Bruyn occurs in the important town of Exeter where wealthy merchants were very aware of contemporary continental ornament.[193] One unnamed merchant's or clothier's house near Exeter (now in the Victoria and Albert Museum, 4870-81-1856) displays a knowledge of Cornelis Floris and Vredeman de Vries in the horizontal frieze panels of the hall panelling. Another of these[194] was adapted from the frame of Abraham de Bruyn's print of Atlas.

Nicolaes de Bruyn (1571–1656) studied in Antwerp under his father, Abraham de Bruyn, and under Assuwerus van Londerseel and Crispijn de Passe. In 1617 he settled in Rotterdam where he died nearly forty years later. His output was similar to that of his father – it includes biblical illustrations, suites of prints of animals, birds and fishes, and friezes incorporating animals and children. A river god, from his suite *Libellus Varia Genera Piscium*, has been identified as being copied in painted glass at Gorhambury in Hert-

fordshire.[195] His ornament style was also similar to his father's, particularly the grotesque frames to one of his two series of the Nine Worthies, published in 1594, the only prints of his whose influence has been identified in England.

125 (*above*) Blickling Hall, Norfolk, ceiling of the north-east turret, 1620s.

93

Chapter 6

THE INFLUENCE OF NETHERLANDISH PRINTS
II SUBJECT PRINTS

Ornament prints were an ideal medium for transmitting style, and, as a result, Antwerp Mannerism became, in Elizabethan and Jacobean England, inseparably grafted on to what was essentially a late-medieval architectural stock. Whether ornament prints were originally conceived by their authors, or later selected by their users, as propaganda for – in the case of these Netherlandish artists – the Protestant cause, is a question whose answer will have to be postponed. Subject prints, particularly biblical illustrations, undoubtedly have the potential to transmit ideas as well as style and this section tries to assess how influential Netherlandish subject prints were in England during the period covered in this book.

First impressions suggest that their impact was substantially less than the ornament prints, perhaps because, being so much more important artistically, they were considerably more expensive and so less affordable. Indeed, any expectation of finding their influence in English painting will largely be disappointed. Painters may have used subject prints more than now appears, but relatively little of their work has survived. Where the influence of subject prints is most apparent today is in the products of the building trades – masonry, plasterwork and joinery. The quality of the work is rarely first-rate, particularly that of native-born and native-trained craftsmen. All prints were by their nature more readily translated into two-dimensions than into three: even the most elaborate ornament such as strapwork cartouches could be cut in stone by a skilled mason, whereas the ability to carve a single anatomically convincing human figure – not to mention composing a natural-seeming group of figures – was one that could only be achieved through long apprenticeship to an experienced master, precisely the conditions that were conspicuously lacking for most of Elizabeth's reign.[1] Englishmen learnt to draw and to trace existing designs (Robert Pytt's triumphal arch is one example, see p.12), but this ability was little use when it came to converting a flat image into the round.

There was no counterpart for English artists and craftsmen of the *Wanderjahre*, the continental practice whereby a journeyman travelled around Europe, perhaps first visiting Italy where he gained first-hand experience of early Renaissance ornament, then working as a journeyman in one or more different European towns, making contacts and collecting prints, before establishing a workshop himself with apprentices and journeymen.[2] As a result, technical skills and a knowledge of source material were harder for a novice to acquire. It is hardly surprising, therefore, that the most skilled artists working in England during the sixteenth century were almost invariably foreigners, or the sons of foreigners.

The use of subject prints as sources of inspiration in England had begun, as seen, during the later fifteenth century with the occasional use of prints by Dürer, van Mekenem, Burgkmair, Lucas van Leyden and others. Now the influence of Flemish artists of a later generation must be traced, in particular Maarten van Heemskerck, Frans Floris and Maarten de Vos, as well as a number of their contemporaries, both familiar and lesser-known.

These three were amongst the leading artists of their day in the Netherlands, and their style was significantly influenced by the fact that all three had, like many artists from the Netherlands, visited Italy and had fallen under the spell of Italian art and architecture. When they returned to their native country, their work was disseminated through the publication of reproductive prints either from paintings or, more frequently, after specially made drawings. As early as 1829 Thomas Kerrich listed more than three hundred and fifty prints after Heemskerck, and his list has since been extended to almost six hundred. There are nearly a hundred prints after Frans Floris and in the region of twelve hundred after Maarten de Vos.[3] In spite of this considerable body of material, few instances of derivation from these prints have been noted in England until now, and most of those are in textiles.

126 (*facing page*) Lydiard Park, Wiltshire, detail of relief depicting Susanna and the Elders.

Maarten van Heemskerck was born in 1498 at Heemskerk, a little village a few miles north of Haarlem in North Holland.[4] His father was a farmer. He received his first artistic training in Haarlem and later in Delft, returning to Haarlem in 1527 to study under Jan van Scorel who (after a six years' journey from 1519 which took him to Strasbourg, Basle, Nuremberg, Venice and Rome) had returned to Utrecht but spent some months in 1527–8 in Haarlem. In the second half of 1532 Heemskerck himself left for Italy and stayed for nearly five years, completing several large paintings and making numerous pen and ink sketches of architecture and sculpture he saw there.[5] He returned via Mantua, where he came under the influence of Giulio Romano and his assistants, and on his return to Haarlem received commissions for large altarpieces, establishing himself as one of the leading citizens of the town where he remainded for the rest of his life, dying in 1574. Heemskerck was a prolific painter (and had at least three pupils), but he was also a tireless designer of prints, working with professional engravers such as Cornelis Bos, Dirck Coornhert, Philips Galle, Herman Jansz. Muller and Cornelis Cort. The years he spent in Italy proved crucial for his work, and his prints are characterised by purposely over-sculptured musculature and by invariable references to Classical architecture, which he had experienced at first hand.[6]

Heemskerck was directly affected by the religious turmoil in sixteenth-century Netherlands. Many of his paintings were destroyed in the iconoclasm of 1566, and in 1572, when Haarlem was sacked, others were commandeered and sent to Spain. Heemskerck's religious sympathies in general, and his attitude to the iconoclasm in the Netherlands in 1566 in particular, have been explored by Ilja Veldman and Eleanor Saunders.[7] Heemskerck was officially a Catholic and he is known to have been a churchwarden of St Bavo in Haarlem from 1552 until his death.[8] On the other hand, several series of Old Testament prints dealing with the destruction of idols seem at first sight to suggest a sympathy with the contemporary iconoclasts. However, Heemskerck continued to paint traditional altarpieces for churches right up to his death and was evidently not hostile to the idea of art in churches. Probably the most important factor in his thinking was his friendship with several leading humanists and politicians in Haarlem, including Dirck Volkertsz. Coornhert (who engraved several of his designs from the mid-1540s onwards), Philips Galle, who took over from Coornhert, Hadrianus Junius, Hendrik van Wamelen and Jan van Zuren. Like these intellectuals, he would probably have professed sympathy for a biblical humanism, the foundations of

which had been laid by Erasmus and were characterised by an ethical philosophy of life, a return to the text of the Bible and a refusal to accept that any one religious persuasion had a monopoly of the truth. As H.A. Enno van Gelder has said, most of the humanists

remained or were called Catholic, but . . . they were not Catholic in the orthodox sense, and some were Protestant, but not in the Reformation sense. Nor, as is often stated, did they stand midway between the two. On the contrary, while they submitted directly to the dogmas of the Catholic Church or joined one of the evangelical or reformed Churches, they gave an entirely individual interpretation to the dogmas and rites of these churches.[9]

It is clear that Heemskerck's graphic output did more to spread his influence amongst the artistic community of Europe than his paintings. Rembrandt admired Heemskerck's work and sometimes used his prints as the basis for compositions of his own; like most of the leading artists of the seventeenth century, he collected prints by contemporaries as well as artists long dead, including 'One [book] of engravings by Heemskerk, containing all his works'.[10] Another artist who demonstrably drew on a print after Heemskerck for paintings of his own was Francisco de Zurbarán (1598–1664).[11] It was in the medium of stained glass, however, that Heemskerck's impact on the Continent is chiefly seen.[12] Numerous panels of stained glass closely follow his prints but, although many of these now survive in England, most have come into this country only as the result of the decline in the fortune of continental monasteries during the nineteenth century, and cannot have exercised any influence over Elizabethan work here.

The main focuses of Heemskerck's extensive graphic oeuvre are the series of Old and New Testament subjects and allegories. The Old Testament series were intended to serve as 'picture Bibles' reminding viewers of the moral messages that had a particular relevance for his own time. Books of Heemskerck's prints were certainly known in England during (and a little after) the period covered here. William Boswell wrote to Lord Arundel from The Hague in January 1633: 'A kinsman of [Mr. Overbeck] (who dwells in this towne) telles me of a Book of Hemskerks (wch he can procure upon reasonable termes) conteyning many pieces of diverse sorts.' A book of this kind, having prints by Heemskerck and others, and bearing inscriptions in an early seventeenth-century English hand, came to light recently.[13] One of the more popular of these series was *The Story of Esther,* which was engraved by Philips Galle. Three of the prints, including his illustration of Ahasuerus holding out the golden sceptre to Esther, were copied for the cast plaquettes on a gilt and enamelled standing cup and cover known as the *Landschadenbundbecher* commissioned (probably from the Augsburg goldsmith Hans Schebel)[14] by the Munich court as a gift to the Archduke Carl of Steiermark on his marriage in 1571. The set was also popular in England probably because Esther was one of the Old Testament prototypes for Queen Elizabeth.

If surviving instances are reliable evidence (which they may well not be) Heemskerck's biblical prints seem to have achieved only limited currency in this country during the sixteenth and seventeenth centuries. Certainly the attitudes his biblical illustrations demonstrate towards religious questions were complex and his allegorical prints are obscure and literary, which would have limited their appeal here to an intellectual and political élite. The best illustration of the use in England of prints after Heemskerck for the purposes of religious propaganda is the group portrait *Edward VI and the Pope*, now in the National Portrait Gallery, which has been exhaustively studied by Margaret Aston in a recent book.[15] Two prints were adapted by the unknown, presumably Flemish painter. One is Heemskerck's depiction of the insomniac King Ahasuerus listening to the reading of the chronicles, from *The History of Esther* (Esther 6:1), a set that was captioned with lines written by the humanist Hadrianus Junius: this print was reversed and employed for the figure of Henry VIII, recumbent in a canopied bed, gesturing towards his enthroned son Edward VI who presides over a fallen figure of the Pope. The other is Heemskerck's illustration of the Destruction of the Tower of Babel, from Genesis 11:1–9, which was included in a set dealing with biblical disasters: this was adapted for the inset in the upper right-hand corner of the painting. Heemskerck's preliminary drawings are dated 1563 and 1567 respectively and the engravings were published by Philips Galle in the following years. This has enabled Aston to redate the painting from 1548 (the dating favoured since 1960)[16] to the late 1560s or early 1570s and to relate it to the momentous religious and political events occurring in England during this period. Commissioned by an unknown patron as a reminder of the necessity of adhering to the reformed faith and to the removal of the idolatrous images of the Roman Catholic Church, its target is also unknown. It might have been Thomas Howard, Duke of Norfolk, who was contemplating a reckless marriage with the royal adulterer, Mary Queen of Scots, a plan that brought him to the block in June 1572; or another candidate is Queen Elizabeth herself, for her intransigence in refusing to abolish the cross and candlesticks in her own private chapel even as late as the 1580s.[17]

The story of Esther is that of a young orphaned Jewish woman who had been brought up by her cousin Mordecai. She was chosen by Ahasuerus (Xerxes, a fifth-century king of Persia) to replace his queen, Vashti, who had displeased him. Haman, the King's chief minister, was an enemy of the Jews in general and of Mordecai in particular, and he induced Ahasuerus to give him the authority to have Mordecai and all the Jews in the Persian Empire killed. Mordecai persuaded Esther to intercede with Ahasuerus, despite the threat of death to anyone who dared to enter into the King's presence; when she did, Ahasuerus offered her the golden sceptre as a symbol that he would receive her. Her pleading was successful and it was Haman who suffered death on the gallows. The story was sometimes seen as a prefiguration of the Virgin in her role of intercessor on the Day of Judgement,[18] but it also demonstrated to Heemskerck's sixteenth-century audience how a faithful subject could be wrongfully accused of breaking the ruler's laws, although ultimately saved from destruction.

Besides being used for *Edward VI and the Pope*, the suite inspired a set of the painted leather wall hangings that were commonly used to draught-proof and enliven Tudor and Stuart interiors. This set, from an unknown country house, was sold from Walsingham Abbey, Norfolk, in September 1916. Two panels were illustrated in the sale catalogue and are again reproduced here (Fig. 127). In the first, King Ahasuerus gives his ring to Haman to seal the orders for the destruction of the Jews.[19] In the second, Ahasuerus offers Esther the golden sceptre. The derivation from the Heemskerck prints (Fig. 128) raises doubts about the dating of these painted leather panels as well as others, now at Dunster Castle in Somerset, which were probably executed in the same workshop.[20] There is nothing in the Walsingham hangings that is stylistically inconsistent with a date around 1600.

These Old Testament suites were not the only ones designed by Heemskerck that were used in England and others will be considered in Part II when looking at the decoration of Elizabethan Chatsworth and Hardwick.[22] Heemskerck's New Testament suites had less impact in England, for reasons that will become clearer in due course. Amongst those that were known in this country are his illustrations of the parable of the Prodigal Son (see pp.271 and 285), while prints illustrating the parable of the Unmerciful Servant which have sometimes been attributed to Heemskerck were also used here, if only for one of their decorative borders, which were probably designed by Vredeman de Vries.[23]

A significant part of Heemskerck's graphic output took the form of allegories on topical themes such as the 'transitoriness of life and the vanity of such human

Aſt animum recipe, en tibi Rex gemmantia tendit   Sceptra ultro, expleti prima argumenta furoris.

127 (top) Two painted leather wall-hangings from Walsingham Abbey, depicting scenes from the story of Esther, c.1600.

128 Philips Galle after Maarten van Heemskerck, Esther Before Ahasuerus, from *The History of Esther*, 1564. Museum Boijmans Van Beuningen, Rotterdam.

features in the first triumph in Petrarch, this was such a potent image that in most series each print depicts one. Heemskerck was not the first to do so – his series are based on Georg Pencz – but in his hands the triumphal procession reaches a climax of elaborate symbolism. His series generally feature a figure seated on a triumphal car drawn by other associated figures and leading the conquered, and the series usually end with the Triumph of Christ.

One of Heemskerck's earlier sets, *The Triumph of Patience*, was used several times in England in the most interesting contexts. The preliminary drawings and the prints, which were engraved by Dirck Coornhert, are all dated 1559. The suite consists of eight prints in the form of an allegorical triumph: it opens with the triumph of Patience herself and continues with Isaac, Joseph, David, Job, Tobias, and St Stephen; in the final scene, Christ by his crucifixion triumphs over the world, the flesh and the devil. The series can be read as 'a succession of stages through which man passes on his way to the ultimate goal of divine mercy'.[24]

The earliest instance identified so far occurs on one of a set of six silver spice bowls made in London in 1573–4, perhaps by an English maker, but engraved almost certainly by a foreigner. The bowls are decorated with a variety of scenes whose sources have not been found, except for one depicting the Sacrifice of Isaac (Fig. 129). This subject was extremely popular amongst artists and printmakers of the period, illustrating as it did Isaac's trust in his father and prefiguring Christ's crucifixion, but the engraver of the silver bowl used none of the more obvious sources, turning instead to Heemskerck's illustration, which appears as an incidental scene in the second print in *The Triumph of Patience* (Fig. 130).

This depicts Isaac riding a camel which pulls behind it the sacrificial altar (of Classical Roman form), Abraham's sword and the ram, symbolising the fate that Isaac so narrowly avoided, with, in the upper right corner, the scene faithfully reproduced on the dish. An armorial on the bowls identifies an early owner as being a member of the Montagu family of Boughton, not the original builder of the sixteenth-century house, Sir Edward, but presumably his son.

The Triumph of Patience was used again, around 1600, in the decoration of Hardwick Hall (pp.264, 277ff.) and perhaps a decade later at Charlton House, Greenwich, built by Sir Adam Newton, tutor to Henry Prince of Wales, between 1607 and 1612. Some of its plaster overmantels have already been mentioned in connection with engravings by Abraham de Bruyn. One of these overmantels, in the White Drawing Room, surmounts a chimneypiece supported by powerful caryatids (Fig. 131). Its carved frieze has two horizontal panels and these show the

preoccupations as money and social position'. Like the biblical prints, these were often designed in sets and the most distinctive take the form of triumphal processions, of the kind based on the *triumphus* of a general or ruler in classical times. They had been popularised by the literary example of the *trionfi* of Petrarch and became established as part of the triumphal entries and other civic festivities in sixteenth-century Europe. Although the triumphal car only

Triumph of Tobias, on the right, with the Triumph of Christ on the left. These are respectively prints 6 and 8 in Heemskerck's *Triumph of Patience* (Figs 132, 133), engraved by Dirck Coornhert. The Triumph of Christ has been reversed to give a better balance with its pair. The text beneath Tobias emphasises the relevance of this Old Testament story: Tobias endured the loss of his sight and his possessions but, though blind, 'saw in faith him whom the wisdom of the world cannot perceive, and upon him alone he placed his trust for evermore'. The Triumph of Christ shows that patience, drawn by hope and longing, leads to union with Christ, who symbolised for Heemskerck and Coornhert 'the only hope of mankind and the true life', the conqueror of the sins of the world and the giver of eternal life. These were wholly appropriate messages for the man who had been tutor to Prince Henry.

I have devoted some time to discussing the appearances of *The Triumph of Patience* in Elizabethan and Jacobean England because the idea of allegorical triumph cycle, though common in sixteenth-century Netherlands (and to a lesser extent in Tudor England), is generally unfamiliar today – traces of the practice survive in the floats of village carnivals. A still more richly detailed suite, *The Cycle of the Vicissitudes of Human Affairs*, was designed by Heemskerck in 1562–3, engraved perhaps by Cornelis Cort and issued in 1564.[25] Its influence on the visual arts even on the Continent seems to have been limited,[26] and in England I have found only one instance of its use, probably two generations after its publication (see pp.191–3). Similarly, Heemskerck's suite *The Triumphs of Petrarch*, which was engraved by Philips Galle and published in or shortly after 1565,[27] is known in a single English context during the sixteenth century, along with several other allegorical sets, representing by far the largest demonstrable concentration of prints by Heemskerck in this country (their use is summarised later, on pp.294–5).

The comparatively few instances of Heemskerck's influence in England all occur in courtly circles, just the elevated intellectual and social milieu to which, with their complex imagery and multi-layered messages, his prints might be expected to appeal. Margaret Aston has suggested a very plausible means by which the engravings that inspired the painter of *Edward VI and the Pope* arrived in England. The accompanying verses were composed by the celebrated Haarlem humanist, physician, poet and scholar, Hadrianus Junius (Adriaen de Jonghe, 1511–75). Junius had found employment during the last years of Henry VIII as physician and informal tutor to the children of Henry Howard, Earl of Surrey, the son of Thomas Howard, 3rd Duke of Norfolk. His career in the Norfolk household had come to an abrupt end with

129 Silver spice bowl, London 1573–4, engraved with the Sacrifice of Isaac. Victoria and Albert Museum, London.

130 Dirck Volkertsz. Coornhert after Maarten van Heemskerck, the Triumph of Isaac, from *The Triumph of Patience*, 1559. Rijksmuseum-Stichting, Amsterdam.

131 Charlton House, Kent, chimneypiece, in the White Drawing Room, *c.*1612.

132 (*facing page top*) Dirck Volkertsz. Coornhert after Maarten van Heemskerck, the Triumph of Tobias, from *The Triumph of Patience*, 1559. Rijksmuseum-Stichting, Amsterdam.

the execution of Surrey in 1547 but Junius attempted to attract the royal patronage of Edward VI and Mary Tudor successively by dedicating a number of books to them. No later than 1556 he returned to Haarlem,[28] where he compiled his popular *Emblemata* (1565), and during the 1560s collaborated with the print publisher Philips Galle, providing verses to accompany Heemskerck's compositions. In 1568 Junius was back in England making contact with William Cecil and renewing his acquaintance with his former pupil, Thomas Howard, Duke of Norfolk. What could be easier than to bring with him some fruits of his collaboration with Heemskerck and Galle?

FRANS FLORIS

Heemskerck outlived by four years another artist twenty years his junior. This was Frans Floris (c.1518–70), and through the prints engraved after his paintings or drawings he exerted a small but significant influence on decoration in Elizabethan England. Frans was the elder brother of Cornelis and Jacob Floris who, as already seen, also made designs for engravings, mostly grotesques and cartouches.

Frans Floris was a pupil of the academic painter Lambert Lombard (1505–66) who, although some of his designs were engraved, himself exerted no apparent influence in England. Floris became a history painter, concentrating on religious, secular and allegorical subjects. He entered the Guild of St Luke in 1540, but left for Italy the following year and came under the spell not only of Michelangelo's *Last Judgement*, which had recently been finished, but also of artists of the next generation, Vasari, Salviati, Bronzino and the Zuccari.

On his return Frans Floris settled in Antwerp where his studio became, like that of Rubens in the next century, the focus of artistic activity in the city. He was a prominent member of a chamber of rhetoric called De Violieren, the Violets, an Antwerp example of a peculiarly Netherlandish phenomenon: these chambers included rhetoricians who composed verses, took part in recitations and acted in plays, but also included artists who designed and painted stage scenery, costumes and shields. Like his sculptor brother Cornelis, Frans Floris's studio received commissions far beyond the limits of the city of Antwerp and his stature was such that he was said (by van Mander, probably overestimating) to have had at least a hundred and twenty pupils, no doubt employed in working up designs into altarpieces.

Sometimes his paintings were disseminated by means of reproductive engravings, and it was in this form that his influence seems first to have come to England, being discernible amongst the decorative work done for the Earl and Countess of Shrewsbury

at their house at Chatsworth after 1565 at the earliest and more probably after 1570 (see p.254).

Many of Frans Floris's drawings for prints were commissioned by Hieronymus Cock and engraved by Cornelis Cort. Amongst these was an influential set of *The Five Senses*, the designs for which are dated 1561. They depart from medieval representations of the

133   Dirck Volkertsz. Coornhert after Maarten van Heemskerck, the Triumph of Christ, from *The Triumph of Patience*, 1559. Rijksmuseum-Stichting, Amsterdam.

134 Cornelis Cort after Frans Floris, Gustus, from *The Five Senses*, c.1561. Museum Boijmans Van Beuningen, Rotterdam.

theme in their choice of symbolic creatures, an eagle for Visus, a stag for Auditus, a dog for Olfactus and a tortoise for Tactus, accompanied by a pecking bird: the monkey is retained for Gustus (Fig. 134). The style of the prints is clearly influenced by Italian art.

The Five Senses, together with other groups of allegorical figures such as the Four Parts of the World, the Seven Virtues and so on, were popular in Elizabethan and Jacobean England, in which representations of saints and martyrs were banned. Floris's set of the Five Senses was used at least twice by Bess of Hardwick or her family, Auditus for a cushion-cover in the New Hall, all five Senses in lunettes on the upper walls of the Pillar Parlour in the Little Castle at Bolsover, built for Sir Charles Cavendish, Bess's favourite younger son, between 1612 and 1619.

The Senses were influential elsewhere, Gustus being used for a Sheldon tapestry cushion-cover in the last decade of the sixteenth century, and again, with Visus and Odoratus, on the ceiling of the Great Chamber at Boston Manor, Brentford, Middlesex (Fig. 135), in the first decade of the seventeenth. The only other instances of the use of prints after Frans Floris identified so far occur in Sheldon tapestries in 1588 (see pp.223–6) and in the north-east of the country, on a chimneypiece that is discussed on page 187.

JOHANNES STRADANUS (JAN VAN DER STRAET)

Another artist who had a limited influence in England through engravings after his designs was Johannes Stradanus (Jan van der Straet). He was born in Bruges in 1523 and was a pupil of his father and later of Pieter Aertsen in Antwerp. He became a member of the Guild of St Luke in 1545 but later worked in Lyons and in Venice. Despite being a Protestant, Johannes Stradanus was employed by Cosimo I de' Medici in Florence between 1553 and 1571, designing a series of twenty-eight tapestries with hunting subjects for the Villa Medici at Poggio a Caiano, which were woven between 1567 and 1578. He also collaborated with Vasari and worked on the catafalque of Michelangelo in 1564. He died in Florence in 1605.

The success of the hunting tapestries led Johannes Stradanus to produce several suites of designs for engravings, six of which were published by Hieronymus Cock in Antwerp in 1570, with another set of forty published by Philips Galle in 1578, and a third somewhat later. The first two sets were combined under the title *Venationes Ferarum, Avium, Piscium, Pugnae Bestiorum* in 1596 and were subsequently re-issued several times.[29] His hunting scenes supplied the inspiration for plasterwork and embroidery at Hardwick New Hall in Derbyshire, for a beast in a Sheldon tapestry and for wall paintings at Madingley Hall near Cambridge. His suite of designs of the Seven Planets was copied at Burton Agnes in Yorkshire. All these examples are discussed below, in Part II. Stradanus also designed sixteen prints to continue the series of fifteen by Heemskerck illustrating the Acts of the Apostles, all of which were engraved by Philips Galle, but these biblical scenes seem not to have been used in England.

135 Boston Manor, Middlesex, figure of Gustus on the ceiling of the Great Chamber, c.1623.

★ ★ ★

PIETER BRUEGEL

Pieter Bruegel was born within a few years of Frans Floris, at some time during the later 1520s, but he occupied the opposite end of the artistic spectrum, his work owing much more to the realism of fifteenth-century Flemish paintings than to contemporary Italian art. Although he did visit Italy, in 1552–4, he seems to have more impressed by the Alps than by Roman architecture or Italian painting. His only excursion into ancient mythology is his famously eccentric painting *The Fall of Icarus* (*c*.1555–8, Musées Royaux des Beaux Arts, Brussels) and his allegories are depicted in terms of everyday rather than classical life. He designed more than two hundred and fifty prints, engraved by numerous artists including Hieronymus Cock and Philips Galle, and these rather than his paintings formed the basis of his reputation during his lifetime. Two instances in England of derivation from his prints – one an illustration of a New Testament parable, the other depicting warships at sea – will be considered later.[30]

MAARTEN DE VOS

Maarten de Vos (1532–1603) was in Italy at the same time as Bruegel, but his art – and his influence in England – was of a very different order. After his apprenticeship in Antwerp, probably in the studio of Frans Floris, he left to continue his training in Rome, Florence and, in particular, Venice, where he worked in the studio of Tintoretto.[31] He returned to Antwerp and can be followed from 1562 to the end of his life.[32] For a number of years he was employed by Count Wilhelm the younger of Brunswick-Luneburg on paintings for the Lutheran *Schloss-Capelle* at Celle (*c*.1569–72), but de Vos decided to make his artistic career in Antwerp under Catholic rule, presumably signing the necessary papers to say that he would become a Catholic within four years. From the late 1570s onwards de Vos was much in demand by the Church, brotherhoods and guilds for painting substantial altarpieces to replace those destroyed by the iconoclasts in the *Beeldenstorm*, but as late as 1584 he was documented as being a Lutheran and it seems probable that his sympathies were never actually transferred to the Catholic Church.

Maarten de Vos was a very prolific draughtsman, producing numerous designs for a whole series of engravers including Adriaen, Hans and Jan Baptiste I Collaert, Hendrick and Julius Goltzius, Pieter I de Iode, Aegidius, Johannes I and Raphael Sadeler, Pieter Cool, the Wierix brothers and Crispijn de Passe the elder. The latter continued to engrave designs by de Vos even after he had himself left for Germany –

he was an Anabaptist – and this is probably explained by the fact that the artist and the engraver were related by marriage: de Vos was de Passe's maternal uncle.[33] Approaching fifteen hundred prints were issued after designs by de Vos: most of the dated examples belong to the period from the early 1570s to the 1590s, reaching a climax around the publication of Gerard de Iode's *Thesaurus veteris et novi Testamenti* in Antwerp in 1579. Maarten de Vos was one of the major contributors to this highly influential picture Bible.

A balanced assessment of the influence of de Vos in England is difficult because of the sheer number of prints engraved after his designs, although the recent publication of fully illustrated volumes in the Hollstein series has made the task less arduous. Present indications are that much late sixteenth-century figurative work in this country – both biblical and allegorical – was based on his designs.

In the sixteenth century, often disparate groups of engravings were brought together into books, some by collectors for their own purposes, some by publishers either in response to a perceived demand or perhaps to test the market. In both cases the intention was to provide as comprehensive a range of biblical illustrations as possible. The so-called Heemskerck-album in the Rijksprentenkabinet in Amsterdam is an example of the collector's sort; the *Thesaurus veteris et novi Testamenti* is an example of the publisher's.

The Heemskerck-album, as its name suggests, consists largely though not exclusively of prints after Maarten van Heemskerck, usually in first editions; it was bound up into one volume sometime after 1575 (the date of the latest print) although the collection may have been begun some years earlier. The *Thesaurus*, on the other hand, is the work of the publisher, Gerard de Iode, and the prints mostly date from a few years before 1579 when the first edition appeared.[34] A second edition was published in 1585. Unlike the Heemskerck-album, the *Thesaurus* contains prints by Maarten de Vos and provides a convenient anthology of his engraved biblical illustrations. It also includes prints after a number of other artists, although there are more engravings after de Vos's work than any other artist's. The individual suites that made up the book must also have been available separately so we cannot be sure in every instance that it was from the *Thesaurus* that a workman learnt of his source, although this does seem probable. For convenience, the overall influence of the *Thesaurus* will be assessed here, whether or not the prints were after designs by Maarten de Vos.

The *Thesaurus* seems to have been an especially popular quarry for decoration in England, and instances are concentrated in the first half of the seventeenth century, when the fact that Maarten de

de Vos in Eng.

Vos was serving the Counter-Reformation cause (by
painting alterpieces for churches ransacked during the
Beeldenstorm or iconoclasm of 1576) was less important
to the English monarch. In a seminal article published
in the 1940s,[35] Nancy Cabot recorded some instances
of derivation from designs in the *Thesaurus* in needlework. As Mrs Cabot's article is somewhat inaccessible,
it is worth summarising her findings here. She discovered that some subjects proved particularly popular
for the designers of textiles (mostly embroidered
pictures), the story of Abraham being perhaps the
favourite. This was told in the *Thesaurus* in six prints
by de Vos and inspired no fewer than twenty-five
embroideries. The list given in her Appendix could
no doubt be extended without much difficulty: the
scenes on two Bruges tapestries were copied from the
same source. After the story of Abraham, those of
David and Bathsheba (after de Vos), of Esther and
Ahasuerus (after Jan Snellinck), and of Susanna and
the Elders (after Gillis Coignet) were most favoured,
accounting (in Mrs Cabot's estimation) for sixteen
separate needlework pictures. More recently,
Margaret Swain noted that ten (out of total of
twenty-nine) Old Testament needlework pictures in
the Burrell Collection in Glasgow were dependent on
the *Thesaurus*.[36]

So textiles provide excellent evidence of the popularity of this book of biblical illustrations in England,
but a growing number of instances in other media are
being identified too. A wall painting from a house
at Waltham Holy Cross, Essex (Fig. 136), for instance,
representing Jonah being thrown into the sea and
painted probably at the beginning of the seventeenth
century, derives from the design by de Vos,[37] which
was included in de Iode's *Thesaurus* (Fig. 137). From
the other end of the seventeenth century there is a

painted ceiling in a house called The Dean in Edinburgh, with (amongst other subjects) a Sacrifice of
Isaac in which the position of the intended victim –
and the appearance of some of the background buildings – relates closely to the print after de Vos in the
Thesaurus. The same scene also inspired the design of
a window in the chapel at Hatfield House in
Hertfordshire.[38]

One figure (and perhaps a second) from a set of
wall paintings at St Guthlac, Passenham, Northamptonshire, also derives from the *Thesaurus*. The decoration here dates from some time after the chancel was
rebuilt by Sir Robert Banastre in 1626.[39] The upper
walls are articulated by pilasters separating shell-arched
niches peopled by Old and New Testament figures.
More than one set of prints must have been used for
Jeremiah and perhaps Ezekiel can be identified with
prints after Jan Snellinck in the *Thesaurus*, while the
others have not been traced to their source.

Amongst other instances of derivation from de

Vos's *Thesaurus* illustrations is a set of painted panels of three of the Evangelists: they have no provenance but are now in the Victoria and Albert Museum. St Matthew, St Mark and St Luke are clearly copied from prints by Jan Wierix after de Vos (Figs 138, 139).[40]

The influence of the collection was equally strong in plasterwork. The gallery at Lanhydrock in Cornwall, with its magnificent plaster ceiling with Old Testament scenes and two chimneypieces, was probably completed shortly before the Civil War broke out in 1642. For some reason, most of the scenes in the compartments of the ceiling were not taken from the *Thesaurus* (and their sources have not been identified), but the figurative reliefs in the overmantels

and over the north door of the gallery, illustrating scenes from the life of King David (Figs 140, 142, 143), were all copied from plates after Ambrosius Francken published in the *Thesaurus* (Figs 141, 144, 145). On stylistic grounds alone it seems likely that another Cornish ceiling, at Prideaux Place near Padstow (Figs 146, 147), was executed by the plasterers who worked at Lanhydrock, so it is not very surprising that here too the *Thesaurus* was used: it provided the source for Moses Striking the Rock after Maarten van Cleve (Fig. 148) and for some (though not all, for several were clearly the plasterers' own invention) of the scenes from the story of Susanna and the Elders after Gillis Coignet (Fig. 149).[41] Incidentally, the use of the same book of prints in these two

138 (*above left*) Painted panel, St Matthew, English, late sixteenth-century. Victoria and Albert Museum, London.

139 (*above right*) Jan Wierix after Maarten de Vos, St Matthew, from a set of the Four Evangelists in the *Thesaurus* (Antwerp, 1585). Bibliothèque Royale Albert 1er, Brussels.

141 (*below right*) Hans Collaert after Ambrosius Francken, David and Goliath, from the *Thesaurus* (Antwerp, 1585). British Museum, London.

Infidys Dauida petit rex Saulus, et ipsum Dextra dei mira pro bonitate tegit. 1.Reg.19.

Accessit noctu tentoria regia Dauid, Hinc aufert regis pocula et arma sui. 1.Reg.26.

142 and 143 (top) Lanhydrock, Cornwall, gallery overmantels, Saul Attempts to Kill David (*left*) and David Spares Saul's Life (*right*), *c*.1640.

144 and 145 Hans Collaert after Ambrosius Francken, Saul Attempts to Kill David (*left*) and David Spares Saul's Life (*right*), from the *Thesaurus* (Antwerp, 1585). British Museum, London.

houses suggests that the work at Prideaux may be roughly contemporary with that at Lanhydrock and therefore later in date than has sometimes been suggested.[42] These West Country uses of illustrations from the *Thesaurus* in plasterwork suggest that the craftsmen may have been introduced to the picture Bible by William Arnold, who, as will be seen later (pp.147, 149), copied some of their title cartouches in his own work.

Maarten de Vos, however, designed many more suites of biblical illustrations than those which appeared in the *Thesaurus*, and it has been exciting to discover that another set was also used as the basis for decoration in England, if only in a handful of self-contained parts of the country.[43] Engraved by several different artists and consisting of fifty-one prints, this was published in Antwerp by Adriaen Collaert under the title *Vita, Passio, et Resurrectio Iesv Christi, variis Iconibus a celeberrimo pictore Martino de Vos expressa, ab Adriano Collart nunc primum in aes incisa . . .*[44]

A single instance occurs in the north-east and is discussed on page 89, but here we should investigate occurrences in the south-west. Amongst the latter is the plasterwork decoration of the Court House at East Quantoxhead in Somerset. This house preserves some fabric dating back to 1272 and more may belong to a building campaign around 1500, but most of the visible structure today dates from the first half of the seventeenth century when the owner was George Luttrell,[45] who was also busy altering Dunster Castle. At the Court House the work was done between 1614 and 1619, the dates on two of the chimneypieces. There are four plaster overmantels with elaborate strapwork cartouches (one adapted from a Vredeman design, see p.63) enclosing New Testament subjects. All derive from the de Vos designs and depict the following scenes, in order of their occurrence in the Bible: Christ blessing little children, from print no.29, in the drawing room (Figs 150, 151); Christ prophesying the destruction of Jerusalem, from no.32, in the North Bedroom (Figs 152, 153); the Agony in the Garden, from no.36, in another bedroom (Figs 154, 155); and the Descent from the Cross, from no.46, in the nursery (Figs 156, 157). It is probable that it was the owner of the house, George Luttrell, who acquired the book and gave it to his plasterers to copy; if so, they must have made

copies of other prints from the suite, for two of the subjects reappear in plasterwork attributed to the Abbott family on stylistic grounds in several buildings in Barnstaple.[46] The Annunciation (Fig. 160) was used twice, as an overmantel panel in 69 High Street (Fig. 158) and for one of the panels on the ceiling of the Golden Lion Hotel in Boutport Street, while the Adoration was used on the ceiling of 7 Cross Street.[47]

Besides biblical illustrations, Maarten de Vos also designed a whole range of allegorical subjects, together with a comprehensive suite of illustrations of Ovid's *Metamorphoses*. So prints following his designs were commonly used, in masonry, plasterwork, wall-painting and textiles. Borrowings from his secular designs tend to be somewhat earlier in date than those from his religious illustrations, perhaps reflecting their less controversial, indeed non-sectarian, content.

There is no need to spend much time on the most

146 and 147   Prideaux Place, Cornwall, ceiling in the Great Chamber, Moses striking the Rock (*left*) and Susanna and the Elders (*right*), c.1635–40.

148 (*bottom left*)   Hieronymus Wierix and Jan Sadeler after Maarten van Cleve, Moses Striking the Rock, from the *Thesaurus* (Antwerp, 1585). British Museum, London.

149 (*bottom right*)   Jan Baptiste Collaert after Gillis Coignet, Susanna and the Elders, from the *Thesaurus* (Antwerp, 1585). British Museum, London.

150 (*above*) The Court House,
East Quantoxhead, Somerset,
overmantel, Christ Blessing
Little Children, early
seventeenth century.

151 Jacob de Bye after
Maarten de Vos, Christ Blessing
Little Children, from *Vita,
Passio, et Resurrectio Iesv Christi*
(Antwerp, n.d.). Rijksmuseum–
Stichting, Amsterdam.

152 (*above*) The Court House, East Quantoxhead, Somerset, overmantel, Christ Prophesying the Destruction of Jerusalem, early seventeenth century.

153 Jacob de Bye after Maarten de Vos, Christ Prophesying the Destruction of Jerusalem, from *Vita, Passio, et Resurrectio Iesv Christi* (Antwerp, n.d.). Rijksmuseum-Stichting, Amsterdam.

154 The Court House, East Quantoxhead, Somerset, overmantel, the Agony in the Garden, early seventeenth century.

155 Cornelis Galle after Maarten de Vos, The Agony in the Garden, from *Vita, Passio, et Resurrectio Iesv Christi* (Antwerp, n.d.). Rijksmuseum–Stichting, Amsterdam.

156 The Court House, East
Quantoxhead, Somerset,
overmantel, the Descent from
the Cross, early seventeenth
century.

157 Jan Baptiste Collaert after
Maarten de Vos, the Descent
from the Cross, from *Vita,
Passio, et Resurrectio Iesv Christi*
(Antwerp, n.d.). Rijksmuseum-
Stichting, Amsterdam.

2. *Ingreſſus Angelus, ad eam dixit, Aue gratia plena, Dominus tecum, benedicta tu in mulieribus.* Luc. 1.

M. de Vos inuent. Corn. Galle sculpsit. Alr. Collaert excud.

PHLEGMATICVS

Nil sapit os humet, fastidit somniat vndas
Trqúitur lentæ crimine pigritiæ.

Segnuag. obliquat male mundus pectora torpor
Humida ch nimio Phlegmate membra madent.

M. de Vos inuentor. Rephael Sadler sculps et excud. Antverpiæ

160 (*bottom left*) Cornelis Galle
after Maarten de Vos, the
Annunciation, from *Vita, Passio,
et Resurrectio Iesv Christi*
(Antwerp, n.d.). Rijksmuseum-
Stichting, Amsterdam.

obvious instances of derivation from prints after de
Vos which have been noticed by earlier writers:
during the 1590s three of the Four Elements were
copied for overmantels at Hardwick Old Hall, while
in the New Hall two figures representing Spring and
Summer appear in the plaster frieze of the High Great
Chamber flanking the window bay. During the next
decade, the Four Ages of Man were copied on the
walls of the painted staircase at Knole by Paul

Isaacson, while in 1611 all four Seasons were
employed for the central scenes of the well-known set
of Sheldon tapestries made for Toddington Manor in
Bedfordshire;[48] they are probably the last significant
commissions of the Sheldon works. Also in the
Cavendish–Smythson orbit are the wall paintings in
the ante-room of the Little Castle at Bolsover, dating
from shortly before 1620: three of de Vos's Four
Temperaments were reproduced in the lunettes

around the upper walls.[49] I am not the first to notice that another of his sets of the Four Temperaments (Fig. 161), of 1583, formed the basis of the relief on a chimneypiece in the Guildhall in Guildford (Fig. 159), perhaps in the 1630s.[50]

To these already identified instances of borrowing from de Vos can now be added a number of others. Some occur at Hardwick, a set of the Virtues together with suites illustrating the Seven Acts of Mercy and the Last Judgement, and the Divine Charge to the Three Estates (see pp.266, 285, 284). The last-named suite may have been rare in England: the only other instance of borrowing from it I have come across occurs on the pargetted exterior of Sparrow's House in Ipswich (Fig. 162, see Fig. 488), work which may date from as late as 1670, representing a time-lag from the publication of the print of around eighty-five years.

The Sheldon tapestry works, besides copying the Four Seasons on the great set of tapestries now at Hatfield, also used de Vos's print of Iustitia (see Fig. 455) on a panel now at Sudeley Castle, which probably dates from about 1600. The source of the remainder of the allegorical figures has obstinately defied identification, but a tendency by the Sheldon works to use prints after de Vos is suggested by the similarity – no more – of one of his Susanna scenes, reversed, and a cushion-cover.

Very occasionally (as perhaps at the Sheldon tapestry works) workmen were able to modify designs – beyond the problem of translating a two-dimensional image into three dimensions – that were not absolutely right for their purposes. Here there is a danger of stepping outside the 'sibling relationship' criterion, but one instance should be enough to suggest that this was sometimes achieved. The staircase newel posts from Thame Abbey in Oxfordshire (one of which is dated 1612) are carved with figures of the Four Parts of the World, presented – appropriately for newel posts – as standing figures (as on the exactly contem-

porary Adam and Eve Staircase at Hatfield). The most likely source, however, shows seated figures. This is a series of designs by Maarten de Vos, which were engraved by Adriaen Collaert (c.1560–1618). Details of Asia's costume provide convincing evidence that it was these prints that were copied (Figs 163, 164, 165): the Continents on newel and print accord perfectly in costume, while the carver (as if to make things certain) included with Europa two of the animals in the middleground to the left of the print for his subsidiary decoration (Figs 166, 167, 168).

The same suite of The Four Parts of the World, engraved by Adriaen Collaert, was used for the relief on the lintel of a chimneypiece at Rawdon House, Hoddesdon in Hertfordshire, and (with other borrowings from designs by de Vos) on an overmantel from north-east England (see p.193). Europa from this set was also copied for the very handsome overmantel in the dining room at Crewe Hall in Cheshire (Fig. 169), while another de Vos invention was adapted for the overmantel relief in the Carved Parlour (Fig. 170). Here the panel has a winged figure flanked by two more, one reclining with head on elbow, the other bending his back to his digging. The scene depicts Time between Labour and Idleness, and the source is a print by Raphael Sadeler after Maarten de Vos published in 1582 (Fig. 171).[51] Another borrowing from de Vos occurs on an overmantel at Ampney Park in Gloucestershire, where a knight in armour, the Miles Christianus, tramples a female figure, flanked by Death, the Devil, Sin and the World (Fig. 172). It derives from the engraving by Hieronymus Wierix of about 1600 (Fig. 173), which is a complex allegory of a kind favoured by the artist, who treated the subject more than once.[52] The date of the overmantel is a matter of some doubt: Pevsner considered the flanking figures between columns to be stylistically about 1625, but the centrally placed shaft, which pierces the lower frame of the panel is perhaps an alteration of the nineteenth century. The relief may be the work of the Gloucestershire tomb-maker Thomas Baldwin, who described himself as 'carver' in Stroud in 1615 but later worked in Gloucester.[53] If so, it would be good to know whether he had any connection with the drawing master Thomas Trevelyon who copied a related print – along with the Speculum Peccatoris designed and engraved by Hieronymus Wierix – into one of his manuscript Miscellanies.[54]

Maarten de Vos's sets of allegorical figures were ideally suited to the caryatid-like supports that often flank overmantels in England. Justice, from a set of the Virtues, appears in this position on the chimneypiece in the dining room at Burton Agnes in east Yorkshire (see p.179). Two of de Vos's figures depicting the Liberal Arts and engraved by Crispijn

158 (facing page top left) Barnstaple, Devon, ceiling at 69 High Street, the Annunciation.

159 (facing page top right) Guildhall, Guildford, Surrey, detail of the chimneypiece.

161 (facing page bottom right) Raphael Sadeler I after Maarten de Vos, Phlegmaticus, from The Four Temperaments. Warburg Institute, London.

162 Ipswich, Suffolk, Sparrow's House, detail of pargetting illustrating the Task of Worldly Power, c.1670.

Burton A.

163 and 164 (*left*) Thame Abbey, Oxfordshire, staircase newel post with the figure of Asia, and detail.

165 Adriaen Collaert after Maarten de Vos, *Asia*, from *The Four Parts of the World* (copy by Gregorius Fentzel). Stedelijk Prentenkabinet, Antwerp.

168 Adriaen Collaert after Maarten de Vos, *Europe*, from *The Four Parts of the World* (copy by Gregorius Fentzel). Stedelijk Prentenkabinet, Antwerp.

166 and 167 (*left*) Thame Abbey, Oxfordshire, staircase newel post with the figure of Europe, and detail, 1612.

de Passe the elder were copied on an overmantel at
South Wraxall Manor in Wiltshire, and more were
copied, along with figures of the Virtues, in a Scottish
context (see pp.143 and 154).

Maarten de Vos designed several sets of the Five
Senses, which achieved rather less popularity in
England than might have been anticipated from their
number. One set was adapted by an important carver
in the north east (see p.193) while another (Fig. 174)
supplied the inspiration for a carved relief reset in the
grotto – in reality a tunnel built under the main road
to Bath – at Arno's Court in Bristol: this was depicted
in a pencil sketch by Hugh O'Neill dated 1820 (Fig.
175).[55]

PHILIPS GALLE

Maarten de Vos may have designed a suite of prints
identified here for the first time as the source that
unites several instances of the appearance of the Nine
Worthies in England. It introduces a man met briefly
as a print-publisher and repeatedly encountered as an
engraver of other men's work. Earlier writers have
commented on the similarities between the instances
known to them – the figures in stone on the east front
of Montacute, after 1588 (see Fig. 238), in plaster in
the Great Chamber at Aston Hall near Birmingham
(Fig. 179; 1618–35), in seventeenth-century wall
paintings in a house in Amersham, Buckinghamshire
(Fig. 178), and in the manuscript embroidery-design
books compiled by Thomas Trevelyon (1608 and
1616) – but had to conclude that the models from
which they were copied were lost.[56] To these
instances of the Nine Worthies can now be added
the figures of the Worthies on an Elizabethan overmantel at Wiston Park in Sussex (after 1575), on a
painted cloth at Hardwick Hall in Derbyshire
(c.1600), on a carved frieze at Burton Agnes in east
Yorkshire and in stone on the conduit from Carfax in
Oxford (both c.1610).[57]

The Worthies were a popular subject during the
sixteenth century. Suites were designed by Hans
Burgkmair, Daniel Hopfer, Lucas van Leyden,
Cornelis van Oostsanen, the monogrammist MG,
Virgil Solis, Maarten van Heemskerck and Nicolaes
de Bruyn, Maarten de Vos and Antonio Tempesta; a
less familiar set was engraved by Nicolaes de Bruyn,[58]
and individual figures also appear in single prints, for
instance in a titlepage border by Hans Holbein,
Michael Kirmer, Conrad Hillebrand and Johann
Hauer.[59]

Although the suite that inspired all these English
instances of the Nine Worthies could have been
designed by Maarten de Vos, the prints were signed
by their publisher Philips Galle (1537–1612).[60] Galle

169 Crewe Hall, Cheshire, dining room overmantel, Europe, 1615–39.

115

was certainly capable of executing, and designing, the prints himself (Figs 176, 177). Besides being a reproductive engraver and print publisher, Galle was an artist in his own right,[61] specialising in depicting themes that had not previously been illustrated: these included suites on the subject of the Wretchedness of Human Existence (1563) and the Four Elements (1564), the first appearance of what was to become a popular theme in Netherlandish art.[62] His pictorial style while in Haarlem was much influenced by that of Maarten van Heemskerck and Frans Floris, whose designs he regularly engraved, but underwent a transformation after his move to Antwerp in 1570, where he came under the spell of Anthonie Blocklandt, Johannes Stradanus and Maarten de Vos. His dependence on humanist writers continued, although his allegiance switched from the Haarlemmer, Hadrianus Junius, to the southerners Cornelius Kilianus and Hugo Faviolus. From now on his designs were usually engraved by others and his prints were signed 'Phls Galle excudit' (i.e. published).

Galle's most important work as artist was perhaps the rare suite of forty-three allegorical figures he published under the title *Prosopographia, Sive Virtutum, Animi, Corporis, Bonorum Externorum, Vitiorum, et Affectuum Variorum Delineatio, Imaginibus Accurate Expressa a Philippo Gallaeo* . . . between 1585 and 1603 (probably *c*.1590).[63] Galle explained his purpose in publishing them:

Tu as ici, amy lecteur, les images de Patience, Penitence, Experience, Humilité, Pieté & autres semblables Vertus, comme pareillement les images des Vices, & autres choses, lesquelles tu voiras ornees & embellies de leurs symboles & appertenances peculieres; fort necessaires à tous peintres, engraveurs, entaileeurs, orfevres, statuaires & memes aux Poëtes rimeurs & rhetoriciens vulgaires, pur eux conseiller à ce livre, qui leur furnira des moyes pour pouvoir imiter toutes sortes deffigies . . .

170 (*facing page left*) Crewe Hall, Cheshire, Carved Parlour overmantel, Victorian replacement by E.M. Barry for the early seventeenth-century original destroyed in the fire of 1866.

171 (*facing page top right*) Raphael Sadeler I after Maarten de Vos, *Time between Labour and Idleness* (1582). Rijksmuseum-Stichting, Amsterdam.

172 (*above*) Ampney Park, Gloucestershire, overmantel, *c.*1625.

173 Hieronymus Wierix after Maarten de Vos, *Miles Christianus* (The Christian Knight), *c.*1600. Bibliothèque Royale Albert 1er, Brussels.

174 (*above left*) Adriaen Collaert after Maarten de Vos, Taste, from *The Five Senses*. Stedelijk Prentenkabinet, Antwerp.

175 (*above right*) Hugh O'Neill, pencil sketch (dated 1820) of antique sculpture in the grotto at Arno's Court, Bristol. Bristol City Museums and Art Gallery.

GODEFRIDVS BVLONIVS.

Phls Gall. excud.

176 (*right*) Philips Galle, Godfrey, from *The Nine Worthies*. Stedelijk Prentenkabinet, Antwerp.

177 (*far right*) Philips Galle, Julius Caesar, from *The Nine Worthies*. Stedelijk Prentenkabinet, Antwerp.

IVLIVS CAESAR.

These French-language comments suggest that Galle may have intended his set to be bought by potential patrons for their workmen rather than by the workmen themselves.[64] Nevertheless, on the very infrequent occasions when the *Prosopographia* was employed for decoration in England, it was probably the individual craftsman responsible who owned the book. One was a joiner or carver in north-east England whose work is examined on pages 172–200, and the other an artist who designed the titlepage of a book printed in London (see note 18 on p.311).

THE WIERIXES

The Wierix family, Johan (1549-after 1615), Hieronymus (1553–1619) and Antonie (died 1604), practised as reproductive engravers from the 1560s and 1570s, providing numerous illustrations for books published by Christopher Plantin. With Crispijn de Passe, Johannes and Raphael Sadeler, they were amongst the most prolific engravers of designs by Maarten de Vos. But they also designed their own prints and there is evidence that some of these were known in England during the reign of James I, when the climate was not perhaps so hostile to Catholic devotional imagery. Two prints were copied by Thomas Trevelyon into the books of pictures with text he compiled in 1608 and 1616 (see p. 236). Another inspired an overmantel in the Charterhouse in London, and a set of the Virtues designed and engraved by Hieronymus Wierix supplied the figures

179 Aston Hall, Birmingham, Godfrey, one of the Nine Worthies, in the plasterwork frieze of the Great Chamber, *c*.1625–35; from William Niven, *Monograph of Aston Hall, Warwickshire* (London and Birmingham, 1879).

of Justice and Charity used on the hall overmantel at Charlton House, Wraxall in north Somerset.[65]

THE COLLAERTS

The Collaert family were also rather more than merely engravers. Adriaen Collaert (*c*.1560–1618) may have designed some prints himself, perhaps the one copied for an overmantel at Longford Castle in Wiltshire (see p.146). His best-known work as a designer in his own right is set of engravings of flowers published as *Florilegium* by Philips and Theodore Galle, which was certainly used in England. This suite was sometimes bound up with another entitled *Florae Deae* which was also used in this country, notably in painted glass at Gorhambury in Hertfordshire and at Lydiard Tregoze in Wiltshire (see p.219).[66] Hans Collaert (fl.1555–81) with his son Jan Baptiste I (1566–1628) designed two suites of pendants and other jewellery, *Monilium Bullarum Inaurumque Artificiossimae Icones* (1581) and *Bullarum inaurumque . . . archetypi artificiosi* (1582), a plate from the latter being used in one of the most surprising ways of any print in England (see pp.165–6).

✳ ✳ ✳

Reproductive engraving reached a peak of virtuosity in the hands of Netherlanders in the late sixteenth and early seventeenth centuries, particularly when they engraved the designs of artists working at the court of Rudolf II in Prague, Bartholomeus Spranger (1546–1611), Hans von Aachen (1552–1615), Roelant Savery (1576–1639), Adriaen de Vries (?1545–1626) and others. Amsterdam, Haarlem and Utrecht were also important artistic centres where the humanist emphasis of Maarten van Heemskerck was continued by artists such as Karel van Mander (1548–1606), Hendrick Goltzius (1558–1617) and Cornelis Cornelisz. van Haarlem (1562–1638), who formed the so-called Haarlem Academy between about 1586 and 1591.[67] The engravers who helped to disseminate their style included Domenicus Custos and Lucas Kilian in Augsburg, members of the Sadeler family (Jan I, Raphael and Aegidius), Jan Muller, Jan Saenredam and Hendrick Goltzius himself. Despite political links with the northern Netherlands and cultural links between individuals at the courts of Elizabeth I (and later Henry Prince of Wales) and Rudolph II at Prague,[68] the apparent influence in England of these artists and engravers was slight. I know of no derivations from van Mander and only two from Cornelisz. van Haarlem, both at Lydiard Park in Wiltshire: a painted glass window there incorporates a quarry decorated with a sailing boat which appears in the background of his design of *Arion and the Dolphin* engraved by Jan Muller (see p.219), and a marble panel depicting Susanna and the Elders (Fig. 180) comes from the engraving by Jan Saenredam (Fig. 181). The glass was probably made between 1628 and 1631 and the panel, which incidentally retains traces of its original polychromy, is likely to be contemporary. Both must have been part of the decoration of the earlier house which was partly remodelled in the Palladian-revival style in the 1740s.[69]

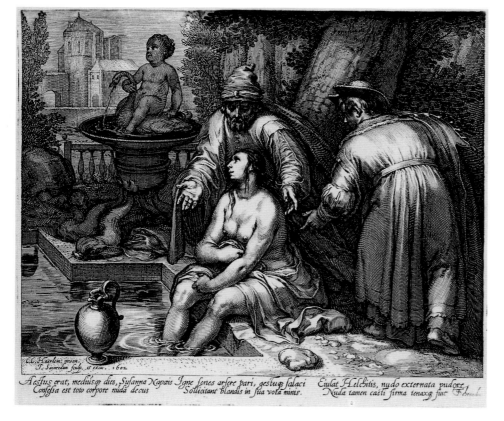

Hendrick Goltzius had slightly more impact in England. He was born in the town of Muhlbracht near Venlo in 1558, but his parents moved to Duisburg about thirty miles away when he was three. Apprenticed to his father as a glass painter, Goltzius learnt the craft of engraving from Dirck Coornhert around 1574 or 1575: Coornhert, poet and engraver, had lived in exile in Xanten from 1568 to 1576 but returned to Holland after the Pacification of Ghent (1576), and persuaded Goltzius to do the same. They settled in Haarlem, where Goltzius remained until his death. Probably at Coornhert's instigation, he met Philips Galle who was now based in Antwerp and in 1582 Goltzius set up his own publishing house which he directed until about 1600. Goltzius's artistic reputation rests on some 433 prints executed during these years; many more of his designs were engraved by his stepson Jacob Matham (1571–1631), who was active in Rome and Haarlem, Jan Saenredam (c.1565–1607), who worked in Assendelft, Jan Muller (1571–1628) in Amsterdam, and others.[70] Early influences had included Flemish masters of earlier generations (Adriaen de Weert, Jan van der Straet and Maarten de Vos, for example) but in 1590–91 Goltzius travelled to Italy via Hamburg and Munich, and his interests turned towards such Old Masters as Raphael, Dürer and Lucas van Leyden. By 1600 Goltzius turned to painting and his workshop was taken over by Jacob Matham, whom he had adopted as his son in 1579.

For all his success in his own country, there are no more than a handful of contexts in which his prints were adapted for decoration in England. Amongst the earliest must be a coverlet depicting Lucretia's Banquet, which C.E.C. Tattershall discovered in 1918 had three figures derived from Goltzius's engraving published by Philips Galle.[71] Approximately contemporary with this is the decoration of Hardwick Hall, where another print after a Goltzius design was employed (p.268); and Rosalys Coope discovered that his suite The United Virtues was copied for wall paintings in the lunettes of the Marble Closet at Bolsover Castle during the second decade of the seventeenth century. The virtuoso suite The Virtues and Vices was clearly known to the craftsmen who worked at Burton Agnes in Yorkshire (p.178) as well as to a goldsmith working in the 1630s or 1640s who may or may not have been English (see p.205). Additionally, prints of Mars and Venus were copied for stained glass at Gorhambury in Hertfordshire in the 1620s. During the following decade, Goltzius's 1583 engraving Moses with the Tablets of the Law may have inspired one of the paintings executed by the house painter John Carleton for the private chapel of Sir Arthur Ingram at Temple Newsam in Yorkshire.[72]

Jacob Matham (1571–1631) specialised in engraving, but was also capable of producing his own designs, a set of the Virtues providing the English glass painter Richard Butler with material for windows in the chapel at Lincoln's Inn in London (p.218). One of Goltzius's pupils also had some influence on decoration in England. This was Pieter de Iode who was born in Antwerp in 1570. In his mid-twenties he travelled to Italy, Holland and France but returned to Antwerp where he died in 1634. He worked as a reproductive printmaker, engraving designs by artists including Bassano, Titian, Giulio Romano and Francesco Vanni, Spranger, Rubens, Vrancx and Maarten de Vos. Sometimes he engraved his own designs, sometimes they were reproduced by other printmakers.

A suite of plates by Pieter de Iode was used in the decoration of the painted staircase at Knole in Kent, executed by Paul Isaacson during the first decade of the seventeenth century. But much the most popular of his designs was The Sacrifice of Isaac (Fig. 182), which was engraved by Egbert van Panderen around 1600. The earliest use of this engraving may be the embroidered front cover of a copy of the Geneva or 'Breeches' Bible in the edition of 1610 (Fig. 183), which was worked by Elizabeth Illingworth in 1613.[73] It appears, reversed, in an auricular cartouche on the titlepage of John Downame's A Guide to Godlynesse (London, 1622). The design was also chosen for carved reliefs in overmantels. Examples occur at Woodstone Manor, a house dating from the 1620s near Peterborough (where it is accompanied by a scene apparently depicting the Dance of Salome, from an unidentified source, Fig. 184); in the almost exactly contemporary gallery in Boston Manor, Brentford in Middlesex (see Fig. 121) – a house owned at the time of building by the wife of Sir William Reade – and in Sir Paul Pindar's house in Bishopsgate, London (see Fig. 123). Further afield it was used in the overmantel of a house in the High in Oxford. It is not clear why this particular print, rather than the innumerable alternatives by artists such as Maarten de Vos, was chosen for use in English contexts that have no immediately evident relationship one with another.

PETER PAUL RUBENS

At the very end of the period, during the second quarter of the seventeenth century, a new source of inspiration for artists and craftsmen working in England emerged in the form of reproductive engravings after paintings by Peter Paul Rubens. He had painted portraits of the Earl of Arundel in 1620 and the Duke

182 Egbert van Panderen after
Pieter de Iode, *The Sacrifice of
Isaac c.*1600. Rijksmuseum-
Stichting, Amsterdam.

183 (*below*) Embroidered book
cover worked by Elizabeth
Illingworth, 1613. Victoria and
Albert Museum, London.

of Buckingham five years later, but eventually visited England for himself while on a diplomatic mission lasting nine months during 1629 and 1630.

Given the scale and intensity of much of his work it comes as a shock to encounter a Rubens composition translated into the genteel medium of embroidery. Examples have been known for many years, however,[74] his painting *The Judgement of Solomon*, known through the engraving by Boetius Adam à Bolswert, being particularly popular: it was reproduced in at least two needlework pictures dating from the seventeenth century and its influence evidently persisted into the eighteenth.[75] Margaret Swain has reinforced our knowledge of the extent of Rubens's influence on textiles by illustrating a needlework picture depicting the Feast of Herod based on a reproductive print of the original painting now in the National Gallery of Scotland.[76]

Engravings after Rubens were also used as the inspiration for painted glass and, on one occasion at least, for architectural decoration during the 1630s (see p.194). Peterhouse Chapel, Cambridge, which was built between 1628 and 1632 during the mastership of Matthew Wren, has an east window

depicting the Crucifixion based on Rubens's painting *Le Coup de Lance*.[77] The glass painter may have been Bernard van Linge from Emden who painted glass for the chapel of Lincoln's Inn in London, for the chapels at Lincoln and Wadham Colleges and at Christ Church Cathedral in Oxford. To the 1670s or later belong two magnificent limewood reliefs based on his paintings *Queen Tomyris with the Head of Cyrus* and *The Battle of the Amazons*.[78]

Besides being a painter, Rubens was a prolific designer of titlepages and book illustrations, tapestries and triumphal arches (the latter marking the triumphal entry of Ferdinand of Austria into Antwerp in 1635, published as *Pompa Introitus Ferdinandi* in 1642). Architectural details in his book *I Palazzi di Genova* (1622) seem to reappear on the south-western range of the Great Court at Bolsover Castle in Derbyshire, perhaps about 1635–40, as well as at Nottingham Castle (*c*.1674–9).[79] The influence of this important publication on later seventeenth-century English architecture has still to be fully assessed.

Chapter 7

THE INFLUENCE OF ENGLISH PRINTS

It may seem somewhat perverse to include in a book on the continental sources for Elizabethan and Jacobean art and decoration a chapter on the influence of English prints. The perversity lies not so much in including them but in describing them as English, when so many prints made in the country either themselves display continental influence or were actually produced by foreigners working in England.

There are several kinds of potential sources, pattern-books of various sorts (for instance John Shute's *First and Chief Groundes of Architecture*, published in 1563, and Walter Gedde's *A Booke of Sundry Draughtes*, which appeared in 1615 or 1616, are perhaps the best known);[1] other possibilities are the records of actual events (such as Marc Geerarts's *Procession of the Knights of the Garter* (1576) or Stephen Harrison's *Archs of Triumph . . . of London*),[2] herbals, bestiaries, emblem books and other illustrated publications, such as Foxe's *Book of Martyrs*, not to mention the decorated page borders in books, as well as independent prints including broadsheets. A unique instance of the use of a royal genealogy, occurs in the decoration (by the engraver P over M) of a ewer and basin made in London in 1567–8, although the publisher of the genealogy was Gyles Godet, a Frenchman denizened in 1551 (see pp.201–2).

John Shute's *First and Chief Groundes of Architecture* can be disposed of in a sentence or two. Besides the titlepage border and woodcuts borrowed from an edition of Vitruvius there are five plates illustrating the orders of architecture: each gives a column, the measurements and an atlas or caryatid figure showing the influence of contemporary Flemish Mannerism. It is well known that the woodcut decoration of the titlepage border was copied for pilasters at Kirby Hall in Northamptonshire, built for Sir Humphrey Stafford by the mason Thomas Thorpe from 1570.[3] In addition, it does seem possible that the exactly contemporary screen in the hall of Middle Temple derived its Roman Doric order from Shute. Otherwise, the influence of this treatise seems to have been nonexistent, probably because it had no readily-copied decorative patterns of the kind that had made Serlio so popular in England.

One text-book that did was Thomas Hill's book *The Gardener's Labyrinth*, published in 1571. From this the gardeners at All Souls College, Oxford, derived the four knot-patterns visible in Robert Hovenden's bird's-eye view of the college of about 1585. Hovenden had acquired the garden shortly after becoming Warden in 1573 and levelled the ground in the week before Easter the following year.[4] There is little evidence that these knots, which might have been adapted from French garden design, exerted much influence elsewhere in England, although one seems to have been copied in the painted decoration of the parlour at Haddon Hall in Derbyshire,[5] while the drawing-master Thomas Trevelyon copied other knots in one of his manuscript books of embroidery patterns (see p.236).[6]

Walter Gedde's *A Booke of Sundry Draughtes* is another book whose illustrations consisted almost entirely of linear patterns of the kind that craftsmen found easy to adapt to their own purposes.[7] Its lengthy title makes it clear at what clientele Gedde aimed: *A Booke of Sundry Draughtes, principaly serving for Glasiers: And not Impertinent for Plasterers, and Gardiners: be sides sundry other professions.*[8] From the instructions that precede the plates and the brief treatise on glass painting, apparently published in 1616, that follows them, it has been assumed that Gedde was a glazier by trade, but there are no facts known about him, not even the dates of his birth and death.

The introductory text, illustrated by figures, demonstrates how the patterns are built up from squares, 'devisions', and circles. Of the 103 patterns that follow, some originated with glaziers,[9] others were simplified from ceiling designs in Serlio's Book IV which was first published in Robert Peake's English translation only four years before Gedde's book appeared.[10] These simplified patterns were then elaborated by division – that is to say, by adding more lines to subdivide areas further – which gave Gedde several more.[11] A small handful of the plates are familiar Renaissance patterns.[12] In short, it is clear that *A Booke of Sundry Draughtes* is both derivative and heterogeneous in character: Gedde – like so many before and after him – collected patterns from a wide

range of origins, simplifying some, elaborating others, recording past achievements in his own putative trade as glazier, as well as in disciplines quite unrelated to his own. Because he borrowed as a matter of course from sources that were equally accessible to his contemporaries, his influence as a pattern-designer is still incalculable, but many examples of the decorative arts do correspond with his plates.

Although Gedde for sound financial reasons intended his book to reach the widest possible readership, not surprisingly it is the patterns of leading in windows that most often correspond with designs found in *A Booke of Sundry Draughtes*, instances sometimes predating its publication. Examples of correspondence are very widely distributed throughout England, although Levens Hall in Westmorland offers a particularly delightful show of geometrical leading patterns in Gedde's manner.[13] An unusually intricate pattern involving an illusion of three dimensions, included by Gedde as his page 23, is recorded at East Sutton Place in Kent in an early nineteenth-century drawing by the architect, C.J. Richardson.[14] Paving patterns also coincide with designs in *A Booke of Sundry Draughtes*. The simple pattern of octagons, hexagons and greek crosses in Gedde's page 25 was certainly used for the paving of the Pillar Parlour in the Little Castle at Bolsover, which may be almost precisely coeval with the publication of *A Booke of Sundry Draughtes*, although the paviour could equally easily have himself adapted the design in Serlio.[15]

Apart from glazing, it is actually in plasterwork that the greatest correspondence with plates of *A Booke of Sundry Draughtes* is found. The seventeenth-century sketchbook of the Abbott family of plasterers from north Devon contains two examples and many English ceilings either derive from Gedde – a fine example in Devon is the ribbed ceiling of the hall at Nutcombe Manor, copied direct from Gedde's page 103 (Figs 186, 188)[16] – or from the common source, Serlio's ceiling designs. But four patterns are specially interesting. Gedde's page 34, divided into rectangular panels of equal size (Fig. 187), is perfectly acceptable as a design for leading but also happens to correspond with the plaster ceiling of the Cartoon Gallery at Knole (Fig. 189). It would be easy to dismiss this as coincidence, were it not for the fact that three other patterns also correspond precisely with ceilings at Knole.[17] All these ceilings were in rooms remodelled by Thomas, 1st Earl of Dorset, after he came into possession of the house in 1603, the staircase between 1605 and 1608, the ballroom around 1607, and the Cartoon Gallery in 1608. The plasterer was Richard Dungan, who was described in the accounts at Knole as the 'King's Plaisterer', receiving substantial amounts for plaster of Paris and 'fretts' in 1607–8. The ceilings at Knole, therefore, precede the publication of *A*

Booke of Sundry Draughtes by at least seven years. Gedde must somehow have become familiar with them. Did he work at Knole as a glazier and abstract these patterns for his book? Or did he devise the patterns for Richard Dungan and many years later decide to publish them in his book? Or did the prints circulate separately before being brought together? We simply do not know.

Besides these pattern-books, the many woodcut or engraved titlepages of sixteenth- and early seventeenth-century books (which often incorporated cartouches or other ornament) were another potential channel for the transmission of inspiration for designers, although no consistent attempt to prove this has hitherto been made. Often inhabited by allegorical figures, these titlepages provided a foretaste – which may always have been difficult for the potential reader to understand – of the contents of the volume they introduced;[18] in Antwerp at least they were actually printed in advance of the book as a form of pre-publication advertisement. Individual titlepages were gathered together in scrapbooks of ornament perhaps for educational purposes.[19] They were probably kept in booksellers' shops as a form of catalogue for sale. Bibliographical interest drove Samuel Pepys to collect nearly a thousand titlepages, mostly seventeenth-century, some English but most continental.[20]

Titlepages seem to have been employed as source material pretty infrequently in England so that, when they were, it must be assumed that it was done for a purpose. One obvious point to make is that the titlepages – unless collected specifically as separate prints – would have been the only illustration of any kind in most books, so that they are more likely to have belonged to a patron than to his employee. The best-known instances are the use of Robert Record's *The Castle of Knowledge* (1556) in the plaster decoration of the gallery at Little Moreton Hall in Cheshire, and the choice of an ornamental pilaster from Shute's *First and Chief Groundes of Architecture* for decoration at Kirby, already mentioned.

A handful of other instances have also been noted. A small-scale example is the book of statutes of Corpus Christi College, Cambridge, in which an actual printed titlepage has been cut out, pasted on and overpainted and gilded with an elaborate frame with grotesques and a hint of strapwork: the titlepage was a woodblock first used in 1569 for an edition of the Bible printed by R. Jugge and later for Matthew Parker's *De Antiquitate Britannicae Ecclesiae* in 1572.[21] Similarly, in 1580–81 the Hilary Roll portrait of Queen Elizabeth was painted over an engraving pulled from the plate used for the frontispiece of Saxton's *Atlas* which had been published first in 1579. In Erna Auerbach's words: 'The artist cut out the royal figure with its throne and immediate

Similarly, the frontispiece to Robert Barker's edition of the Bishops' Bible printed in London in 1585 may have supplied the inspiration for someone to embroider a binding for her copy of *The Book of Common Prayer* and *The Holy Bible* both printed in London by Robert Barker in 1607, while another embroiderer copied a figure of David playing the lyre from the titlepage of *The Holy Bible* printed in Cambridge in 1629 by Thomas and John Buck for her copy of the New Testament (1633) and Book of Common Prayer (1636).[23] The same titlepage was also used by plasterers in Devon (see Figs 264, 263). Again, the woodcut of the Garden of Eden – used at the end of the preliminary pages in a number of editions of the Bishop's Bible in folio, for instance in Christopher Barker's edition of 1583 – was adapted for an embroidered binding for a Book of Common Prayer and a Bible (both printed by Robert Barker in London in 1607).[24]

Three strapwork compartments also appear early on in Thomas Trevelyon's 1608 manuscript book of embroidery designs: all must have been copied from English or Continental titlepages. Only one of the

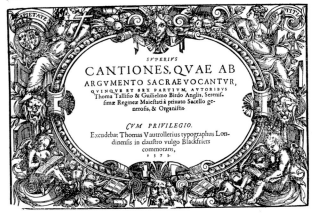

sources has been identified, a titlepage compartment, used to introduce numerous books printed by John Day from the mid-sixteenth century onwards (see p.236).[25]

Two other intriguing adaptations of printed titlepage borders spring to mind, both dating from the 1580s. It has already been remarked that the carver of the hall screen at Cuckfield in Sussex used the suite of cartouches enclosing French proverbs by Cornelis Bos, one plate of which was copied for the armorial cartouches over the pair of doors (Fig. 190). Between these is another, bearing the date 1581. This is distinguished by figures of Pietas and Iustitia above the oval cartouche, and two putti below, and these enable the source to be identified as the titlepage of *Cantiones,*

190 (*above left*) Cuckfield Park, Sussex, hall screen, 1581.

191 (*above right*) Thomas Vautrollier (publisher), titlepage to Thomas Tallis and William Byrd, *Cantiones, quae ab argumento sacrae vocantur . . .* (London, 1575).

background and covered up the plate where it represented the architectural canopy and the two figures of an astronomer and geographer who supported the throne on both sides. The used part of the plate is skilfully rounded off to fit the old-fashioned strapwork initial . . . The painting produces a rich and deeply coloured effect.'[22]

The same frontispiece (as shall be shown later, p.223) provided figures used in the lower borders of some Sheldon tapestries, and their designer also incorporated the titlepage border from *The Common Places of . . . Peter Martyr*, published in 1574; likewise, the vertical borders of Thomas Buckminster's *A Prognostication for . . . 1582*, which appeared that year, were also adapted for use in tapestries (see p.222).

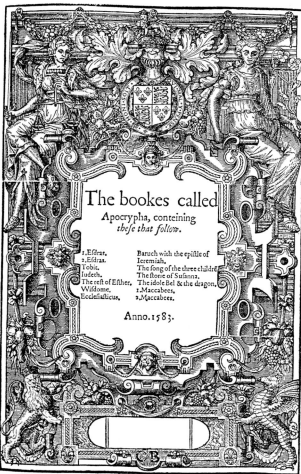

quae ab argumento sacrae vocantur, quinque et sex partium (Fig. 191), with music by Thomas Tallis and William Byrd, published in London in 1575, the first publication after they had been granted a twenty-five-year music-printing monopoly from Queen Elizabeth. Their woodblock was copied, with certain differences, from an earlier titlepage block used on the Continent for Orlando di Lasso's *Primus Liber Modulorum*, published in Paris in 1571, but the differences show that the Cuckfield carver had the later English publication in front of him.[26]

The second noteworthy instance of the use of a printed titlepage for decorative purposes occurs in the church at Clovelly in north Devon. Here there is the tomb of Sir Robert Carey who died in 1586 (Figs 185, 192). As Pevsner says, it is an 'odd design, the solid superstructure with six engaged columns, the interstices between adorned with big strapwork cartouches'.[27] Perhaps Sir Robert designed it himself. In any event, the choice of the cartouches was probably his, for they were copied from the titlepage of the Bible first printed by Christopher Barker in 1578 (Fig. 193), with a quarto edition the next year.[28]

There is no doubt that these uses of titlepage borders afford us an impression of the personal interests of the patron. At Cuckfield it must have been the owner's (rather than the carver's) interest in music, presumably for Protestant use – although Byrd certainly and Tallis probably remained staunchly faithful to Catholicism throughout the decades of doctrinal change.[29] At Clovelly, the patron was surely publicising in the most permanent way his adherence to the Protestant faith, for this Bible must have been very familiar at the time and (one would imagine) the cartouche instantly recognisable. On the other hand, rather different signals were presumably being sent by the use, in the borders of Ralph Sheldon's tapestry maps, of the titlepage copied from *The Common Places . . . of Peter Martyr*, the notable reformer, for Sheldon was a Catholic convert (see pp.222, 226).

English emblem books were certainly a more widely used source of inspiration than individual titlepages – derivations appear in paint and plaster, metal and wood, tapestry and embroidery – but these, as explained in the Preface, lie outside the range of printed images I have been able to study to my satisfaction. Some isolated instances will be mentioned in part II, generally when they occur in conjunction with other source material. Here we only need to note the most popular books, Geffrey Whitney's *A Choice of Emblemes* published by Christopher Plantin in Leiden in 1586, George Wither's *Emblemes* (1635), and Henry Peacham's *Minerva Britanna* (1612). Individual prints occasionally influenced the design of textiles[30] and on one occasion a suite of the Five Senses engraved about 1625 by the Dutchman Johannes Barra for Thomas Jenner at the Exchange in London was copied for wall paintings at Hilton Hall in Huntingdonshire.[31] The increased availability of English prints as a result of the abolition of censorship is demonstrated by the stock in Peter Stent's print shop, established around 1642 in London's Newgate.[32]

Part II

DESTINATIONS

Chapter 8

MASONRY

The first part of this book concentrated on sources, examining the influence of prints by designer. It has been seen that, by studying complete suites in libraries and print rooms rather than using published modern illustrated anthologies, it is possible to suggest otherwise unsuspected links between buildings (for instance) whose decoration depends on two different prints from the same suite.

This second part looks at destinations – where the prints were used, particularly work which displays a dependence on more than one set of prints, keeping in mind all the time that prints were only one of the agents of stylistic change. In dealing with the work of masons (and later, an architect in the modern sense) I shall attempt to demonstrate how a knowledge of print sources can help build up a conjectural picture of one of the houses built by the powerful courtiers in the circle of Edward Seymour, Duke of Somerset and Protector during the reign of Edward VI, unravel the decorative style of a significant provincial mason-architect, and incidentally explain one of the crazier buildings in an age of unpredictable (and therefore exciting) architecture. Over much of this chapter the spectre of Elizabethan Longleat will hover.

First of all we must look at drawings. One measure of a sixteenth- or early seventeenth-century mason's or architect's artistic personality is his awareness of, and ability to synthesise, continental fashions, which came through his contacts with foreigners or with foreign prints. Four men working during the period left a substantial number of drawings which can readily be assessed from this point of view, Robert and John Smythson, John Thorpe and Inigo Jones. Others have to be judged only by their executed work, where this can be identified: among these is the provincial mason-architect William Arnold. So before considering the buildings themselves I shall briefly review the Smythson and Thorpe drawings, with which those of Inigo Jones will provide a fitting comparison to end this chapter.

The Smythson drawings in the collection of the Royal Institute of British Architects (RIBA) represent the work of several generations of the Smythson family who originated in Westmorland: Robert, John

the elder, Huntingdon and John the younger.[1] From the latter they may have descended in the Byron family of Bullwell and Newstead Abbey; in 1778 they were sold to the Coke family who eventually (after a fifth of the 125 late seventeenth-century or eighteenth-century mounts on which they were pasted, several to a mount, had been destroyed in a fire at Colwick near Nottingham) gave them to the RIBA in the 1920s. The survivors have been catalogued by Mark Girouard.[2]

A small number of the drawings by Robert Smythson may date from his years at Longleat. One is his design for a window-bay,[3] which shows a clear awareness of Serlio while this drawing (with others for a gatehouse and several for screens and funerary monuments) displays the largest unit of classical currency in his repertoire; Smythson also copied a term figure from Agostino Veneziano, J.A. Ducerceau or Cornelis Bos for a chimneypiece (Figs 195, 196), but abstracted its frieze from a design by Vredeman de Vries (Fig. 197).[4] Smythson was probably introduced to Vredeman's work during the 1580s by his bookish patron Sir Francis Willoughby for whom he built Wollaton: Vredeman's influence is particularly apparent in drawings for that house and in the building as executed. So Smythson lifted features from Vredeman's three-part *Architectura, Das Erst Büch, Das Ander Buech* of 1565, and *Architectura, 3e Stuck* of 1571, for the metopes and decorated lower columns of the screen (I/27), copied details of the titlepage of Vredeman's *Caryatidum . . . sive Athlantidum* of 1565, and adapted strapwork from the *Pictores, Statuarii . . .* of 1563 for the panel in the centre of the hall screen.[5] Above this panel Smythson drew from two prints in *Deorum Dearumque Capita* (1573), which has cartouches designed by Vredeman: it is a suite whose presence in England at this date is otherwise difficult to establish. How Smythson, on the screen as executed, substituted a different design for this feature has already been noted (see p.64).

Robert's knowledge of continental prints would certainly have been shared by his son John: if the designs for monuments are his (II/24, III/27), he certainly had access to Vredeman's *Pictores*

A Wollaton

Vredeman
↓
R.W. Smythson
↓ John Smythson

See p. 141

194 (*facing page*) Wiston Park, Sussex, Elizabethan chimneypieces of *c*.1580 reassembled on an outside wall.

133

195 Robert Smythson, drawing for a chimneypiece. British Architectural Library, RIBA, London.

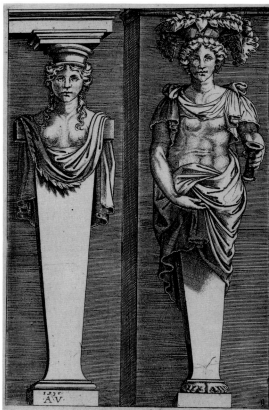

196 (*right*) Agostino Veneziano, term figure. Metropolitan Museum of Art, New York.

197 (*far right*) Jan Vredeman de Vries, *[Architectura] Das Ander Buech* (Antwerp, 1565), pl.14. Victoria and Albert Museum, London.

Statuarii . . . New influences must have included Wendel Dietterlin's *Architectura*, one design being simplified for a chimneypiece and overmantel (III/28) subsequently executed at Clifton Hall, Nottinghamshire,[6] and perhaps Philibert de L'Orme, one of whose plates he may have adapted for the Marble Closet in the Little Castle at Bolsover (III/1). Ludovico Scalzi has also been suggested as an alternative to Dietterlin for the inspiration for drawings of heavily rusticated doorways associated with the gallery range at Bolsover (III/1 (5–8) and III/15 (8–9)).[7]

John Thorpe's use of continental prints is slightly different, for he was first and foremost a surveyor rather than a mason-architect, although he does seem to have designed and built Aston Hall near Birmingham for Sir Thomas Holte and Campden House – next to Holland House – in London, as well as a handful of houses in Lincolnshire – Dowsby Hall, the Red Hall at Bourne and Thornton College. A generation younger than Robert Smythson, he was born into a family of masons. Summerson, in his catalogue,[8] fully explored Thorpe's debt to continental books, and to his list I can make only one addition, though this is an interesting one.

Thorpe's repertoire is more varied than the Smythsons'. He was clearly aware of Serlio and Palladio, Hans Blum and Vignola. He made several copies from J.A. Ducerceau's *Le Premier Volume des Plus Excellents Bastiments de France* of 1567, and derived a method of perspective from Ducerceau's *Leçons de perspective pratique* of 1576, a treatise which he prepared for an English-language version, never published.[9] He also knew Vredeman's *Architectura* of 1577, his *Caryatidum . . . sive Athlantidum* of about 1565 and owned a plate from an untitled 1562 suite of architectural perspectives (included with two other suites in Vredeman's *Variae Architecturae Formae* in 1601); the print had once covered one of Thorpe's drawings, T216.

To these can be added for certain Jacques Perret's *Des Fortifications et Artifices . . . Architecture et Perspective* first published in 1601.[10] Taking plate x of this book (Fig. 198; probably from a later, Oppenheim edition, published as *Architectura et Perspectiva* in 1613 with reversed plates), Thorpe simplified Perret's design (which was for a Protestant temple) to make it suitable for a house (Fig. 199). He omitted the architectural orders and ran the four traceried windows in the upper floor of Perret's central block into a single huge mullioned and transomed window. What Thorpe retained from the original was the fanciful balustrading, the hipped roof and corner turrets of the central block (adding more to the corner towers) and the crowned heraldic achievement over the front door. The result is much plainer and more English than the design on which it was based. Summerson

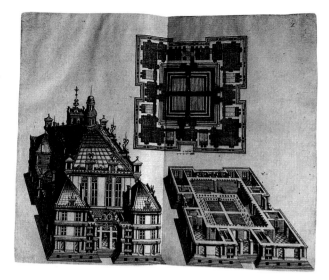

198 Jacques Perret, *Architectura et Perspectiva* . . . (Oppenheim, 1613), pl.x. Skokloster Slott, Sweden.

199 John Thorpe, drawing of a perspective-elevation of a house. Sir Soane's Museum, London.

noted the similarity of Thorpe's drawing with the plan and elevation of Wollaton,[11] and the agent of this resemblance was this plate of Perret's, which Girouard believes was itself inspired by Wollaton.[12]

Now for actual buildings. Mark Girouard has given an exciting account of the houses associated with the Smythson family, and as most of their source material is obvious from their drawings there is nothing to add. Perhaps the most tantalising question for anyone interested in the architecture and decoration of the Elizabethan era is this: What did the interiors of Sir John Thynne's Longleat look like? A knowledge of prints can help.

Longleat is the greatest survivor of the houses built by men in the circle of the Duke of Somerset around the middle of the sixteenth century,[13] the 'momentary

135

"High Renaissance" of Tudor architecture'. William Chambers in the eighteenth century destroyed Somerset House, built during the years 1547–52. The pure classical style of its façade (Fig. 200), which set the style for the next generation, may well have been, as has been argued in recent years, politically inspired, the architectural equivalent of the vernacular text of the Bible or the simpler liturgical music required in Protestant worship:[14] it certainly had its stylistic origins in Serlio and in France.

Externally Longleat survives remarkably complete, internally little was left unchanged in the alterations of Sir Jeffry Wyatville in 1801–11 and the redecoration by J.D. Crace in the 1870s. As Pevsner has pointed out, not a single whole Elizabethan room remains. Is it not presumptious even to begin to suggest what the interiors looked like, let alone what continental prints inspired them?

And yet, working by analogy, both can be attempted. In fact, one of the drawings associated with Longleat and the few precious surviving features of the Elizabethan decoration tell us a surprising amount about the actual pattern-books used in the design of the house. Moreover, Mark Girouard has shown that it is possible to track the movements around the country of masons associated with Longleat, by concentrating on individual details and investigating other appearances of them. He did it, for example, for what he called the 'Longleat motif' – an oeil-de-boeuf wreathed by paired fronds – which he found on several monuments in West-Country churches. By extending the search other houses can be brought in and the repertoire of possible source material used in the decoration of Longleat can be broadened.

So let us start with the design for an entrance front which Girouard has attributed to Allen Maynard (Fig. 202).[15] Quite rightly he identified its overall character as French, although of an earlier generation than the 1560s when the drawing was probably made. For all its general competence, it displays signs of having been cobbled together from disparate elements: a façade of pedimented and pilastered windows linked vertically, on to which has been grafted a triumphal arch to serve as the frontispiece. In fact this was precisely the designer's method. He took a triumphal arch with its decoration of 'gross and slug-like monsters which huddle and grin so distressingly between these chaste windows' straight from a book of triumphal arches published by Jacques Androuet Ducerceau in 1549 (Fig. 201), and the flanking figures, hunched against the pedimented window, from another – Ducerceau's suite of furniture designs (Fig. 203), some of which resemble so strongly the tables carved by John Chapman at Lacock in 1553. A cartouche from the same suite might have been adapted for a cartouche on the monument to Bishop Stephen Gardiner (d.1555) in Winchester Cathedral.[16]

Now to motifs that still survive at Longleat. These occur principally (though not exclusively) on the three sixteenth-century chimneypieces, which were probably carved by the French mason Allen Maynard. But before looking at these it should be remembered that the hall screen has decoration derived from the set of cartouches by Vredeman published as *Multarum variarum'que* in 1555, and that this suite provides a link with overmantels at Grafton Manor in Worcestershire[17] and the Red Lodge in Bristol, a

monument at Bruton in Somerset and previously unexplained decorative panels at Wilton (see pp.69–70).[18]

And so to the Longleat chimneypieces. Each has at least one feature derived from a print source. The first, in the Upper Gallery (Fig. 204), is characterised by vigorous leafy Vitruvian scrolls and massive leaf brackets, with rams' heads and drapery swags on the pilasters. Here the frieze of four leafy Vitruvian scrolls

202 (*above*) Allen Maynard, design for a classical façade.

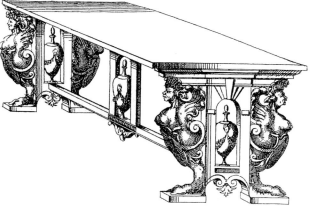

201 (*far left*) Jacques Androuet Ducerceau, *Arcs* (Orléans, 1549), 'Arc selon lordre Salomonique'. Victoria and Albert Museum, London.

203 Jacques Androuet Ducerceau, design for a table, *c.*1560. Victoria and Albert Museum, London.

137

was copied from Serlio, specifically from the plinth of a window surmounting a gate in a mixture of the Tuscan, Doric and Ionic orders (Fig. 207). Little wonder that Girouard felt that the various decorative panels were 'a trifle clumsily combined'.[19]

The second (Fig. 205) has a heavy entablature supported on term figures bearing Ionic capitals on their heads: a band of Vitruvian scroll appears above the arch while the frieze is carved with acanthus leaves and stylised shells alternating. This distinctive frieze was adapted from the chimneypiece of the Composite order in Serlio's Book IV (see Fig. 4). The woodcut has a band of stopped flutes interrupted by acanthus leaves at intervals and with curious low scrolls at the lower edge of the frieze: at Longleat, the flutes are omitted but the acanthus and the scrolls survive, the latter surmounted by shell motifs; with the band of Vitruvian scrolls, there can be no doubting the Serlian ancestry of this chimneypiece.

The third (Fig. 206), in the hall, has a fluted and gadrooned fire-arch surmounted by a frieze carved with a repetitive leaf motif; its overmantel has a frieze of isolated sprays above a pair of round arches with a variation of a guilloche moulding in the pilasters and the arch, and containing strapwork cartouches separated by a single central term figure with twisted tails

138

and flanked by paired figures. The repetitive leaf motif of the chimneypiece motif may have been adapted originally either from Palladio – similar friezes occur on the Temple of Mars in Book IV, chapter 15, page 52 – or from Philibert de L'Orme – a frieze illustrated in the 1648 edition, Book VII, folio 210r, which (given that the mason who carved the Longleat chimneypiece and overmantel was probably French) may have been the inspiration.

Mark Girouard has shown how an impressive list of work can convincingly be associated with Longleat by the appearance of one or more of these Longleat motifs. His original list can be considerably extended and must include chimneypieces at Upper Upham and Woodlands Manor, both in Wiltshire, a door architrave and other work at Wolfeton in Dorset, two monuments in Gloucestershire (at Almondsbury commemorating Edward Veele (d.1577), at Sapperton, Sir Robert Atkyn),[20] and several monuments in Hampshire – among them the tomb commemorating Sir James Worsley and his wife (d.1536 and 1557) of Appledurcombe, at Godshill on the Isle of Wight (this also has Longleat-like leaf brackets), and the Gardiner Chapel and the Mason tomb in Winchester Cathedral.[21] Similarly, the tombs of Sir John Leweston at Sherborne Abbey, Dorset, and of the Delamores at Nunney in Somerset, must belong to the Longleat group for they both have the oeil-de-boeuf motif which appears on the parapet of the house.

Although these examples demonstrate the movement of Longleat masons (before, during and after the building of Thynne's house) around the southern counties of England and add other patrons to the list of those who employed them, they do not materially enlarge the range of continental source material which might also have been employed at Longleat – with one exception, ironically the most fragmentary survivor.[22] The Mason monument in Winchester Cathedral (Fig. 210) was erected to Thomas Mason on his death in 1559 by his father, Sir John, but dismantled c.1818. Decorative elements that survive include a band of Vitruvian scroll copied feature for feature from Serlio, and figures apparently depicting Adam and Eve who lean against the hard edges of some chunky strapwork cartouche. What little of the latter is left is enough to show, without doubt, that the sculptor's original inspiration was an allegorical print by Cornelis Bos (Fig. 211). The date is right, for the print was probably published about 1554, no more than five years before the monument was executed.[23] Cornelis Bos may therefore have been one of the designers whose prints were used at Longleat and in other houses where Longleat artificers worked.

We have not finished with Longleat motifs yet. A design by Allen Maynard for the façade of Longleat

208 (left) Allen Maynard, design for the façade of Longleat, detail.

204 (facing page top left) Longleat, Wiltshire, chimneypiece in the Upper Gallery.

207 (facing page top right) Sebastiano Serlio, design for an arch, 1537 (from the London edition of Book IV, 1611, Chapter 7, folio 46r).

205 (facing page centre) Longleat, Wiltshire, chimneypiece.

206 (facing page bottom) Longleat, Wiltshire, chimneypiece and overmantel in the hall.

209 (left) St Peter, Bristol, monument to a member of the Newton family, 1570s or 1580s.

210a–c Winchester Cathedral, Hampshire, three fragments from the monument to Thomas Mason (died 1559).

211 (*bottom centre*) Cornelis Bos, cartouche framing an allegorical subject, *c*.1554. The Royal Library – National Library of Sweden, Stockholm, Maps and Prints Department, De la Gardie Collection.

(Fig. 208) which was superseded by the continuation of the window bays to second-floor height includes a scrolled feature which probably provided the inspiration for several instances of masons' work elsewhere in the region. The single scroll encloses a plain field which is drawn out to a point between the ends of the scroll. This feature occurs, as Girouard has pointed out, on overmantels at Woodlands Manor, Mere, and at Dodington Park, both in Wiltshire. But it is also a feature of an extremely distinguished (and hitherto unremarked) monument in St Peter's church in Bristol which unhappily was destroyed during the Second World War (Fig. 209). It commemorated a member of the Newton family as the inscription, transcribed in a watercolour dated 1826, recorded:[24]

> This Monument was Erected to the Memory of a Maiden Lady an Ancestor of the Family of the Newtons of Barrs Court in the County of Gloucester about 250 Years Since And Repaired by Mrs Archer Sister to the late Sr Michael Newton 1750

The monument belonged stylistically to the 1570s or 1580s. The scrolled feature appears unmistakably in the gables (complete with fluting in the curved section terminating in leaf stops at the scrolls, as at Woodlands) proving that a Longleat mason was also working here. Another similarity is the treatment of the body of the tomb-chest which seems to have been carved with a pattern resembling overlapping fish-scales, very much like the turret roofs at Longleat, and recalling a projecting hooded chimneypiece at the Manor House, Upper Swell in Gloucestershire.[25] The most tantalising feature of the monument, however, is the frieze which combined foliate decoration with figures: the pattern must have been derived from a print source (possibly Italian or French, though I have yet to discover it), particularly as it is repeated exactly in the decoration of a house in Sussex.

This is Wiston Park near Steyning, which had been started on 'an optimistically grand scale' by Sir Thomas Shirley about 1573, with some interiors complete by 1576.[26] From the 1580s Shirley was in straightened financial circumstances because of debts incurred while Treasurer at War to Elizabeth I (goods at Wiston were seized in 1588, in 1591 he was committed to the Marshalsea Prison, in 1597 his lands were seized and in 1602 sold to the Queen) and it likely that he was never again in a position to build much. So the house was probably built during the 1570s and early 1580s. The evidence that Longleat masons were engaged here is slight – just a characteristic interlaced rope pattern over a door in the gallery of the hall, which appears at Longleat decorating the pilasters of the hall overmantel. However, it is confirmed by the design of the hammer-beam timber roof, which Pevsner describes as having 'pendants and plenty of braces like the Middle Temple Hall in London, not much fun'. Not much fun it may be, but it is identical to that of the Middle Temple and of Longleat itself: both were constructed by Thynne's carpenter John Lewis.[27]

So Wiston can be accepted as a Longleat house, built during the last years of Sir John Thynne's life (he died in 1580), and for suggesting further prints that could have been used at Longleat it is invaluable. In terms of planning and elevations Wiston is nothing like as advanced as Longleat, only the porch betraying signs of a classicism quite refined for the date. The most precious survival is a feature, now deteriorating on an outside wall, which must originally have formed at least two separate chimneypieces (Fig. 212).[28] These offer perfect indications of the range of source-material – Italian, Flemish and German for certain – that was brought to bear on the decoration of a house at that period.

What survives of these overmantels is classical in character, plain architraves, richly decorated friezes and dentil cornices. Superimposed above these is a curved-sided element flanked by griffins which comes straight from a design for a chimneypiece (or a door) of the Corinthian order by Serlio (Figs 194, 213): the text specifies that this is suitable for 'a Hall or a Greate Chamber [where] there is a great Chimney required . . .'[29] The mason at Wiston gave the sides a greater splay but in other respects the similarity is close. There is a roundel surrounded by vermiculation where Serlio seems to suggest a marble veneer. This Serlian feature is somewhat too short for the entablature it surmounts, suggesting perhaps that it once had the pilasters and term figures of Serlio's design. At Wiston an obelisk crowns the chimneypiece, derived from the obelisk that Serlio identified by the letter R on folio 29r of his Book III: he recorded it in the 'circo Antonino Caracalla'.

Serlio was not the only Italian source used at Wiston. The lower of the two decorated friezes has low-relief carving of repeated lengths of scrolled foliage with figures, and three strapwork cartouches. The repeated figure, on examination, turns out to be an archer bending one arm behind his back to withdraw an arrow from his quiver. This enables the source to be pinpointed accurately: this archer appears at the end of the frieze of the Temple of Jupiter 'Upon Monte Quirinale, now called Monte Cavallo' in Rome, where the figures of the Horse-Tamers stood (see p.16), and was published by Andrea Palladio in I Quattro Libri d'Architettura in 1570 (Fig. 214),[30] only a very few years before Wiston was begun.

The upper frieze is tantalising: three lengths of mirror-imaged motifs are interrupted by term figures with arms raised, and, in the centre, another figure with legs splayed. The frieze seems to consist of scrolled foliage inhabited by further figures and a dog or lion. No source has yet been found for this – it is not in Palladio – but, by analogy with the lower frieze this too might be Roman, although the closest analogies so far found are with the decorative compartments in mid-century French books: closest of all is the head-piece on folio 6 of Philibert de L'Orme's Architecture.[31]

From Antwerp come the six cartouches of four different designs in the lower frieze and in the plinth course immediately above. All derive from one suite of cartouches enclosing French proverbs perhaps designed by Cornelis Bos which proved very popular in England (see pp.51–2, Fig. 53). From Antwerp too come the figures between the columns supported on this plinth. They represent the Nine Worthies and they derive from the popular – but these days rarely surviving – prints that inspired so many other such sets.[32]

The sources brought into play by the mason at Wiston are not yet quite exhausted, for there remain the two scenes in the roundel at the top (Fig. 218), contained within a gadrooned frame strongly reminiscent of mouldings surviving at Longleat. They depict, as Pevsner surmised, scenes of combat if not of battle, from early Roman history: the upper shows Tarquinius Priscus Axed to Death on the Throne, from Livy, I.40, the lower depicts The Death of Lucretia, Livy I.58. These scenes are only identifiable because I managed to find the prints that inspired them, woodcuts designed by Jost Amman and published in Philip Lonicer's verse adaptation, Icones Livianae, in 1572.[33] The upper scene shows two soldiers with axes raised above the head of Tarquin as he falls from the throne, one arm up in an attempt to protect himself. The term figure supporting the drapery of the canopy, and the throne itself, together with the falling figure, are – when pointed out – readily identifiable, but the double-arched building to the right derives not from this woodcut (Fig. 215) but from the background of the next illustration in the book (Fig. 216), showing Tullia driving over her murdered father's corpse.[34] The lower scene on the roundel shows, on the left, the Rape of Lucretia and, on the right, her suicide. Slight alterations were made from the woodcut (Fig. 217) to accommodate it in the new format. Tarquinius Priscus was a member of

212 Wiston Park, Sussex, Elizabethan chimneypieces of *c.*1580 reassembled on an outside wall.

214 (*far right*) Andrea Palladio, *I Quattro Libri d'Architettura* (1570), Book IV, folio 47r.

213 Serlio, chimneypiece, 1537 (from the London edition of Book IV, 1611, folio 58r).

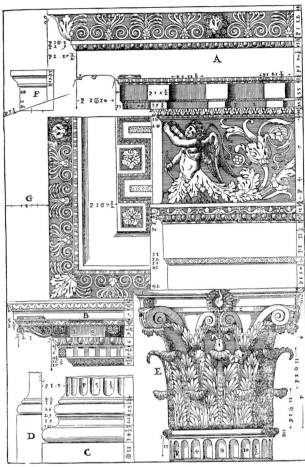

the Tarquin dynasty, an Etruscan family which provided two kings of Rome. He was the fifth, traditionally reigning 616–579 BC, and was believed to have brought Etruscan craftsmen to Rome and built the temples on the Capitol. Tarquinius Superbus, a tyrannical king, was his son, and Sextus Tarquinius his grandson. Amman's woodcut shows the latter forcing himself on Lucretia, the virtuous wife of a nobleman, at knife point, threatening to kill both her and a servant to give the appearance of her being caught in adultery with him. She yielded to him but later confessed her shame to her father and husband, and is depicted on the right of the print taking her own life, despite the entreaties of Brutus, the nephew of Tarquinius Superbus, and two others.

After Wiston it is more difficult to find similarities with Longleat. One house where Longleat masons almost certainly worked – albeit nearly twenty years after the death of Thynne – is South Wraxall Manor in Wiltshire, which was altered by Sir Walter Long in the late sixteenth century – the date 1598 occurs on the chimneypiece in the hall. The motif common to both houses is the band of intricate rope-like inter-

142

lace, found over the door to the minstrels' gallery in the hall at Wiston and on the hall overmantel at Longleat: at South Wraxall it forms the frieze of an Ionic chimneypiece.

This is one of five impressive chimneypieces in the house, all carved in the local stone. The Great Chamber has the most important, a veritable thesaurus of Flemish Mannerist ornament (Fig. 221). The entablature of the chimneypiece itself is supported not by columns but by term figures, which derive from a plate in Vredeman de Vries's *Caryatidum* published

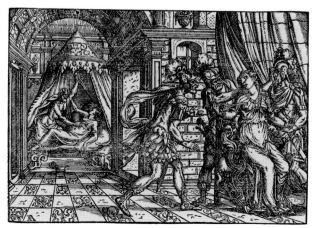

in 1565 (Fig. 219); the cartouches on the lintel of the chimneypiece, in the zone between the fireplace opening and the entablature, were copied from Benedetto Battini's *Vigilate quia nescitis diem neque horam* published in Antwerp in 1553 (see Fig. 16; this suite also provided the plate from which both the cartouches on another chimneypiece in the house were copied, see below). The small cartouches flanking the figures of Arithmetica and Geometria come from a metope design in Vredeman's *[Architectura] Das Erst Büch* of 1565 (the joiner who panelled the Raleigh Room used a design from the contemporary *Das Ander Buech*). The distinctive pattern carved on the frieze of the overmantel (which reappears on a chimneypiece from a house in St Nicholas Street, Bristol, see p.82) probably derives from a print source which is as yet unidentified. All the allegorical figures on the overmantel derive from prints after Maarten de Vos, Prudentia and Justicia between the paired columns, Arithmetica and Geometria (Fig. 220) in the main panels; the latter were engraved by Crispijn de Passe the elder, with inscriptions that were also transcribed precisely on the overmantel.[35]

Another chimneypiece (Fig. 222) was clearly executed by the same craftsman who carved the monument to George Lloyd and his wife, at Ampney Crucis in Gloucestershire (see Fig. 13), for it too features both alternative cartouches of a Battini print (Fig. 223).

Potentially, therefore, any of these prints might also have been used at Longleat, though not necessarily during Sir John Thynne's lifetime. One connection that has been known for many years but never docu-

218 (*above*) Wiston Park, Sussex, roundel surmounting the chimneypieces.

215 (*far left top*) Jost Amman, Tarquinius Priscus Axed to Death on the Throne, from *Icones Livianae* (Frankfurt, 1572). British Library, London (196.a.18).

216 (*far left centre*) Jost Amman, Tullia Drives over Her Murdered Father's Corpse, from *Icones Livianae* (Frankfurt, 1572). British Library, London (196.a.18).

217 (*far left bottom*) Jost Amman, The Death of Lucretia, from *Icones Livianae* (Frankfurt, 1572). British Library, London (196.a.18).

GEOMETRIA.

Mensuras rerum spatiis dimetior æquis:
Quid Cœlo distet Terra, locusque loco.

Martin d. V. inuent.   *Crispian de Passe excu.*

at Longford Castle, a link which deserves to be explored. Longford was built by Sir Thomas Gorges and has been the subject of much speculation on account of its triangular plan and traditional connection with the celebrated Danish astronomer Tycho Brahe's country house at Uraniborg. Sir Thomas cer-

219 Lucas or Johannes Duetecum after Jan Vredeman de Vries, *Caryatidum* (Antwerp, *c*.1565), pl.10. Victoria and Albert Museum, London.

220 (*far right*) Crispijn de Passe the elder after Maarten de Vos, Geometria, from *The Seven Liberal Arts*. British Museum, London.

221 (*facing page*) South Wraxall Manor, Wiltshire, chimneypiece and overmantel in the Great Chamber, *c*.1600.

mented by stylistic comparisons is that between Longleat and Elizabethan Chatsworth, which Bess of Hardwick was decorating in the grandest manner during the 1570s. She wrote to Thynne asking him for the loan of his 'cunning plasterers' and may also have tried to persuade him to lend her other craftsmen as well. Now it is possible to indicate a tenuous, indirect stylistic link. The chimneypiece in Dame Eleanor's Room at South Wraxall (Fig. 224) has a conventional architectural framework of superimposed Doric (the triglyph derived from Vredeman's *Das Erst Büch*, plate C) and Ionic orders but the other details are somewhat unusual. The opening, for example, is bordered by a moulding consisting of raised blocks alternately square and rectangular, and above the lintel is a band of carving with inverted acanthus and circles contained in a strapwork frame. Oddest of all are the cartouches in the overmantel which are linked by horizontal bands of strapwork with the pilasters in the centre which enclose a vase of flowers. There is nothing quite like this anywhere else in England, except in the gallery at Hardwick. Here the two overmantels have much the same combination of cartouche and strapwork, with patterns of raised blocks, albeit executed in different coloured stone and loosely based on designs by Serlio.[36] If they were made by William Griffin, did he also work at South Wraxall? And Longleat?

Another characteristic Longleat motif (perhaps not itself based on a print source) is a frame-moulding consisting of bands of fluting and nulling with leafy corners, which surrounds the fire-arch in the great hall. One context in which the nulling on its own forms the frame moulding is a panel of relief sculpture

tainly married a Swedish wife, Helena Snakenborg, but she had apparently left her native country by the early 1560s (fifteen years before Uraniborg was started), settling in England in 1565 and marrying the Marquess of Northampton.[37] The house dates from Sir Thomas's marriage to the widowed Marchioness in 1584 and it was finished in the 1590s. Apart from its triangular plan, probably associated with an earlier trinitarian project, in its original form it was distinguished for its north-west façade, which had an open loggia on the ground and first floors, where shell-head niches appear; otherwise the details are close to Vredeman's *Architectura* of 1577: niches between caryatids, pilasters with blocks at intervals, cross-windows and (simple) shaped gables.

144

222 (*above*) South Wraxall Manor, Wiltshire, chimneypiece in the dining room, *c.*1600.

223 (*right*) Benedetto Battini, 'Faber est . . .' and 'Aequa laus . . .', from *Vigilate quia nescitis . . .* (Antwerp, 1553), pl.12. The Royal Library – National Library of Sweden, Stockholm, Maps and Prints Department, De la Gardie Collection.

224 (*far right*) South Wraxall Manor, Wiltshire, overmantel in Dame Eleanor's Room, *c.*1600.

Inside there are two notable overmantels, mostly of sixteenth-century date. The first is in the south-west tower, next to the hall, and has a relief carved with an unidentified subject. Before Salvin's alterations of the 1870s, the chimneypiece itself had a cartouche enclos-

ing a carved figure, perhaps of Venus and Cupid.[38] No source for either of these has been found. The second chimneypiece (Fig. 225), in the room in the same tower adjoining the gallery, has an excellent-quality relief depicting Orpheus Charming the Beasts. This has emerged as a copy of one of at least three allegorical engravings by Adriaen or Hans Collaert, probably after designs by Jan Snellinck (Fig. 226).[39] Pevsner says that this Orpheus relief came from another room at Longford and, before that, from another house. If this is true, it is tempting to suggest Longleat, on the basis of the frame moulding: and Longleat had undergone substantial structural and decorative alterations during the nineteenth century, as a result of which this overmantel could have been removed. But this is pure speculation, particularly as decorative pieces of this kind usually remained in the same family. What seems certain is that a Longleat mason carved this overmantel relief.

If there was an individual who bridged the gap between Longford and Longleat he may be the master mason William Arnold, alias Gouerson, who was born perhaps around 1560, the son of a joiner who had worked at Longleat, and died in 1636/7 after a successful career.[40] Arnold's securely documented work comprises only the remodelling for Sir Robert Cecil, 1st Earl of Salisbury, of Cranborne Manor in Dorset (1608–12); Wadham College in Oxford (for the executors of Nicholas Wadham, 1609–12); and

Dunster Castle in Somerset which he remodelled
for George Luttrell from 1617. Many other houses
have been attributed to him on the basis of stylistic
comparison: work at Wayford Manor in Dorset, for
instance, and at Montacute in Somerset closely
resembles Arnold's distinctive Mannerist additions to
Cranborne in Dorset, as does decoration at Sherborne
Castle (granted to Sir John Digby in 1617) and
Lulworth Castle in the same county; and Ruperra in
Glamorgan, built by Sir Thomas Morgan in 1626.[41]

For an appreciation of Arnold's use of continental
print sources Montacute is crucial. The house was
built for Edward Phelips who took over the property
in December 1587, was knighted in 1603 and became
Speaker of the House of Commons the following
year; in 1605 he opened the case for the prosecution
of the conspirators in the Gunpowder Plot. The evidence for Arnold's involvement at Montacute comes
from a letter from Dorothy Wadham to her half-
brother, Lord Petre, on 10 February 1610 in which
she pressed him to 'ymploye one Arnold in the work
[at Wadham College, Oxford], who is an honest man,
a perfectt workman, and my neere neighboure, and
soe can yeld me contynewall contentmentt in the
same', adding that Arnold had been commended
to her by her 'good frend and lovinge neighboure Sr
Edward Phelipps'.[42] Arnold may have been involved
at Montacute for fifteen years or more: a *sala terrena*
south of the main building is dated 1588, while the
house itself is dated 1601 over the east door.

His artistic personality is neatly summarised in the
monument to Sir Thomas Phelips (d.1588), which on
grounds of style must be his work (Fig. 227). This is
traditional in form but contemporary in ornamentation: Arnold derived the strapwork from Jacob Floris's

Compertimentorum of 1566 (see Fig. 435), and the
inscription cartouche from one of the anonymous
designs associated with Geerarts's suite, *Diversarum
Protractationum*, and with Gerard de Iode's *Thesaurus* of
1579 or 1585 (Figs 228, 229).

Montacute (Fig. 230) is an archetypal Elizabethan
house in its combination of traditional form, demonstrated by the placement of the hall to the right of
the entrance instead of axially, and use of continental
decoration. The house shares a distinctive print-
derived motif with both Longleat (where it may first
have appeared) and Longford, a shell-headed niche
used singly or in pairs. This was probably adopted
from one of several Serlio woodcuts, such as his
design for a façade of the Corinthian order, which
incidentally features both the types found in West-
Country buildings – with the whorl at the top or the

225 (*above left*) Longford
Castle, Wiltshire, overmantel
with Orpheus Charming the
Beasts, 1590s Private Collection.

226 (*above right*) Adriaen or
Hans Collaert after Jan
Snellinck, *Orpheus, with the
Muses*. Stedelijk Prentenkabinet,
Antwerp.

Sacred to the memory
of Edward Phelips Jun.r
who succeeded his Father, in his
life time in the representation of
this County, and died in it.
August 4.th 1792.

Occidit, heu valde deflendus, juvenis!
O ite nimis agitata fati.
Inexpiatum quod scelus amicis
Et patriæ tantam ramum detulit!
Nec secula priora parem viderunt
Futura nec similem videbunt.

Likewise in memorial, of
his Aunt Elizabeth Phelips Spinster,
who died universally lamented,
on the first of June 1796.

Edvardus Phe.
Elizabethæ Uxor Oli
Memoriæ Sacru.
Marmor Hoc
Pie Grateque Vovet,
Edvardus filius natu Maxim.
—— Hoc saltem Fungar

Tho.s Phelips Esq.r
1588.

Eliz.th Phelips,
1598.

bottom of the arch.[43] Both types appear on the gate-house at Clifton Maybank in Dorset.[44]

Inside Montacute, Arnold employed the same suites for the decoration of chimneypieces and overmantels (in both stone and plaster) as he had used on the monument to Thomas Phelips in the church: the anonymous cartouches associated with those of Marc Geerarts for the overmantel of the Great Chamber (Figs 231, 233), Jacob Floris's *Compertimentorum . . .* for the stone overmantel in the Parlour (Fig. 232, see Fig. 61 left) and the plaster ones of at least two further rooms. The latter are probably the work of John Abbott the elder from Frithelstock near Barnstaple in north Devon, whom Arnold seems to have employed for most of his commissions. There is no evidence of Philibert de L'Orme, one of whose plates conceivably suggested the basket arch of the monument,[45] but Arnold added two sets of prints after Vredeman de Vries, his *[Architectura] Das Erst Büch* and *Das Ander Buech* which gave him the scrolled gable of the exquisite wind-porch in the Great Chamber (Figs 235, 236), the capitals and ornamental taffrils on the hall screen (Figs 234, 235, 237; see Fig. 73) and the frieze of the Great Chamber chimneypiece; and a third suite – in the only identified instance of its use in England – for the lower cartouche in the chimneypiece in the parlour, Vredeman's strapwork titlepage compartment for the *Theatrum Vitae Humanae* of 1577, engraved by Hieronymus Wierix (Fig. 239).[46]

Externally, Arnold copied the figures of the Nine Worthies in the niches on the east front (Fig. 238) from Philips Galle's set used at Wiston Park in Sussex only a few years earlier, adapting them to achieve more consistent poses. (Is this enough to suggest that Wiston, where other Longleat artificers were at work, was another building on which William Arnold – and perhaps his joiner father – had been employed?)

Arnold – it is safe to suggest – similarly adapted Galle's prints of the Worthies (Fig. 240) on the early seventeenth-century conduit erected in Carfax in Oxford: he was in Oxford between 1608 and 1612 building Wadham College, whose frontispiece shares with the conduit a distinctive form of canopied niche. The Carfax conduit (Figs 241, 242), which was removed to the park at Nuneham Courtenay in 1787, is a remarkable edifice, essentially a cube from which four flying ribs rise to support a *tempietto*-like structure set with niches containing the Worthies separated by Mannerist terms, beneath an ogee roof with scales. With its picturesque profile and forest of sculpted figures, it is a cousin of the many granite calvaries erected in Breton villages to ward off a particularly severe epidemic of the plague in 1598. Paintings of the Nine Worthies had decorated the conduit in Gracechurch Street, London, for the visit to the City of Queen Mary and her consort Philip of Spain in

228 (*above*) Montacute, Somerset, detail of the monument to Sir Thomas, Phelips.

229 Unidentified designer, cartouche associated with Gerard de Iode's *Thesaurus* (Antwerp, 1579 or 1585). Victoria and Albert Museum, London.

July 1554,[47] and some inherited recollection of this might have informed Arnold's Carfax design.

In all, the decoration of Montacute depends on no fewer than seven distinct suites of continental prints, and an eighth – a set of cartouches designed by Cornelis Bos – was employed for the overmantel in the gallery at Wolfeton.[48] Various combinations of these recur elsewhere. The use of the rare Geerarts-like cartouches in combination with Vredeman's *Das Erst Büch* is probably enough to suggest that the Exeter mason John Deymond and William Arnold may have been associated in some way.[49] But the

227 (*facing page*) Montacute, Somerset, monument to Sir Thomas Phelips (died 1588).

149

230 (*facing page*)   Montacute, Somerset, from the east.

233 (*right*)   C.J. Richardson, chimneypiece and overmantel in the Great Chamber at Montacute, Somerset, watercolour, 1834.

231   Unidentified designer, cartouche associated with Gerard de Iode's *Thesaurus* (Antwerp, 1579 or 1585). Victoria and Albert Museum, London.

232   C.J. Richardson, the overmantel in the Parlour at Montacute, watercolour. Victoria and Albert Museum, London.

234 (*right*) Jan Vredeman de Vries, *[Architectura] Das Erst Buech* (Antwerp, 1565), pl.E. Victoria and Albert Museum, London.

235 (*far right*) Jan Vredeman de Vries, *[Architectura] Das Ander Büch* (Antwerp, 1565), pl.19. Victoria and Albert Museum, London.

237 (*below right*) C.J. Richardson, the wind porch in the Great Chamber at Montacute, watercolour. Victoria and Albert Museum, London.

236 (*below left*) C.J. Richardson, the hall screen at Montacute, Somerset, watercolour (for the taffrils see Fig. 73). Victoria and Albert Museum, London.

238 Montacute, Somerset, east front with figures of the Nine Worthies, Julius Caesar on the left (see Fig. 177), Judas Maccabeus on the right.

combination of cartouches copied from Battini and Vredeman at Brereton Hall in Cheshire (pp.64–68) is not sufficiently exceptional for an attribution of this eccentric house to Arnold or anyone of his acquaintance.

How Arnold acquired his knowledge of prints is unknown. Perhaps his father was exposed to some at Longleat. Arnold's involvement with the sophisticated Robert Cecil at Cranborne came too late to influence his work at Montacute, so perhaps Edward Phelips introduced his master mason to prints. What is certain is that Arnold's familiarity with continental prints was considerably more extensive than that of most of his contemporaries. The unknown carver of the series of continental-style monuments in Buckinghamshire, Bedfordshire and Northamptonshire relied on designs by Cornelis Floris and Vredeman de Vries (pp.48–9, 86), the mason working in Shropshire mostly used Vredeman's suites of architectural decoration (p.60). Perhaps surprisingly, the Southwark-based masons, most of them Netherlanders who found employment in England from the 1560s, almost never needed prints, except occasionally for specific features or incidental details.[50]

One mason working north of the border at Edzell, which lies six miles north of Brechin, between Dundee and Aberdeen, copied several suites of prints for figures decorating the remarkable walled pleasure garden (Fig. 251) constructed in 1604–10 by Sir David Lindsay, Lord Edzell, and his second wife, Dame Isobel Forbes. The garden wall is articulated into compartments by pilasters and in some of these compartments are panels with moulded frames enclosing sculptures. There are three series, on the east side the Planetary Deities, on the south side the Liberal Arts and on the west the Virtues. Of these, the planets, with the exception of Saturn, were copied from a set of prints dated 1528–9 by the Master I.B

239 Hieronymus Wierix after Jan Vredeman de Vries, *Theatrum Vitae Humanae* (Antwerp, 1577), titlepage. Stedelijk Bibliotheek, Leeuwarden.

240 Philips Galle, David Rex, from *The Nine Worthies*. Stedelijk Prentenkabinet, Antwerp.

DAVID REX.

(Figs 247, 249), identified as Georg Pencz (Iorg Bentz).[51] The source of the Liberal Arts was a Flemish suite, designed by Maarten de Vos and engraved by Johannes Sadeler (Figs 248, 250).[52] The Virtues also derive from a set of prints after de Vos, engraved this time by Crispijn de Passe the elder (Figs 243, 245). Sir David Lindsay had given authority to prospect at the head of Glenesk for copper, lead and alabaster to two German mining engineers, Bernard Fechtenburg and Hans Ziegler from Nuremberg: it may have been a compatriot of theirs who carved these reliefs.

Sir David Lindsay died in 1610 before his garden was fully finished. About the same year, Inigo Jones produced a design for the monument to Lady Cotton, at Norton-in-Hales in Shropshire, based on continental precedents which may have included Floris or

242 (*far right*) Nuneham Courtenay, Oxfordshire, conduit from Carfax in Oxford from a late eighteenth-century engraving.

241 Nuneham Courtenay, Oxfordshire, detail of the conduit with the figures (from left to right) of Hector, David and King Arthur.

Vredeman as well as Ducerceau.[53] By the time he designed it, Jones had been to Italy (*c.*1601) and Denmark (1603–4). From 1608 onwards, Jones was patronised by Robert Cecil, Lord Salisbury, at that time building Hatfield House and the New Exchange in London. Another foreign visit followed in 1609, this time to France. In January 1610 Jones, as

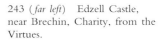

243 (*far left*) Edzell Castle, near Brechin, Charity, from the Virtues.

244 (*left*) St Olave's, London, gate into the churchyard, dated 1658.

CHARITAS.
Spemque, fidemque ratam DILECTIO (quam bene Græci
(Disserunt Agapen) maior vtraque facit.

245 (*far left*) Crispijn de Passe the elder after Maarten de Vos, Charity. Rijksmuseum-Stichting, Amsterdam.

246 (*left*) Hendrick de Keyser, design for a gateway, published in Salomon de Bray (ed.), *Architectura Moderna* (Amsterdam, 1631), pl.XVII. Victoria and Albert Museum, London.

247 (*right*) Edzell Castle, near Brechin, Mars, from the series of carvings depicting the Planetary Deities.

248 (*far right*) Edzell Castle, near Brechin, Geometria, from the series of carvings of the Seven Liberal Arts.

249 (*right*) Georg Pencz, Mars, 1528. Warburg Institute, London.

250 (*far right*) Johannes Sadeler I after Maarten de Vos, Geometria, from *The Liberal Arts*. Rijksmuseum-Stichting, Amsterdam.

Surveyor to Henry Prince of Wales, designed the costumes and setting for *Prince Henries Barriers*, a dramatic tourney written up by Ben Jonson. Of this nothing survives and of all Jones's work for the short-lived Prince (he died in November 1612 aged eighteen) there is little left. For eighteen months between April 1613 and November 1614 Jones travelled on the Continent with Thomas Howard, Earl of Arundel, one of the foremost collectors of the age. Besides seeing continental buildings with his own eyes, Jones was introduced to and acquired architectural treatises, prints of all kinds and original drawings.

As so much has been written on Jones's continental source material, it need only be summarised here. In his early work – Jones's career as Surveyor (1615–38) falls half within this period and half outside it – he adapted details from non-Italian sources, Stephen Harrison's *Archs of Triumph . . . of London*, treatises by Philibert de L'Orme and Jacques Androuet Ducerceau, Jan Vredeman de Vries and Jacques Francart, and (surprisingly) René Boyvin's engravings after Leonard Thiry's *Livre de la Conquête de la Toison d'Or* (1563). Otherwise most of the publications from which he derived inspiration whilst working for James I and Anne of Denmark were Italian, principally Serlio, Palladio and Vitruvius.[54] The French content of his interior decoration increased dramatically during the 1630s, when Jones worked for Charles I's French-born Queen Henrietta Maria. In his designs for chimneypieces and overmantels at Somerset House in 1636,[55] and the Queen's House in Greenwich in 1637, he introduced detail from the recently published work of Pierre Collot, Jean Barbet and D. Antoine Pierretz. There is no evidence that he used Salomon de Bray's *Architectura Moderna* (Amsterdam, 1631), which celebrates the later work of the Amsterdam sculptor and architect, Hendrick de Keyser,[56] but one design (Fig. 246) was copied by an unknown mason for the gate into the churchyard of St Olave, Hart Street in London (Fig. 244), which is dated 1658. Jones did, however, press into service two widely differing suites – Hieronymus Cock's engravings after Sebastiaan Noyen, *Terme Diocletiana Imp . . .* (1558) and Peter Paul Rubens's *I Palazzi di Genova* (1622) – for his restoration of St Paul's Cathedral.[57]

It is as well to remember that prints were only one source of Jones's inspiration;[58] nevertheless, at the height of his architectural career his ability to synthesise print sources in his designs far exceeded that of men who were not much older than he – Smythson born around 1550, Arnold perhaps ten years later, Jones in 1573.

Chapter 9

PLASTERWORK

Elaborate plaster ceilings and overmantels are amongst the glories of English houses in the Tudor and early-Stuart period. Highly-decorated rib-work ceilings in particular have much in common aesthetically with the hybrid late-Gothic stone vaults with early-Renaissance ornament characteristic of the middle years of the reign of Henry VIII, even though most of the patterns can be traced back to Serlio. A period of considerable activity in the study of plasterwork in the years around the First World War was followed by a longer period of comparative neglect, so that recent studies of plasterwork in London, the Home Counties, north Derbyshire and south Yorkshire, and Somerset are particularly welcome.[1] These have succeeded in clarifying the organisation of the trade and the working of the networks of patronage on which plasterers depended, but have been generally been rather less successful in tracing sources of design. Interesting in themselves, print sources sometimes illuminate what may have been a special relationship during the period covered here between plasterwork and carving in wood.

There was probably always some cross-over between the two trades. The Gunby brothers, Thomas and Francis, for instance, were highly skilled plasterers. Based in Leeds, they together executed the plasterwork of Gawthorpe Hall in Lancashire (1600–5)[2] and of many houses throughout Yorkshire, while Francis worked for Sir Arthur Ingram at Sheriff Hutton (1621–2) and Temple Newsam (1626–9). But they were also noted for their woodcarving and joinery, Francis cutting the moulds at Gawthorpe and ending his career carving the screens in Wakefield Cathedral (1634–5) and – probably – St John, Briggate, Leeds, where he also must have done the plasterwork ceilings.

Print sources reinforce this picture. As seen in Part I, the repeated motif in the plaster frieze of a room above the gateway at Corpus Christi College, Oxford, derives from the same set of cartouches designed by Vredeman de Vries as those on overmantels at Levens Hall in Westmorland and Lanercost Priory in Cumberland. The infrequency of their use suggests that the plasterer's moulds were made by a wood

carver who, as will be demonstrated below (p. 197), was probably based in Newcastle. Again, similarities between carved stone and moulded plasterwork have been noted in the south-west, and between timber and moulded plaster at Chastleton in Oxfordshire.[3] The practice of joiners carving moulds for casting in plaster is supported by further contemporary evidence. Hugh Platt, writing in *The Jewell House of Art and Nature* first published in 1594, describes an economical manner in which friezes could be manufactured:

> Or else if some excellent carver in wood or stone did carve some excellent piece of a border, of half a yard long, and a foot in breadth, with antick faces and personages, or other frutages thereon, and with the coat-armours of Gentlemen, and other pleasing devices to garnish the same; the aforesaid Artist might easily, and with small cost, cast off whole borders for chambers or galeries, in the aforesaid substances or compositions, which would seem to be of infinite charge.[4]

The best plasterwork from the early years of Elizabeth I is the overmantel in the Star Chamber at Broughton Castle in Oxfordshire, executed sometime after 1554 and based on French prints of the Fontainebleau school (see Figs 36–8). We may speculate that the plasterers who executed the Broughton work were based in Oxford, which must have been an important centre for the building trades.[5]

Amongst several productive traditions of plasterwork in England at least two display a dependence on a variety of continental prints. One flourished in Devon and the West Country in general from the 1570s to the end of the Stuart period and beyond, the other was centred around London and must have been almost precisely contemporary. Each possessed its favourite stock of printed source material only some of which was common to both geographical areas.

The plasterwork of the West Country is justly famous and much of it has been attributed to members of the Abbott family who settled in north Devon in the mid-sixteenth century. William Abbott

254 (*far right*) Abbott sketch-book, term figures copied from Jan Vredeman de Vries's *Caryatidum* (Antwerp, 1565). Devon Record Office, Exeter (404M/B1).

255 (*facing page top left*) Abbott sketch-book, cartouche copied from an untitled and undated set by Jan Vredeman de Vries. Devon Record Office, Exeter (404M/B1).

256 (*facing page top right*) Abbott sketch-book, cartouche copied from Benedetto Battini's *Vigilate quia nescitis . . .* (Antwerp, 1553). Devon Record Office, Exeter (404M/B1).

257 (*facing page centre right*) Abbott sketch-book, cartouche. Devon Record Office, Exeter (404M/B1).

258 (*facing page bottom*) Lucas Kilian, cartouche, from his *Newes Schildtbylin* (Augsburg, 1610), pl.19. The Royal Library – National Library of Sweden, Stockholm, Maps and Prints Department, De la Gardie Collection.

253 Abbott plasterers' sketch-book, rounded knot pattern copied from William Lawson's *The Country Housewife's Garden* (London, 1617). Devon Record Office, Exeter.

was the first to establish himself in the county. He was Knight of the Cellar to Henry VIII and was granted the dissolved Abbey of Hartland. One of his many sons settled at Culleigh in the parish of Frithelstock, whose abbey had been an appurtenance of Hartland. John Abbott (1565–1635) may have been the first of the family to take up the business of plasterer, and he was succeeded by his son Richard, born in 1612, and grandson John Abbott the younger (1639–1727).

The importance of the Abbott family rests on their documented work and on other plasterwork attributed to them both on stylistic grounds and by comparison with designs recorded in the remarkable sketch-book which they compiled over a period of as much as a century and a half.[6] It offers a unique insight into sixteenth- and seventeenth-century craftsmen's design methods. It consists of a small leather-bound volume of 318 pages measuring three and a half inches by five, and contains copies of recipes, freehand drawings based on continental prints and exercises in overall pattern-making. Many of these fall outside the period: but there are plenty that must date from about 1575 onwards and represent the work of John Abbott the elder.

Let us look first at the overall patterns. Leaving aside compartment designs, for the moment, these fall into two groups. One comprises many overall patterns that derive from Serlio's ceiling designs in his Book IV. Their variety is achieved by adding lines to form smaller compartments and though this process results in a blurring of the original pattern, once this fact is understood these patterns are easy to read. But there is another group of designs (Fig. 253) which are equally certainly derived from a different source. For one thing, they are drawn with a double rather than a single line and for another they are less rectilinear,

more rounded in character. The origin of these is not hard to find: they all derive from a contemporary English gardening book, William Lawson's *The Country Housewife's Garden*, published in London in 1617 – in fact they are designs for knot gardens.[7] An interesting feature of the sketch-book are the drawings of the Classical orders of architecture, quite small and rather simplified. These have the distinction of placing the columns on pedestals decorated with standing figures, for which there is an English precedent in John Shute's *The First and Chief Groundes of Architecture* published in 1563. Figures also appear in the form of caryatids or terms (Fig. 254) and these derive from Vredeman de Vries's *Caryatidum . . . sive Athlantidum* of 1565 (see Fig. 219).

The sketch-book contains numerous designs for cartouches, to be used for overmantels and for panels on ceilings. Some are angular in character (Fig. 256). These derive for the most part from one suite of cartouches, designed by the Italian Benedetto Battini and published in Antwerp in 1553 (pp.20–22). The drawing is almost ludicrously infantile to modern eyes, often leading to some initial uncertainty as to which print was being copied, but when the drawings are placed side by side with the prints there really is no doubt about it. Another source used for their

cartouches is a Jacob Floris suite which appeared in the following decade. Here the evidence of the sketch-book coincides with that of surviving ceilings in Barnstaple and neighbouring areas of the West Country (see p.55). A third source may be significant: at least one cartouche was copied from an untitled and undated Vredeman suite (Fig. 255; probably of the early 1560s) which was rarely employed in England, (see p.72). Several of the cartouches in the sketch-book are more curvilinear and certainly derive from auricular-style ornament dating from after 1600 at the earliest. In fact, five were adapted from a set designed by Lucas Kilian and published under the title *Newes Schildtbylin* in Augsburg in 1610 (Figs 257, 258). The sketch-book is the only evidence that these cartouches were known in England.

Smaller compartments formed by intersection of the plaster ribs were often inhabited by beasts, and drawings of these appear in the sketch-book as well. Once again, they seem to derive mainly from one source, Edward Topsell's book, *The History of Foor-footed Beasts and Serpents*, which was published in London in 1607 and 1608. Topsell's woodcuts were taken from Konrad Gesner's famous illustrations. Alternatively, these compartments might be populated by emblematic figures (so the sketch-book seems

to suggest) and a considerable number of these come from George Wither's book, *A Collection of Emblemes, Ancient and Moderne*, published in London in 1635 using engravings by the de Passe family; the remainder have yet to be traced.

The few figurative scenes included in the sketch-book depict Adam and Eve, the Sacrifice of Isaac (twice), the Judgement of Solomon (with the head of the king, Charles I), and two allegorical scenes: Time Rewarding Industry and Punishing Idleness, and one which has been taken to represent the Four Seasons. I have been unable to find a source for the biblical scenes and it is disappointing that the allegory of Time – an uncommon subject in surviving overmantels – does not derive from the print after Maarten de Vos that supplies the single instance in plasterwork in England (p.113). The scene once thought to depict the Four Seasons,[8] on the other hand, which actually represents the Triumph of Time over Fame (Fig. 259), has now been traced to its source. The drawing is extremely perfunctory but the two overmantels related to it, at Dean Head, Swimbridge in Devon, and Binham Farm, Old Cleeve in Somerset (Fig. 260), are very much better quality and enable the details to be made out. Though the number of figures in each is reduced (and the Dean Head panel is reversed from the woodcut), both the position of the figure of Time and the overall composition are virtually identical to a print from a suite designed by Georg Pencz (Fig. 261). What clinches it is the appearance of the infant in the baby-walker, which is a notable feature of Pencz's composition. This source is extremely surprising, for there is no other surviving evidence that prints by Pencz were used anywhere else in England, although there is what may be an isolated instance in Scotland (see pp.153–4).

Not unexpectedly, the repertoire of continental prints used in actual plasterwork during the period extends that of the sketch-book: it would have been surprising if the plasterers had drawn every print they used. The main characteristics of work attributed to them are overall patterns on ceilings derived from Serlio – we have seen them playing around with these in the sketch-book – and ceiling and overmantel cartouches copied from Jacob Floris designs: these are just about identifiable in the sketch-book.

Their drawings, however, give no hint that they employed two particular series of biblical illustrations, Gerard de Iode's *Thesaurus veteris et novi Testamenti* published in Antwerp in 1579 and 1585 and Adriaen Collaert's slightly later publication, *Vita, Passio, et Resurrectio Iesv Christi*. The former supplied the inspiration for plasterwork reliefs in the overmantels and above the north door of the gallery at Lanhydrock, the overmantel relief at Trewarne Manor, as well as in some of the figurative panels in the Great Chamber

ceiling at Prideaux Place, all three in Cornwall (see pp.105–6). The latter included plates copied on the plaster overmantel reliefs at the Court House, East Quantoxhead, in Somerset, and contained within Jacob Floris cartouches on the ceilings of houses in Barnstaple, at the Golden Lion in Boutport Street, at 69 High Street and 7 Cross Street (see p.55). In addition, the Abbotts made use of some of the figurative scenes with which Jacob Floris filled his cartouches in the prints: Moses and the Brazen Serpent in an overmantel at Holcombe Court, the Judgement of Paris on an overmantel at Montacute. In one instance, for an overmantel in a house in the Butterwalk in Dartmouth (Fig. 263; related stylistically to their overmantels at Lanhydrock and datable between 1635 and 1640), they used a print of the Pentecost engraved by Johan Wierix after a design probably by Crispijn van der Broeck (Fig. 262). This print appeared in an edition of the Bible printed by Christopher Plantin in Antwerp in 1583. The figures of Moses and David which frame this scene were, by contrast, derived from an English source, the titlepage engraved by John Payne to *The Holy Bible* printed in Cambridge by Thomas and John Buck in 1629 (Fig. 264). The same print was used for the embroidered book-binding of a New Testament and Book of Common Prayer reputed to have belonged to Archbishop Laud.[9]

263 (*above*) Dartmouth, Devon, overmantel in a house in the Butterwalk, *c*.1640.

262 (*far left*) Johannes Wierix after Crispijn van der Broeck, Pentecost, from Christopher Plantin's *Biblia Sacra* (Antwerp, 1583). Bibliothèque Royale Albert Ier, Brussels.

264 (*left*) John Payne, engraver, titlepage of *The Holy Bible* (Cambridge, 1629). British Library, London (4.d.9).

259 (*facing page top*) Abbott sketch-book, drawing depicting the Triumph of Time over Fame. Devon Record Office, Exeter (404M/B1).

260 (*facing page centre*) Binham Farm, Somerset, plaster overmantel depicting the Triumph of Time over Fame.

261 (*facing page bottom*) Georg Pencz, *The Triumph of Time*. Warburg Institute, London.

At times the Abbotts must have worked with the mason-architect William Arnold: at Montacute they contributed overmantels derived from Jacob Floris

163

and the amusing relief in the frieze at the east end of the hall, copied from a popular print that I have not identified.[10] It was probably William Arnold who insisted on prints which they would not themselves have considered suitable for overall patterns on ceilings, as in the use of a Vredeman design for ceilings at Beckington in Somerset and Cold Ashton in Gloucestershire, and a Jacob Floris design for the remarkable ceiling of a ground-floor room at Wolfeton in Dorset. And it was probably Arnold who suggested cartouches derived from Cornelis Bos for overmantels at Claverton Manor and at Beckington Abbey, and one of Vredeman's cartouches for Clemens Perret's 1569 *Exercitatio Alphabetica* at Nettlecombe Court in Somerset. No evidence of either of these suites appears

265 Blickling Hall, Norfolk, plaster ceiling of the Gallery, early 1620s.

in the sketch-book. A rare instance of a print by Virgil Solis inspiring plasterwork decoration occurs at Chevithorne Barton with a panel of Orpheus Charming the Beasts, although Haddon Hall in Derbyshire has an overmantel in which the Solis woodcut was considerably elaborated (see Figs 20, 21).

Apart from the widespread use of ceiling designs copied or adapted from Serlio in the West Country and in London, none of the sources employed by the Abbotts was copied by plasterers working in or near the capital, with one exception. This is a ceiling at Forty Hall, Enfield in Middlesex, where a plate from Vredeman's 1565 *[Architectura] Das Erst Büch* was used just as it had been at Beckington Abbey. Differences in detail suggest that the same plasterers were not employed in these two houses, but the fact that the same idea occurs in both suggests that there may have been some connection between their owners, or their craftsmen.

A curious and unexplained relationship exists, as seen earlier (pp.125–7), between patterns disseminated by Walter Gedde in his glazier's pattern-book, *A Booke of Sundry Draughtes*, published in 1615, and ceilings in the London area; in the West Country the relationship seems to have been the straightforward one of source and destination (see p.127). Other patterned ceilings have completely resisted elucidation so far. Notable amongst them are those in the drawing room and dining room at Langleys in Essex and in the gallery at Charlton House, Greenwich: the latter looks as though it should derive from a design by Johann Jakob Ebelmann,[11] but it actually does not. Again, the handsome tunnel-vaulted ceiling at Slyfield Manor in Surrey, a house of about 1625–40, must have been adapted from a print source but this still remains to be discovered.

For panels in their ceilings, London plasterers tended to favour allegorical figures rather than biblical scenes, although there are exceptional instances (on the ceiling of the private chapel in Sir Paul Pindar's house, as well as on an overmantel at Boston Manor, Brentford) of the use of a print after Pieter de Iode for the Sacrifice of Isaac. Particularly popular were sets of the Nine Worthies from prints by Nicolaes de Bruyn, and his father Abraham's prints depicting mythological characters (Atlas, Andromeda, Medusa, Perseus, Phineus and Danaë) were used for the series of plaster overmantels at Charlton House, Greenwich, and Boston Manor.[12] There are two ceilings (see p.93) whose overall pattern was cleverly adapted from the grotesques framing the scene of Andromeda in Abraham de Bruyn's print, the ceiling of the chapel in Sir Paul Pindar's house in Bishopsgate, London, about 1624, and of the closet off the gallery at Blickling in Norfolk, contracted by Edward Stanyon (who worked for Sir Henry Hobart between 1620 and

1623) at a cost of 4s. 6d. a square yard.[13] The gallery ceiling at Blickling (Fig. 265) has twenty figures in the compartments which have long since been recognised as deriving from Henry Peacham's *Minerva Britanna, or A Garden of Heroical Devises* published in London in 1612, together with the Five Senses from a source as yet unidentified.

Doctrina (Fig. 266), or Learning, is one of the figures derived from Peacham (Fig. 267) and she reappears in plasterwork which has not hitherto been connected with Blickling, although it must be precisely contemporary, or with Stanyon, who must have executed it. This is the barrel-vaulted ceiling of the library at Langleys at Great Waltham in Essex, an earlier house which was altered by Hugh Everard who inherited in 1617: glass in the parlour was said to bear the date 1621, and evidence of the heraldry suggests a date between 1621 and 1628 for Hugh's alterations.[14] Doctrina dominates the centre of one of the tympana at either end of the room (Fig. 268) and was clearly derived from Peacham where she is described in the following terms:[15]

Heere Learning sits, a comely Dame in yeares;
Upon whose head, a heavenly dew doth fall:
Within her lap, an opened booke appears:
Her right hand shewes, a sunne that shines to all;

267 Henry Peacham, Doctrina, from *Minerva Britanna* (London, 1612).

268 Langleys, Great Waltham, Essex, plaster tympanum of the library with the figure of Doctrina, 1621–8.

Blind Ignorance, expelling with that light:
The Scepter shewes, her power and soveraigne might.

Her out spread Armes, and booke her readiness,
T'imbrace all men, and entertaine their love:
The shower, those sacred graces doth expresse
By Science, that do flow from heaven above.
Her age declares the studie, and the paine;
Of many yeares, ere we our knowledge gaine.

The Five Senses themselves appear in the library overmantel, but they derive from a different suite from that used for the figures at Blickling. The most interesting and individual feature of this overmantel is the relief in the central compartment depicting Tobias and the Fish (Fig. 272). Like most pieces of decoration in England which depend on a print, this was copied absolutely faithfully from the source. The source is the more surprising because of the difference in scale between the object it depicts and the overmantel it inspired. The print is a design for a jewel-encrusted pendant, from the second of two suites entitled *Monilium Bullarum Inauriumque*

Eng c/c

266 Blickling Hall, Norfolk, detail of the Gallery ceiling with the figure of Doctrina.

165

Artificiocissimae Icones (1581) and *Bullarum inaurumque . . . archetypi artificiosi* (1582; Fig. 271); these were designed by Hans Collaert, engraved by his son and published by Philips Galle in Antwerp.[16] The design was intended to be executed in gold or silver with translucent enamel for the body of the fish; many pendants of the kind survive, of English as well as Antwerp manufacture. It is interesting that the plasterer saw this print not in terms of its designer's intention, but simply as a design source like any

other engraving. There may be an equally eccentric source for the figures of Concord and Peace in the overmantel in the dining room: perhaps they originally populated some undiscovered titlepage border. Even less well known than the plasterwork at Langleys is an unusual relief of the Theological Virtues at Charterhouse (Fig. 269), which was adapted from a print designed and executed by Johan Wierix (Fig. 270); a more accurate rendering of the same design was done in tapestry, see Fig. 395. London plasterers also made use of allegorical figures after Marc Geerarts (see p.90).

All in all, these two regional traditions of fine plasterwork, with the exception of their common dependence upon Serlio, could hardly have been more different in their choice of continental source material, the Londoners not surprisingly favouring rather more up-to-date publications.

It would be useful to know the precise relationship between plasterwork of the London area and that of Scotland. Closer contacts between the two countries followed the accession to the English throne of James VI of Scotland, and elaborately decorated plaster ceilings in the English manner became commoner north of the border. Sometimes the same subjects appear: at Balcarres House, a ceiling was decorated with the Nine Worthies after Nicolaes de Bruyn, as at Mapledurham in Oxfordshire, the Old Palace,

272 Langleys, Great Waltham, Essex, plaster overmantel in the drawing room depicting Tobias and the Fish, surrounded by the Five Senses, 1621–8.

270 (*facing page bottom*) Johan Wierix, *The Theological Virtues*, 1572. British Museum, London.

273 (*right*) Craigievar Castle, Aberdeenshire, plasterwork frieze in the hall, *c.*1626.

274 (*far right*) Theodor de Bry, design from *Grotis for die goldtsmit und andern khunstiger* (1589). Victoria and Albert Museum, London.

Bromley-by-Bow in London, Boston Manor and Kew Palace. Which plasterer was responsible for the plasterwork executed around 1626 in the hall at Craigievar Castle in Aberdeenshire (Fig. 273)? This has a pattern of decorated ribs enclosing panels, one with a medallion of King David; the frieze has a combination of strapwork and flowers and foliage, and this frieze was copied (upside down) from an engraving by the Flemish-born engraver and designer, Theodor de Bry (1528–98), who worked in Frankfurt (Fig. 274). The suite, entitled *Grotis for die goldtsmit und andern khunstiger*, was published in 1589.[17] Further minute scrutiny of the subsidiary ornament – for instance, the characteristic low-relief decoration of the ribs – will be necessary before the extent to which plasterers were still dependent on specific examples can be determined, and whether these examples were increasingly coming from Germany rather than from Antwerp.

Chapter 10

JOINERY AND CARVING

As in masons' work during the reign of Elizabeth I so in that of joiners and carvers Longleat makes its presence felt, even though only its hall screen and wonderfully carpentered hammerbeam roof now survive, the latter made by John Lewis. Some of the networks of patronage suggested by the joiners' use of prints are now familiar, others will be new and introduce centres of artistic activity not already noted.

As might be expected, joiners in England mirrored their mason contemporaries in matters of style: a brief period of Frenchified classicism lasting from the middle years of the sixteenth century to about 1580 gave way to thirty or forty years of dependence largely on Netherlandish prints, before new source material gradually became popular in the second quarter of the seventeenth. However, most Elizabethan and Jacobean joiners and carvers probably went through their careers entirely unaware of prints as potential sources of decorative ideas: there is little or no evidence that small workshops in country districts had a copy of Serlio or something by Vredeman to hand. Indeed, pieces of domestic furniture displaying any perceptible debt to continental prints are exceptional – the Eglantine and Seadog Tables now at Hardwick are two examples, and the latter may have been made in France. It is as if there were a recognised hierarchy in the matter of decoration, domestic furniture falling below the threshold at which it was worth a joiner's while to make any special efforts towards up-to-date continental appearance. Joinery was anyway a comparatively humble calling, bringing modest rewards: analysis of probate inventories in Exeter, for example, have shown that a joiner's £4 of goods compared very unfavourably with a weaver's gross estate which might be worth £90,[1] and this was a weaver of functional woollen textiles not luxurious tapestries.[2]

The principal contribution of the joiner to continental-style decoration was in the carving of room panelling, chimneypieces and overmantels, decorative screens and staircases. Some very significant works dating from the early 1570s – after the massive immigration of Protestant refugees from abroad and before their return around 1577 – give a vivid picture

of the diversity of style that resulted from different groups of joiners adapting, in some cases, the same stock of source material.

The so-called Haynes Grange Room – it may have originated at Chicksands Priory in Bedfordshire – was, from its eschewing of Flemish excesses, a rarity in England.[3] Stylistically it comes from Serlio's illustrations of details of the Pantheon in Rome, perhaps modified by elements derived from Palladio, whose treatise was first published in 1570. No comparable joiner's work survives from Elizabethan England.

The screen in the hall of Middle Temple in London (Fig. 276) may be contemporary with the Haynes Grange Room but displays little of its classical purity.[4] Like so many screens, its five-bay design with two openings, corresponding to the doors of buttery and pantry across the passage, resembles Roman triumphal arches (known chiefly through the publications of such architects as Serlio and Ducerceau, Palladio and Vignola) or their Renaissance successors, the temporary arches constructed in timber, canvas and plaster, to mark the triumphal entry of a ruler or other grandee into a town. One English screen, made for Holdenby House and surviving altered in the church, may have been inspired by the illustrated souvenir publication issued to commemorate such an entry, Cornelius Graphaeus's *Le triumphe d'Anvers, faict en la susception du Prince Philips, Prince d'Espagne* published in 1550, recording the event that occurred the previous year.[5] There is no evidence that the Middle Temple screen depends on any such continental precedent for its overall design but, like most decorative work in England, its details show that its creators were well aware of continental prints.

The screen spans the east end of the hall – a building of impeccable legal conservatism built during the 1560s – in two storeys, of which the lower is somewhat taller than the upper. The six free-standing Roman Doric columns of the lower storey are united in pairs by lengths of distinctly uncanonical architrave and frieze, which are not continued over the arched openings. Consolidating these pairs of columns is a second, more correctly Doric entablature which breaks forward in six places to support, with scrolled

275 Benedetto Battini, *Vigilate quia nescitis . . .* (Antwerp, 1553), pl.13. Victoria and Albert Museum, London.

276 (*facing page*) Middle Temple, London, hall screen, early 1570s. The cartouche on the extreme left derives from Benedetto Battini's *Vigilate quia nescitis*, see Fig. 275.

consoles, the term figures that articulate the upper stage. The resulting bays are further divided by arched niches flanked by Ionic pilasters and panels decorated with strapwork cartouches in relief – these form the balustrade of the gallery front which is topped by a heavy entablature.

Subscriptions were being taken to meet the expense of building the screen in 1574 but neither the designer nor the joiner is recorded.[6] The designer cannot have been an experienced mason-architect: the solecism whereby the columns of the lower storey support not one but two entablatures militates against it. Stylistically, the two storeys suggest mixed parentage: the lower is by Italy out of France or England, the upper is all Netherlands. The Roman Doric order, below, with the Hercules figures on the pedestals strongly recalls the Italianate illustrations of Shute's *The First and Chief Groundes of Architecture* published in 1563; the boldly pulvinated frieze of the uncanonical entablature, its elaborate interlacing strapwork which resembles designs by Ducerceau,[7] even the caryatid figures at this level are French in character; the double guilloche carved on the soffits of the arched openings probably comes from Serlio.

In the upper storey the mood changes abruptly to heavy Flemish Mannerism. In overall design the gallery front, with its syncopated rhythm of bays, is a distant echo of the famous rood-screen designed by Cornelis Floris in Tournai Cathedral which – constructed in 1571–4 – is precisely contemporary.[8] The detail too is Netherlandish, boldly carved terms, masks, pendants and cartouches, the latter derived from at least two series of engravings: one was the Italian artist Benedetto Battini's suite, *Vigilate quia nescitis diem neque horam* (Fig. 275), and the other was Jacob Floris's *Compertimentorum quod vocant multiplex genus*; both were published by Hieronymus Cock in Antwerp in 1553 and 1566 respectively (see pp.20, 54).

It is almost as if a different man had taken over the direction of the work in mid-stream. But the fact that the French-looking strapwork frieze of the lower storey and Floris cartouches in the upper occur together on decoration made for Chatsworth in Derbyshire and for Canonbury House in Islington, London, suggests that the stylistic dog's-dinner was the product of a single mind. From Chatsworth came the celebrated overmantel depicting Apollo and the Muses, and from Canonbury House two overmantels dated 1599 and 1601 (see Figs 427, 65).[9]

It is beginning to look as though the same carver was working on all these objects, a man having first-hand knowledge of French architectural decoration but perhaps inexperienced in Antwerp Mannerism and needing engravings to help him reproduce this complex style. The Longleat joiner Adrian Gaunt matches this profile admirably,[10] and is the more likely as a candidate because another Longleat craftsman had recently worked on Middle Temple Hall. John Lewis, though employed by Sir John Thynne at Longleat from 1552 until 1580, was forcibly impressed into the Queen's Works in 1562 and with her permission was diverted to Middle Temple Hall to construct the hammerbeam roof. It is a pair to those at Longleat and at Wiston, and at Burghley.

So the Middle Temple screen may be the work of Adrian Gaunt, and he could equally have been the author of the Apollo overmantel, carved in alabaster, from Chatsworth.[11] Although there is no documentary evidence that they actually went to the Midlands, Longleat craftsmen are known to have been canvassed by Sir William Cavendish who wrote to Thynne in 1555 asking him for the loan of a 'conning plaisterer' for Chatsworth; and that in 1560 Bess, now married to Sir William St Loe, herself wrote to Sir John asking him to 'spare me your plasterer' for work at this great Midlands house.

There is also a strong scent of Longleat in the five-bay Ionic screen in the hall of Gray's Inn, London (Fig. 277). It is to be sensed not in the elaborate patterns of low-relief strapwork decorating the column drums and the frieze above, which is Flemish in character, but in the gallery front which features exaggeratedly tapering French-style term figures and curious Italianate gable-like features with fluted friezes. The latter have their origin in two chimney-piece designs in Serlio's Book IV, the superstructure from folio 32r and the fluted frieze from folio 62r (see Fig. 4).[12] Terms and fluted Serlian frieze both appear on an original chimneypiece at Longleat (see Fig. 205).

Longleat was where the West-Country mason William Arnold may have had his training (see pp.146–53), and he developed the design of his stone screen in the hall at Montacute in the 1590s for the timber screens he devised for the hall and chapel at Wadham College, Oxford, which were erected about

SOCIETATIS INSIGNIA E SENATU TRANSLATA FUERE
ET LECTORUM INSIGNIA RENOVATA A.D. 1755 & 1791
DECORATA ET PICTÆ TABULÆ RENOVATÆ.

1613. These, and the screen in the Spencer Chapel at Yarnton Church in Oxfordshire, are surmounted by strapwork crestings derived, as at Montacute, from elements in Vredeman de Vries's *Das Ander Buech*. Vredeman was also the main stylistic influence on the Flemish-style screens constructed by joiners who enjoyed court patronage in the greatest houses of the early seventeenth century, Knole, Hatfield and Audley End; but their designers were largely independent of actual prints.[13]

Significant joiners' workshops were undoubtedly supported in a number of provincial towns in England. Many were ports, and the patrons were wealthy merchants. Bristol was one. Anonymous joiners fitted out interiors of houses on both sides of the Bristol Channel, the Red Lodge for Sir John Yonge in Clifton, Bristol, and Raglan Castle near Monmouth in Wales.[14] If these were inspired by continental prints, however, these remain to be identified.

Exeter boasted another, a shop where the joiners were probably members of the Garrett or Hermon family and must surely, from their surnames (which were interchangeable), have been immigrants from the Netherlands. They probably worked with the mason John Deymond, whose output of funerary monuments and possible relationship with the mason-architect William Arnold have been referred to earlier. Many Flemish-style interiors were fitted by this workshop in houses of the landed gentry and urban merchants during the last decade of the sixteenth century and the first two of the seventeenth.[15] The

panelling of an unprovenanced house near Exeter[16] – the finest survival since the destruction of Bampfylde House in Exeter during the Second World War – shows that the joiners shared with Deymond a knowledge of Vredeman's *[Architectura] Das Erst Büch* of 1565, which supplied the pattern for two panels in the frieze; another panel derives from a print after Cornelis Floris, while a fourth was adapted from a design by Abraham de Bruyn; some of the panels centre on Classical gods and goddesses whose sources remain to be found. So have those for the woodwork of the Job Room at Bradninch, the parlour at Bradfield, and The Grange at Broadhembury, all within a few miles of each other (and of Exeter) in Devon, for which the same joiners were probably responsible.

Judging by survivals of important woodwork, other provincial centres likely to have harboured significant joiners' shops probably included cathedral cities such as Gloucester, Canterbury, Norwich and York, the university towns of Oxford and Cambridge, and busy ports such as Ipswich, Great Yarmouth and King's Lynn.[17] Further research is needed at a local level to determine the amount of activity during the period and the nature of any foreign influence. This approach has proved highly successful in the case of a house where, with the exception of some fine plaster ceilings, carved woodwork comprises the major part of its surviving decoration. The house is Burton Agnes near Bridlington in the old East Riding of Yorkshire, and the woodwork shows the joiner to have been exceptionally well-informed about continental prints. Many of the suites he employed can be identified and used to establish links between this house and further work in another urban centre.

Burton Agnes (Fig. 278) was built chiefly during the first decade of the seventeenth century, from about 1601 to 1610,[18] for a man born during the first full year of Elizabeth's reign. Like Hardwick, Burton Agnes is associated with the mason-architect Robert Smythson, but it is very different in character – Hardwick essentially tall, compact and forward-looking, Burton Agnes built in the traditional way around an internal courtyard. Smythson provided the surviving ground plan,[19] which was modified for the house as built, and the placement of the gallery on the second floor is another Smythson characteristic; but the eclectic decoration must represent the patron's highly idiosyncratic taste.

The patron was Sir Henry Griffiths. He seems to have spent the early years of his life at the family estate at Wichnor in Staffordshire, marrying Elizabeth Throckmorton, a member of the leading Catholic family who lived at Coughton Court. In 1594 he became High Sheriff of Staffordshire, but only five years later, in 1599, was a member of the Council of

the North; this position entailed attendance at York and he must have decided, as a result, to build a new house at Burton Agnes, an estate which had come into the Griffiths family in 1355. Henry became High Sheriff of Yorkshire in 1606; he died in 1620.

Three very remarkable features mark out the decoration of Burton Agnes from that of most of its contemporaries: the extraordinary number of allegorical figures, the fact that the majority are labelled for identification and the range and variety of print sources used. Labelling was recommended by Cesare Ripa in the introduction to the 1603 edition of his *Iconologia*:

This dressing up signified the composition of bodily images in colour in a great variety of proportions with fine attitudes and exquisite *finesse* . . . so that there can be no-one who is not moved at first sight by a certain desire to investigate the reason why they are represented and arranged in this particular manner. This curiosity is even strengthened by seeing the names of the things written under these Images, and I think the rule of writing the names underneath should always be observed except when a king of Enigma is intended, for without knowing the name it is impossible to penetrate to the knowledge of the signification except in the case of trivial images which will be recognised by everyone thanks to usage.[20]

It is almost as if the deviser of the iconographical programme wanted Burton Agnes to embody Ripa's message, to be at once easy to understand and a 'king of Enigma' at the same time.

There is nothing about the exterior of the house – except perhaps the Flemish strapwork of the bays in the south front and the superimposed classical orders crammed into the narrow space of the east face of the entrance bay – to indicate the riot of allegorical decoration inside. This begins immediately the hall is entered. Alterations were made to the room during the ownership of Sir Griffith Boynton, 3rd Baronet, who inherited in 1695 and died in 1730: to improve circulation from the 'high' end of the hall he introduced three round arches ornamented with seventeenth-century carvings.[21] Also, much of the carving here and elsewhere in the house looks as if it has been rearranged; but there seems to be no reason to doubt that most of it originated at Burton Agnes.

Screens, as seen, traditionally provided the carver with the largest single area for lavish decoration in the hall. However, there is nothing in England quite like this oak screen whose towering plaster superstructure reaches right up to the eighteenth-century ceiling (Figs 279, 280). It is the nearest surviving visual equivalent (lacking only colour) of the *Archs of Triumph Erected in honor of the High and mighty prince James the first . . . at his Maiesties entrance and passage through his Honorable City and chamber of London . . . 1603*, designed and published by Stephen Harrison, 'Joyner and Architect'; Henry Griffiths was knighted by James I that same year.

279 (*right*) and 280 (*below*) Burton Agnes, Yorkshire, hall screen and detail.

More than fifty figures appear on the screen in several registers. Most are likely to have been copied from print sources, but there are some that clearly were not, including a man and a woman in contem- porary dress. The man, perhaps to be identified as the builder, Sir Henry Griffiths, makes his entry in the lower right-hand corner of the plaster superstructure, at the level occupied by the four Evangelists. These were copied from engravings by Johan Wierix after Maarten de Vos (Fig. 281).[22] The man ascends to the next level, peopled by the Twelve Apostles (from an unidentified print series), and in the level above he is led by an angel. In the top tier he takes his place amongst the Theological Virtues, of whom Charity derives from Jacob Matham's engraving after Hendrick Goltzius, which was used elsewhere at Burton Agnes (see Figs 295, 296).

On the oak screen itself, the spandrels over the arched door openings are carved with now-mutilated figures in pairs, of whom Jupiter seated on the Eagle enables them to be identified as the Planets, derived, as will shortly be seen, from the same set of prints as the larger figures flanking the arched doorways leading eastwards out of the Great Hall. Above these, in the frieze, appear for the first time figures who are labelled with their name and accompanied by a text. These are personifications of the tribes of Israel, or the Twelve Patriarchs (Fig. 282). Each figure comes from one of several sets of such illustrations that appeared in the Netherlands during the sixteenth century, wood- cuts first published (and perhaps designed) by Joos Lambrecht in Ghent in 1552 under the title *De*

D. Joannes omnium postremus Euangelium scripsit a: que a Domitiano missus est, in Pathmum et post obitum eius reuersus, obyt cum esset 90 annorum.

282 (*above*) Burton Agnes, Yorkshire, hall screen, figures of the Patriarchs with Gad on the right.

281 (*far left*) Johan Wierix after Maarten de Vos, St John. British Museum, London.

testamenten der twalf patriarcken Jacobs kinderen (Fig. 283).[23] From the inscriptions it is certain that the inspiration was actually provided by one of the English editions printed from 1576 onwards.[24]

The blocks over the columns are carved with figures of the Sibyls from a source still to be discovered, but all the remaining panels at this level are carved with an apparent miscellany of allegorical figures. In the keystones are Honor and Liberalitas (Fig. 284), with Pax and Concordia in the blocks above. From left to right the other figures are Diffidentia Dei, Experientia (Fig. 285) and Foedus (on the centre block, left and right faces), Obedientia and Pietas (right-hand block), with Potestas and Inquietas on the extreme right-hand end of the frieze.

All these allegorical figures were derived from engravings first published by Philips Galle in his book, *Prosopographia, Sive Virtutum, Animi, Corporis, Bonorum Externorum, Vitiorum, et Affectuum Variorum Delineatio, Imaginibus Accurate Expressa a Philippo Gallaeo, et Monochromate ab Eodem Edita: Distichis a Cornelio Kiliano Dufflaeo illustrata*, published in Antwerp about 1590 (Figs 286, 287).[25] This book provides the key to much of the other decoration in the house.

The three openings at the east end of the hall introduced in the early eighteenth century have arched frames made of oak featuring substantial caryatid figures of the Planets and numerous tiny figures

Gads testamēt/ van den Haat.

283 Joos Lambrecht, Gad, from *De testamenten der twalf patriarcken Jacobs kinderen* (Ghent, 1552). Koninklijke Bibliotheek, The Hague.

representing the Virtues and the Nine Worthies, all (despite rearrangement) probably indigenous to Burton Agnes. The Moon and the Sun (Luna and Phoebus Apollo, or Sol) flank the arch leading to the staircase (Fig. 288), Saturn and Jupiter, Mars and Venus the central opening, with Fame and Mercury to the south. With the exception of Fame, all derive

284 (*right*) Burton Agnes,
Yorkshire, hall screen,
Liberalitas.

285 (*far right*) Burton Agnes,
Yorkshire, hall screen,
Experientia.

286 (*right*) Philips Galle,
Liberalitas, from *Prosopographia*
(Antwerp, *c*.1590). Warburg
Institute, London.

287 (*far right*) Philips Galle,
Experientia, from *Prosopographia*
(Antwerp, *c*.1590). Warburg
Institute, London.

288 (*far left*) Burton Agnes, Yorkshire, arch from hall to staircase, Sol (Apollo).

289 (*left*) Burton Agnes, Yorkshire, Saturn and Jupiter.

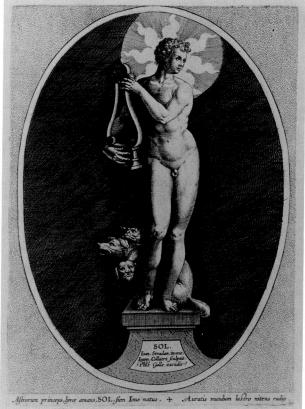

290 (*far left*) Jan Baptiste Collaert after Johannes Stradanus, Sol, from *Septem Planetae* (Antwerp, n.d.). Warburg Institute, London.

291 (*left*) Jan Baptiste Collaert after Johannes Stradanus, Saturnus, from *Septem Planetae* (Antwerp, n.d.). Warburg Institute, London.

from a suite of engravings by Jan Baptiste I Collaert
after Johannes Stradanus, published as *Septem Planetae*
by Philips Galle (Fig. 290). The carver here showed
himself capable of considerable versatility, transforming the seated Jupiter of the print into the standing
figure of the doorcase and managing a frontal pose for
Saturn (Fig. 289) from the three-quarter view of the
original (Fig. 291). He also simplified the images
somewhat. In the case of Sol or Apollo he omitted –
perhaps because he did not understand its significance
– the strange canine-bodied tricephalous monster
which, in the engraving, lurks menacingly behind the
figure's legs, investigating the present but also reflecting on the past and the future.[26] It is clear that this
suite also provided the source for the mutilated figures
of the Planets in the spandrels of the hall-screen
arches.

Over the arched opening into the Little Hall is
a frieze, also now rearranged, with numerous small
figures representing the Seven Virtues and the Nine
Worthies. The Virtues were easy to identify as straight
copies from engravings by Jacob Matham after
Hendrick Goltzius,[27] but the source of the Nine
Worthies remained a puzzle for a long time: they
were evidently copied from the same suite of prints
used, for instance, by Thomas Trevelyon and the
painter who decorated a house in High Street,

Amersham, Buckinghamshire. I have indicated earlier
that this common source was the set published by
Philips Galle around 1590. One of the plates was
probably adapted for the military figure in the centre
of the plaster superstructure of the hall screen.

Rather than consider at this point the
chimneypiece and overmantel, which are carved in
alabaster, let us move on to the overmantel of the
drawing room (the parlour or Low Dining Room of
the original house). Surmounting a plain stone
chimneypiece with term figures, this consists of a
horizontal oak panel carved in high relief, flanked by
caryatids. These are identified by labels as Quiet and
Libertie, but no source has yet been found for them.
The panel is, with the relief of the Wise and Foolish
Virgins over the hall chimneypiece, the outstanding
piece of carving in the house. It represents Death (Fig.
294). In the middle a ghastly skeleton brandishing a
dart tramples on symbols of earthly power, while to
left and right the Just and Unjust go to their desti-
nies.[28] Unlike the relief depicting the Wise and
Foolish Virgins, or for that matter any other decoration in the house, this panel was not copied straight
from one readily accessible source but seems to have
been composed from several quite disparate images
with considerable ingenuity and resourcefulness.

Not all the identifications are completely secure.
The figure of the semi-reclining naked man on the
left, for instance, might have been adapted from that
of Hercules being tended by the midgets in Cornelis

178

Cort's engraving after Frans Floris, and the standing female figure with the looking glass on the right personifying Pride seems to have been borrowed from the print by Jacob Matham after Hendrick Goltzius (Fig. 292); this comes from the same suite of the Virtues and Vices that was used for figures at the east end of the hall. The winged devil in the upper right-hand corner might have been adapted from the titlepage border of Foxe's *Ecclesiastical History . . . or Actes and Monuments* in one of its many editions from 1563.[29] The way in which the symbols of temporal power are strewn around on the ground is reminiscent of a print by Cornelis Cort after a design by Frans Floris, although this does not provide the source here. Of the origin of the main figure of the skeleton, however, there can be little doubt, although this too has been subtly altered from the source, a Fontainebleau-school print designed by Martino Rota (Fig. 293). The position of the right arm is different (it might derive from another Rota print of Venus and Adonis) but the distinctive treatment of the wings and the overall character of the skeleton are very close indeed.[30]

There are at least two more overmantels carved with allegorical figures. One is now in the dining

room (Fig. 295) but it came from the gallery and was originally much wider, having two extra panels flanked by taller caryatids. In its present form the Theological Virtues occupy the main panels with the Cardinal Virtues separating them. For some reason these derive from more than three different suites, Justice from a set of engravings by Adriaen Collaert after Maarten de Vos (see Fig. 455), Faith and Charity from the engravings by Jacob Matham after Hendrick Goltzius (Fig. 296); the Seven Deadly Sins in the frieze above, however, were copied from a suite entitled *VII Peccatorum Capitalium Imagines Elegantissime a Philip Gallaeo Depictae et Aere Incisae*; the plates were probably engraved by Hieronymus Wierix.[31] The architect C.J. Richardson illustrated the overmantel when it was in the gallery and his lithograph shows that the relief figures now missing were Pandora and Honour. The latter had already appeared on the hall screen and both instances were inspired by Galle's *Prosopographia*; so Pandora was probably adapted from Liberalitas in the same publication.

The State Bedchamber is a handsomely panelled room whose panels have a geometric pattern derived from one of the ceilings in Serlio's Book IV. No fewer

294 Burton Agnes, Yorkshire, overmantel panel in the parlour representing Death, perhaps originally made for Barmston Hall near Bridlington and brought to Burton Agnes in the eighteenth century.

295 Burton Agnes, Yorkshire, overmantel in the dining room.

296 Jacob Matham after Hendrick Goltzius, Caritas. Warburg Institute, London.

Omnia Dia Agape diuino nectit amore
Et Stupens uinclo nos propiore ligat. N.G.

than eighteen figures inhabit the overmantel and plaster frieze above (Fig. 297), and all derive from Galle's *Prosopographia*. The relief panel has figures of four Virtues, arranged in pairs separated by columns, each named below and holding her proper attributes: from the left they are Patientia, Veritas, Constantia and Victoria. The articulation of the panel by columns was suggested to the carver by Galle's depiction of Constantia (Fig. 298) who is shown holding a sword in her left hand over a blazing cauldron, like Gaius Mucius Scaevola, whilst grasping a column – in an allusion to Samson's destruction of the Temple – with her right.

Above this panel is a frieze carved with three of the Vices – Tribulatio, Fraus and Periculum – with Ratio (Reason), whilst Mensura and Misericordia take their place on the face of the blocks above the columns with Virtus and Maiestas on the inner faces. In the plaster frieze above, Sanitas and Inquietudo appear over the blocks and four further figures between these. Arthur Oswald identified Kindness and Frailty among them, but actually they represent the Four Parts of the World: Europa holds a huge bunch of grapes and a sceptre (Fig. 299), Africa brings a sprig of sweet balsam, Asia magnificently attired bears a censer or thurible, and America grasps a head in one hand

Sanitas   Euro√   Africa√   Asia√   Amer!   Inquietudo

Sanitas   4 P+s of world   Inquietudo

Mensura → Trib./ Fraud/ Danger Miseria

297 Burton Agnes, Yorkshire, overmantel in the State Bedchamber, dated 1610.

CONSTANTIA.

Firma, columnæ instar, maneo; ceu Sceuola dextram
Urens, sum constans, propositiq́ tenax.

8.

EVROPA.

Sceptrum Europa gerit, pars præstantissima mundi
Lætaq́ fert vinum munus Iacche tuum.

40.

298 (far left) Philips Galle, Constantia, from Prosopographia (Antwerp, c.1590). Warburg Institute, London.

299 (left) Philips Galle, Europa, from Prosopographia (Antwerp, c.1590). Warburg Institute, London.

300 (*right*) Burton Agnes, Yorkshire, State Bedchamber, Eternity.

301 (*far right*) Philips Galle, Aeternitas, from *Prosopographia* (Antwerp, *c.*1590). Warburg Institute, London.

and a spear in the other. The source of Judith and St Barbara in the elaborately carved doorcases remains to be discovered, but the figure of Eternity (Fig. 300) over the north door undoubtedly derives from Galle's *Prosopographia* (Fig. 301): she has lost her attributes but fortunately is labelled underneath.

Having examined this multitude of allegorical figures carved in oak, let us finally return to the chimneypiece and overmantel in the Great Hall. Here it is necessary to distinguish the work that certainly belongs to Burton Agnes – the chimneypiece itself and the relief with term figures – from the three heraldic panels with separating term figures which were brought from the Boyntons' lesser house at Barmston during the eighteenth century and topped by a broken pediment. The Burton Agnes chimneypiece and overmantel (Fig. 302), although of stone and alabaster, could easily have been executed by the same carver. Coupled Ionic columns carved with strapwork in low relief flank the fireplace. The blocks above the columns and in the centre of the frieze have half-length female figures in contemporary dress personifying the Five Senses, probably adapted from

engravings, and prints surely lie behind the caryatid figures representing Wisdom and Innocence.[32] But it is the relief itself which is not only the masterpiece of carving in this room but has claims to be the most fascinating piece of decoration in the whole house. The subject is the parable of the Wise and Foolish Virgins from Matthew 25:1–13:

Then the kingdome of heauen shalbe likened vnto ten virgins, which toke their lampes, and went to mete the bridegrome. And fiue of them were wise, & fiue foolish. The foolish toke their lampes, but toke none oyle with them: but ye wise toke oyle in their vessels with their lampes. Now while the bridegrome taryed long, all slombred and slept. And at midnight there was a crye made, Beholde the bridegrome cometh; go out to mete him. Then all those virgins arose, & trimmed their lampes. And the foolish said to the wise, Giue vs of your oyle, for our lampes are out. But the wise answered, saying, We feare lest there wil not be ynough for vs & you: but go ye rather to them that sel, and bie for your selues. And while they went to

182

302 (*above*) Burton Agnes, Yorkshire, alabaster overmantel in the hall, illustrating the parable of the Wise and Foolish Virgins.

DATE NOBIS DE OLEO VESTRO, QVIA LAMPADES NOSTRÆ EXTINGVN NEQVAQVAM, NEQVANDO NON SVFFICIAT NOBIS ET VOBIS *math 25*
TVR·

303 Philips Galle after Pieter Bruegel, *The Wise and Foolish Virgins*, 1555–65. British Museum, London.

bie, the bridegrome came: & they that were readie, went in with him to the wedding, and the gate was shut. Afterwardes came also the other virgins, saying, Lord, Lord, open to vs. But he answered, and said, Verely I say vnto you, I knowe you not. Watche therefore: for ye knowe nether the day, nor the houre, when the Sonne of Man wil come.

The relief consists of six or seven panels of alabaster forming a horizontal composition. On the left, the wise virgins, with their lamps burning brightly, are engaged in spinning; on the right, the foolish virgins are occupied in dancing. Separating the two scenes is a tree above which appears an angel in a cloud, flanked on either side by another trumpeting, and holding a band with the inscription, 'Ecce sponsus venit exit obviam ei'. Between these three angels, and forming almost a relief, the virgins appear again, now naked, presumably to symbolise their virginity. On the left, the wise virgins with their lamps are admitted by the bridegroom; on the right, the foolish virgins knock on the door in vain.

It is a memorable image, conveying a powerful message. But it is one for which the able carver was not ultimately responsible. For the scene was copied, element for element, from − and it is a measure of the lack of interest in and understanding of the origins of Elizabethan and Jacobean decoration that the source has not hitherto been suspected let alone identified − an engraving by Philips Galle, published in Antwerp by Hieronymus Cock in the late 1550s or early 1560s, after a design by Pieter Bruegel the elder (Fig. 303).[33] All that is missing is the late-Gothic architecture in the upper register of Bruegel's design, and the characteristically mysterious atmosphere, so hard to translate into stone. Otherwise the carver's interpretation is pretty accurate and remains, so far as I know, one of only two adaptations from a print after Bruegel in Elizabethan or Jacobean England.[34]

It has been seen that the carving of the chimneypieces and overmantels, hall screen and panelling depended on more than a dozen different publications − some right up to date, others rather old-fashioned − and this does not take into account the movable furnishings of which there is unfortunately no record. The sheer number of allegorical figures, the fact that they are mostly identified by name, the high quality of the carving and a selection and variety of source material virtually unparalleled in England − particularly the choice of prints after Martino Rota and Pieter Bruegel − are the really remarkable features of the decoration of Burton Agnes. What do all these figures and subjects add up to? Two themes appear to run through the house: figures drawn from the Old and New Testaments (together with the story of the Wise and Foolish

Virgins), and the Virtues and Vices, the Four Parts of the World, the Nine Worthies and the Planetary Deities, together with the Vanitas relief, the Dance of Death. All have a overtly moralistic purpose.

The choice of particular books as sources for the decoration enables it to be said with some degree of certainty that it was the carver rather than his patron, Sir Henry Griffiths, who owned the prints. There is, regrettably, no record at Burton Agnes of his identity, but we can make a confident suggestion as to where he had his workshop. Two of the books used as source material at Burton Agnes were employed almost nowhere else: Joos Lambrecht's *De testamenten der twalf patriarchen Jacobs kinderen*, though certainly a popular book in England, with eight English editions from 1576, was only otherwise used to my knowledge at Burton Latimer in Northamptonshire (see p.210); Philips Galle's *Prosopographia*, in its sole edition of about 1590, was scarcely used more often.

One instance occurs on an overmantel now in the collections of Beamish Open Air Museum in County Durham (Fig. 305). It features a pair of allegorical figures flanking a well-carved relief, the whole com-

304 Philips Galle, Gratia Dei, from *Prosopographia* (Antwerp, c.1590). Warburg Institute, London.

305 Overmantel from the Beehive Inn, Sandhill, Newcastle-upon-Tyne, 1630s. Beamish (the North of England Open Air Museum).

position in its previous form being articulated by columns. Both the figures were copied from the *Prosopographia* which enables them to be identified correctly. From her upturned cornucopia it would be tempting to identify the figure on the left as Liberality. But Galle gives Liberality two cornucopiae, and the *Prosopographia* shows that the overmantel figure actually personifies Gratia Dei (Fig. 304). Her companion holds a double-headed mask in her left hand, but the other hand is missing: again the *Prosopographia* indicates that it was a circle formed by a snake biting its tail, so this figure personifies Aeternitas. Eternity is, as we have seen, one of the figures standing over a door in the State Bedchamber at Burton Agnes and comparison shows that, despite their losses, the two are indeed very similar. The use of the same unusual source and the repetition of Eternity, not to mention the quality of the carving, indicates that this carver

was responsible for the work at Burton Agnes. Who was this man and where was he based?

The history of the overmantel now at Beamish is complicated. It came to the museum from the keep of the Castle in Newcastle-upon-Tyne, but had been in the Mansion House in The Close, from the early nineteenth century until the dismantling of the building; before that it was in the Beehive Inn on Sandhill.[35] So the location of this exceptionally talented carver's workshop should be sought in Newcastle, and it soon becomes apparent that something very interesting was going on at Newcastle in architectural decoration during the thirty years from about 1605, something very different, it is beginning to seem, from anything happening elsewhere in England at that time.

Newcastle was a highly significant port, the most northerly in the country (Berwick-upon-Tweed being an English garrison town on the foreign soil of Scotland). The Tyne was one of the busiest rivers, not just in England but in the world. It has been shown that the development of Newcastle as a commercial centre was a key factor in the industrial development England as a whole, for her wealth was founded substantially (though not exclusively) on coal. Along with a poorish quality of salt used in preserving food-stuffs (principally fish, the main source of protein in Elizabethan and Jacobean diets), coal was shipped in huge quantities to other ports in England during the later sixteenth century.[36] Newcastle also exported coal, wool and hides, particularly to the Baltic and Norway. In view of the amount of goods that left the port undeclared, it is hardly surprising that Newcastle merchants built up considerable wealth, which they invested not only in ships but in their houses.

No description of the parts of the town built up by the merchants could improve on that given by William Grey whose *Chorographia, or a Survey of Newcastle upon Tine* was first published there in 1649.[37] Most of the work to be looked at here was executed during his lifetime, only a few years before he wrote. Describing 'The Highest and North Parts of the Town', Grey says:

In after ages the Burgesses and good men of the Town began to trade, and venture beyond the seas,

into forraigne places; they builded many ships; pro-cured a Charter from the Kings of England to carry Fels beyond seas, and bring in forraign commodi-ties. The Staple was then at Antwerp in Brabant, called Commune totius Europa Emporium. This charter of the Merchant Adventurers, was the first charter that was granted by any King to any Town. After which Grant, this town flourished in trading; builded many faire houses in the Flesh Market, (then called the Cloath Market.) The Merchants had their shops and warehouses there, in the back parts of their houses; the River of Tine flowed and ebbed, where boats came up with commodities; which trade of merchandizes continued many years. In that street the Mayors, Aldermen, and richest men of the Town lived. In after times, the Merchants removed lower down towards the River, to the street called the Side, and Sandhill, where it continueth to this day.

The Sandhill.

Now let us describe unto you the other Streets and Markets in the Town: First of the Sandhill, a Market for fish, and other commodities; very con-venient for Merchant Adventurers, Merchants of Coales, and all those that have their living by ship-

306 Samuel and Nathaniel Buck, Panorama of Newcastle, 1745, detail extending from the Mansion House on the left (which backs on to the river and fronts the narrow street called The Close) to the Guildhall on the right (with the Sandhill fish market behind it).

ping. There is a navigable River, and a long Key or Wharfe, where ships may lye safe from danger of stormes, and may unlode their commodities and wares upon the Key. In it is two Cranes for heavy commodities, very convenient for carrying of corn, wine, deales, &c. from the Key into the Water-Gates, which is alongside the Key side, or into any quarter of the Town.

In this market is many shops and stately houses for Merchants, with great conveniences of water, bridge, garner, lofts, cellars and houses of both sides of them. Westward they have a street called the Close. East, the benefit of the houses of the Key side.

Then Grey moves on to describe the Town-Court or Guild-Hall, the Court of Admiralty, the Court of Pye-powder, the Weigh-house, the Town-house, the Almes-house or 'Mason de Dieu'; above this is 'the stately Court of the Merchant Adventurers, of the old Staple, resident at that flourishing City of Antwarps in Brabant; since removed to the more Northern Provinces under the States. Their Charters are ancient, their priviledges and immunities great; they have no dependance upon London, having a Governour, twelve Assistants, two Wardens, and a Secretary'. The general lay-out of the quay, with the old bridge and the jumble of merchants' houses just upstream of it on Sandhill and The Close is vividly evoked by the Bucks' mid-eighteenth-century prospect from the south-east (Fig. 306).

The Beehive Inn, where the Beamish overmantel was, was probably one of these merchant's houses on Sandhill before it became an inn. The main relief in the overmantel seems to depict Lot embracing his daughters (Fig. 307), but the protagonists are accompanied by two further allegorical female figures. The meaning of this seemingly inexplicable relief is made clear only by the print from which it derives. The old man, Lot, personifies Honour, who embraces his daughters Virtus and Dignitas, while Gloria, standing behind this group, shows the way to Immortalitas; symbols of temporal and spiritual authority lie discarded with the fruits of the earth. The whole is an allegory on the Immortality of Virtue. The source is an engraving by Cornelis Cort after a design by Frans Floris (Fig. 308), published by Hieronymus Cock in 1564, and its use here is unique in England. The Beehive Inn overmantel is undated[38] but it must be nearly contemporary with the decoration at Burton Agnes, from c.1610 onwards.

Philips Galle's *Prosopographia* was also used, around the same date, on another overmantel, formerly at Hunwick Hall, seven miles south-west of Durham, which must therefore have been made by the same Newcastle workshop. The chimneypiece was

removed from Hunwick in about 1900, and its present whereabouts are unknown, but fortunately photographs of it survive in the archive at Beamish Open Air Museum (Fig. 309).[39] They show that the overmantel had a frieze above the principal register

308 Cornelis Cort after Frans Floris, *Allegory of Virtue*, 1564. British Museum, London.

187

309 Hunwick Hall, County Durham (partly demolished), overmantel with Orpheus and Arion, 1630s (whereabouts unknown).

310 (*right*) Crispijn de Passe the elder, Orpheus, from *The Elements*, 1602. Rijksmuseum-Stichting, Amsterdam.

311 (*far right*) Crispijn de Passe the elder, Arion, from *The Elements*, 1602. Rijksmuseum-Stichting, Amsterdam.

where three main panels – depicting Orpheus and Arion with the royal arms in the middle – were separated by standing figures personifying the Four Parts of the World. These latter, like Gratia Dei and Aeternitas on the Beehive Inn overmantel, were adapted from Galle's *Prosopographia*. The figures of Orpheus and Arion were derived from a different source, a set of prints depicting the Elements (Figs 310, 311) designed and engraved in Cologne by Crispijn de Passe the elder, and dated 1602.[40] In Ovid's *Metamorphoses*, Orpheus, a legendary Thracian poet, charmed wild beasts and the trees and rocks with the music of his lyre: he therefore represents Terra, Earth. Arion, known from Herodotus, was a Greek poet of the seventh century BC who was cast from a ship by its villainous crew and rescued by a dolphin attracted to the sound of his lyre: he represents Aqua or Water.

Very similar to the Hunwick Hall overmantel is another, allegedly from the Mansion House in Newcastle (Fig. 312). It was installed at Clervaux Castle, a castellated mansion built 1839–44 for Sir William Chaytor near Croft in the North Riding of Yorkshire and demolished in 1950–51.[41] Here the figures personify the Four Parts of the World and, as at Hunwick, derive unaltered from the *Prosopographia*. However, the two reliefs flanking the central coat of arms and representing Orpheus Charming the Beasts (left) and Arion, though surely based on Flemish prints, derive not from the de Passe engravings but from a source as yet unidentified. There are representations of both in George Wither's *A Collection of Emblemes, Ancient and Moderne* (1635), and his Apollo is just possible as a source (fol. 234); however, Arion is rather different and suggests that further searches are needed.[42]

A second chimneypiece and overmantel formerly at Clervaux also came from the Mansion House in Newcastle (Fig. 313).[43] There are single figures including Hope in the topmost frieze, but their source remains to be identified. The main panels of the overmantel depict the Adoration of the Magi and the Presentation in the Temple. These were copied direct from a set of biblical illustrations mentioned earlier. This undated set was published under the title *Vita, Passio, et Resurrectio Iesv Christi* by Adriaen Collaert, presumably in Antwerp.[44] The designs were made by Maarten de Vos and several engravers contributed. The Adoration (Fig. 314) was copied from Jan Baptiste Barbé's engraving (Fig. 316) which is inscribed beneath 'Procidentes adoraverunt eum, et apertis thesouris suis obtulerunt ei munera, aurum, thus, et myrrham'. The Presentation (Fig. 315) was copied from the next plate, engraved by Jacob de Bye (or Bie) and inscribed 'Accipit in ulnas suas . . .' (Fig. 317). This suite seems to have been used only very

rarely in England: surviving instances are the plasterwork overmantels at the Court House, East Quantoxhead in Somerset, and the ceilings of houses in Barnstaple on Devon (see pp.106–7). Could there be any connection between them? It seems unlikely, but the answer may be found by exploring genealogies.

Whoever this accomplished carver was, he executed a further chimneypiece now at Haughton Castle, north-west of Hexham in Northumberland, but originating in Derwentwater House in Newcastle (Fig. 318).[45] Here the two reliefs depict Cain and

312 (*top*) Clervaux Castle, Croft-on-Tees, North Riding of Yorkshire, nineteenth-century photograph of overmantel with Orpheus and Arion.

313 Clervaux Castle, Croft-on-Tees, nineteenth-century photograph of biblical overmantel.

6. *Procidentes adorauerunt eum, et apertis thesauris suis obtulerunt ei munera, aurum, thus, et myrrham.* Matth. 2.

M. de Vos inuent.   Ioan. Baptista Barbè sculp.   Adrian. Collaert exc.

7. *Accepit cum in vlnas suas, et benedixit Deum, et dixit, Nunc dimittis seruum tuum Domine, secundum verbum tuum in pace.* Luc. 2.

M. de Vos inuent.   Iacob. de Bye sculp.   Adr. Collaert eccud.

316 (*above*)   Jan Baptiste Barbé after Maarten de Vos, Adoration of the Magi, from Adriaen Collaert's *Vita, Passio, et Resurrectio Iesv Christi* (Antwerp, n.d.). Rijksmuseum-Stichting, Amsterdam.

317 (*above*)   Jacob de Bye after Maarten de Vos, the Presentation in the Temple, from Adriaen Collaert's *Vita, Passio, et Resurrectio Iesv Christi* (Antwerp, n.d.). Rijksmuseum-Stichting, Amsterdam.

314 (*top*)   Overmantel relief depicting the Adoration of the Magi, from Clervaux Castle, Croft-on-Tees, 1630s. Private collection.

315 (*top*)   Overmantel relief depicting the Presentation in the Temple, from Clervaux Castle, Croft-on-Tees, 1630s. Private collection.

Abel, and David and Goliath, both characterised by sunbursts in one corner, like those on the Clervaux overmantel; articulating the whole composition are four figures personifying the Four Elements. None of these has yet been traced to its source but the latter appear to be in the style of Pieter de Iode or Maarten de Vos. Behind the heads of the outer figures are consoles supported on carved brackets. These are close relatives of the brackets and carved shields that appear on yet another elaborately carved chimney-piece and overmantel, now in the Billiard Room of Chipchase Castle not far from Haughton but again originally from a house in Newcastle (Fig. 319).

The Chipchase overmantel has been dated around 1625, but a date approaching 1640 is more likely, with some re-arrangement on its transfer to Chipchase and further work in the Victorian period.[46] Here the upper shields are carved with the Seven Virtues, the lower with emblematic or heraldic devices and figures of Fame and Victory. The main panel has a brilliantly carved relief depicting a pair of winged horses (representing the sun and moon) drawing a triumphal car which is driven by Time: riding on the car are seated female figures personifying the Four Elements and they have a globe with the signs of the zodiac. The source is evidently an engraving of a triumph of the kind illustrated by Maarten van Heemskerck. In fact, this relief depicts the Triumph of the World and was based on a print from a suite designed by Heemskerck, engraved perhaps by Cornelis Cort[47]

and published by Hieronymus Cock in 1564 (Fig. 320). The cycle was entitled by Thomas Kerrich the *Circulus vicissitudinis rerum humanarum* – the Cycle of the Vicissitudes of Human Affairs, a title borrowed from a later suite of plates designed by Maarten de Vos (see Fig. 357). The print is the first in the suite that is a record of an actual event, the allegorical section of the Circumcision Procession – an annual event held in honour of the circumcision relic – in Antwerp on 1 June 1561. Heemskerck may have witnessed this procession but anyway based his designs, which he began the following year, on the official printed programme.[48] The Triumph of the World introduces the series. The Latin caption reads in translation: 'Time, the charioteer of the World, tirelessly whips on the winged horses of Night and Day in a cycle. With him he carries the sisters Fire, Air, Earth and Water and brothers South, North, East and West Winds, equal in number. How swiftly do immutable laws on earth engender the rotary motion which reveals everything in its turn.'

The carver has rendered the scene with remarkable faithfulness: the pair of horses and the figure of Time are virtually unchanged though the mountain fastness between them has been simplified: behind Time, Fire, Earth, Air and Water are much as in the print, as are the four Winds which are nicely rendered. The carver even copied the scrolled spokes of the wheels, merely repairing their broken rims which must have struck him as too improbable. The only significant alteration

was his moving of the terrestrial globe from between the Elements to a central position behind the figure of Time. This made the composition more symmetrical, appropriately for an overmantel.

The culminating print sums up the purpose of the series:

So shall it be seen that Riches, Pride, pernicious Envy, War, Want, Humility and Peace, the begetter of Riches, shall follow each other in turn as in a circular motion until the Final Day shall break upon the world. On that day the son whose father is God and who is both man and God shall deliver the Last Judgment as an impartial judge and shall make an end to the earth and shall return the dominion previously entrusted to him by his father, so that God alone shall be all in all.[49]

This relief is the only instance of derivation from Heemskerck's cycle of the Vicissitudes of Human Affairs that I have come across in England.

Returning to the overmantel, the supporting cast of figures and smaller scenes is also derived from con-

tinental prints. Above the panel appear the Four Parts of the World (Fig. 321), based on well-known engravings by Adriaen Collaert after designs by Maarten de Vos (Fig. 323). Flanking the overmantel relief are figures – two on either side – of four of the Five Senses. From left to right these are Taste, Smell, Sight and Hearing. They have the true *hauteur* of the Antwerp specimen and display such a convincing *contrapposto* that it seems difficult to believe that they were (I am certain) adapted from figures that were shown seated in the original prints. The change from seated to standing was necessary for them to substitute for columns. The prints were designed by Maarten de Vos and engraved by Adriaen Collaert (Fig. 324).[50] There is strong supporting evidence that this is the correct interpretation. Beneath the relief panel, the frieze of the chimneypiece itself includes four horizontal panels carved with biblical subjects, Christ's feet anointed by Mary Magdalene (Fig. 322), Christ healing a blind man, Christ multiplying the loaves and fishes, and John the Baptist preaching in the wilderness. What can this disparate group of subjects add up to?

With the help of prints the answer is simple: the Five Senses. In his designs, Maarten de Vos reworked the sixteenth-century formula, in which the Senses were depicted as female figures with standard attributes, introducing a supplementary idea in the

form of biblical scenes in the background introduced as 'a moralising exegesis to the main figure'. Five scenes from the story of Adam and Eve, with five from the life of Christ form the old device of types and anti-types. The carver of the Chipchase chimneypiece chose the New Testament scenes, omitting both the main figures and the Old Testament stories. These scenes were taken from the very same suite from which, it is argued here, he adapted the caryatid figures of the Senses. The conclusion must be that the carver had but a limited stock of prints available, and was forced to make the maximum use of those he did possess, winning two groups of figure subjects from a single resource. The chimneypiece is an admirable piece of make-do-and-mend.

The date of the Chipchase chimneypiece must be in the 1630s, for there is a very similar chimneypiece with overmantel in the Merchant Adventurers' Hall in the Guildhall at Newcastle-upon-Tyne, which is dated 1636 (Fig. 325).[51] The history of the Guildhall is complicated and work done there during the seventeenth century was re-set in alterations during the nineteenth. The Merchant Adventurers' Hall was itself rebuilt between 1823 and 1825 and the chimneypiece was certainly re-arranged or rebuilt at this time. Biblical scenes of Mary Magdalene (Fig. 326), Christ and John the Baptist are identical to those now at Chipchase; they appear in precisely equivalent

325 Guildhall, Newcastle-upon-Tyne, chimneypiece and overmantel in the Merchant Adventurers' Hall, 1636.

positions and derive from the same suite of prints after Maarten de Vos. It seems highly probable that standing figures personifying the Senses have been lost. Additionally, blocks on which we would expect to find subsidiary figures are left plain, and the main reliefs lack the heavily-moulded frames of other Newcastle overmantels.

The large reliefs in the Guildhall overmantel depict the Judgement of Solomon and the Miraculous Draught of Fishes (Figs 327, 328). These derive from designs by another Flemish artist, Sir Peter Paul Rubens, a fact which was known in 1842 but has been lost sight of since.[52] The prints were engraved by two brothers who specialised in reproducing the master's work, *The Judgement of Solomon* by Boetius Adam à Bolswert (Fig. 329), and *The Miraculous Draught of Fishes* by Schelte à Bolswert (Fig. 330). This is an unusual though not entirely unparalleled instance of the use of prints after Rubens in English architecture and decoration (see pp.121–3).

The frieze above these panels has horizontal reliefs depicting the Planetary Deities, figures seated in wheeled cars drawn by a variety of birds and beasts. There are seven over the chimneypiece and a further thirty-four in the frieze around the rest of the room. From left to right on the overmantel are Saturn, Jupiter, Mercury, the Sun, Venus, Mars, and Mercury again (Fig. 331).

The Planetary Deities were a popular subject in sixteenth-century Europe and there is a well-known suite of woodcuts dated 1531 usually attributed to Hans Sebald Beham or Georg Pencz, and another (based on them) engraved by Herman Jansz. Muller after designs by Maarten van Heemskerck.[53] However, the Newcastle panels were actually derived from one of two rather similar suites designed by Maarten

326 Guildhall, Newcastle-upon-Tyne, detail of the overmantel with panel depicting Christ's Feet Anointed by Mary Magdalene.

194

327 Guildhall, Newcastle-upon-Tyne, overmantel panel showing the Judgement of Solomon.

328 Guildhall, Newcastle-upon-Tyne, overmantel panel showing the Miraculous Draught of Fishes.

329 Boetius Adam à Bolswert after Peter Paul Rubens, *The Judgement of Solomon*. Victoria and Albert Museum, London.

330 Schelte à Bolswert after Peter Paul Rubens, *The Miraculous Draught of Fishes*. Victoria and Albert Museum, London.

331 Guildhall, Newcastle-upon-Tyne, overmantel, frieze with Mercury (right).

332 Crispijn de Passe the elder after Maarten de Vos, Mercury, from *The Planetary Deities*. British Museum, London.

de Vos, the set engraved by Crispijn de Passe the elder (Fig. 332).[54] The Newcastle carver understandably omitted the 'children' of the planets who appear, engaged in appropriate activities, in the lower part of the de Vos designs, but he reproduced the Planets in their cars very accurately. Two features of these Planets are noteworthy. The first is the omission of

the Moon. As she is also absent from the remainder of the frieze panels around the room (which appear to be in every way consistent with those in the overmantel and so must be original) it must be assumed that the carver had an incomplete set of prints, including six of the Planetary Deities but lacking Luna. Secondly, they do not appear in the traditional order starting with the Moon which occupies the sphere nearest Earth and moving outwards through Mercury, Venus, the Sun, Mars, Jupiter to Saturn, furthest from Earth: this is additional evidence that the set was rearranged, presumably in the rebuilding of the room in the 1820s.

Still more evidence of this is provided by the blocks flanking the fireplace, which have cartouches carved with figures representing Aqua, water, on the left and Terra, earth, on the right (Fig. 333). These were adapted from the title-print from the same suite (Fig. 334), in which the artist – in this case probably Crispijn de Passe rather than Maarten de Vos[55] – demonstrated Man's position in the cosmos according to Plato's Golden Chain. In this scheme Man occupies the region immediately below the Moon, linked both to the lower orders of animals, plants and minerals, and to the Four Elements, all of which he is able to influence. This suggests that the corresponding figures of Ignis, fire, and Aer, air, were lost when the chimneypiece was rebuilt.

Before considering who this exceptionally able Newcastle-based carver might have been, two possible outlying examples of his work should be examined. The first is suggested by the craftsman's rare ability to transform his original. As seen, he adapted the seated figures of de Vos's Five Senses to produce standing figures, whilst retaining some of the subsidiary figures for separate panels. This is precisely what the carver of the newel posts at Thame Abbey in Oxfordshire had done (p.113) and the sources were again prints after de Vos.

The second instance is suggested by a presentational similarity and the use of a common source. This is the staircase from Slaugham Place in Sussex which now survives in Lewes Town Hall, a building which dates only from 1893. Its newel posts are carved with five groups of figures, neatly labelled as in some of the Newcastle work: Classical gods and goddesses, the Five Senses, the Four Elements, three of the Four Parts of the World, and four miscellaneous Virtues.[56] Some of the rectangular panels also have musical and military trophies. As at Burton Agnes and in the Newcastle group of overmantels, one of the sources is Philips Galle's *Prosopographia*, which certainly supplied the figures of three of the Four Parts of the World (from which America was omitted, probably because the set was incomplete) as well as those of Constantia, Experientia (Fig. 335, see Fig. 287), Justitia and Vic-

toria. The gods and goddesses were copied from Philips Galle's set, *De Deis Gentium Imagines Aliquot Iconicae . . .* , published in Antwerp in 1581 (Figs 337, 339).[57] For the Elements the carver selected the set designed, engraved and published by Adriaen Collaert, illustrating couplets by Cornelis Kilian (Cornelius Kilianus): these he adapted from their oval format, simplifying their detail (Figs 336, 338). The source used for the Senses remains to be identified.

So rare are instances of the use of Galle's *Prosopographia* (which, published around 1590,[58] conveniently provides a *terminus ante quem* for the Slaugham carving) that it seems likely that the staircase and the north-eastern work are related by means of the complex web of patronage that existed during the period, in which one patron recommended either printed material or actual craftsmen to another. The latter is certainly possible here. The staircase was probably part of the alterations made to the original

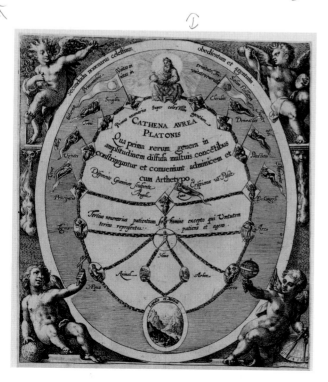

house (which had been built by Richard Covert before 1579)[59] by the mason and surveyor John Thorpe for Covert's son Walter (1543–1631) sometime after he was knighted in 1591: a date in the last decade of the sixteenth century or the first of the seventeenth would accord well with the style of the staircase and with its unusual source material.

We are not quite finished with Newcastle even now, for the very remarkable decoration of a house in The Close should be considered.[60] Until the nineteenth century when one side was demolished for the High Level Bridge, The Close was a narrow street with the tall houses of merchants facing each other across it. This house is one of the few survivors and though the fabric is earlier its decoration dates from the first quarter of the seventeenth century. Not just one but two long rooms, on the first and second floors, have close-set plastered beams 'with Renaissance decoration (Fig. 344), in a style reminiscent of Scottish painted ceilings of the sixteenth century. The sides have quasi-classical mouldings, the soffits a variety of repeated motifs, with pairs of herons, thistles, flowers and arabesque patterns filling the surfaces.'[61] The astonishing thing about this building is that its decoration derives from a suite of engravings apparently used nowhere else in England. These are engravings after designs by the Nuremberg engraver and silversmith Theodor Bang, first published in 1601.[62] There are four major patterns of decoration used, two on the ceiling itself and two on the underside of the beams; these alternate, and I have identified three as copies from Theodor Bang. The derivation is absolutely unmistakable, for the relationship between the plasterwork and the prints used is extremely close. Easiest to recognise are aquiline birds with their heads protruding through splits in a curved strapwork element in an otherwise vegetal arabesque (Figs 340, 341). The pairs of herons, each attacking the other, derive from another plate in the series (Figs 342, 343), and a narrow border on a third print supplied the other identifiable element.

It is all very odd, for there is virtually no contemporary work in England that depends on German prints of this date. The explanation must be that the moulds were carved in wood by the astonishingly cosmopolitan carver whose work we have been following through these pages. The use of Theodor Bang invites the question as to whether his nationality might have been German rather than Flemish: Newcastle certainly had a northern focus to its trade at this date. It must also be significant that, later in the seventeenth century, Newcastle silversmiths (and their York contemporaries) produced a distinctive form of tankard closely resembling Scandinavian and Russian models.

In these overmantels, perhaps in the Thame newels

TERRA *parens, qua non elementum est firmius vllum,*   *Fert gramen, flores, lætas fert denique fruges,*
In media mundi parte locata manet.   *Et reliqua vnde animans viuere quodqʒ queat.*

Adriæn Collaert inuent. sculp. et excud.   *Corn. Kd Duffl.*

CVPIDO   19.
Fusus hic veneris, facibus telisqʒ Cupido
Instructus, vexat pectora nostra Deus.

338 (*above left*) Adriaen Collaert, Terra, from *The Elements*. Warburg Institute, London.

335–7 (*top row*) Lewes Town Hall, Sussex, staircase from Slaugham Place: (*left*) Experientia, early seventeenth century; (*centre*) Terra, and (*right*) Cupido, both early seventeenth century.

339 (*above right*) Philips Galle, Cupido, from *De Deis Gentium Imagines Aliquot Iconicae . . .* (Antwerp, 1581). Victoria and Albert Museum, London.

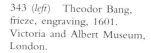

340 (*far left*) Nos 28–30 The Close, Newcastle-upon-Tyne, detail of the ceiling.

342 (*left*) Nos 28–30 The Close, Newcastle-upon-Tyne, detail of the ceiling.

341 (*below left*) Theodor Bang, frieze, engraving, 1601. Victoria and Albert Museum, London.

343 (*left*) Theodor Bang, frieze, engraving, 1601. Victoria and Albert Museum, London.

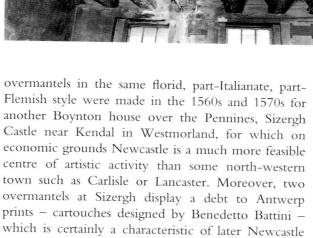

(see Figs 163, 164, 166, 167), the Slaugham staircase and the moulded plaster ceiling, there is a canon of work executed in Newcastle by a carver both exceptionally able and unusually conversant with Netherlandish prints of an allegorical nature. It is frustrating that he remains anonymous. The wood-workers of Newcastle became united in 1579 under the title 'House Carpenters' Company' which received incorporation three years later.[63] As a result of 'great debates, quarellings, malice and strife', the joiners separated from the carpenters and established the incorporated 'Company of Joiners of Newcastle-upon-Tyne' in 1589. However, the lists of joiners who, having completed their apprenticeships, became freemen of the town appear to survive only from 1617, by which time the work at Burton Agnes, at least, was presumably complete.[64] A notable feature of their constitution was that no Scot or alien was to be admitted as an apprentice. Whether a Flemish or German carver could therefore have had a workshop in the town is debatable.

How did Sir Henry Griffiths of Burton Agnes come to employ this Newcastle-based carver? A likely answer is that Griffiths had him recommended by a neighbour, in which case Sir Thomas Boynton of Barmston, High Sheriff of Yorkshire in 1576, is a strong candidate, or his son Sir Francis, who became a fellow-member of the Council of the North in 1602. Sir Thomas's painted wood overmantel (subsequently superimposed above the indigenous overmantel in the hall at Burton Agnes) would therefore have been made in Newcastle rather than somewhere like York – perhaps by an earlier carver – between 1573 and Sir Thomas's death in 1581. Lending weight to this idea is the fact that several overmantels in the same florid, part–Italianate, part–Flemish style were made in the 1560s and 1570s for another Boynton house over the Pennines, Sizergh Castle near Kendal in Westmorland, for which on economic grounds Newcastle is a much more feasible centre of artistic activity than some north-western town such as Carlisle or Lancaster. Moreover, two overmantels at Sizergh display a debt to Antwerp prints – cartouches designed by Benedetto Battini – which is certainly a characteristic of later Newcastle work.[65]

This is pure speculation, but at Levens Hall nearby there is undoubted Newcastle-type carved decoration of slightly later date in the form of a chimneypiece and overmantel carved with characteristic *rinceaux* and

344 Nos 28–30 The Close, Newcastle-upon-Tyne, general view of the ceiling, first quarter of the seventeenth century.

199

1595 and carved with a cartouche copied from a rarely-used suite designed by Vredeman,[66] is also likely to have been executed there.

And what of the work, some of it just beyond the later limit of the period covered here, commissioned by John Cosin from the time he was chaplain to Bishop Neile of Durham (1623), vicar of Elwick (1624) or rector of Brancepeth (1626)? While combining Gothic-revival forms with decoration strongly continental in style – and recalling designs by Dietterlin and his contemporaries – it displays no precise debt to any actual prints.[67] The carvers – like his masons and glaziers – were apparently all local men, mostly from Durham or Bishop Auckland. For instance, Cosin's joiner in the 1630s was a man named Robert Barker.[68] What his relationship was to the outstanding Newcastle-based carver who worked at Burton Agnes is, at present, anyone's guess, although it is known that in 1633 when church-wardens from All Saints, Newcastle-upon-Tyne, travelled to see Cosin's unfinished furnishing work at Brancepeth they took joiners with them. More-over, these joiners may, on their return to Newcastle, have been responsible for Cosin-style pews installed in the church of St Nicholas (now the Cathedral) in 1635, which alas do not survive.[69]

What is certain, however, is that Cosin's pre-Civil War woodwork, though representing the same desire for the 'beauty of holiness' promoted by Laud and his follower Bishop Neile, is stylistically dissimilar from the fashionable woodwork being produced in and around London at the end of the period. Late-Mannerist in character and to some extent reflecting contemporary Antwerp patterns popularised by Paul Vredeman de Vries's *Verscheyden Schrynwerck* of 1630, London examples include Robert Lynton's 1624 hall screen at Lincoln's Inn (which has, besides fashionable perspective arches, oval frames with brackets at the cardinal points, and much use of raised mouldings and pseudo-architectural blocks), Adam Browne's 1629 overmantel in the Jerusalem Chamber at Westminster Abbey and his screen in Laud's Chapel in Lambeth Palace (1633).[70] Examples may also be found in numerous Oxford colleges and in churches in East Anglia and elsewhere.[71] The copying of a plate from J.J. Ebelmann's 1598 suite (see p.30) on the panel of a cabinet made in the 1630s for William Laud while Bishop of London may follow trends in other media which suggest a slight but perceptible increase in the use of German prints at the beginning of the seventeenth century; but in furniture it is unparalleled (except in a related group) in England.

345 Levens Hall, Westmorland, overmantel, late sixteenth or early seventeenth century.

with numerous allegorical figures (Fig. 345). These are identified for the observer rather as the decoration at Burton Agnes, this time in four lines of verse beneath:

> Thus the Five Senses stand Portraited Here,
> The Elements Foure and Seasons of the Yeare,
> Samson supports one side as in rage,
> the other Heracles in Like Equipage.

If Newcastle was indeed the main northern centre of craftsmanship, another overmantel at Levens, dated

Chapter 11

METALWORK

Goldsmiths in sixteenth-century England succeeded in producing fashionable continental-style Mannerist objects without apparently making much use of actual prints. The picture may, however, be distorted by the fact that plate is more subject than any other artistic commodity to economic fluctuations and political instability because the metal (but not of course the fashion) could be turned back into coin in times of need. This process is reflected in the amounts of plate melted during the Civil War, and accounts for the relative scarcity of surviving examples of Elizabethan and Jacobean precious metalwork.[1]

Many goldsmiths who worked in England were themselves foreigners who fled from religious persecution on the Continent, particularly during the 1560s and 1570s: it has been noted that during the reign of Elizabeth a hundred and fifty Dutch, Flemish and German goldsmiths were working in London, while in her reign and that of her successor James I there were no fewer than sixty-three French goldsmiths in the capital.[2] The majority of foreigners, however, came (like the sources used in England during these two reigns) from Antwerp, so it is not surprising to find Netherlandish-style pieces with London marks.

Philippa Glanville has given the fullest account so far of the patterns and designs that influenced English silver during the period, but the difficulty of relating chased or engraved decoration to particular prints remains.[3] Instances are, with the exception of one silver-engraver's work (discussed below), isolated. The influence in general terms of prints by Nicoletto da Modena and Hans Burgkmair has been remarked upon, as well as the use for silver of various types of borders included in a publication of Hans Sebald Beham.[4] Again, the cups, jugs and vases designed by Cornelis Floris and Jan Vredeman de Vries and Balthasar van den Bos (Sylvius) may have exerted some non-specific influence, while the arabesques published by the Frenchman Thomas Geminus in London in 1548 (arabesques themselves derived from those of Francesco Pellegrino and Peter Flötner) may have resulted in the simplified versions that adorn many a rim, border or band. In one early case, a complex leaf-scroll published by Daniel Hopfer was adopted for the Gatcombe Cup (1540);[5] the Howard Grace Cup has cast Renaissance motifs derived from woodcuts by Hans Burgkmair and there are Elizabethan salts chased after plaquettes by Peter Flötner.[6] Another spectacular salt bearing the arms of the Vyvyan family of Trelowarren House, near Helston in Cornwall, has *verre églomisé* panels with emblems copied from Claude Paradin and Geffrey Whitney, together with four of the Nine Worthies, perhaps adapted from the set after Maarten van Heemskerck.[7] Some pieces, like the Simon Gibbon Salt belonging to the Goldsmiths' Company and Dr Butler's Tankard at Clare College, Cambridge, have Mannerist cartouches which recall those of Jacob Floris.[8] It has regrettably proved impossible to trace the prints adapted for scenes in the life of David on the standing cup (1565–6) belonging to the church of St Peter Mancroft in Norwich, and on the body of the coconut cup (1577–8) belonging to the Art Institute of Chicago.[9]

However, it has sometimes been possible to pin down the source of particular pieces of decoration. One instance is the print depicting Phisique by Etienne Delaune, which was copied for the replacement body of what had been an ostrich-egg or coconut cup made for Richard Goodricke in London in 1563–4 (Figs 346, 347).[10]

The only concerted use of continental prints in the decoration of English silver was made by the foreign engraver known only by his initials P over M, who was responsible for a substantial group of pieces made during the 1560s and 1570s. They have been extensively studied and some of the prints identified.[11]

The engraver's P over M monogram appears on a set of twelve plates, bearing the maker's mark of Richard Bampton and assayed in 1567–8, engraved with the Labours of Hercules after prints by Heinrich Aldegrever (1502–c.1558);[12] on a second set of plates probably made in London between 1565 and 1570 (though marked in Strasbourg) and engraved with Old Testament subjects after Bernard Salomon; and on a ewer and rosewater bowl (Fig. 348), with the maker's mark of a pick or scythe and the date-letter for 1567–8, engraved with Old Testament scenes,

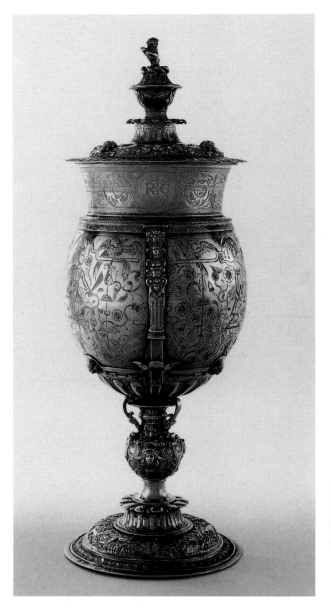

again after Bernard Salomon, and with royal portraits
after Gyles Godet's *Genealogie of Kynges* published in
London in 1562/3.[13]

Unsigned, but perhaps by the same craftsman, is a
set of twelve plates with the maker's mark of Roger
Flynt (1568–9, one 1569–70) engraved with the
parable of the Prodigal Son;[14] another ewer and
rosewater-dish bearing the maker's mark BI in an oval
(1575–6), together with the arms of two German
families, engraved with Old Testament scenes after
Virgil Solis (ewer) and Bernard Salomon (basin): from
the etched grounds these may have been decorated in
Germany.[15] Finally there is a set of six spice bowls
bearing the maker's mark of Roger Flynt (1573–4),
engraved with scenes from the life of Abraham and
with sea monsters.[16]

The engraver P over M showed himself capable

of expanding Salomon's compositions to fit a different
format, and this ability to invent and adapt is even
more apparent in the set of plates depicting the
parable of the Prodigal Son (Fig. 352). Several sets of
prints illustrating this popular subject were available
during the sixteenth century and from one of these –
by Hans Sebald Beham – P over M adapted at least
two of his scenes, the Prodigal Son with the Swine, in
which the pigs but not the standing figure were
copied faithfully, and the Return of the Prodigal Son
(Fig. 349); he may also have had the print depicting
the Prodigal Son Wasting his Fortune, for two of the
figures reappear on the silver plate. The nine remaining silver plates gave him greater difficulty, for no
Prodigal Son suite offered as many as twelve different
scenes. So the engraver turned to Etienne Delaune,
adapting two scenes from Delaune's illustrations of
the story of Abraham for the Prodigal Son Receiving
his Inheritance, and for the feast with which the
Prodigal's father celebrated his return (Figs 350,
351).[17]

So P over M had Delaune's set of the story of
Abraham. Why then, if it was he who, only five years
later, engraved the bowls illustrating this very story,
did he not use the same engravings? Or Salomon's
woodcuts, or those of Virgil Solis which he had used
on other commissions? As Glanville suggested, it was
probably a different engraver who decorated these
bowls. The sources of the scenes, however, have

348   Ewer and rosewater bowl, London 1567–8, engraved by a craftsman with the initials P over M with Old Testament scenes after Bernard Salomon, and with royal portraits after Gyles Godet's *Genealogie of Kynges* (London, 1562/3). Museum of Fine Arts, Boston, Mass.

349 Hans Sebald Beham, the Return of the Prodigal Son from *The Parable of the Prodigal Son*. British Museum, London.

350 Etienne Delaune, scene from the Story of Abraham. British Museum, London.

351 Etienne Delaune, scene from the Story of Abraham. British Museum, London.

← ↑ q.349 ↑ q.351

q 350

proved highly elusive and all that can be said is that more than one set of prints was involved – and all may have been allegorical rather than biblical. The one that I have managed to identify is the Sacrifice of Isaac which derives from an incident in the background of a print illustrating the Triumph of Isaac, the second in the 1559 set entitled *The Triumph of Patience* engraved by Dirck Coornhert after Maarten van Heemskerck (see Figs 129, 130).

Right at the end of the period – indeed, perhaps a little after the end – comes a silver-mounted bookcover enclosing a copy of the Puritan divine John Downame's *A Briefe Concordance to the Bible* (London,

1631). It is unmarked but may date from the 1630s or 1640s.[18] In the corner of each pierced rectangular plaque is an oval engraved with the Seven Virtues (with the addition of Patience), of which the three Theological Virtues – Faith, Hope and Charity – were adapted from Jacob Matham's engravings after Hendrick Goltzius (see Fig. 296).

These are small pickings from what is a surprising quantity of continental-style silver of the period: further concentrated work is clearly needed if any other instances of precise derivation from print sources are to be identified.

352 Twelve plates, maker's mark of Roger Flynt, London 1568–9 (one 1569–70), engraved by P over M with scenes from the parable of the Prodigal Son. His Grace the Duke of Buccleuch.

Chapter 12

PAINTING

Being one of what are now known as the Fine Arts, paintings have been subjected to continuous art-historical scrutiny over many years. This scrutiny has often involved identification of source material so that, in this respect, there are far fewer pickings for today's researcher of paintings – even of the sixteenth century – than there are in the decorative arts. However, recent discoveries show that there is still room for progress, particularly if decorative paintings on cloths or plastered walls, and glass painting, are not excluded from consideration. Their artists' design process was, after all, no different from that of painters on panel or canvas.

Historically there had been during the fifteenth century a trade demarcation between the painters, who worked with oil and varnish, and the stainers, who worked with water and size. However, in 1502 in London their companies amalgamated to form the powerful Company of Painter-Stainers. The lack of differentiation may have been one reason why writers, at least those who compiled inventories, in the sixteenth century made little distinction between paintings on canvas and those on cloth. As Susan Foister has pointed out:

> Use of words sometimes makes it difficult to distinguish between paintings and sculptures, and it can be hard to decide, from written evidence only, when a painted cloth becomes a picture in the modern sense. At the beginning of the sixteenth century it was common for a room to be hung with a variety of painted hangings of different sizes; only towards the end of the century do we encounter the room with pictures neatly defined by being hung in frames, and even then coloured hangings were still used.[1]

During the first half of the century Holbein worked both as a portraitist and as a decorative painter and similarly, a hundred years later, we find Rowland Buckett executing what today would be called easel paintings as well as decorative painting. Holbein certainly, and Buckett probably, used continental prints.[2] However, only in the field of decorative and allegorical painting did artists generally employ more than one or two prints for inspiration.

Artists often borrowed no more than a small detail from a print such as the grotesque masks in Gerlach Flicke's portrait of Thomas Cranmer (pp.34–5) but occasionally a print was copied almost in its entirety: a Fontainebleau engraving for the background of Guillim Scrots's portrait of the Earl of Surrey, architectural and perspective designs by Vredeman de Vries for Hans Eworth's portrait of Henry Lord Darnley and Charles Stuart, and Isaac Oliver's *Unknown Melancholy Man* (pp.78–9, 80).[3] Royal portraits in which allegories of kingship play such a large part seem to have been specially susceptible to the influence of continental prints. The prime example is the complex 'Sieve' portrait of Queen Elizabeth in the Pinacoteca in Siena, which Roy Strong has attributed to Cornelis Ketel,[4] with its borrowings from engravings by Marcantonio Raimondi. During the early seventeenth century the artist Robert Peake based a portrait of Henry, Prince of Wales, which he painted between 1604 and 1610, on a print of Torquatus Manlius by Hendrick Goltzius.[5] These borrowings are hardly surprising in view of the fact that most of the artists were not native-born Englishmen but were foreigners who had not been away from their own countries for many years.

The same is true of more obviously allegorical pictures of which a sizeable number appear to date from the period around 1570, years which were so crucial for the future of Protestantism in England. As already noted on page 97, Margaret Aston discovered that the allegorical picture *Edward VI and the Pope* depends on two engravings after Maarten van Heemskerck, and an equally intriguing painting dated 1570 (now at Hardwick Hall) depends on at least two woodcuts (see pp.250–1). Other more or less contemporary allegorical paintings include the celebrated *Queen Elizabeth I and the Three Goddesses* dated 1569, the *Allegory of the Tudor Succession*, perhaps painted by Lucas de Heere in 1572, and de Heere's *The Sleeping Arts in Wartime*: all are composed of figures which, had they been painted by an English artist rather than

353 (*facing page*) British School. *Allegory with the Story of Phaethon*. Detail of Fig. 356.

207

tyrdom of the Followers of Christ, from the Acts of the Apostles (Fig. 355). The correspondence is incontrovertible: the unknown painter copied the building block by block from the engraving, only altering the perspective to make it less dominating, and peopling the distinctive windows with onlookers. This instance of dependence serves as another warning to art historians not to identify too readily the scenes in the backgrounds of paintings as actual buildings in the English landscape. It also demonstrates how little concern the painter had for the subject-matter of his source, adapting a print showing acts of brutality for the celebration of a happy and propitious event.

The *Procession Portrait of Queen Elizabeth* is very much a courtly painting in which it does come not come as a great surprise to find the artist employing a continental print for an up-to-the-minute piece of architecture. But how far did prints penetrate into the workshops of lesser artists, especially in the provinces? If the example of masons, plasterers and joiners is anything to go by, there is no reason they should not have done so, but there has been relatively little evidence until recently.

In 1964 the Walker Art Gallery in Liverpool bought the *Allegory with the Story of Phaethon* (Fig. 356), a panel perhaps executed for a room at Grafton Hall, Malpas, Cheshire, a house built around 1609. This painting has long been suspected of dependence on prints though no precise source has hitherto been found. It tells the story in a series of episodes from left to right: Clymene informs her son Phaethon that his father is Sol; Phaethon asks him to let him drive the

354 George Vertue, engraving of *The Procession Portrait of Queen Elizabeth I* (London, 1742). Courtesy of John Chichester Constable Esq.

355 Johannes Sadeler I after Maarten de Vos, the Scourging of the Apostles, from *The Martyrdom of the Followers of Christ*, 1580. Rijksmuseum-Stichting, Amsterdam.

357 (*facing page bottom*) Karel van Mallery after Maarten de Vos, Wealth Brings Forth Pride, from *The Cycle of the Vicissitudes of Human Affairs (Circulus vicissitudinis rerum humanarum).* Museum Boijmans Van Beuningen, Rotterdam.

a foreigner, would have seemed certain to depend on prints.[6]

A particularly tantalising example of an artist's possible use of one or more continental prints is the much-discussed *Procession Portrait of Queen Elizabeth I* which hangs at Sherborne Castle in Dorset. Roy Strong called it one of the greatest visual mysteries of the Elizabethan age, and there is much about the painting that remains obscure. Even the event it commemorates is uncertain. George Vertue in the eighteenth century described it as 'The Royal Procession of Queen Elizabeth I to Visit the Right Honble. Henry Carey Lord Hunsdon' in 1571 (Fig. 354): but shortly before he died he concluded that the event was the marriage of Henry, Lord Herbert, and Lady Anne Russell at Blackfriars on 16 June 1600. It is has always seemed possible that the procession in the foreground and, more particularly, the buildings in the middle and background were derived from continental prints. Efforts have indeed been made to link the procession to a tradition of prints representing royal power, a tradition which starts with Hans Burgkmair's woodcut, *The King of Cochin*; but no precise source has ever been found. However, it can now be shown that the Netherlandish-looking building that dominates the right-hand middleground of the composition has an exact continental counterpart in an engraving by Johannes Sadeler I after Maarten de Vos. Published in 1580, this depicts the Scourging of the Apostles, from the five-print series, *The Mar-*

ET CONVOCANTES APOSTOLOS, CÆSIS DENVNTIAVERVNT NE LOQVERENTVR IN NOMINE IESV.

chariot of the son; driving out of control past the signs of the zodiac he causes fires on earth; Zeus strikes him with a thunderbolt and he falls into the River Eridanus; he is buried by Naiads. Maarten de Vos designed a print series illustrating this story, but the painter must have used a different set, still unidentified. However, in the lower part of the painting, towards the left-hand side, there appears a Renaissance castle, each of whose corner towers is topped by a pedimented banqueting house. The castle is set in a knot garden with a bower in which people are seated. Behind the bower there is what seems to be an elaborate tree house with a topiaried leaf canopy. The whole of this little composition is far too fantastic to be the original invention of an artist as naïve as the painter of this picture, and the answer is that it was copied straight from a print. This is one of the set of eight (including the title print) designed by Maarten de Vos entitled *Circulus vicissitudinis rerum humanarum* published by Philips Galle. The cycle depicts the endless progression from wealth to pride, from pride to envy, and then successively to war, poverty, humility, peace and back to wealth. In the first print, *Wealth Brings Forth Pride* (engraved by Karel van Mallery, Fig. 357), the castle and its setting appear to the right of the figure. This panel painting is the only evidence to date that this important moralistic print series was known in England.[7]

Celebrated wall paintings were commissioned by Sir Thomas Smith for Hill Hall near Theydon Mount in Essex – the house he built between 1557 and 1575.[8] Educated at Cambridge, later lecturing there and

eventually becoming Vice Chancellor, Smith travelled to Paris during the 1540s, Orléans (where the architect Jacques Androuet Ducerceau was to publish a suite of prints of Triumphal Arches in 1549) and Padua. Entering politics he served the Protector Somerset and presumably became involved, like Sir William Sharington and Sir John Thynne, in the building of

356 British School, *Allegory with the Story of Phaethon*, oil on panel, perhaps executed for a room at Grafton Hall, Malpas, Cheshire, *c*.1609. National Museums and Galleries on Merseyside.

DIVITIÆ.

Diuitijs *oritur plerunque* Superbia: *cum sit*
Flixarum paucis cognitus vsus opum.

M. de Vos inuenit.   *Carol. de Mallery sculp.*   *Phls Galle excud.*

Somerset House in the fashionable French style. His own house, particularly in the work undertaken from 1568–9, was also mainly French in architectural and decorative character.[9] The cycle of paintings illustrating scenes from the life of King Hezekiah, executed c.1570, depends principally on compositions by Bernard Salomon in the Protestant *La Sainte Bible en François* (Lyons, 1554), a copy of which was certainly in Smith's library in 1566.[10] The Cupid and Psyche wall paintings, on the other hand, are literal copies from Italian sources, engravings by the Master of the Die and Agostino Veneziano after designs by Michiel Coxie. The diametrically different compositional methods suggest that these two series may have been the work of different artists, or at least were executed at different times. F.W. Reader has pointed out that the Cupid and Psyche paintings, with their tapestry-like borders, are very similar to painted cloths such as those painted for the chapel at Hardwick.

A man who enjoyed the same educational and social background as Sir Thomas Smith was Charles Seckford, the assumed author of a series of lost allegorical pictures now known through a group of manuscript programmes in the Sloane Collection of the British Library. These also shed a flood of light onto the vexed question of the relationship between patron and artist.[11] Charles Seckford – a Cambridge man who was evidently a considerable scholar besides having powerful contacts at the court of Elizabeth I – is seen devising paintings of the most complex nature, allegories of the Tempest, of the Epicure, of Fortuna, of Pluto, of Justitia–Injustitia; they include more than one drawing. The paintings, at least one of which seems to have been carried out, would have resembled the elaborate compositions devised for engraving as titlepages of books. The patron, who must have owned or had access to a considerable library, can be observed instructing his artist to go to the illustrations in Gesner for animals, Matthioli for plants, Alciati and Cartari for mythological personages;[12] but these four visual sources are far outweighed by standard classical authors and contemporary commentaries and scientific textbooks which number approaching a hundred. These manuscripts provide powerful evidence of the taste for ingenious and sophisticated allegories, of a predominantly literary kind, amongst the social and intellectual élite in sixteenth-century England.

Much more straightforward from the point of view of source material is a set of Elizabethan decorative wall paintings that survive in the church of St Mary, Burton Latimer in Northamptonshire. These are remarkable for having been painted in the first place, at a time when all the 'ornaments of the church' – 'lights, incense, holy water, gay and rich cloths and garments, crosses, images, paintings, bells, organs, merry songs, steeples, gay carved roofs with painted windows' – were obnoxious to the opponents of imagery on the grounds that they served idolatry.[13] On the north aisle wall are scenes of the life and martyrdom of St Catherine which date from the fourteenth century, but the Elizabethan paintings appear in the spandrels of the nave arches (Fig. 358). They take the form of individual figures personifying the Twelve Tribes of Israel or the Twelve Patriarchs, each set in a strapwork cartouche of decidedly Netherlandish character. The subject is certainly a rare survival today,[14] although it may have been relatively popular at the time. That they were allowed at all may be explained by the choice of book from which these figures were copied. They originate in a mid-sixteenth-century book, *De testamenten der twalf patriarchen Jacobs kinderen*, published by Joos Lambrecht of Ghent (Fig. 359). He is described as '*lettersteker*' (letter-cutter) and may therefore have designed the woodcuts himself.[15] From a Protestant English point of view, Lambrecht's credentials were excellent: he was always falling foul of the ecclesiastical authorities in the Netherlands for criticising the Pope and the Church, and the *Testamenten* was itself placed on the list of proscribed books in 1570.[16] The strapwork borders derive from none of the editions examined to date[17] and I have searched for some source without success; indeed, they show some misunderstanding of Flemish strapwork cartouches, suggesting that they were devised by the painter himself or designed for him perhaps by a glass painter.

Flemish prints also provided the inspiration for at least two sets of wall paintings at North Mymms Park, a large late-Elizabethan house north of London.[18] In the Marble Hall, paintings covering the upper walls in a wide horizontal zone were derived, as already seen (p.50), from an Italianate grotesque designed and engraved around 1548 by Cornelis Bos. Another set of wall paintings at North Mymms represents the Worthies, eight of whom have been shown to derive from the suite engraved by Herman Muller from drawings by Maarten van Heemskerck (see note 55 on p.306). A third set takes the form of Netherlandish grotesques, including arbours, strapwork and cartouches, but no source has yet come to light for these, which are paralleled in the King Charles I Room at Childerley Hall, Cambridgeshire.[19]

Few houses of the late sixteenth and early seventeenth centuries survive sufficiently unaltered for any coherent overall iconographic programme to be discerned. The decoration of Burton Agnes has already been discussed, while that of the most complete Elizabethan house, Hardwick Hall, will be tackled later (pp.247–95). Otherwise there are tantalising fragments of decorative schemes. One is a single room from Hawstead Hall in Suffolk, known as Lady

Drury's Oratory and deriving most of its painted decoration from a number of emblem books.[20] Although the relationship is not always so close as to be considered 'sibling', the sources the artist consulted seem to include Georgette de Montenay, *Emblemes, ou Devises Chrestiennes* (1571), Paolo Giovio, *Dialogo dell'Imprese Militari et Amorose* (1574), Valeriano *Hieroglyphica . . .* (1586), Geffrey Whitney *A Choice of Emblems* (1586), Joachim Camerarius, *Symbolorum et Emblematum . . . Centuriae* (1590–1604), Claude Paradin, *Heroical Devises* (1591) and Peacham's *Minerva Britanna* (1612).

The Ages of Man and the Virtues seem to be the theme of the decoration of the Great Staircase at Knole (Fig. 360), which was part of the remodelling done by Thomas Sackville, Earl of Dorset, between 1605 and 1608. Apart from the identification of one printed source, the decoration of this staircase has never been fully interpreted. Some more identifications can be offered here, demonstrating a choice of sources rather unusual for this country. In addition, the painter's identity is known. He was probably Paul Isaacson, who was paid for the decoration of the Cartoon Gallery here in 1607, and may previously have painted the hall screen at Greenwich Palace for Queen Elizabeth in 1594. If it was indeed he who was responsible for the Knole staircase he was certainly a versatile artist, able to copy, adapt or invent at will.

From the ground floor upwards the paintings show the Four Ages of Man (Fig. 361), derived from engravings by Crispijn de Passe after Maarten de Vos published in 1596 (Fig. 362). This source has been recognised for many years. Netherlandish strapwork, probably of the painter's own devising, is employed to fill every available wall surface: further up the stairs appear cartouches very freely adapted from Jacob Floris's *Velderhande cierlijcke Compertementen . . .* of 1564. Moving up again, there are paintings of the Five Senses after prints by Pieter de Iode (Figs 363, 364), Virtues Conquering Vices from prints by Johannes Sadeler I after Maarten de Vos published in 1579 (Figs 365, 366); at the top are depictions of other Virtues, after prints by Crispijn de Passe (Figs 367, 368). Beneath these there are grotesques, adapted from a design by Cornelis Floris, published by Hieronymus Cock in 1554 (Figs 369, 370). The wall paintings convey a moral message: vanity, certainly, in the inevitability of death, but the path of virtue as

360 Knole, Kent, Great Staircase, general view from the first floor, c.1605–8.

the means of salvation. An inescapable aspect of the decoration of this staircase is that, while the subject prints chosen were relatively new in 1605–7 and were perhaps supplied by the owner, the ornament prints were half a century old and may have been in Isaacson's stock-in-trade.

The Virtues underlie the most complete series of decorative paintings surviving from Jacobean England, those in the Little Castle at Bolsover, built by Robert and John Smythson for Bess of Hardwick's younger son Sir William Cavendish between c.1612 and c.1621. Although greatly inferior in quality, these paintings are the nearest equivalent to those of the castle of Bučovice near Brno in the Czech Republic.

Wall paintings decorate rooms at every level above ground and the sources of most have been identified by Rosalys Coope.[21] The ante-room has three of the Four Temperaments from engravings by Pieter de Iode after Maarten de Vos, the hall has the Labours of Hercules, after the Italian artist Antonio Tempesta, published in 1608: these represent the triumph of virtue (in the form of Hercules) over the baser instincts of mankind (represented by the beasts). Then follow, in the Pillar Parlour, the Five Senses adapted from engravings by Cornelis Cort after Frans Floris. Christ in Glory, and putti carrying symbols of the Passion (with the date 1619), are the subjects of the paintings in the Heaven Room; the loves of the pagan

361 <u>Knole</u>, Kent, Great Staircase, wall paintings depicting scenes from the Four Ages of Man. *1605-08*

362 (*below*) Crispijn de Passe the elder after <u>Maarten de Vos</u>, Adolescence (Adolescentia Amori), from *The Four Ages of Man, 1596*. Rijksmuseum-Stichting, Amsterdam.

gods and goddesses are depicted in the Elysium Room, the composition and figures deriving mainly from engravings after Primaticcio, the Italian artist working at Fontainebleau in the 1530s and 1540s. The Virtues occupy four lunettes in the Marble Closet and were copied from the suite of United Virtues by Hendrick Goltzius, while the walls of the Star Chamber (painted in 1621) are inhabited by figures from the Old and New Testaments, of whom two derive from prints by Marco Dente after Marcantonio Raimondi. Rosalys Coope has interpreted the cycle as concerning the nature of man and his ability through virtue to overcome his baser nature and progress to a true understanding of God.[22]

Two decades earlier a versatile artist had decorated an organ-clock sent as a gift by Queen Elizabeth on behalf of the Levant Company to the Sultan of Turkey, Mahomet III. The painter was Rowland Buckett and this is his first recorded work, dating from 1599–1600.[23] Not long afterwards he painted the timberwork arch erected by the Dutch community in honour of James I's accession in March 1604. In 1608 he was first employed by Robert Cecil, 1st Earl of Salisbury, at Salisbury House in London, and

213

365 (*above*) Knole, Kent, Great Staircase, wall paintings depicting Virtues Conquering Vices.

363 (*top left*) Pieter de Iode, Auditus (Hearing), from *The Five Senses*. Victoria and Albert Museum, London.

364 (*top right*) Knole, Kent, Great Staircase, wall painting depicting Hearing.

366 (*right*) Johannes Sadeler I after Maarten de Vos, Maiestas, from the series *Virtues Conquering Vices*, 1579. Rijksmuseum-Stichting, Amsterdam.

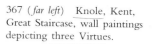

PATIENTIA.

Sis sapiens, et sis patiens, silendo, ferendo;
Perfer et obdura, dolor hic tibi proderit olim.
Et licet immerito patiáre grauissima quæque
Si tamen æquo animo tuleris, eris usque beatus.

367 (*far left*) Knole, Kent, Great Staircase, wall paintings depicting three Virtues.

368 (*left*) Crispijn de Passe the elder, Patientia, from a series of the Virtues. Warburg Institute, London.

369 (*far left*) Knole, Kent, Great Staircase, panel of grotesque ornament.

370 (*left*) Lucas or Johannes Duetecum after Cornelis Floris, cartouche with grotesque ornament, from a series of six enclosing Maxims of the Wise Men of Greece, 1554. Victoria and Albert Museum, London.

the Angel ap[peareth] to the Sheppards for the Chappell at Hatfield . . .' and a variety of decorative painting 'donne in the lawer parte of the Chappell on the wall, and one the sydes of the windowe, they are wrought with figures of the small prophetts and with borders and skrowles gilded about them and very much other work'.[24] More work is also needed to ascertain whether Buckett used continental prints for his painted decoration of the chimneypiece and overmantel in the Governor's Room or Great Chamber of the Charterhouse in London. This is dated 1626, the chimneypiece featuring three Christian Virtues, the overmantel the arms and cipher of Charles I surrounded by spandrels with the Four Evangelists, flanked by figures of Peace and Plenty and coloumns of grotesques incorporating figures of the Apostles; below there are representations of the Annunciation and the Last Supper. Unfortunately this was badly damaged in 1941 and, though restored in 1955–7, the figures and compositions are difficult to make out in detail.

Related in character to Buckett's work at the Charterhouse is the almost exactly contemporary painted decoration of the Kederminster Library in the church at Langley Marish in Buckinghamshire. The structure was apparently ready in 1623 but the fitting up was not complete until 1631. The room is panelled and entirely painted, the frieze with landscapes, the remainder with cartouches (one design after Jacob Floris) and individual figures including the Apostles. The frieze of the chimneypiece has very Germanic-looking grotesques in the style of Lucas Kilian – suggesting that Buckett could have been involved here, too – separated by three masks deriving from the set pirated from Cornelis Floris and extended by the Italian engraver, Adam Scultori.

The overmantel panel is flanked by columns which are painted and gilt (Fig. 371). Their decoration consists of several elements arranged vertically, female figures (possibly the Sibyls) in grotesques, trophies of arms, male figures in architectural compartments. Of these, the male figures, Mars and Mercury, derive from prints by Jacob Matham after Hendrick Goltzius (Fig. 372), and it is likely that all the elements derive from prints.

The panel itself appears to be straightforwardly heraldic, eighteen armorials describing the ancestry of the Kederminster family (but they include the arms of the Harveys who acquired the manor in the late eighteenth century). They are, however, arranged in an oval format, the spandrels having seated figures of the Cardinal Virtues, and they are united by chains. The whole composition may, like the individual components that make up the decoration of the entire room, have been copied or adapted from a particular print. The panel does bear a striking resemblance to

371 Kederminster Library, Langley Marish, Buckinghamshire, overmantel, *c*.1631. The figure of Mars appears at the top of the right-hand column.

the following year began work at Hatfield House in Hertfordshire. His work there included painting another musical instrument, the celebrated Dutch chamber organ bought in 1609, which he decorated with grotesques after prints by Lucas Kilian (see p.32), an appropriate source as Buckett's father had been a German immigrant.

There is every likelihood that Buckett was introduced to the potential of prints by the glass painters working at Hatfield. Further research might prove that he applied his knowledge to other work he did there besides the painted organ-case. This included 'painting two picktures upon cloth, the one is the Angells salutacon to the Virgin Marie and thother is

372 Jacob Matham after Hendrick Goltzius, Mars, from *The Planetary Deities*. Warburg Institute, London.

3. M A R S.

Whitney's *A Choice of Emblemes* (1586), while at Largs in 1638 grotesques designed by Etienne Delaune were copied by the painter J. Stalker (see pp.40–41). It seems likely that prints lie behind the majority of these decorative paintings but the repertoire of source material is certainly very different from that most commonly employed south of the border.

Alexander Seton, Earl of Fyvie and first Earl of Dunfermline, had the boarded ceiling of his gallery at Pinkie Castle, Musselburgh, near Edinburgh, painted with emblems. These derive from a number of sources, amongst which Michael Bath has identified Otto van Veen's *Emblemata Horatiana* (Antwerp, 1607, etc.) and Jean Jacques Boissard's illustrations to Denis Lebey de Batilly's *Emblemata* (Frankfurt, 1596). In England, Lady Bullard has identified the sources of the paintings in the Upper Reading Room of the Bodleian Library in Oxford where there are 202 portraits.[25] She has discovered that these derive mainly from three publications, Boissard's *Imagines L Doctorum vivorum qui bene de studiis literarum mervere* (Antwerp, 1587), Thevet's *Portraits et Vies des hommes Illustres*, and Verheiden's *Praestantium aliquot Theologorum qui Romum antichristum Praecipue oppugnarunt Effigies*. The paintings were executed between 1616 and 1629 by Thomas Knight who subsequently became Master of the Painter-Stainer's Company. Two generations later, John Cosin, Bishop of Durham, had portraits painted for his library which faces on to the green by the castle, and some of these may derive from Theodore de Beze's *Icones id est Verae Imagines* (Geneva, 1580).[26]

Some mention has already been made of painted cloths which were so common in England up to the middle of the seventeenth century and perhaps beyond. They occur in inventories at every level of society but very few now survive. Two are now at Christchurch Mansion in Ipswich and depict the Labours of Hercules (from a source I have yet to identify), four others survive in the chapel at Hardwick and are discussed in some detail later (see pp.275–85). Equally rare survivals are painted leather wall hangings, although these too must have been widespread at the most elevated levels of society. Many of Lord Leicester's thirty-seven sets of hangings inventoried at Kenilworth Castle in 1588 were of leather and most of their subjects were recorded (see p.297). One such set, depicting scenes from the story of Antony and Cleopatra, and thought to be of late seventeenth-century date, survives at Dunster Castle in Somerset, while a set painted with scenes from the story of Esther and Ahasuerus, from prints after Maarten van Heemskerck, was sold from Walsingham Abbey in 1916 (p.97).[27]

Another related medium in which continental prints played a vital part was glass painting. During the

the titlepage of the suite of *The Planetary Deities* engraved by Crispijn de Passe after designs by Maarten de Vos, which supplied some supplementary figures for the carved oak overmantel in the Guildhall in Newcastle (see Figs 333, 334). The panel would then allude to the Neo-Platonic scheme in which all things are bound together in a hierarchy of three levels, the *intellectualis mundus*, the world of angels and saints, the *caelestis mundus*, the heavenly realm of stars and planets, and the *sensibilis mundus*, the material world in which mankind lives. In this system, man can only reach God via the planets and angels, that is, through astrology or faith, and the presence in the painted decoration of the flanking columns of two of the planets suggests that this was indeed in the artist's or the patron's mind.

The Kederminster Library would amply repay further investigation, and the same is true of the numerous painted ceilings in Scotland (which I have been obliged to leave to others to explore systematically). These form a geographically distinct group having closer stylistic links with continental Europe and Scandinavia than with England. Some of the paintings have been traced to their source – those at Culross Abbey, for instance, derive from Geffrey

reign of Elizabeth opportunities had been severely curtailed by a virtual embargo on devotional subjects, so that painted glass tended to be heraldic or chivalric in nature – there are excellent examples at Middle Temple Hall in London (1570), Gilling Castle in Yorkshire (1585), Montacute in Somerset and Stoneleigh in Warwickshire (late sixteenth-century).[28] After the accession of James I, it evidently was possible, without undue danger, for patrons in remoter parts of the country to commission Crucifixion windows, particularly for their private chapels which 'whether aristocratic, collegiate, or royal, were accepted, to some degree, as a law unto themselves'.[29] Michael Archer's invaluable detective work in the neglected area of Jacobean glass has revealed the extent of designers' debts to continental prints and a few paragraphs must be devoted to summarising his discoveries.

Painters have already been mentioned copying prints for the windows of the chapel at Hatfield in 1609–10. There were three craftsmen, the Frenchman Lewys Dolphin (probably anglicised from Louis Dauphin), Martin Benton (Martin van Bentheim) from Emden, and Richard Butler of whose origins nothing is known. Butler was paid for a window depicting scenes from the story of Jonah in both of which the figures of the whale (but nothing else in the composition) were copied from a suite of prints by Hieronymus Wierix after Maarten de Vos.[30] The window depicting Samson and Delilah is stylistically unlike Butler's documented work and may have been painted by one of the other craftsmen. Whoever was responsible copied a print after Maarten van Heemskerck. It could have been Butler: he certainly had a stock of such material for, when he died in 1638, he left to one of his sons, William, 'all my droughtes and patterns that I . . . use for work in and about my . . . occupation of painting of glass'.[31] One of his two windows in the chapel of Lincoln's Inn, London, painted in 1623, depicts Apostles (presumably copied from prints not yet identified) standing on elaborate plinths set with armorial cartouches flanked by figures of the Virtues in niches: the figures derive from prints by Jacob Matham, some following designs by Hendrick Goltzius.[32]

Richard Butler was also employed by Archbishop Laud to repair the glass in the chapel at Lambeth Palace. Although it did not survive the Protestant iconoclasts, Butler's detailed bills are still extant and something of the subject-matter is also recorded in Laud's defence at his trial in 1644.[33] Laud was accused of causing

> these demolished superstitious Pictures in the Glasse windowes to be repaired, furbished, beautified, and made more compleat and accurate with new painted Glasse, than ever before, setting them up againe in fresh lively colours, according to the very Patterne in the great Roman Missall, or Masse Book (which he had diligently noted with his own hand almost in every Page) so as no chappel in Rome could be more Idolatrous, Popish, superstitious in regard of such offensive Pictures, than his at Lambeth . . .

To this Laud replied in spirited terms:

> The Truth is, they [the windows] were all shameful to look on, all diversly patched, like a Poor Beggars Coat. Had they had all white Glass, I had not stirred them . . . And it was utterly mistaken by Mr. *Brown*, that I did repair the Story of those Windows, by their like in the *Mass-Book*. No, but I, and my Secretary made out the Story, as well as we could, by the Remains that were unbroken, Nor was any Proof at all offered. That I did it by the Pictures in the *Mass-Book*; but only Mr. *Pryn* Testified, that such Pictures were there; whereas this Argument is of no consequence: There are such Pictures in the *Missal*, therefore I repaired my Windows by them. The Windows contain the whole Story from the Creation to the Day of Judgment: Three Lights in a Window: The two Side-Lights contain the Types in the Old Testament, and the middle Light the Antitype and Verity of Christ in the New: And I believe the Types are not in the pictures in the *Missal*. In the mean time, I know no Crime, or Superstition in theis History: And though *Calvin* do not approve Images in Churches, yet he doth approve very well of them which contain a History; and says plainly, that these have their use, *in Docendo & Admonendo*, in Teaching and Admonishing the People: And if they have that use, why they may not instruct in the Church, as well as out, I know not. . . .[34]

This is a rare reference to the practice of copying illustrations from a printed book, and Laud's defence of his repair, on the basis that windows contained a 'History' and were for 'Teaching and Admonishing the People' is highly significant.

Two other glass painters worked at Lincoln's Inn, the brothers Bernard and Abraham van Linge from Emden. Bernard came to England in 1621 after spending two years in France but had left again by 1628: Abraham probably arrived in this country around 1620 and stayed until his death sometime in the 1640s. His work therefore spans the end of the period covered here. He was entirely at ease with printed source material, reproducing a print of *The Deposition* by Rogier van der Weyden for a window he painted in 1629 for Hampton Court, Herefordshire. His two painted glass windows made for Sir Francis

Bacon at Gorhambury, Hertfordshire, a few years before, between 1620 and 1626, draw on an extraordinarily wide variety of sources. Birds were copied from Adriaen Collaert's *Avium Vivae Icones*, fishes from Jan Sadeler's *Piscium Vivae Icones* and animals from Conrad Gesner's *Icones animalium* (1560), Collaert's *Animalium Quadrupedum* and Antonio Tempesta's suite of fighting animals (1600). Flowers were taken from Sadeler's *Florae Deae* and Crispijn de Passe's *Hortus Floridus* (1614). Figure subjects came from Tempesta's illustrations to Ovid's *Metamorphoses* (1606), Jost Amman's *Kunstbüchlein* (1599), Nicolaes de Bruyn's *Libellus Variae Generis Piscium* and prints by Jan Saenredam after Hendrick Goltzius. Rearranged glass in the heads of these windows was adapted from suites of the Continents and the Elements by Marc Geerarts, while the pattern of the leading was taken from Walter Gedde's *A Booke of Sundry Draughtes* (1615).

Abraham van Linge employed some of the same sources in a window at Lydiard Park in Wiltshire which he executed probably between 1628 and 1631.[35] This survives in a room which may always have been a closet to the state bedchamber, even before the remodelling of the house in 1743. The window consists of 108 whole or partial quarries delicately painted with flowers, birds and animals, figures and figurative scenes. Collaert's flower and bird prints were used again, together with de Passe's *Hortus Floridus* and Sadeler's *Florae Deae*, but some different prints were also available to him, Johannes Stradanus's hunting suite *Venationes Ferarum, Avium, Piscium*, Abraham Bloemaert's *Natus Dei Solius ad Servitium* and, on a quarry signed by van Linge with his monogram, a print of Arion and the Dolphin engraved by Jan Muller after Cornelis Cornelisz., from the background of which a distinctive sailing boat was derived.[36]

In few other media were so many different suites of prints plundered for decoration, and further research would perhaps eventually add to the tally, particularly of those which inspired van Linge's glass in Oxford, at Queen's College and Christ Church (both 1635), Balliol (1637) and University College (1641). In view of the consistency with which the same prints were employed for windows in different buildings it seems that in each case it must have been the artist who owned the originals. It is worth noting that contacts forged at university or Inns of Court helped to secure commissions for craftsmen and thereby spread the influence of continental prints.[37]

Chapter 13

TAPESTRY

Tapestries in the early-Renaissance style and apparently woven in England are mentioned in French inventories, classified as 'vieille fabrique d'Angleterre', from designs by Lucas van Leyden and Albrecht Dürer; there were nearly a hundred such hangings in the inventory of Louis XIV, including sets of the Life of Christ, in wool, silk and gold; the Triumphs of Petrarch, the Virtues, King Priam, Hercules, King Ahasuerus, Joseph, Moses, Vine-dressers and Vintagers, Faggot-makers and Shepherds.[1] Tapestry-weaving enterprises were set up in many towns in England during the mid-sixteenth century: at Sandwich, Maidstone and Canterbury in Kent, at Colchester and Norwich in East Anglia, and at York. The workers seem to have been mostly immigrants from the Netherlands. Similarly, a high proportion of the weavers who worked in the Great Wardrobe for the Crown were foreigners. Sometime after 1561, however, William Sheldon set up an important factory at Barcheston in the West Midlands, which was staffed almost exclusively by Englishmen, under the direction of Richard Hickes.

Investigation of the tapestries generally attributed to the Sheldon workshops shows that their designers relied on continental prints to an extent remarkable even in this country. Not only was the range of source material extremely wide – much has still evaded capture – but a good many prints were employed which were apparently never used anywhere else. Moreover, we know the names of the weavers though not which pieces they were responsible for. In some instances these tapestries allow a rare insight into the relationship between the patron and the tapestry designer.

William Sheldon (d.1570) bought the manor of Weston near Barcheston in Warwickshire in 1534, but moved to his family's manor house at Beoley in Worcestershire in 1546–7. Having purchased the manor of Barcheston in 1561, he established a tapestry works there (and later at Bordesley in Worcestershire), apparently to provide employment for weavers in the counties of Worcester and Warwick and, failing them, in Herefordshire, Gloucestershire, Shropshire, Staffordshire, Oxford-

shire and Berkshire.[2] By way of preparation it seems that he sent his son Ralph (1537–1613) abroad in the company of the man who later became director of the works, Richard Hickes (1524–1621). Their travels probably took place between 1555, when Ralph left Oxford, and 1557, when he married.[3] A century later, the antiquary Anthony Wood (1632–95) wrote: 'The first Rich. Hycks here mentioned was bound prentice to a Dutch arras weaver in Holland by Ralph Sheldon (who built the great house at Weston in Com. Warw. in 1588) and being out of his time setled at Barcheston a mannor yt belongs to the Sheldons, and made and weaved those fair hangings yt are in ye dining roome at Weston.'[4]

This is very significant. The privilege of travel in foreign countries was common amongst continental craftsmen who expected to spend their *Wanderjahre* in the workshop of a master craftsman, but it was rare indeed amongst their English equivalents. Hickes clearly put the opportunity to good use, collecting continental prints for source material at the tapestry works.

The Sheldon looms supplied tapestries, cushion-covers and other furnishings, such as valances for country-house use. Some small pieces, displaying a charming and characteristically English naïvety, are generally attributed to Bordesley (where Thomas Chance was the director) while larger, better quality pieces have been given to Barcheston, which Hickes himself directed. But the picture is complicated by the close association from 1584 of the Sheldon weavers with those of the Queen's Great Wardrobe: Richard Hickes left Barcheston temporarily, with his elder son Francis, to repair tapestries at Windsor Castle, the Tower of London, the Palace of Westminster, Hampton Court, Richmond, Oatlands, Woodstock and elsewhere, appearing in the Lord Chamberlain's accounts from 1584/5 to 1587/8 when he returned to Barcheston.[5] Francis's name appears until 1605–6. Tapestries woven in the Great Wardrobe have never satisfactorily been identified but are likely to have been Netherlandish in character and may for this reason have gone unrecognised.

Unquestionable products of the Sheldon looms

373 Tapestry with the arms of Robert Dudley, Earl of Leicester, perhaps designed by Richard Hickes and woven in England *c*.1585. Victoria and Albert Museum, London.

appear to be the tapestry maps and the tapestries from Chastleton House illustrating the Story of Judah and the Judgement of Paris, with two smaller heraldic panels and at least three long cushion covers. Others can reasonably be attributed to the looms either by stylistic similarities or by inscriptions: several small panels with biblical scenes, cushion-covers both long and short, either illustrating the stories of Abraham, Jacob, Tobias and Susanna, or depicting the Virtues; valances and two panels at Sudeley Castle. The tapestries representing the Four Seasons, now at Hatfield, are probably the last important pieces to be woven at Barcheston before the establishment of the Mortlake looms in 1619.

Numerous other tapestries have also at one time or another been attributed to the Sheldon factories with varying degrees of probability. Amongst these are the famous tapestries displaying the arms of the Earl of Leicester (Fig. 373). In the 1920s these tapestries were included in the Sheldon *corpus* both on stylistic grounds and because Leicester was well acquainted with Sheldon's undertaking; almost immediately they were excluded and ascribed to a Dutch or Flemish factory, commissions by Leicester while he was Governor in the Netherlands shortly before his death in 1588.[6] However, documentary evidence has been discovered which associates them with tapestries mentioned in inventories three years earlier, in 1585.[7] Moreover, a memorandum dated 13 January that same year mentions 'One new peece for the banketting howse wth Hickes to be called for when ye rest are made', and 'Three new peeces bought of Hix: with my Lo Armes in the middell therof verie

large & faire: made for the banqueting howse'. This must be Richard Hickes and it is possible that in this instance he was merely acting as middleman on the Earl's behalf and passed the commission on to some factory in the Netherlands. On the other hand the choice of source material suggests that they were designed by Hickes in England, even if they were woven abroad.

All three surviving tapestries (there was a fourth matching panel at Drayton House in the 1920s but it has since disappeared), have the Earl's armorial achievement placed against a verdure ground inhabited by birds, with borders of flowering and fruiting plants within strapwork baskets and frames, and stylised guard-stripes consisting of grotesques incorporating demi-figures supporting armillary spheres. The large horizontal tapestry has, either side of the achievement, a decorative cartouche framing a fountain in a landscape setting. It has been suggested that these represent views of fountains installed at Kenilworth Castle for the famous entertainments staged there when Queen Elizabeth visited the Earl in 1575,[8] and the memory of these events may have been in the designer's (and his patron's) mind. But they were, in fact, copied with only minor adaptations – such as the addition of the Earl's distinctive bear and ragged staff crest – from a well-known suite of plates designed by Vredeman de Vries and published by Gerard de Iode in Antwerp in 1568 under the title *Artis Perspectivae . . .* (Fig. 374; and see pp.79–80).[9]

One of the elements in the vertical guard-stripes, on the other hand, derives not from a continental print (at least not in the first instance) but from an English publication: this is the winged figure supporting an armillary sphere which appears in the woodcut titlepage compartment of T. Buckminster's *A Prognostication for M.D.LXXXII*, as well as for several subsequent English almanacs and prognostications.[10] All the individual plants and flowers that make up the verdure grounds, and the many species of birds that inhabit them, may derive from prints as well but the source of only one has so far been found: the eagle beneath the word 'LOYAL' on the large Leicester tapestry seems to have been taken – having first been deprived of its crown and lance – from a woodblock head-piece used on page 213 of *The Second Part of The Common Places of Peter Martyr*.[11] Both the Flemish and the English sources were used on unquestioned Sheldon tapestries, a plate from Vredeman's *Artis Perspectivae* on the borders of one of the tapestry maps, the English titlepage border with the armillary sphere on an armorial panel from Chastleton in Oxfordshire. From their superior quality and the suggestive combination of source material, Lord Leicester's tapestries could, I suggest, have been woven in 1584–5 by skilled foreigners at the Great Wardrobe in London,

to the designs of Richard Hickes who was working there at that date.

The famous set of four tapestry maps were woven for Ralph Sheldon's house Weston Park in Warwickshire in 1588, and bear not only the names of Richard Hickes and his son Francis but also the Sheldon arms.[12] Replacements for these originals, with picture-frame borders and the arms of Ralph Sheldon the younger and his wife Henrietta Maria, were woven around 1647, the date of their marriage, and as already seen were noted by Anthony Wood in the dining room at Weston; these and the originals, by now in a dilapidated state, were sold in the Weston Park sale in 1781 and fragments are now distributed amongst various collections.[13]

I have explored the range of pictorial source material used on these tapestry maps elsewhere, so it is only necessary here to summarise my discoveries and bring them up to date.[14] It has been known for many years that the maps were based on the pioneering county maps of Christopher Saxton, which were engraved and published individually during the 1570s, but brought together in his *Atlas* in 1579.[15] In the field of the map of Worcestershire (Fig. 375) is a whole cartouche framing a scale of miles – not present on Saxton's printed map – and this was copied from the cartouche beneath the portrait of Queen Elizabeth on the dedication page of Saxton's 1579 *Atlas* (Fig. 378), proving that the weavers worked from the compilation rather than from individual maps. The rest of the cartouches in the main field of the tapestries, where their source has been identified, derive from those designed by Vredeman de Vries to frame specimen alphabets in the very popular copybook, Clemens Perret's *Exercitatio Alphabetica* (Antwerp, 1569): one of these appears on the tapestry map of Oxfordshire, others, either whole or fragmentary, on the surviving portions of Gloucestershire and Worcestershire.

The sixteenth century maps have elaborate Flemish-style borders, similar features being repeated at regular intervals with small variations. All the upper corners have apparently been lost, but some of the lower corners survive in whole or in part. These depict four of the twelve Labours of Hercules and there is enough of them intact to show that their source was a suite of ten plates designed by Frans Floris, engraved by Cornelis Cort and published in Antwerp in 1563; their iconographical programme was based on a small tractate of Albricus Philosophus, *De Imaginibus Deorum*, in which the majority of the Labours were interpreted as symbols of the victory of virtue over sin.[16] The manner in which the designer of the tapestries used these engravings is particularly intriguing. He made few changes in the scenes in which Hercules stands over the dead Diomedes (on

Oxfordshire) and kills the Lernaean Hydra (on Worcestershire) – apart from the fact that they are reversed from the originals, because the weavers worked on what became the back of the tapestry. For his own Cerberus scene (on Gloucestershire; Fig. 376) the designer did not use Floris's version; instead, he took the figure of Hercules clubbing the Hydra (Fig. 377), reversed it and introduced a completely different three-headed figure of Cerberus, whose source I have yet to identify. For Hercules's conquest of the Erymanthean Boar (on Oxfordshire) the tapestry designer chose the moment before the boar leaps to the attack (Fig. 379): although he was perhaps inspired by Floris's vision of the episode (in the background of the print depicting the slaughter of Geryon) his boar is quite unlike Floris's and the appearance of the tip of his club and his sandalled foot indicate that the figure of Hercules would have taken up the stance of the Hercules in the Hydra scene.

Two conclusions are possible. Either the tapestry designer possessed only two or three of the Cort/Floris originals and was obliged to invent the Cerberus and the Erymanthean Boar compositions using whatever he could extract from the engravings. Or he indeed had the full suite of originals but decided to go his own way with these two Labours. This is perhaps the more likely explanation, for the designer not only needed compositions that would effectively turn the corner from the vertical to the horizontal but also would have welcomed the possibility of standardising portions of the design to reduce the cost of weaving. Significantly, three of the four surviving lower corners have identical figures of Hercules. Had the upper corners of the 1588 tapestries survived it might be possible to know whether this is the correct explanation for the manner in which the prints were used. Either way, the figures of Cerberus and the Erymanthean Boar must have been adapted from some other publication: I have not found the source of the former but the boar was copied from a suite of hunting plates designed by Johannes Stradanus, engraved by Philips Galle and published as *Venationes Ferarum, Avium, Piscium . . .* in 1578 (Fig. 380). The significance of this discovery will be discussed below (p.234).

The upper and lower borders of these three sixteenth-century tapestries mainly consist of arbour-like constructions of the kind that originated in Italy but were popularised by Cornelis Bos, J.A. Ducerceau and Vredeman de Vries.[17] Their source ought to be identifiable: they are clearly individual elements repeated laterally in order to fill the horizontal format. The arbours are inhabited by figures personifying some of the Theological and Cardinal Virtues – Charity in the form of a maternal figure surrounded by three children, and Temperance, a female figure

375 (*following pages*) Sheldon tapestry map of Worcestershire, *c*.1588. Bodleian Library, Oxford, on loan to the Victoria and Albert Museum, London.

MERIDIES

THIS SOWTHLY
PART WHICH HEAR
BELOW TOWARDS
GLOCESTER FALL
OF CORNE AND
GRASSE GREAT
PLENTIE YELDS BVT
FRVIT EXCEDITHE ALL

376   Lower right corner of the Sheldon tapestry map of Gloucestershire, *c*.1588. Private Collection.

377   Cornelis Cort after Frans Floris, Hercules and the Lernaean Hydra, from *The Labours of Hercules* (Antwerp, 1563). Victoria and Albert Museum, London.

dedication page of Saxton's *Atlas* which, as already seen, served as a useful quarry for decorative material (see Fig. 378).

The same compositional method was applied to the vertical borders of all three tapestry maps which, on examination, naturally divide into individual elements superimposed on one another. Only one of these can so far be traced to a specific source, a feature consisting of Salomonic columns entwined with vines and separated by a vase of flowers, below, and a distinctive cartouche, above. This was copied precisely from a titlepage border used in two books published in England – *The Common Places of . . . Peter Martyr* (1574, second edition 1583; Fig. 382), and *Sermons of Master Iohn Calvin, vpon the Booke of Iob* (also 1574, second edition 1579).[20] The printed title of the original book naturally had to be removed when the titlepage border was used on the maps. On Worcestershire it was replaced by other appropriate inscriptions; on Gloucestershire and Oxfordshire it gave way to views of arched buildings seen in perspective, both taken from suites designed by Vredeman, the former from his *Scenographiae, sive Perspectivae* (1560, second edition 1563), the latter from his *Artis Perspectivae* (1568) which had earlier been used for the fountains on Lord Leicester's tapestries.[21]

Next, the tapestries associated with Chastleton, beginning with the set of four illustrating the story of Judah in elaborate strapwork cartouches (Fig. 384). One is dated 1595. They bear the initials of Walter and Eleanor Jones and their son Henry, but must have been made for some house owned by the family before they bought Chastleton in 1602. (A fifth tapestry of very similar design depicts the Judgement of Paris and has the initials of Henry Jones alone.) As on the tapestry maps, the cartouches derive from those in Clemens Perret's *Exercitatio Alphabetica* of 1569 (Fig. 385). The sources of the figurative

pouring liquid from one vessel to another, diluting wine with water, to represent moderation in liquor (see Fig. 379). Despite differences, particularly in the lower parts of the figures (perhaps explicable by some common source) both the Virtues seem to have been derived, in reverse, from a suite of engravings by Herman Muller (Fig. 381). Mercury nearby with his winged sandals, hat and caduceus, was reversed from a print showing a frieze of the Seven Planets by the Nuremberg master Virgil Solis (Fig. 383).[18]

The upper and lower borders of Oxfordshire and the surviving lower border of Worcestershire (see Fig. 375) centre on architectural features copied virtually unchanged from two designs in Vredeman's untitled suite of fountains (Antwerp, 1573).[19] The exaggerated perspective and specific architectural details of the originals were faithfully translated into the new medium, and filled with terrestrial globes in one and an inscription in the other. The flanking figures holding spheres (on Worcestershire) come from the

378   Remigius Hogenberg
(attributed), dedication page to
William Saxton, *Atlas* (London,
1579). Devonshire Collection,
Chatsworth.

379 Two fragments from the Sheldon tapestry map of Oxfordshire, c.1588. Victoria and Albert Museum, London.

cf.381   cf383

scenes, however, have so far defied every attempt at identification.[22]

Also from Chastleton came two small heraldic tapestry panels. One (Fig. 386) has guard-stripes which derive from the same woodcut as those of Leicester's armorial tapestries. The arms are contained in a cartouche copied from one (probably designed by Vredeman) framing illustrations of the parable of the Unmerciful Servant, engraved by Dirck Coornhert after designs once attributed to Maarten van Heemskerck (Fig. 387).[23] A companion piece (Fig. 388) takes its inspiration from a strapwork cartouche (enclosing a quotation from Seneca) by Cornelis Bos dated 1554 (see Fig. 51).[24] Amusingly, the print was used upside down.

Two cushion covers, which, from the initials T and E.I. may have been woven for a member of the Jones family of Chastleton, can also be connected with print sources. The first is a long cushion-cover with three scenes under a triple colonnade (Fig. 393). These illustrate episodes from the life of Christ, the Annunciation, the Nativity and the Adoration of the Magi. The second, a short cushion-cover, adds the Flight into Egypt (Fig. 394). All these scenes can now be shown to derive from a suite of fifteen prints illustrating the life of the Virgin, with a pictorial titlepage that reads: *Vita Divae Mariae Virginis* (Figs 389–92). The suite was presumably designed and engraved by Hieronymus Wierix and published by Hans van Luyck, probably in the 1580s.[25] The way in which the prints were used is instructive. The two outer scenes on the long cushion-cover appear as they do in the prints but the central scene, the Nativity, was woven in reverse. Most of the Flight into Egypt was woven in reverse, but the figures of the Virgin and Child are as in the print. This procedure, in

which figures were reversed or not, was based on artistic choices which exactly correspond in kind with those made in the weaving of the tapestry maps.

The best of the later Sheldon tapestries rely almost equally heavily on continental prints. The tapestries

380 (*above left*) Philips Galle after Johannes Stradanus, Boar-Hunt, from *Venationes Ferarum, Avium, Piscium . . .* (Antwerp, 1578). Victoria and Albert Museum, London.

381 (*above right*) Herman Jansz. Muller, Temporantia and Iusticia. British Museum, London.

383 Virgil Solis, Mercury, from a print depicting the Seven Planets. Warburg Institute, London.

382 Block-cutter with the initials C.T. after N.H. (?Nicholas Hilliard), titlepage to *The Common Places of . . . Peter Martyr* (London, 1583). British Library, London (3705.f.11).

229

384 (*top left*) Detail of a Sheldon tapestry from Chastleton House, Oxfordshire, depicting a scene in the Story of Judah, 1595. Aston Hall, Birmingham.

386 (*centre left*) Sheldon tapestry panel from Chastleton House, Oxfordshire, late sixteenth or early seventeenth century. The Barber Institute of Fine Arts, Birmingham University.

388 (*right*) Sheldon tapestry panel from Chastleton House, Oxfordshire, late sixteenth or early seventeenth century.

385 (*top right*) Lucas or Johannes Duetecum after Jan Vredeman de Vries, pl.XXXIIII from Clemens Perret, *Exercitatio Alphabetica . . .* (Antwerp, 1569). The Royal Library – National Library of Sweden, Stockholm, Maps and Prints Department, De la Gardie Collection.

387 (*centre right*) Dirck Coornhert after an unknown artist (formerly thought to be Maarten van Heemskerck), scene from the parable of the Unmerciful Servant, in a cartouche attributed to Jan Vredeman de Vries. Victoria and Albert Museum, London.

ANVNTIATIO CONCEPTIONIS.

NATIVITAS IESV CHRISTI.

389 (*far left*) Hieronymus
Wierix, the Annunciation, from
Vitae Divae Mariae Virginis
(Antwerp, probably 1580s).
Bibliothèque Royale Albert ler,
Brussels.

390 (*left*) Hieronymus Wierix,
the Nativity, from *Vitae Divae
Mariae Virginis* (Antwerp,
probably 1580s). Bibliothèque
Royale Albert ler, Brussels.

TRIVM REGVM OBLATIO

FVGA IN AEGYPTVM

391 (*far left*) Hieronymus
Wierix, the Adoration of the
Magi, from *Vitae Divae Mariae
Virginis* (Antwerp, probably
1580s). Bibliothèque Royale
Albert ler, Brussels.

392 (*left*) Hieronymus Wierix,
the Flight into Egypt, from
Vitae Divae Mariae Virginis.
Bibliothèque Royale Albert ler,
Brussels.

393 Sheldon tapestry long cushion-cover, with three scenes from the Life of the Virgin: the Annunciation, the Nativity and the Adoration of the Magi, c.1600. The Metropolitan Museum of Art, New York. Bequest of Mary Stillman Harkness, 1950.

depicting the Four Seasons, one of which is dated 1611,[26] are similar to the maps in deriving their main fields from one set of engravings and elements of their borders from quite different prints. The tapestries bear the arms of Tracy of Toddington, Gloucestershire, impaling those of Shirley of Wiston in Sussex, for Sir John Tracy and his wife Anne, daughter of Sir Thomas Shirley of Wiston (a man already encountered, incidentally, as an enlightened patron himself, pp.140–42). The marriage took place in 1590 and it has been pointed out that the Tracy family and the Sheldons were connected by marriage with the Throckmortons, which was presumably the means by which the Sheldon weavers received this commission.[27] The tapestries were probably woven at Barcheston under the direction of Richard Hickes's son Francis, who had been working with the royal arras-workers until 1602–3 at least.[28] He may indeed have left London to weave them, as his father had done to weave the tapestry maps.

Their main fields have adaptations of engravings of the Four Seasons after designs by Maarten de Vos,[29] to which were added animals apparently copied from Edward Topsell's *History of Four-footed Beasts and Serpents* (1607–8). The borders have a series of oval compartments with mottoes and emblems which have been shown to derive mostly from Geffrey Whitney's *Choice of Emblemes* (Leyden, 1586) and Andrea Alciati's *Emblemata*.[30] The Hatfield Seasons are in the same tradition as the maps woven twenty-five years earlier: their design was built up from a number of different printed sources, but it involved less adaptation and as a result they are less convincingly continental in appearance. They also lack the sheer number and variety of sources and consequently reveal less of their designer's (or patron's) thoughts.

Smaller tapestries from the early seventeenth century survive in some numbers but the search for the sources used has met with far fewer rewards: particularly tantalising are the many cushion-covers depicting

scenes from the story of Susanna. It is almost as if – when Francis Hickes returned from London in 1603 to direct the Sheldon works – an entirely new range of sources was deliberately introduced which have so far proved rather resistant to identification. However, there is little doubt that further intensive study would probably reveal all the prints employed. In the meantime some comparisons can be made.

On one panel, which may be nearly contemporary with the Seasons,[31] the figure of Justice derives from a suite of prints by Hans Collaert after Maarten de Vos. Figures of Justice and Charity from the same prints appear on the upper corners of a Sheldon tapestry cushion-cover,[32] with Ceres and Pomona in the lower corners: the main scene depicts the Circumcision and was derived from a print which so far eludes me. The three Theological Virtues, Faith, Hope and Charity, feature on another tapestry (Fig. 395) consisting of borders of flowers and exotic and other fruits enclosing the central panel where the

three figures sit, identified by labels in rudimentary cartouches beneath their feet.[33] The Virtues were copied from a print designed and engraved by Johan Wierix and published in 1572 (see Fig. 270). It has the figures labelled by the head of each figure, and is of a much more elongated format, but otherwise the tapestry designer followed it very closely.[34]

* * *

The impressive variety of source material used in the Sheldon workshops included some unusual items rarely if ever employed in decoration elsewhere. One is the titlepage border from a book by one or other of two leading Protestant reformers – probably the *Common Places of . . . Peter Martyr* was on the designer's drawing board. A highly educated and literate man, Ralph Sheldon probably owned this well-known book, even though he had converted to Catholicism, perhaps on his marriage in 1557 to

394 Sheldon tapestry short cushion cover, with the Flight into Egypt, *c*.1600. Victoria and Albert Museum, London.

discounted by other writers – that documentary mention of 'Mr Sheldon's man' in the Hardwick Accounts actually does refer to these tapestry weavers; and they were employed in the borders of the Bradford embroidery table-carpet now in the Victoria and Albert Museum, made for a member of the family at Castle Bromwich in the Midlands. These instances do suggest that Hickes, who had a wide circle of friends, acquaintances (and opponents – he frequently resorted to the law) may have acted as some kind of design consultant to Queen and courtiers – employed by the Queen at the Great Wardrobe, by the Earl of Leicester, known to Bess of Hardwick. I cannot help thinking that Richard Hickes may emerge as one of the pivotal figures in Elizabethan domestic design.

It is not known precisely when the Sheldon works closed, but it may have been after the weaving of *The Seasons* that are now at Hatfield. In 1619 a rather different enterprise was set up by James I, probably at the instigation of Charles Prince of Wales. This was the celebrated Mortlake factory established in two houses in that part of Surrey, having two first-floor weaving rooms with eighteen looms and an artist's studio, and two galleries above with three rooms each. More than fifty weavers arrived secretly from the Netherlands under the leadership of Philip de Maecht: amongst them were weavers like Louis Dermoulen, who specialised in heads, and Pieter de Craigt, who specialised in flesh parts. With royal patronage and first-class foreign weavers, this was a far more prestigious operation than the provincial looms of a landed family.

The first tapestries to be woven (1620–22) were a set depicting the Story of Venus and Vulcan from tapestries that had belonged to Henry VIII. The difference in quality between these and the last major products of the Sheldon looms is immediately apparent, for the three-dimensional quality of the figures and the spatial recession are brilliantly realised. These were followed by a set of the Months, also from hundred-year-old designs. About 1623 Francis Cleyn was persuaded to leave his native Rostock to join the factory as official artist and the Raphael cartoons of the Acts of the Apostles, purchased in Genoa for £300, provided the subject for the next series, while Cleyn himself designed a set telling the story of Hero and Leander, grotesques of the Five Senses and many others.[35] Van Dyck designed a set for the Great Hall at Whitehall Palace, which was unfortunately not woven. By the end of period, the Mortlake factory had established itself as a court enterprise to match those of Paris and Brussels and relied on celebrated cartoons by Renaissance masters or on new designs by continental artists.

Anne, daughter of Sir Robert Throckmorton, a leading Catholic recusant. Despite being constantly under investigation, Sheldon continued to practise his faith in his chantry chapel in Beoley Church.

A second source used uniquely in the Sheldon works is the set of prints by Hieronymus Wierix depicting scenes in the Life of the Virgin, which has a distinctly Counter-Reformation character that would surely have been unacceptable earlier. Apart from these tapestry cushion-covers (which are likely to postdate the relaxation of Elizabethan restrictions on the type of religious subject-matter acceptable in England), all the Sheldon tapestries with biblical scenes, whether made before or after the death of the Queen, fall clearly into the narrative type approved by Protestants.

A third source calling for comment is the suite of plates designed by Johannes Stradanus and published under the title *Venationes Ferarum, Avium, Piscium . . .* The prints were rarely used elsewhere, so instances may suggest contacts between patrons and Richard Hickes. They were used in the decoration of Hardwick Hall, re-introducing the possibility –

Chapter 14

EMBROIDERY

Like paintings, embroideries have been much studied in the past. The reason lies in their great charm as 'pictures in needlework' and the result has been the discovery of many of the sources popular during and just after the period covered here. By far the best collection of Elizabethan embroideries dependent on continental prints are those made by or for Elizabeth Countess of Shrewsbury and preserved at Hardwick Hall in Derbyshire and Oxburgh Hall in Norfolk. Because these are an integral part of her overall artistic patronage, which included the building of three great houses and several smaller ones, consideration of them will be left until the next chapter. They demonstrate clearly the wealth of source material used by the embroiderers both professional and amateur during the last three decades of the sixteenth century. What is needed here, therefore, is a summary of the discoveries of others – with additions where possible – together with a brief investigation of some other evidence.

It is fortunate that, as with masons' and plasterers' work, there is invaluable manuscript evidence to show what kinds of prints were being used around the turn of the century. These are the two huge books of pictures with texts compiled by Thomas Trevelyon or Trevilian (1548–post 1616), probably an embroiderer by trade. They are dated 1608 and 1616 and belong respectively to the Folger Shakespeare Library in Washington DC and to Mr J.P. Getty, KBE (from the collection of Boies Penrose). Both have been investigated by John Nevinson,[1] who recorded that the 1608 book contained

a picture calendar with the Occupations of the Months, a gazetteer related to Thomas Bretnor's Almanach, an illustrated epitome of Old Testament and British History, partly derived from Giles Godet's Chronicle and later series of Royal Portraits, a number of allegories and proverbs from broadsheets, scriveners' alphabets and copy-book texts, portraits of theologians and reformers from Boissard, Verheiden and Henry Holland, the Gunpowder Plot Conspirators, and finally the Lord Mayors of London. Before these last, undescribed

and without any text are grouped about 80 folios of patterns which could have been used for embroidery.[2]

Thomas Trevelyon is a shadowy figure. The Trevelyan family is of Cornish origin, but many were found in the sixteenth and seventeenth centuries in Somerset, including several Thomases; there was also a Thomas Trevilian, a barber-surgeon of St Martin, Vintry, London, whose will was proved in 1646: he may have been the son of Thomas Trevilian the embroiderer. Part of both books consists of alphabets, some resembling those in the writing manual of Jean de Beauchesnes.[3] Nevinson concluded that Trevelyon was evidently familiar with 'a fairly wide range of prints from the Low Countries, English woodcuts, title-pages and portraits'.

The most important aspect of Trevelyon's compilations, from the point of view of this study, is what material he copied and where he obtained it. Nevinson continues: 'It is worth recording that eight of his 1608 portraits of Protestant divines are not copied from Verheiden but anticipate the iconography of the portraits engraved by Magdalena and Willem van de Passe, and not published till 1620 in Henry Holland's *Herωologia*.' Indeed, Trevelyon must have copied the portraits while they hung in shops in Blackfriars, the Strand and elsewhere, leading to the conclusion that he himself may have worked in a shop in that part of London.[4] Nevinson also asserted that 'Apart from their carpentry and garden patterns, [the Trevelyon manuscripts] undoubtedly contain copies of lost woodcuts, popular prints and broadsheets, which were more likely to have been pasted on walls than preserved in libraries'. If Nevinson is correct in his supposition that Trevelyon may have worked in a shop in Blackfriars or the Strand, the commonplace books potentially offer the best evidence for the actual prints and suites of prints available in London at the beginning of the seventeenth century. It is, therefore, worth exploring these manuscripts further.

Nevinson managed to identify a considerable number of the originals copied by Trevelyon. Some were suites of portraits – which strictly lie beyond the

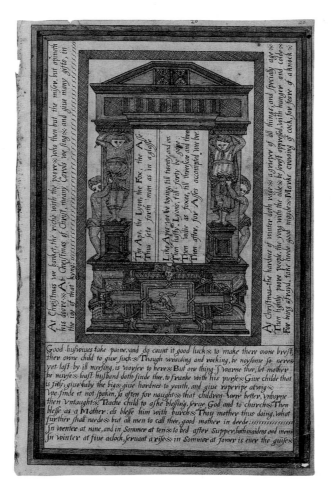

scope of this book – of theologians and reformers, which he discovered were derived from A. Boissard, *Icones Quinquaginta virorum* (1585), J. Verheiden, *Praestantium aliquot theologorum effigies* (1602), and H. Holland, *Herwologia Anglica* (1620).[5] Trevelyon also copied portraits from *A view of the Right Honourable the Lord Mayors of London,* (W. Jaggard; 1601). Nevinson also demonstrated that Trevelyon was able on occasion to alter prints in a straightforward manner to suit his own purposes. So he adopted

> the figure of Albert Meyer, the draughtsman honourably depicted in Leonard Fuchs's *De historia stirpium*, 1542, for the Unjust Steward . . . ; a figure of Peace similarly does duty for the mother of Zebedee's children . . . , while the captive Netherlands, personified by M. Gheeraerts as Andromeda rescued by Perseus (William the Silent) from the Spanish monster, is copied mural crown and all for the woman taken in adultery . . . and also for Cordelia, King Lear's daughter. . . .

It is now possible to extend quite considerably Nevinson's list of Trevelyon's borrowings from printed material. Early on in the 1608 Miscellany strapwork compartments enclosing text appear. Two

have so far eluded identification but the third (Fig. 396) is easily recognisable as deriving from a titlepage compartment that was used to introduce numerous books in the later sixteenth century: its first appearance was in *The Byble* printed by John Day in London in 1551 (Fig. 397), and it can also be found in the same printer's *The whole booke of psalmes* in 1565, as well as in many later editions.[6] The several sheets of knot patterns (Fig. 398) are equally evidently derived from Thomas Hill's *The Gardener's Labyrinth* of 1577.[7]

The Seven Liberal Arts (Folger manuscript, fols 158r and 158v; Getty manuscript, pp. 385–6, Fig. 399), seem to have been copied from the set designed by Hans Sebald Beham (Fig. 400), except that they were reversed.[8] It is interesting that Trevelyon had access to prints of a blatantly devotional character by the Wierix brothers, for he copied or adapted at least two for his Miscellany (Fig. 401): the *Speculum Peccatoris* designed and engraved by Hieronymus Wierix, and the *Miles Christianus* by the same artist (Figs 402, 403).[9] A particularly brazen adoption of one print to tell a different story is exemplified by his copying The Prodigal Son leaving his Father's House from the suite by Crispijn de Passe after designs by Maarten de Vos (Fig. 404) to illustrate the departure

Grammev, teacheth men to speake aptlye, and to make congruetye of speach in all languages, and ioyne, perfict sentences to geather: by the rulles of Grammer:

Dialectica:

Logicke theacheth men to reason and dispute, and by arguments to proue the truthe, from falsehode, whose rules being obserued they dee shewe an order to all other arts:

Rhetorica teacheth men to delate, and of a small matter to make alonge talle, and as the olde prouerb is to make along haruest of alittell corne, or to set manye colours vpon alittle peice of woode:

Arithmatike:

Arithmatike, teacheth men to number, and hath foure parts, addition substraction multiplication and diuision, by which foure partes one number is parted in to manye, or manye are collected in to one:

399 Thomas Trevelyon, four of the Seven Liberal Arts, on page 385 of his *Miscellany*, 1616. Mr J.P. Getty, KBE.

398 (*above left*) Thomas Trevelyon, knot patterns on folio 263 of his *Miscellany* (1608). The Folger Shakespeare Library, Washington, D.C.

400 (*left*) Hans Sebald Beham, Arithmetria, from *The Seven Liberal Arts*. Warburg Institute, London.

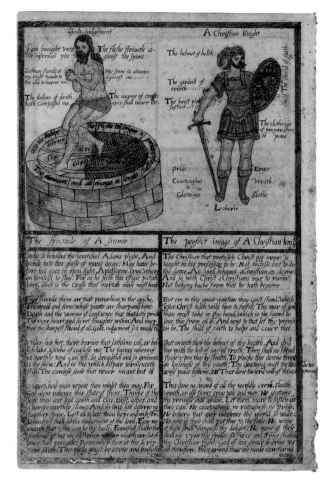

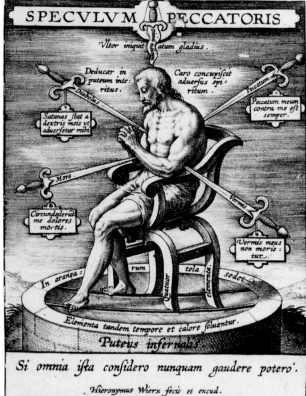

of Mordecai, in the story of Queen Esther (Fig. 405).[10]

Later in the Miscellany appear drawings of the Twelve Patriarchs, and these Trevelyon copied from the suite of prints engraved by Jan Sadeler after designs by Crispijn van der Broeck (Figs 406, 407).[11] He might have had these as a set complete in itself, but it is more likely that he had access to a much larger publication in which this set was included, Gerard de Iode's *Thesaurus veteris et novi Testamenti* (Antwerp, 1579, 1585). The *Thesaurus* was one of the principal sources used in actual embroidery, as shall shortly be seen. Prints after Vredeman de Vries were also amongst the sources used by Thomas Trevelyon: for instance, he copied a plate from Vredeman's *Caryatidum* on to one of the sheets of his 1616 commonplace book (Getty, p. 599).

The source used by Trevelyon for his drawings of the Nine Worthies which he included in both the 1608 and the 1616 Miscellany proved enduringly elusive.[12] It was specially pleasing, therefore, to track it down to the set of prints bearing the signature of the publisher Philips Galle.[13] Trevelyon followed the originals to the best of his ability (which in figure painting was admittedly limited), reproducing most

details of the armour fairly accurately (see Fig. 177) although, for example, he omitted the plume on Alexander's helmet. This suite proves to have been quite widely known in England during the decades either side of 1600, appearing at Wiston in Sussex probably in the 1580s and at Aston Hall near Birmingham as late as the 1620s or 1630s.

Prints bearing the signature of Philips Galle also provided the source for the next series of figures, depicting the Muses, in the 1608 and 1616 Miscellany. Trevelyon's drawing of Therpsichore, for instance (Fig. 409), demonstrates that they were copied, with the omission of background details, from the suite designed by Maarten de Vos (Fig. 408).[14]

Trevelyon also copied prints by Claes or Nicolaes Breau after Jacob Matham for figures of David, Samson, Judith and Jael (Getty, pp. 355–8), and a

M. de Vos *figuravit.* Filius acceptis opibus minor exterae quaerit *Coffin Pass Sculpt*

print designed by Jacob Savery between 1591 and 1603 for a delightful interior scene in the 1616 Miscellany (Getty, p. 428). But the most exciting discovery is that he adapted a set of etchings designed by Pieter van der Borcht around 1595–1600 for four spectacular double-page spreads illustrating the parable of Dives and Lazarus, one scene of which is illustrated in Fig. 411. The original prints were copied (probably in reverse) by Johannes Barra (1581–1634), and these were re-issued by the publisher Jan Thiel (Fig. 410).[15] Although elsewhere Trevelyon must have copied woodcuts that do not survive, painstaking comparison

405   Thomas Trevelyon, scene from the story of Queen Esther, on page 413 of his *Miscellany*, 1616. Mr J.P. Getty, KBE.

404 (*above left*)   Crispijn de Passe the elder after Maarten de Vos, The Prodigal Son Leaving his Father's House, *c.*1599–1600. Rijksmuseum-Stichting, Amsterdam.

239

of his drawings with continental prints would reveal other sources he used and provide a fuller picture of the variety of printed material available in London in the generation before Peter Stent became the leading print-seller in the metropolis.

Turning now to surviving embroideries, much detective work on the sources has been done over the past half-century, particularly by Nancy Graves Cabot, Yvonne Hackenbroch, John Nevinson, Margaret Swain and latterly Xanthe Brooke (see the

Dan. 7.

The Copie of Dan his words, which hee spake vnto them in his last dayes: In the hundreth and fiue and twentieth yeere of his life, hee called his tribe vnto him and sayd, ye Children of Dan, heare my sayings, and giue heed to the words of your fathers mouth, I liked in my heart, and shewed in my life the thing that is good: for trueth ioyned with right dealing pleaseth God well, I haue hated hurtfull things, as lying and anger, because they teacheth a man all manner of naughtines, I confesse vnto you my Children this day, that I was glad in my heart at the death of Ioseph, and reioyced at the selling of him, because our father loued him mor then vs, For the spirite of spitefulnes and pride sayd vnto mee: thou art his sonne to as well as hee, And one of the spirites of Beliall wrought with me saying: take this Swoorde and slay Ioseph with it, and when he is dead thy father shall loue thee, this was the spirit of spitefulnisse, which counselled mee to deuour Ioseph: as the Leoparde deuoured a kid, But the God of our father Iacob, did not put him into my hands, nor suffer me to find him alone, that I might dispatch two Scepters in Israell, by committing that wickednesse, and now my Children, I tell you of a trueth, that vnles yee keepe your selues from this spirite of lying and wrath, and loue trueth, and long sufferance, ye shall perish. wrath is blinde my Children, and no wrathfull man looketh trueth in the face. if they were his father and mother, yet he think they his enemies: In saying these words, hee sayd burie mee by my fathers, hee kissed them and died. And his sonnes buried him by Abraham, Isaake, and Iacob: in y 125 yeere of age

406 Thomas Trevelyon, Dan, one of the Twelve Patriarchs, from his *Miscellany*, 1616. Mr J.P. Getty, KBE.

407 (*above right*) Jan Sadeler after Crispijn van der Broeck, Dan, from *The Twelve Patriarchs*. Victoria and Albert Museum, London.

Bibliography). From their discoveries it is clear that the sources were numerous and varied. Bernard Salomon's woodcuts provided much inspiration, a figure from his *Metamorphose d'Ovide figurée* being used for a seated soothsayer on a bed-hanging in the Untermyer Collection in New York.[16] Salomon's illustrations for Jean de Tournes's *Quadrins Historiques de la Bible* inspired the design of two other embroideries, while emblems in Claude Paradin's *Devises Heroïques* reappeared on the celebrated Shepheard Buss Coverlet in the Victoria and Albert Museum. Some scenes were derived from Jost Amman's illustrations in the *Biblia Sacra* of 1564, but otherwise the sources are almost exclusively Flemish. In at least two instances, however, the titlepage or frontispiece of an English-printed book supplied the design for needlework (see p.128).

Two of Maarten van Heemskerck's illustrations of the story of Daniel, published by Hieronymus Cock

409   Thomas Trevelyon, Therpsichore, one of the Nine Muses, from his *Miscellany*, 1616. Mr J.P. Getty, KBE.

408 (*above left*)   Philips Galle after Maarten de Vos, Therpsichore, from *The Nine Muses*. Victoria and Albert Museum, London.

410 (*left*)   Jan Thiel (publisher), the Rich Man at Dinner, from *The Rich Man and the Poor Lazarus*. Copy of an etching after Pieter van der Borcht, *c*.1595–1600. Rijksmuseum-Stichting, Amsterdam.

411 Thomas Trevelyon, the Rich Man at Dinner, on pages 514–15 of his *Miscellany*, 1616. Mr J.P. Getty, KBE.

...iftly the word of God, being deliuered by the *Prophetes*, *Chrift*, and the *Apoftles*:
...reuerently to be hard, and dutifully to be obeyed: because it talleth vs to repentaunce:
...he effect of this parable is to withdrawe vs from the abuse of our *Riches* and to
...oue vs to bountifullnes, and liberalitie towards the *Poore* that want: ssssssssssssss

ORPHEVS

ORPHEVS *arte lyræ doctus, rapidas ſtitit amnes,*
Et mouit ſyluas, perdomuitæ; feras.

ORATOR *ſapiens dicendiq; arte peritus,*
Dura hominum eloquio mitigat ingenia.

412 Adriaen Collaert after Adam van Noort, *Orpheus Charming the Beasts.* Rijksmuseum-Stichting, Amsterdam.

413 Needlework picture of Orpheus Charming the Beasts, early seventeeth century. Present whereabouts unknown.

in 1565, were copied on an embroidered valance at Drumlanrig Castle, while prints by Philips Galle (after Hans Bol) were adapted for three bed valances in the Untermyer Collection,[17] and for the needlework coverlet depicting the Banquet of Lucretia (after Hendrick Goltzius) that is now in the Victoria and Albert Museum.[18] It was Gerard de Iode's *Thesaurus veteris et novi Testamenti*, however, with its illustrations after Maarten de Vos and others (see pp.103–6) that was the single most influential publication for needlework, its influence lasting for at least a century after its

publication in Antwerp in 1579 and 1585. Nearly a dozen pieces of embroidery in the Untermyer Collection alone depend upon plates in the *Thesaurus*,[19] and so do many examples in other collections. One is a needlework picture in the Burrell Collection in Glasgow which depicts the story of David and Bathsheba, another, in the Victoria and Albert Museum, shows two scenes from the Story of Abraham: all are derived from the *Thesaurus*. Needleworkers also liked to incorporate allegorical figures designed by de Vos in their pictures.[20] These comparisons have all been published before, and so have the interesting developments of the early seventeenth century, when prints after Rubens began to be influential, particularly the Judgement of Solomon, Tomyris with the Head of Cyrus and the Feast of Herod.[21]

The application with which earlier writers pursued the embroiderers' use of continental prints has left me with little to add, except for sources for the needlework at Hardwick. However, I have found that Pieter de Iode's illustration of the Sacrifice of Isaac, engraved by Egbert van Panderen (see Fig. 182) achieved a certain currency in England and was used in the design of needlework, while Adriaen Collaert's engraving after Adam van Noort's *Orpheus Charming the Beasts* (Fig. 412) was copied on a needlework picture formerly in the F.H. Richmond Collection (Fig. 413).[22] It is surprising that no one seems hitherto to have noticed that several figures of humans and animals from Philips Galle's engravings after Johannes Stradanus's suite *Venationes Ferarum, Avium, Piscium, Pugnae Bestiorum* (Fig. 415) were incorporated into the borders of the celebrated late sixteenth-century Bradford table-carpet (Fig. 414) in the Victoria and Albert Museum.[23]

414 (*above*) The Bradford Table-carpet, English, late sixteenth century, detail of the border. Victoria and Albert Museum, London.

415 Philips Galle after Johannes Stradanus, Fishing by Night, from *Venationes Ferarum, Avium, Piscium . . .* (Antwerp, 1578). Victoria and Albert Museum, London.

Chapter 15

THE DECORATION OF ELIZABETHAN
CHATSWORTH AND HARDWICK

So finally, having skirted all round the place hitherto, we arrive at Hardwick, to look at both the Old and New Halls. All the skills and a good many of the artists considered earlier are represented in the decoration of these two great houses and in the earlier houses associated with Elizabeth Hardwick, who became by successive marriages Elizabeth Barlow, Lady Cavendish, Lady St Loe and Countess of Shrewsbury, but is best known today by her nickname, Bess of Hardwick.

Although little of her work at Chatsworth and the houses in Sheffield survives, and the Old Hall is but a ruin, some of their decoration and furnishings found their way at various times (starting in Bess's own lifetime) to Hardwick New Hall (Fig. 417), the pinnacle of her building works. It would be wrong to think that the house remains comparatively little altered from her day to this, for much work was done there after Bess's death in 1608, particularly by the 6th Duke of Devonshire during the first half of the nineteenth century. But the losses can be measured by comparing the contents of the house today with what was recorded there in admirable detail in the celebrated inventory of 1601. If the two Hardwicks, Old and New, are approached from the viewpoint adopted throughout this book, we shall begin to get an idea, as never before, of their purpose and meaning.

The redoubtable Bess of Hardwick has been described as 'neither cultured nor religious'.[1] If by the end of this chapter it can finally be accepted that the decoration of her houses had any central purpose and that she was involved in the decisions that brought the decoration into existence, we shall inevitably be led to the contrary opinion, that she was actually both cultured, not just superficially, and religious – in her own way.

The problem is that no library or book room was mentioned in the 1601 Inventory, in either the Old or the New Hall; indeed, only a handful of books were specified, as follows: 'In my Ladies Bed Chamber . . . my Ladies bookes viz: Calvin uppon Jobe, Covered with russet velvet, the resolution, Salomans proverbes, a booke of meditations, too other bookes Covered with black velvet . . .'[2] However, this looks much more like Bess's bed time reading than a catalogue of her entire library. Perhaps other books were packed in some of the many 'trunckes', 'Deskes', 'Cofers' and boxes piled up in her bedchamber and in the Maid's Chamber nearby. Alternatively, there may have been a library in the Old Hall (as there was during the seventeenth century) and an entire book-list may simply have gone missing. This gives even more purpose to this investigation.

Only one book is actually mentioned by name – 'Calvin uppon Jobe'. This was presumably one of the editions of the *Sermons of Master Iohn Calvin, vpon the Booke of Iob*, in the English translation by Arthur Golding, of which the first was published by L. Harrison and G. Byshop in London in 1574, with another the same year and later editions in 1579 and 1584. (I shall return to it later.) The 'resolution' can also be identified, probably as a book by the recusant Catholic Robert Persons (or Parsons). From a work of the Italian Jesuit Gaspar Loarte, entitled *The Exercise of a Christian Life*, Persons developed his own *The First Booke of the Christian Exercise, appertayning to resolution* – more generally known as the *Resolution* – and published it in Rouen in 1582. It was revised by a Protestant minister, Edmund Bunny, as *A Booke of Christian exercise, appertaining to Resolution* (London, 1584), its publisher describing it as 'one of the most vendible books ever issued in this country'. Essentially uncontroversial, it became the most popular book of devotion among both Catholics and Protestants in Elizabethan and Jacobean England. Alas, it is not known which version Bess owned![3] 'Salomans proverbes' might just be one of the books illustrated by Bernard Salomon for Jean de Tournes in Lyons which were so popular in the second half of the sixteenth century, perhaps the *Quadrins Historiques de la Bible* published in Lyons in 1553, with an English edition the same year entitled *The true and lyuely historyke*

416 (*facing page*) Hardwick Hall, Derbyshire, detail of an appliqué wall hanging depicting Temperance with Sardanapalus, c.1580.

418 (*facing page top*) Hardwick Hall, Derbyshire, the Eglantine Table, *c*.1567.

419 (*facing page bottom left*) Hardwick Hall, Derbyshire, detail of the Eglantine Table.

420 (*facing page bottom right*) Pieter van der Heyden after Jacob Floris, cartouche from *Compertimentorum quod vocant multiplex genus* (Antwerp, 1566). Victoria and Albert Museum, London.

purtreatures of the vvoll Bible. However, it is more likely that it was one of the 'Books of Solomon' retailing some of the wise words of the Old Testament king that were published in many editions around the middle of the century.[4] It is certainly noteworthy that these two were religious in character.

It is now accepted that Bess was born in 1527. She made the first of her four marriages, probably in 1543, to her cousin Robert Barlow when he was just thirteen and she not many years older: the Hardwick finances were in desperate straits and this short-lived union – Barlow died in December 1544 – did nothing to rescue them. In the two and a half years before her second marriage she was probably a lady-in-waiting to Frances Brandon, wife of Henry Grey, 3rd Marquess of Dorset, and a grand-daughter of Henry VII. This gave her the entree into court circles where she met Sir William Cavendish, whom she married in 1547. He was a successful government servant and had been twice widowed with three surviving daughters from his first marriage. As one of the ten auditors to the Court of Augmentation from 1536, Sir William had been involved in the work of dissolving the monasteries and in 1546 he became Treasurer of the King's Chamber and Privy Councillor, acquiring property in many counties. But he sold all of it to enable him and Bess to buy land at Chatsworth, on 31 December 1549, and elsewhere in Derbyshire and the east Midlands. The choice of godparents for their children provides evidence of their religious sympathies and of their circle of friends. For their first daughter, Frances, they chose Frances Grey, her brother, Lord Suffolk, and his wife; for their second daughter, Temperance, they asked Lady Warwick (later to become mother-in-law to Jane Grey, Frances Grey's daughter), Jane Grey herself and the Earl of Shrewsbury. Their first son, Henry, had the Princess Elizabeth herself, the Earl of Warwick (the future father-in-law of Jane Grey) and Henry Grey, Jane's father. William, the second son, had William Paulet, the Lord Treasurer, William Herbert, Earl of Pembroke, and Elizabeth Brooke, Marchioness of Northampton. When Charles Cavendish was born in 1553, Sir William asked Queen Mary to be godmother – a diplomatic choice if ever there was one – together with Henry Grey, Duke of Suffolk, and Stephen Gardiner, Bishop of Winchester. With the obvious exceptions of Queen Mary and Stephen Gardiner, all ended up on the Protestant side.[5] Bess became as good a friend to Princess Elizabeth as a commoner could, and remained loyal to her throughout her long reign.

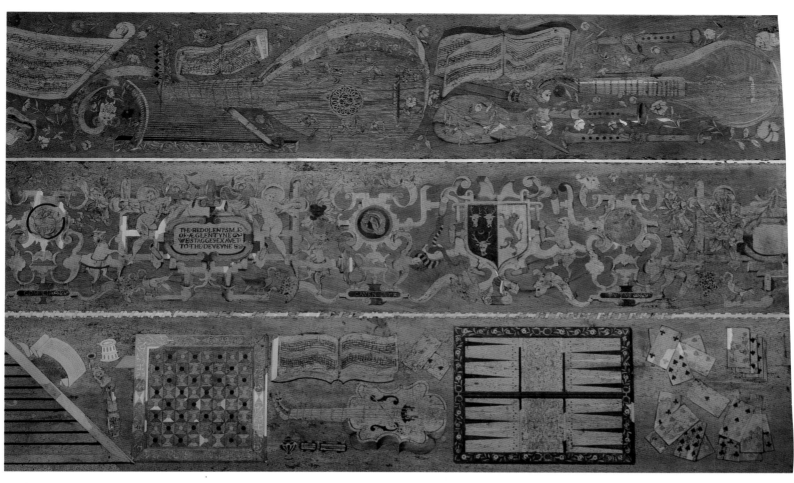

During her marriage to Sir William, Bess was first able to indulge what became a passion for building. Chatsworth was started about 1551, on the site of an earlier house which was demolished to make way for it, and she was ordering materials for embroidery for it during this decade.[6] But the house was incomplete on Cavendish's death in 1557 when work was probably interrupted. Bess was left with a life interest in Chatsworth and six children who survived infancy. Two years later she married again, this time Sir William St Loe, a wealthy West-Country landowner who was a favourite of the Queen. Work at Chatsworth resumed again and continued until his death in the winter of 1564–5; Bess inherited much of his property outright. She married for the last time in 1567 George Talbot, 6th Earl of Shrewsbury, the richest and grandest by far of her four husbands, with half-a-dozen houses besides his wife's house at Chatsworth. The marriage has been described as to some extent resembling the merging of two companies.

It was probably to celebrate this marriage, and those at the same time of Henry Cavendish to Grace Talbot and Mary Cavendish to Gilbert Talbot, that the so-called Eglantine Table (Figs 418, 419) was made. The earliest surviving object that can be associated with Bess, its decoration was adapted from at least one set of continental prints. The top is inlaid with musical instruments and sheet music, one with the four-part motet 'O Lord in Thee is all my trust', together with board-games and the arms, crests and mottoes of the Talbot, Hardwick and Cavendish families. These appear in cartouches with elaborate strapwork frames which were ingeniously adapted from at least three different continental prints, all designed by Jacob Floris and published in the suite titled *Compertimentorum quod vocant multiplex genus lepidissimis historiolis poetarumque fabellis ornatum* (Fig. 420) in Antwerp in 1566, only a year or two before their use on the table. This minimal delay suggests that the craftsman was

particularly well informed about continental prints – indeed, he may well have been a foreigner who fled during the religious turmoil of 1566. In any event the table was probably made in England, for this suite of prints was used more than once in Bess's later commissions.[7]

Her marriage to the Earl of Shrewsbury gave Bess the opportunity of resuming work on Chatsworth which continued on the most lavish scale, accounts from 1577–80 showing that the labour force varied between eighteen in winter and eighty-four in summer. Lord Shrewsbury was also obliged to build on his own account, for in 1569 he was entrusted by Queen Elizabeth with the custody of her half-sister Mary Queen of Scots who had fled from Scotland and was threatening to concentrate forces to establish her on the throne of England. Amongst these houses were Tutbury Castle, Sheffield Castle and Sheffield Manor, Wingfield Manor and Worksop Manor.

There can be little doubt that some of the furnishings that now survive at Hardwick were made for one or other of these. From its presumed subject, the striking but mysterious panel painting which is known today as *The Return of Ulysses to Penelope* (Fig. 423) was probably made for Bess's house at Chatsworth: by 1601 it had been moved to the Withdrawing Chamber of the New Hall at Hardwick and was described as 'Ulisses and Penelope'. This is one of the very few pictures belonging to Bess that were not either portraits or religious.[8] It was painted in 1570 (the date is on the entablature, upper left) and has been somewhat misinterpreted in the past by writers unaware that the painter based his composition on prints.[9] These are two woodcuts by Jost Amman from the *Biblia. Das isst die gantze heylige Scrifft Teutsch. D. Mart. Luther* . . . (known as the *Biblia Sacra*), which was published in Frankfurt in 1564. They were also used, the same year, in a picture Bible entitled *Neuwe Biblische Figuren dess Alten und Neuwen Testaments. The*

architecture, consisting of an arched entrance to an interior with a balustraded court leading to another building in which a lady can be seen at her loom, derives from Amman's illustration of Nebuchadnezzar's Dreams, in Daniel 2 (Fig. 421). It was simplified but the resemblance is otherwise very close, the peacocks in the foreground and the dogs playing on the steps putting the matter beyond doubt. The figure on the left of Amman's print, however, was replaced in the painting by a group of six soldiers, one of them mounted. These were copied from a second woodcut in this Bible, illustrating the Triumph of Mordecai from Esther 6 (Fig. 422) which also provided the classical arch on the left, with the

buildings beyond. The fact that the painting depends so heavily on illustrations by Jost Amman suggests that the artist might have been German, but as the woodcuts were presumably popular in Protestant circles he could equally have been English, Flemish or, indeed, French. What a pity that, though dated, the picture is unsigned. We would dearly like to know for certain the name of the artist, and indeed the actual subject. Alastair Laing has tentatively suggested[10] that the painting depicts not Ulysses and Penelope but the return of Tarquinius Collatinus to his faithful and virtuous wife Lucretia. There is good reason to suppose, as will be explained before long, that Bess sympathised equally with Lucretia and Penelope.

423 John Balechouse (attributed), *The Return of Ulysses to Penelope*, 1570. The National Trust.

424 Hardwick Hall, Derbyshire, intarsia panel, c.1570.

425 Jost Amman, Solomon's Palace, from *Neuwe Biblische Figuren* (Frankfurt, 1564). British Library, London (680.a.9).

426 Frans Huys after Frans Floris, *Apollo and the Muses*, 1565. British Museum, London.

Another woodcut from the same Protestant Bible was adapted for one of the four inlaid and painted panels, one dated 1576, that are amongst the finest survivals of decoration that may have originated at Elizabethan Chatsworth: they are at present shown at Hardwick in the gloom of the north staircase. All four take the form of architectural perspectives but although superficially similar they were not derived from the same set of prints. From Amman's *Neuwe Biblische Figuren* comes the scene depicting a building within a circular walled enclosure (Fig. 424) and the woodcut shows that this represents Solomon's Palace in Jerusalem (Fig. 425). A second panel derives from the early set of architectural capricci – *Scenographiae,*

sive Perspectivae . . . (Antwerp, 1560) – designed by Jan Vredeman de Vries. The set was certainly used in England, but only by artists who were themselves foreigners or had received some training on the Continent, such as Hans Eworth and Richard Hickes (see pp.78–9 and 226). I have so far been unable to identify the source of the two remaining intarsia panels. The combination of the Frankfurt source of one panel and the demanding intarsia technique suggests that the craftsman responsible was German rather than English, though he might have been working in this country. The 1601 inventory of Chatsworth makes it clear that the house was indeed provided with fine marquetry work of this kind:

High Great Chamber	verie fayre waynscotted with coulored woodes markentrie and set fourth with planetes

High Gallerie	verie fayre waynscotted with coulored woodes markentrie and pelasters fayre set foarth	My Ladies withdrawing chamber	portals verie fayre waynscotted deep french panell markentrie
Savills Chamber	verie fayre waynscotted or seeled with coulored woodes markantrie pelasters and carving	My Ladies bedchamber	verie fayre waynscotted to the height with coulored woodes
Round Turrett	verie fayre waynscotted and with alabaster blackstone and other devices of carving	ffynishers Chamber	fayre waynscotted markentrie[11]
Another turrett	fayre waynscotted with coulored woods and piramides		
Matted gallerie	fayre waynscotted to the height markentrie with		

Unquestionably from Chatsworth is the overmantel depicting Apollo and the Muses (Fig. 427) probably made originally for the 'Muses Chamber', the name given in the 1601 Inventory to the High Great Chamber or the withdrawing chamber to the Earl of Leicester's chamber.[12] Carved in alabaster, it is a work

253

Dafur Sara Tobiæ, vxor. Epulati funt benedicentes deum. Tob. 7

428 Unidentified engraver after Maarten van Heemskerck, the Marriage of Tobias and Sarah, from *The Story of Tobias*, 1556.

of high quality and has an integral frame consisting of a narrow band of Vitruvian scroll and a much broader band of shells in roundels with interlacing ribbons of strapwork.[13] The latter may have been derived from a French print now lost, but an incidental feature, the strapwork cartouche enclosing the initials of the Queen, was derived from a suite designed by the Antwerp artist, Jacob Floris: his *Compertimenta pictoriis flosculis . . . variegata* (1567) may well have been bound up with the *Compertimentorum . . .* published the previous year, which was employed for the decoration of the Eglantine Table.

But what of the main scene? Apollo was a popular figure during the sixteenth century because he represented the rational, civilised aspect of man's nature, particularly when accompanied by the nine Muses, the goddesses of poetic inspiration and of the creative arts in general. Of the many prints depicting the scene, one, an engraving by Giorgio Ghisi (an Italian who had worked for the print publisher Hieronymus Cock in Antwerp), had more than once been used by decorative artists in mainland Europe[14] and several figures borrowed for the titlepage of *The psalmes of David in English meter* printed by John Day in 1579 prove that it was known in England.[15] But neither this nor a print by Maarten van Heemskerck was used for the overmantel.[16] Instead, another Antwerp print was copied, an engraving by Frans Huys after Jacob Floris's better-known brother Frans, published by Cock in Antwerp in 1565 (Fig. 426).[17]

Another probable survivor from the decoration of Bess's Chatsworth is the chimneypiece and overmantel depicting the Marriage of Tobias and Sarah (Fig. 429): in the central blackstone panel of the chimneypiece there is the dim outlined monogram of Mary Queen of Scots, Elizabeth and George Talbot, which was repeated on one of the octagonal embroidered panels now at Oxburgh Hall.[18] The story of Tobias's adventures with the archangel Gabriel is told in the Apocryphal Book of Tobit: charged with a mission to recover money owing to his blind and dying father Tobit, Tobias set out with his dog and took the archangel as his companion on the way; Tobias bathed in the River Tigris and would have been devoured by a fish, but caught it and with its burnt offal he exorcised the demons in Sarah, the daughter of a kinsman with whom they stayed after completing their task. Sarah had been married seven times before, but the demons had each time prevented consummation. The binding of Tobias and Sarah in marriage was a union destined to be blessed with complete success and it may have been for this reason that Bess chose it for the Chatsworth overmantel: her marriage to Sir William Cavendish not only lasted longer than any of her others but also provided her with six children who survived infancy. The Tobias story ends with the healing of Tobit's blindness and the eventual disclosure of Gabriel's true identity. The source for the alabaster relief was an engraving by an unidentified artist after Maarten van Heemskerck, published by Hieronymus Cock in Antwerp in 1556 (Fig. 428). The whole suite of prints must have been available to Bess or her embroiderers, for all ten seem to have been reproduced in the border panels of a needlework table-carpet which bears the Talbot arms, the cypher ES and the date 1579 (Figs 430, 431).[19] Bess seems to have liked the story of Tobias particularly: 'Tobies Chamber' on the first floor of the New Hall at Hardwick in 1601 had 'Fyve peeces of tapestrie hanginges of the storie of Tobie Tenn foote deep'.

A Flemish print also inspired the decoration of another needlework table-carpet, again sporting the intials ES and dated 1574. Here the central scene shows the Judgement of Paris (Fig. 434) and, whilst related to engravings by Marcantonio Raimondi and others who depended ultimately on Raphael, actually derives from a source that is not primarily narrative so much as ornamental: this is an engraving after a design by Jacob Floris (Fig. 435), included in his *Compertimentorum quod vocant multiplex genus* of 1566, a suite which as already noted was used in the decoration of the Eglantine Table made around 1567. There is evidence that this suite was later used at Hardwick and from there its influence spread to at least one smaller manor house in south Yorkshire.[20]

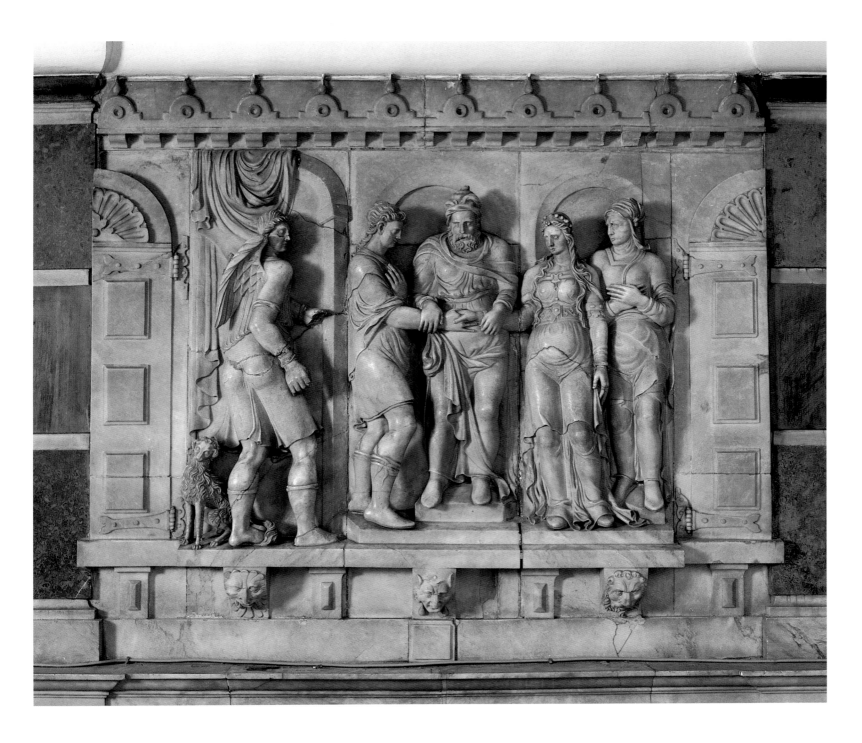

These Flemish sources are rather at variance with the mainly French prints identified by earlier writers as employed in textiles worked by Bess and Mary Queen of Scots during the 1570s, the decade during which the lives of these two ladies were inextricably entwined.[21] In reality, however, French prints can be shown to have mingled with Flemish in the design of many of their embroideries before the latter influence became predominant in the decoration of the two houses at Hardwick.

As early as March 1569, when Mary had only been the prisoner of Bess's husband for a matter of weeks,

Shrewsbury noted that 'This Queen continueth daily to resort to my wife's chamber where with the Lady Lewiston [Livingstone] and Mrs [Mary] Seton she useth to sit working with the needle in which she much delighteth and in devising works'.[22] The best-known of these embroideries are the hangings made by the ladies to celebrate their various marriages and consequently known now as the Cavendish, the Mary Queen of Scots (or Marian) and the Shrewsbury Hangings.[23] These consist of panels, of three different shapes, stitched to green velvet, perhaps in the early seventeenth century: octagons with monograms or

429 Hardwick Hall, Derbyshire, overmantel showing the Marriage of Tobias and Sarah, probably made for Elizabethan Chatsworth, *c*.1570.

430 (*top*) Hardwick Hall, Derbyshire, table-carpet dated 1579, with scenes from the Story of Tobias and Sarah, general view before conservation.

431 Hardwick Hall, Derbyshire, the Tobias table-carpet, detail of Tobias and the Angel Taking Leave of Tobit.

motifs based on woodcuts in herbals, cruciform panels worked with animals or birds from natural history books, and squares which were originally cushion-covers. One of these is dated 1570.

The French sources include Claude Paradin's *Devises Heroïques* (Lyons, 1557) which provided several emblems including the one used in the central square of Bess's Shrewsbury Hanging;[24] Pierre Belon's *La Nature et Diversité des Poissons* and *L'Histoire de la Nature des Oiseaux* (both Paris, 1557) supplied fish and birds. The 1572 Lyons edition of Pietro Andrea Matthioli's *Commentarii . . .* , or herbal, was used for a set of hexagonal embroideries now at Hardwick which were conceivably worked during Mary's captivity. Other sources were the Swiss author Conrad

Gesner's *Historia Animalium* published in four volumes between 1551 and 1558 (and including nearly a thousand woodcuts) and Gabriel Faerno's *Centum Fabulae* first published in Rome in 1563 (with a new Antwerp edition in 1573).

To these can be added two more, which supply

434 Hardwick Hall, Derbyshire, table-carpet dated 1574, with the Judgement of Paris.

432 (*facing page top right*) The needlework cushion-cover in the centre of the Shrewsbury Hanging, worked by Bess of Hardwick and Mary Queen of Scots, *c.*1570. Victoria and Albert Museum, London (on loan to Oxburgh Hall, Norfolk).

433 (*facing page bottom right*) Lucas or Johannes Duetecum after Jan Vredeman de Vries, *Grottesco: in diversche manieren* (Antwerp, 1565). Victoria and Albert Museum, London.

435 (*below*) Pieter van der Heyden after Jacob Floris, cartouche with the Judgement of Paris, from *Compertimentorum quod vocant multiplex genus* (Antwerp, 1566). The Royal Library – National Library of Sweden, Stockholm, Maps and Prints Department, De la Gardie Collection.

the border of the cushion-cover in the centre of the Shrewsbury Hanging, and the two term figures. The border (Fig. 432) was cleverly adapted from elements in a grotesque designed by Jan Vredeman de Vries and published in his *Grottesco* (Fig. 433) while the term was copied not from the same print but from Vredeman's specialised set, *Caryatidum . . . sive Athlantidum* of the same year.

French or German prints may also have contributed to the design of the sumptuous embroideries – also dating from the 1570s, and made out of velvet, cloth of gold and figured silk, partly cut from medieval copes – depicting virtuous wives flanked by figures personifying their virtues. The set originally consisted of five panels[25] and by 1601 they were one of the two alternative sets of hangings for the Withdrawing Chamber at Hardwick: 'Fyve peeces of hanginges of Cloth of golde velvett and other like stuffe imbroidered with pictures of the vertues, one of Zenobia, magnanimitas and prudentia, an other of Arthemitia, Constantia and pietas, an other of penelope, prudentia, and sapientia, an other of Cleopatra, fortituto, and Justitia, an other of Lucretia, Charitas and liberalitas, everie peece being twelve foote deep . . .'

The Artemisia hanging is dated 1573. Made from fifteenth- and sixteenth-century Italian silks and velvets cut from vestments brought to Bess by Sir William Cavendish in 1557 and by Sir William St Loe

436 Hardwick Hall, Derbyshire, appliqué wall-hanging with Lucretia between Charity and Liberality, c.1573.

mostly defied identification. The figure of Lucretia, the classical heroine noted for her chastity and liberality, may have been chosen as a reminder to Bess of her last and short-lived daughter, who bore that name after her birth in March 1557. Lucretia's pose (Fig. 436) closely adheres to the best-known formula of contemporary prints, particularly in her two-handed grasp on the sword, yet I am not satisfied that she was copied from any individual print I have seen. On the other hand, this pose is identical to that of a painting in the Musée des Beaux-Arts in Beaune,[27] although the embroiderer extended the figure to full-length and partly clothed it. As the painting may have belonged to Mary Queen of Scots and no engraved reproduction is known, it may itself have served as the basis for the embroidery. In any case, a French source is implied here. By contrast, an Italian or German print may have been used for Piety, who appears on the Artemisia hanging as Pero suckling her father Cimon in a scene known as Roman Charity.[28] The subject is rarely if ever encountered elsewhere in English art of the period.

Equally uncommon is the appearance of Sardanapalus, the seventh-century BC Persian king and voluptuary, on one of two completely surviving hangings perhaps made for Chatsworth or Sheffield Manor. With its companions, it was amongst the textiles in the Best Bed Chamber at Hardwick in 1601: 'Seaven peeces of hanginges of imbroiderie of Cloth of golde and silver, cloth of tyssue, velvett of sondry Coulors, and nedleworke twelve foote deepe, one peece of the picture of fayth and his contrarie Mahomet, an other peece with the picture of hope, and the contrary Judas, an other peece with the picture of temperaunce and the contrary Sardanapales, the other fowre peeces paned and wrought with flowers and slips of nedlework . . .'

The main source is here identified as a rare series of prints of the Virtues engraved by Hans Collaert perhaps after designs by Crispijn van der Broeck in 1576.[29] Whilst undoubtedly depending on the prints, the embroiderer made significant alterations. In the panel depicting Temperance with Sardanapalus (Fig. 438), Temperance is given a standing pose and is dressed – like the figures of the revellers in the subsidiary scene – in contemporary instead of classical clothes (Fig. 437). The flagon and cup stand not on a stone slab but on an Elizabethan table, while the classical building has been transformed into three stylised columns. More radical changes were made in the hanging depicting Faith with Mahomet (Fig. 440). This has the half-figure of Mahomet (Fig. 439) but a quite different standing figure of Faith (again in contemporary dress). The Moorish-style building in the background with figures in Turkish costume must come from another source, perhaps German rather

in the 1560s, the hangings are remarkable for their architectural composition, the figures being set beneath the graduated openings of a triumphal arch. With the sole exception of a grotesque mask ornamenting one of the keystones, which derives from a set originally designed by Cornelis Floris in about 1555,[26] the sources used for these hangings have

438   Hardwick Hall, Derbyshire, appliqué wall-hanging depicting Temperance with Sardanapalus, *c*.1580.

437 (*facing page bottom*)   Hans Collaert, perhaps after Crispijn van der Broeck, Temperantia, from a set of *The Virtues* (1576). Museum Boijmans Van Beuningen, Rotterdam.

The engraving caption reads:

MACHOMETVS.

6

Croiez en Iesus Christ, et vous serez sauvez,
Et du faux Mahometh le conseil ne suiuez.

SÆVIAT IMPIETAS QVANTV LIBET, ARMA MINASQ2.
RIDET SANCTA FIDES ROBORE FVLTA SVO.

Ghelooft in Iesu Christu, y·dy suet sacliss: sins
En willt ng, als Machum3, back in duals·sns·

439 Hans Collaert, perhaps after Crispijn van der Broeck, Fides, from a set of *The Virtues* (1576). Museum Boijmans Van Beuningen, Rotterdam.

answered until the main body of Bess's patronage has been investigated.

Most of these textiles must have been removed by Bess from Chatsworth, along with plate and many items of furniture (including the celebrated Sea-Dog Table related to a design by Du Cerceau),[33] during her acrimonious wrangle with the Earl of Shrewsbury.[34] The irretrievable breakdown of her marriage in 1584 left the old manor house at Hardwick, which she had bought from her feckless brother James the previous year, as the only one available to her; she had but a life-interest in Chatsworth which would pass to her eldest son Henry whom she heartily detested for siding with her husband.

From about 1587 to 1591 she remodelled and enlarged the house to become what is now called Hardwick Old Hall (Fig. 443). The east wing was built during the first year and the new west wing overlooking the valley was finished within the six months between May and December 1588. Decorative work apparently continued until about 1595 or 1596. Neither architecturally nor practically can Hardwick Old Hall ever have been satisfactory, but it enabled Bess to 'hold to herself all the rest of her living' and, as it turned out, served as a practice run for the New Hall. Bess had started the New Hall by the end of 1590, possibly laying out the foundations a couple of weeks before the Earl of Shrewsbury's death, or at most only a month afterwards. The shell of the building was complete by the end of 1593 and Bess moved in on 4 October 1597; decoration and furnishing continued up until her death in 1608 and beyond. As Girouard has said, 'After a lifetime's experience of building she clearly set out to create the perfect house'.[35]

Though so different from each other, the Old and New Halls are alike in shunning almost entirely details derived from architectural pattern-books, despite the fact that several of the workmen had previously been employed on Wollaton, the epitome of pattern-book architecture. Indeed, the occasional quotations from Serlio and Vredeman in the New Hall are overwhelmingly outweighed by those from biblical and other subject prints.[36]

Although now mostly roofless, the Old Hall retains several chimneypieces with plaster overmantels attributed to Abraham Smith, who had already worked at Chatsworth in 1581,[37] and fragments of two great interiors almost the equal of any room in the New Hall: the Forest Great Chamber on the top floor of the east wing, and the Giants Chamber (or Hill Great Chamber) in the corresponding position in the west wing, overlooking the valley. Some of the overmantels have armorials contained in anglicised strap-work cartouches, others have figurative scenes that

than French or Flemish.[30] More than one set of prints, therefore, lie behind these marvellous embroideries which have finally relinquished some of the mystery of their creation.

Almost as enigmatic are the patchwork embroideries depicting single allegorical figures beneath round arches. All are female and include goddesses, the Cardinal and other Virtues (and Vices), the Elements, the Senses and the Liberal Arts. Such a comprehensive series could not have been culled from a single source – the first illustrated edition of Ripa lay a generation in the future – so their designer probably adapted a number of prints to achieve the desired consistency of appearance. A clue is provided by some of the Virtues, who resemble their equivalents by Virgil Solis without ever being slavish copies, and by the Liberal Arts. Two of the latter in particular – Perspective and Architecture (Fig. 441) – must, from the way in which they hold their attributes, have been adapted from prints by Etienne Delaune (Fig. 442). So it is probable that exhaustive searching would ultimately identify all the sources used for these figures.

It would be very exciting to know how these panels were used originally. At present some are framed up individually and hang on the north staircase at Hardwick, whilst others have been framed in groups to form multi-fold screens, but in 1900 some were shown incorporated into the canopy that hung on the north wall of the High Great Chamber.[31] Could they *ab initio* have bordered one or other set of embroideries just considered?[32] Are there any clues as to who designed them? This question cannot be

440   Hardwick Hall, Derbyshire, appliqué wall–hanging depicting Faith with Mahomet, *c.*1580.

derive quite certainly from continental prints. These are to be found in various rooms in the west wing, either side of the stone staircase and intended for the use of William Cavendish, Bess's younger and favoured son, and his servants. The source of three, the figures of the Elements (Air (Fig. 444), Fire and Water), has long been recognised as prints by Crispijn de Passe the elder after designs by Maarten de Vos, but the remainder proved more elusive.[38]

In what was Mr William Cavendish's chamber a figure is depicted seated astride a deer; in Mr Reason's chamber a man milks a goat (Figs 445, 448).[39] There would really be no way of guessing who these people are without identifying their print source. The former is closely similar to a print depicting Auditus (Hearing) in a well-known suite of the Five Senses engraved by Cornelis Cort after Frans Floris, so much so that it would certainly have been within the competence of a skilled plasterer such as Abraham Smith to have made the necessary changes. But he had no need to, for he was able to copy the scene from a suite of the Twelve Patriarchs, etched in 1550 by Dirck Coornhert after designs by Maarten van Heemskerck. It depicts Nephthali seated on a stag by a statue of Mercury (Fig. 446). The accompanying verse reads in translation: 'Nephthali is likened to a swift hart, and with his mouth he shall speak sweet words.' The man who milks a goat, accompanied by another now virtually invisible figure, is Aser (Fig. 447) – sometimes seen as symbolising virtue and vice, the two paths a person can take – accompanied by Ceres. The significance of these figures will be considered below.

On the west side of the staircase at first-floor level is a room with another handsome plaster overmantel (Fig. 450). Rather more fragmentary, it seems to

442 Etienne Delaune, Arquitraicture. Warburg Institute, London.

show the angel appearing to the Virgin in an interior. But at least one figure is now missing and this suggests that this is not the Annunciation. Again, the discovery of the print source proves beyond doubt that the subject is the angel Gabriel accompanied by Tobias taking leave of Tobit as they begin their journey to Rages in Media. One of the most conspicuous features of the relief is a Serlian window, partially obscured, above a table on the right: this can easily be

443 Hardwick Old Hall, Derbyshire, c.1587–91, seen from the roof of the New Hall.

441 (facing page) Hardwick Hall, Derbyshire, appliqué panel with the figure of Architecture.

recognised in the engraving after Maarten van Heemskerck (Fig. 449) from the suite which Bess had already employed for the Tobias table-carpet in the 1570s (see Figs 430, 431).

The magnificent Hill Great Chamber can still be imagined from the drawing by S.H. Grimm, its walls panelled below and plastered above with a syncopated arrangement of rib-work arches. The freestone chimneypiece is surmounted by a plaster overmantel (probably executed by Abraham Smith some time after March 1596)[40] in which figures, perhaps of Gog and Magog, flank a strapwork cartouche enclosing a winged figure with winged heels (Fig. 453). The cartouche was adapted – with inexplicable alterations to the lower part – from Clemens Perret's very popular copy-book, *Exercitatio Alphabetica* (Fig. 451), published in Antwerp in 1569 with thirty-four cartouches attributed to Vredeman de Vries (see pp.73–6): this overmantel is the only surviving evidence that this book was known at Hardwick.

But who is the winged figure who appears so wild-eyed in the overmantel cartouche? Certainly not Mercury nor precisely Cupid who is usually depicted as a winged cherub. Once again, it is impossible to

444 (*top*) Hardwick Old Hall, Derbyshire, plaster overmantel representing Air, one of the Four Elements, copied from a print by Crispijn de Passe the elder after Maarten de Vos.

445 (*above left*) Hardwick Old Hall, Derbyshire, plaster overmantel in Mr William Cavendish's chamber.

446 (*above right*) Dirck Coornhert after Maarten van Heemskerck, Nephthali, from *The Twelve Patriarchs*, 1550. The Syndics of the Fitzwilliam Museum, Cambridge.

identify the figure or to determine its function in the iconological programme without first discovering the source of the image. This is a print illustrating the Triumph of Patience after a drawing by Maarten van Heemskerck (Fig. 452): it is the first of eight plates in the suite of the same title, engraved by Dirck Coornhert and published by Hieronymus Cock in 1559.[41] It shows a figure, labelled Patientia, seated on a stone plinth on a triumphal car drawn by Spes (Hope) and Desiderium (Desire), the latter supplying the figure used on the overmantel.[42] As will be seen, there are reasons for suggesting that this overmantel provides the clue to the whole programme of decoration in the Old and New Halls at Hardwick.

Hardwick New Hall

Hardwick Hall is distinguished by its biaxial symmetry, its height and compactness, the logic by which the increase in window size reflects the mounting loftiness of the rooms inside, above all the genius of the internal planning and the romance and majesty of the state rooms. Much of this character must have been due to the inspiration of the mason-architect Robert Smythson. Add to it the best masons', plasterers', painters' and embroiderers' work and there is little dispute that for sheer excitement there is no Elizabethan house in England to rival Hardwick.

The form of Hardwick – a rectangular block with six towers attached, two on the long sides and one at each end – is very remarkable and to some extent represents a development of Worksop Manor. The discipline is even more rigorous, however, and it has been suggested that the woodcut of Solomon's Palace,

448 (top right)   Hardwick Old Hall, Derbyshire, plaster overmantel in Mr Reason's chamber.

449 (above left)   Unidentified engraver after Maarten van Heemskerck, Tobias and the Angel Taking Leave of Tobit, from *The Story of Tobias*, 1556. British Museum, London.

450 (above right)   Hardwick Old Hall, Derbyshire, plaster overmantel depicting the Departure of Tobias.

452 (*above*) Dirck Coornhert after Maarten van Heemskerck, the Triumph of Patience, from the suite of the same name, 1559. Rijksmuseum-Stichting, Amsterdam.

451 (*top*) Lucas or Johannes Duetecum after Jan Vredeman de Vries, pl.vi from Clemens Perret, *Exercitatio Alphabetica . . .* (Antwerp, 1569). The Royal Library – National Library of Sweden, Stockholm, Maps and Prints Department, De la Gardie Collection.

453 (*facing page*) Hardwick Old Hall, Derbyshire, chimneypiece and plaster overmantel in the Hill Great Chamber.

which provided the source for one of the intarsia panels (see Figs 424, 425), might have given Bess and Smythson the idea for Hardwick.[43] There are some resemblances: the palace is a more or less regular building with attached towers, situated within a regular enclosure (actually two concentric circles). It would have required a leap of the imagination – indeed a stroke of genius of which Smythson could have been capable – to arrive at the Hardwick we know from this woodcut. But it would give Hardwick the intellectual basis – the purposeful reconstruction of the palace of the wise king of the Old Testament – that the house has seemed to present-day observers to lack. Surprising, perhaps, but not utterly far-fetched in view of the possibility that Wollaton might have been a conscious attempt to reconstruct Solomon's Temple.[44]

The decoration of Hardwick Hall must have been the collaborative effort of Bess, her clerk of works and the band of trusted craftsmen, many of them employed previously at Chatsworth or Wollaton.[45] The derivation of two figures in the plaster frieze of the High Great Chamber from prints by Crispijn de Passe after Maarten de Vos was recognised satisfactorily many years ago, but recent attempts to link decoration with continental prints have been less convincing – for instance the identification of the soldier's head guarding the door from the staircase to 'My Ladys Withdrawing Chamber' with Joshua from Nicolaes de Bruyn's 1594 set of *The Nine Worthies*.[46]

There is little figure-carving at Hardwick, but it is of high quality and was perhaps the work of Thomas Accres, the best-paid of Bess's craftsmen. In the gallery the overmantel cartouches – perhaps inspired by Benedetto Battini's suite *Vigilate quia nescitis diem neque horam* (Antwerp, 1553) – enclose alabaster figures representing Justice (Fig. 454) and Mercy; these are stylistically very similar to that in the Green Velvet Room (the Best Bedchamber in 1601), which represents Charity (Fig. 456). All three derive from a set of the Virtues designed by Maarten de Vos and engraved by Hans Collaert (Figs 455, 458).

Abraham Smith was the main plasterer at Hardwick, although he was also capable of carving stone. He may have been responsible for the overmantel in 'my Ladies Bed Chamber' which has a cartouche derived from Jacob Floris's set *Compertimentorum . . .* (1566), the set that had been used for the Judgement of Paris table-carpet in 1574, but most of the strapwork decoration in the house is completely anglicised. For figure-work, however, the plasterers resorted to engravings. The plaster overmantel relief in what was in 1601 the 'little dyning Chamber' (now the Paved Room) is an example. It depicts a goddess naked but for a cloak which slips from her shoulders (Fig. 459); she holds a cornucopia

454 (*right*) Hardwick Hall, Derbyshire, Gallery overmantel with the figure of Justice.

455 (*far right*) Hans Collaert after Maarten de Vos, Justice and Prudence, two of the Virtues. Warburg Institute, London.

456 Hardwick Hall, Derbyshire, Best Bedchamber overmantel with the figure of Charity.

457 (*far right*) Unidentified engraver after Hendrick Goltzius, Cybele, 1586.

458 (*right*) Hans Collaert after Maarten de Vos, Charity and Grace, two of the Virtues. Warburg Institute, London.

and, from the mural crown she wears, must be Cybele rather than Ceres.[47] She represents Earth, one of the Four Elements, and derives from an anonymous engraving after a design by Hendrick Goltzius (Fig. 457) which he published in 1586.[48] The plasterer omitted a male figure from the background and introduced instead a unicorn and the Hardwick stag.

Together with the gallery, the High Great Chamber provides the climax of anyone's experience of Hardwick (Fig. 460). The room, fittingly positioned at the top of the south staircase, tells two interrelated stories. The Brussels tapestries woven to a design by Michiel Coxie, which were bought by Bess in 1587 and must therefore have to some extent dictated the dimensions of the room, relate the history of Ulysses (Odysseus), the resourceful yet faithful hero of the *Odyssey*, a story perhaps chosen as a symbol of Bess's own loyalty to her husband, to her faith and to her Queen. The plaster frieze, on the other hand, glorifies Diana, here personifying Queen Elizabeth under whose just and virtuous rule the country had

459 Hardwick Hall, Derbyshire, plaster overmantel in the 'litle dyning Chamber' with the figure of Cybele, personifying Earth.

460 Hardwick Hall, Derbyshire, the High Great Chamber.

reaped prosperity for so many years. She is seen with her courtiers in the centre of the north-wall frieze, and beneath, on a chair under a canopy of estate, Bess (or the Queen herself, had she ever visited Hardwick) would have received her visitors as they entered through the door across the room. This great frieze was devised with almost infinite wit and inventiveness as a forest setting of extraordinary variety, inhabited by figures, Hardwick stags and animals and birds of all kinds, and superbly executed by Richard Orton and John Marker.

How was this vast panorama designed? Its origins – unsurprisingly – lie in continental prints. Just as the figures in the reveals either side of the window bay

representing Spring and Summer derive from engravings (by Crispijn de Passe after Maarten de Vos), so do some if not all the figure groups in the main frieze. I have been unable to identify all the sources. The virgin huntress and her group of courtiers, for instance, have yet to be tied to particular engravings,[49] but three groups of figures were copied or adapted from a single suite of hunting prints, *Venationes Ferarum, Avium, Piscium* . . . engraved by Philips Galle after designs by Johannes Stradanus and first published in 1578. The suite accounts for two of the lions in the extreme north-west corner of the room, the bear-hunt (Fig. 461) in the centre of the south wall (with a possible reference to the story of Diana and

270

Callisto),[50] and the three hunters immediately to the left of the overmantel, two of whom adjust their footwear while a third holds their spears (Fig. 463): the bear-hunt was copied almost literally from the engraving (Fig. 462) while the hunters come from a plate illustrating a gazelle-hunt (Fig. 464). Elephants and monkeys, even ostriches and porcupines appear in the suite and were evidently not safe from (imaginary) late sixteenth-century human predators. In its dependence on hunting scenes after Stradanus, this plaster frieze has a painted counterpart at Madingley Hall near Cambridge, dating from the early seventeenth century.[51]

Whereas Chatsworth had marquetry panelling, Bess had to be content at Hardwick with stencilled decoration, mostly taking the form of arabesques which must ultimately depend on prints. The dado panels in the Withdrawing Room have cartouches in their centres which derive from the suite designed by Marc Geerarts and published under the title *Diversarum protractationum quas vulgo Compartimenta . . .* by Gerard de Iode in Antwerp in 1565. The use of a series of late sixteenth-century portrait engravings of Roman emperors and classical authors and philosophers pasted on to the panelling around the window-bay of the High Great Chamber is unusual and may only have been introduced when the panelling itself was added in the early seventeenth century or even later.

It is a tragedy that, richly furnished though Hardwick still seems to us, all the plate listed in the 1601 inventory has completely disappeared. How far it would have added to the picture of dependence upon continental prints is questionable, but it is tantalising, nevertheless, to speculate on the appearance and possible derivation of the 'great guilt salt with a Cover & pictures waying threescore too ounces' – whose description recalls the Vyvyan Salt – and all the other treasures listed in the 'saide newe building'.

In the absence of plate, textiles now constitute the most important surviving furnishings of Hardwick. Those that were made during the 1570s for Chatsworth or one of the Sheffield houses have already been discussed. Next come those that stylistically are later and must have been at Hardwick from the first; most were in the window bays of the gallery by 1601. Some perhaps came to Bess as gifts and hardly concern us here. Two are professionally made embroideries both described in the inventory as a 'long quition of nedledwerke, silk & Cruell . . .', one depicting 'the storie of the sacryfice of Isack . . .', the other 'the Storie of the Judgment of Saloman between the too women for the Childe . . .' They are of a type that include figures in French court clothes of the last two decades of the sixteenth century and were probably, indeed, made in France.[52] Superfluous onlookers flank their central scenes, which appear to have been adapted respectively from Jost Amman's woodcut of the Judgement of Solomon in the German Bible of 1564, and an anonymous Fontainebleau print of the Sacrifice of Isaac.[53]

Contrasting with these are several English-made embroideries which follow printed sources more slavishly. One has already been mentioned, the cushion-cover worked with the Rape of Europa from Virgil Solis's reversed copy of a woodcut by Bernard Salomon. The most charming of them is the embroidery (Fig. 465) which in 1601 was placed in one of the windows of the gallery, where it was described as: 'one long quition the grounde purple velvet, the fancie of a fowler and other personages in nedleworke with blewe silk frenge & tassells & lyned with blewe damask . . .' The scene was not the original invention of the embroiderer nor was the building in the background intended to be Chatsworth. The source was actually an engraving showing the Return from a Bird Hunt (Fig. 466), from the same set of hunting prints that were used for the frieze of the High Great Chamber, by Philips Galle after Johannes Stradanus.

Rather less accomplished is the valance embroidered with the story of the Prodigal Son (Fig. 468). The source for the four scenes here can easily be traced to the suite engraved by Philips Galle after Maarten van Heemskerck and published in 1562 (Fig. 467). This was not the only use of this suite at Hardwick. Another valance, from its identical borders, may have been associated with this. It has a seated female figure playing a lute, flanked by a drum and the pipes of a regal, and by a stag lying behind a tree. She personifies Auditus or Hearing, and comes from Cornelis Cort's engravings of the Five Senses after designs by Frans Floris. The print could hardly have been a more appropriate model for Bess, having a stag that would be taken by every observer as a symbol of Hardwick.

Some of the sources for cushion-covers have defied identification, like the 'long quition of nedleworke of the storie of Acteon and Diana', despite there being numerous sixteenth-century engravings of the scene. Another story from Ovid's *Metamorphoses* is the Fall of Phaethon which appears on a long cushion-cover (Fig. 469) that was in the Withdrawing Chamber in 1601. In 'a classic example of hubris followed by nemesis',[54] Phaethon asked his father Helios for permission to drive the horses of the sun for a day; unable to control them, and threatening to set the world on fire, he was killed by a thunderbolt from Zeus. He fell from his chariot into the river Eridanus (the Po) and was mourned by his sisters until they turned into trees, their tears becoming fossilised resin, or amber. The story was a popular one with painters and the designers of prints – it even appears in one of

461 (*above*) Hardwick Hall, Derbyshire, plaster frieze of the High Great Chamber showing a bear-hunt.

462 Philips Galle after Johannes Stradanus, Bear-Hunt, from *Venationes Ferarum, Avium, Piscium . . .* (Antwerp, 1578). Victoria and Albert Museum, London.

Ioan. Stra. inue.

Sic capitur gladijs, et acutę cuspidis hastis,   Pręceps sanguinea dū se rotat vrsus arena.

463 (*above*) Hardwick Hall, Derbyshire, plaster frieze of the High Great Chamber showing a gazelle-hunt.

Per iuga summa petunt imbelles corpore damas,   Et per muscosos scopules, atq; horrida saxa.

464 Philips Galle after Johannes Stradanus, Gazelle-Hunt, from *Venationes Ferarum, Avium, Piscium* . . . (Antwerp, 1578). Victoria and Albert Museum, London.

465 (*above*) Hardwick Hall, Derbyshire, needlework cushion-cover described in the 1601 inventory as 'the fancie of a fowler'.

Crea fu torto capitur Ficedula reti, Aurea frugiferos dum tollunt tempora vultus.

Filius prodigus accepta portione, substantiæ suæ a patre peregre proficiscitur.

468 (*below*) Hardwick Hall, Derbyshire, needlework valance depicting the parable of the Prodigal Son.

466 (*facing page centre left*) Philips Galle after Johannes Stradanus, Return from a Bird Hunt, from *Venationes Ferarum, Avium, Piscium . . .* (Antwerp, 1578). Victoria and Albert Museum, London.

Jacob Floris's cartouches in the *Compertimentorum quod vocant multiplex genus* of 1566, which had been used for the Judgement of Paris table-carpet in 1574. But the broadside rather than head-on viewpoint and the unusual attitude of the four horses' heads together suggest that the actual source for the cushion cover is an incidental scene (probably supplied on a whim by the engraver, Frans Huys) in a print of a man-of-war between two armed galleys (Fig. 470); this was one of a set of eleven engravings published by Philips Galle in 1564–5 after designs by Pieter Bruegel the elder.[55]

Textiles of a very different calibre are included in the full-length portrait of Queen Elizabeth which hangs at the north end of the gallery. If Janet Arnold is correct, this painting records an exceedingly elaborate gown that was given to the Queen by Bess as a New Year's gift having been made up by the Queen's tailor, William Jones.[56] The white silk forepart or petticoat is decorated with a wealth of flowers, birds and beasts, some of which were apparently derived from Pierre Belon's *L'Histoire de la Nature des Oyseaux . . .* (Paris 1555) and Conrad Gesner's *Historia Animalium* of 1551, both used in the hangings now at Oxburgh Hall. Whether these were embroidered by Bess herself or painted by her painter John Balechouse, the forepart would have been designed at Hardwick.

Balechouse was undoubtedly responsible for treasures that still survive in the house, largely overlooked. These are the four painted cloths that hang on the walls of what is now the Upper Chapel. Notwithstanding the lukewarm opinion expressed in the 1840s by the 6th Duke of Devonshire, who wrote that 'the history of St Paul is there represented with earnest, if not successful effect', these painted cloths are arguably

amongst the most significant Elizabethan works of art in existence. Even if they were the only original furnishings left at Hardwick they would nevertheless, I believe, afford a remarkable insight into Bess's mind.

Painted cloths of different sizes were once a common feature of rooms throughout the Tudor period at all but the lowest levels of society. Less expensive than tapestries, even shopkeepers and joiners had them at the end of the fifteenth century,[57] and a Frenchman, Etienne Perlin, who visited England in 1558 commented: 'the English make such use of tapestries of painted cloths [*tapisseries de toiles*

470 (*above*) Frans Huys after Pieter Bruegel the elder, *Men-of-War*. British Museum, London.

467 (*facing page centre right*) Philips Galle after Maarten van Heemskerck, The Prodigal Son Leaving his Father's House, 1562. Graphische Sammlung Albertina, Vienna.

pinctes] which are very well executed . . . for there are few houses you could enter without finding these tapestries.'[58] So common were they that, during the second half of the sixteenth century, fifty-six per cent of inventories in Nottinghamshire (for example) listed painted cloths or hangings.[59] They had a functional as well as a decorative purpose: like those of Sir William Wangrave in 1555 which were of yellow say 'broydered with painted cloth',[60] their thick textile support (which may be the original) would have provided some protection from draughts. These painted cloths at Hardwick are exceedingly rare survivals of the type. But it is hard to know how typical they actually were: their compositional complexity suggests that they were always more sophisticated than most.

Awkwardly folded around the projections of the walls, the painted cloths now occupy the upper part of the original two-storey chapel[61] where in 1601 there were instead 'too peeces of hanginges imbroidered with pictures'. These cannot be the present hangings of which there are four, painted rather than embroidered and easily identifiable as to subject from the inscriptions and from the name-labels on the hem of garments. In fact they were probably being painted when the inventory was compiled, as a payment made on 8 February 1600 suggests: 'Paynting stuff for John Painter for stayning the cloth hanging, 1lb of fernando bark 1/–, 1lb of brasil fusticle 10d., 2lb of blackwood 6d., 2lb of alloe 6d., 2lb of fusticle 10d., 1lb of copris 6d., 1lb of gumme 16d., 2lb of glew 7d.'[62]

The subjects come from chapters 9, 14, 26 and 28 of the Acts of the Apostles, and depict the Conversion of Saul, the people of Lystra bringing oxen to sacrifice to Paul and Barnabas, Paul's defence before Festus and Agrippa, and Paul being bitten by the viper. These scenes are contained within repetitive borders (resembling those of contemporary tapestries) for which no certain print source has been discovered, although the vases containing irises and other flowers bear a strong resemblance to those bordering Spring in a suite engraved by Crispijn de Passe after Maarten de Vos.[63]

There were at least two readily accessible suites of Flemish prints that might have suggested these particular scenes, one engraved by Philips Galle after designs by Maarten van Heemskerck and published by Hieronymous Cock in 1558, and a second suite after the same artist and Jan van der Straet (Johannes Stradanus).[64] However, with the exception of the Conversion, the subjects of the Hardwick hangings do not correspond at all with those of the prints, so the Galle prints cannot have been available at Hardwick. Significantly, however, all but Paul's defence before Festus and Agrippa do appear in Bernard Salomon's popular illustrations of the New Testament. It is probably safe to suggest that the subjects were chosen by

Bess as a result of her readings in the Scriptures. More than this, Salomon's woodcuts may possibly have provided the underlying compositional structure for the painted hangings. But they did not suggest individual figures: their small format prevented the kind of detail the painter needed for the wall hangings. So for these he turned to other suites of prints which, as will shortly be seen, offer a insight into the working of Bess's innermost thoughts that transcends the apparent subject-matter of these painted cloths.

The story of the Conversion of Saul (Acts of the Apostles, 9:3–8) is very familiar, although the words of the Geneva Bible that Bess would have used are less so:

> Now as he journeyed, it came to passe yt as he was come nere to Damascus, suddenly there shined rounde about him a light from heauen. And he fel to the earth, and heard a voyce, saying to him, Saul, Saul, why persecutest thou me? And he said, Who art thou, Lord? And the Lord said, I am Iesus whome thou persecutest: it is hard for thee to kicke against prickes. He then bothe trembling and astonied, said, Lord, what wilt thou that I do? And ye Lord said vnto him, Arise and go into the citie, and it shalbe tolde thee what thou shalt do. The men also which iorneyed with him, stode amased, hearing his voyce, but seing no man. And Saul arose from the grounde, and opened his eyes, but sawe no man. Then led they him by the hand, and broght him into Damascus . . .

For this scene (Fig. 477), the painter may have based his composition on Salomon who, like several other sixteenth-century artists, placed the Conversion centre-stage, with the figure of Saul falling from a stumbling horse (Fig. 475).[65] But he was faced with the problem of how to expand Salomon's woodcut, which measures two and a half inches in height, to the five feet of the hangings.[66] How did he manage this? The answer is that he borrowed more detailed figures from other suites of engravings and recombined them, generally following Salomon's disposition.

The hanging incorporates, besides Saul and his stumbling horse, six further figures and four horses. The figure of Saul himself was lifted from a print symbolising the Triumph of Death, from *The Triumphs of Petrarch* engraved by Galle *c.*1565 after designs by Heemskerck (Fig. 471).[67] The figure follows the print exactly, except that Saul, instead of being bare-chested, has an elaborately ornamented breastplate, probably a deliberate decision on the part of the artist to indicate that Saul, though Jewish by race, inherited Roman citizenship from his father. There is no mention in the Bible of Saul being mounted on his journey to Damascus. Here, however, he is shown fallen from his horse, in a tradition associated with the medieval custom of representing pride as a fallen horseman. Saul's mount probably derives from some print source as yet unidentified. The horse and rider immediately behind, however, were copied from another suite of prints designed by Heemskerck and engraved by Philips Galle, *The Eight Wonders of the World* published in 1572: the original appears as the horseman gesticulating towards the Colosseum in Rome (Fig. 472).[68] To the right of this figure in the hanging are three more soldiers. Of these, the footsoldier in half-armour derives from one of the 'children' of Mars in a print after Heemskerck (Fig. 473), inscribed 'Cholerici' and representing Choler, from *The Four Temperaments* engraved by Herman Jansz. Muller and published in 1566.[69]

The mounted soldier behind this footsoldier, on the other hand, was reversed from the figure of King Arthur in a third separate suite designed by Heemskerck, this time *The Nine Worthies*, again engraved by Herman Jansz. Muller (Fig. 474) and published c.1567.[70] The same print was used again in this hanging, the figure of Godfrey of Bouillon providing the source for one of the two horsemen on the left. The horse on the extreme left-hand side was copied from that of the Prodigal Son leaving his Father's House in Heemskerck's suite (see Fig. 467).

This first hanging, therefore, has already introduced us to the artist's methods, his use of one print for the composition and different prints – from four separate suites, all designed by Maarten van Heemskerck – for the individual figures, some of which he reversed from the originals. The next painted cloth shows an episode in Paul's first missionary journey (Fig. 482). At Lystra, accompanied by Barnabas, Paul healed a cripple who had never walked (Acts of the Apostles, 14:8–18):

Now there sate a certeine man at Lystra, impotent in his fete, which was a creple from his mother's wombe, who had neuer walked. He heard Paul speake: who beholding him, and perceiuing that he had faith to be healed, Said with a loude voyce, Stand vpright on thy fete. And he leaped vp, & walked. Then when the people sawe what Paul had done, thei lift vp their voyces, saying in the speache of Lycaonia, Gods are come downe to vs in the likenes of men. And thei called Barnabas, Iupiter, & Paul, Mercurius, because he was ye chief speaker. Then Jupiter's priest, which was before their citie, broght bulles with garlandes vnto the gates, & wolde haue sacrificed with the people. But when the Apostles, Barnabas and Paul heard it, thei rent their clothes, & ran in among the people, crying And saying, O men, why do ye these things? We are euen men subiect to the like passions that ye be,

and preache vnto you, that ye shulde turne from these vaine idoles vnto the liuing God . . .

The Authorised Version substituted the more neutral word, 'vanities', for the highly charged 'idols' of the Geneva Bible here.

The overall composition once again recalls Salomon's woodcut, but most of the figures were derived from Flemish prints. Three were ingeniously adapted (and juxtaposed) from a suite known today as *Christ, St Paul and the Twelve Apostles* (1578) engraved by Hieronymus Wierix after designs by Maarten de Vos: Paul from St James the Greater (Fig. 479), Barnabas from St Matthew, and the figure in the yellow cloak behind the priest from the print depicting Christ. The priest, on the other hand, was copied from the figure of Solomon (Fig. 478) in the Triumph of Love from Heemskerck's *The Triumphs of Petrarch* engraved by Philips Galle (Fig. 480).[71] The folds of drapery over arms and legs, together with the distinctive sandals, confirm that this was the source. But the ox bedecked with flowers for the sacrifice was copied from a print illustrating the Triumph of Joseph (Fig. 481), the fourth plate in Heemskerck's suite *The Triumph of Patience*, the suite that supplied the figure in the overmantel relief in the Hill Great Chamber in the Old Hall (see p.264, Fig. 453).

The third hanging (Fig. 487) illustrates Paul's defence before Agrippa on a charge, brought by the chief priests and elders of the Jews, that 'one Iesus, which was dead . . . Paul affirmed to be aliue' (Acts of the Apostles, 25:23–7 and 26:1–32). Paul told Agrippa and Festus of his early life, persecuting Christians, and of his conversion on the road to Damascus.

Neuertheles, I obtained helpe of God, and continue vnto this day, witnessing bothe to smal & to great, saying none other things, then those which the Prophetes & Moses did say shulde come, To whit, that Christ shulde suffer, and that he shulde be the first that shulde rise from the dead, and shulde shewe light vnto the people, and to the Gentiles . . . Then Agrippa said vnto Paul, Almost thou persuadest me to become a Christian.

This scene does not appear amongst Salomon's illustrations and the painter may have devised it for himself. Here, again, we find adaptations from Flemish prints. The figure of Paul, who stands before Agrippa, was based on that of the Greek philosopher Plato (Fig. 486) who accompanies the triumphal car in Heemskerck's Triumph of Fame (Fig. 485), from *The Triumphs of Petrarch*. Behind Paul stands a group of soldiers in classical armour of the kind familiar from engravings after Maarten van Heemskerck and other Netherlandish artists; they hold spears or halberds in their left hands. In fact the positions they adopt are

473 (*above left*)   Herman Jansz. Muller after Maarten van Heemskerck, the Choleric Temperament, from *The Four Temperaments*, 1566. Prentenkabinet, Rijksuniversiteit, Leiden.

474 (*above right*)   Herman Jansz. Muller after Maarten van Heemskerck, the Three Christian Worthies, from *The Nine Worthies*, *c.*1567. Rijksmuseum-Stichting, Amsterdam.

471 (*top left*)   Philips Galle after Maarten van Heemskerck, The Triumph of Death, from *The Triumphs of Petrarch*, *c.*1565. Rijksmuseum-Stichting, Amsterdam.

472 (*top right*)   Philips Galle after Maarten van Heemskerck, The Colosseum at Rome, from *The Eight Wonders of The World*, 1572. Rijksmuseum-Stichting, Amsterdam.

475 (*far left*)   Bernard Salomon, The Conversion of Saul, from the *Quadrins Historiques de la Bible*, printed by Jean de Tournes (Lyons, 1556). Victoria and Albert Museum, London.

476 (*left*)   Detail of Fig. 473.

SAVL SAVL WHY
PERSECVTEST
THOV ME.
SAVL
THE ACTES
CHAP. IX.

477 John Balechouse, painted cloth depicting the Conversion of Saul, *c.*1600–01.

478 (*right*) Solomon, detail of Fig. 480.

479 (*far right*) Hieronymus Wierix after Maarten de Vos, St James the Greater, from *Christ, St Paul and the Twelve Apostles*, 1578. Rijksmuseum-Stichting, Amsterdam.

480 (*below left*) Philips Galle after Maarten van Heemskerck, the Triumph of Love, from *The Triumphs of Petrarch*, *c*.1565. Rijksmuseum-Stichiting, Amsterdam.

481 (*above right*) Dirck Coornhert after Maarten van Heemskerck, the Triumph of Joseph, from *The Triumph of Patience*, 1559. Rijksmuseum-Stichting, Amsterdam.

so closely similar to figures representing the Nine Worthies at Wiston in Sussex, Montacute in Somerset and elsewhere, that it seemed probable that all must derive from a common source long before I discovered that it was the rare set published by Philips Galle.[72] From their use elsewhere it seems likely that the prints were published in the early 1580s. It is notable that the painter reversed the figures of

Joshua and Judas Maccabeus, as he did for one of the horsemen in the first hanging, presumably for compositional reasons (Figs 483, 484).

One of the most exciting discoveries has been the source used for the figures of Agrippa, Festus and Bernice, as well as the canopy of estate under which they sit. For a long time I thought it possible that the painter derived the latter feature from the print

280

482   John Balechouse, painted cloth depicting Paul and Barnabas at Lystra, *c.*1600–01.

483 (*right*) Philips Galle,
Joshua, from *The Nine Worthies*.
Stedelijk Prentenkabinet,
Antwerp.

484 (*far right*) Philips Galle,
Judas Maccabeus, from *The
Nine Worthies*. Stedelijk
Prentenkabinet, Antwerp.

485 (*below left*) Philips Galle
after Maarten van Heemskerck,
the Triumph of Fame, from
The Triumphs of Petrarch, *c.*1565.
British Museum, London.

486 (*below right*) Detail of Fig.
485.

Iudæorum hi tres fortiſſimi fuerunt.
IOSVE DVX.

IVDAS MACHABEVS

PRÆPETIBVS PENNIS CAPVT INTER NVBILA CONDIT
FAMA LOQVAX, ACRIQVE TVBA LATE OMNIA COMPLET.

MARMARICA INMANI QVAM CORPORE BELLVA DVCIT
HAC VIVVNT VATES, ATQVE INCLITA CORPORA BELLO.

487   John Balechouse, painted cloth depicting Paul before Agrippa, *c*.1600–01.

489 Adriaen Collaert after Maarten de Vos, the Reward for Fulfilling the Tasks, from *The Divine Charge to the Three Estates*, *c*.1585–6. Kupferstichkabinett der Staatliche Kunstsammlungen, Dresden.

488 (*top*) Adriaen Collaert after Maarten de Vos, the Task of Worldly Power, from *The Divine Charge to the Three Estates*, *c*.1585–6. Kupferstichkabinett der Staatliche Kunstsammlungen, Dresden.

depicting Achior before Holofernes, from *The Story of Holofernes*,[73] but as this suite was not used elsewhere in these painted cloths this was never completely convincing. So it is satisfying to record that the figures and the canopy derive from one single suite of prints, again completely unrelated to the story of St Paul. This is a set of four prints usually known as *The Divine Charge to the Three Estates* designed by Maarten de Vos and engraved by Adriaen Collaert.[74] In an earlier treatment of the subject, engraved by Philips Galle after Maarten van Heemskerck, the three estates of the feudal Middle Ages, represented by a pope, an emperor and a peasant, are enjoined by God in heaven, 'Tu precare, Tu iustitiam exercere, Tu labora' (Thou shalt pray, thou shalt administer justice, thou shalt work), and are then shown in appropriate activities. In the Collaert/de Vos set, the representatives of the three estates are depicted in triumphal chariots. In the second print, depicting the Task of Worldly Power (Fig. 488), the king provided the painter with the figure of Festus, and Sapientia (Wisdom) that of Bernice. The three representatives are shown together in the fourth print (Fig. 489), which illustrates the Reward for Fulfilling the Tasks, the king supplying the painter with the figure of Agrippa. Their canopy was copied from that under which the bishop travels in the first print (Fig. 490) whose subject is the Task of the Church. This series of prints was designed to illustrate the work ethic, visual expositions of which reached their peak in the Netherlands during the second half of the sixteenth century. The dates 1585 and 1586 on the original drawings, together with the dedication to Jean Sarrazin, who had negotiated the Union of Arras on behalf of Philip II, have suggested to Veldman that the suite was intended to show the Spanish authorities that its author, Maarten de Vos, and publisher, Philips Galle, were prepared to do their duty as citizens of Antwerp by renouncing Protestantism. Would Bess of Hardwick (or her artist) have been aware of these circumstances when acquiring the prints? Would she have minded?

On his journey to Rome, Paul was shipwrecked on Malta (Acts of the Apostles, 28.1–10) where

... the Barbarians shewed vs no litle kindenes: for they kindled a fyre, and receiued vs euerie one, because of the present showre, and because of the colde. And when Paul had gathered a nomber of stickes, and laid them on the fyre, there came a viper out of the heat, and leapt on his hand. Now when the Barbarians sawe the worme hang on his hand, they said among them selues, This man surely is a murtherer, whome, thogh he hathe escaped the sea, yet Vengeance hathe not suffred to liue. But he shoke of the worme into the fyre, and felt no harme ... In the same quarters, the chief man of the yle (whose name was Publius) had possessions: the same receiued vs, and lodged vs thre daies courteously. And so it was, that the father of Publius lay sicke of the feuer, & of a bloodie flixe: to whome Paul entred in, & when he praied, he laid his hands on him, and healed him.

This wall hanging (Fig. 494) offers the clearest indication that the Salomon illustration (Fig. 492) formed the basis of the composition. In each, the viper rising from the fire is placed centrally with Paul on the right and the onlookers on the left; above the figure of Paul can be seen the ship from which Paul and his companions escaped to the island of Malta, while in a small vignette above the onlookers Paul heals the father of Publius. Minor differences in the compositions, such as the addition of extra figures in the hangings, can be attributed to the necessity of achieving a more horizontal format from the vertical of Salomon's woodcuts.

The painter scoured his available stock of prints and copied the figures on the left, who watch as the viper bites St Paul, from those of the family of the Prodigal Son when he leaves on horseback, in Heemskerck's suite (see Fig. 467); he took the head of the man on the extreme right from the Triumph of Fame, from Heemskerck's suite *The Triumphs of Petrarch* (see Fig. 485), and reproduced the architecture beside the house of Publius's father from the background of a print in Heemskerck's set, *The Eight Wonders of the World*, illustrating the Pharos of Alexandria (Fig. 491). These three suites had been used elsewhere in these painted cloths.

Finally there is the scene in the left-hand corner of the viper wall hanging, in which Paul heals the father of Publius: this was copied from the print Visiting the Sick (Fig. 495) from *The Seven Acts of Mercy and the Last Judgement*, engraved by Crispijn de Passe the elder after designs by Maarten de Vos.[75] The bed with its canopy suspended from between the ceiling joists, the window-wall behind and the arch through which the scene is viewed, are unmistakable, as is the position of the bedridden patient. The only difference is that the partly obscured figure ministering to the sick man in the print (Fig. 496) was replaced in the hanging by a repeat of the figure of the Apostle as he leans forward over the fire. The sources for the rest of the figures remain unidentified.

These painted cloths offer invaluable insights into how the painter supplied what his patron wanted and how heavily he relied on the printed page to help him through. What is remarkable about them is the ingenuity with which he selected elements from many disparate sets of prints, and the skill with which he patched them together to form convincing compositions. Only occasionally is awkwardness apparent. The cloths are clearly the work of an experienced artist. Who was John Balechouse and what can be

deduced from these painted cloths about his contribution to the decoration of Hardwick?

Nothing is known of his background for certain. He has been thought to be Flemish[76] from his unusual name, which appears in the Hardwick accounts in a variety of other spellings: Ballechous, Ballechouse, Balleschous are just three. Certainly Flemish nationality would conveniently explain the introduction of Netherlandish source material into work commissioned by Bess during the 1570s, although examples actually precede his first appearance in the Chatsworth accounts in 1578. But there is no published record of his naturalisation or denization in London or anywhere else.[77] Another suggestion is that he was from an old-established French family recorded as living in the vicinity of Hardwick during the thirteenth century;[78] however, a local background of this kind would not explain his greater-than-average ability. A third and more promising possibility is that he is identical with a painter by the name of Jehan Balechou or Baleschoux who is recorded in legal documents in Tours in 1557.[79] These would put his birth date around 1530–35 at the latest. Of his presumed sons (both of whom were goldsmiths) Josue Baleschou was living in Tours in 1587, but Pierre, who was born in Tours, had arrived in England by 1576, being recorded in London in 1593 with his wife Catherine (born in Rouen) and seventeen-year-old daughter born in England.[80] If this painter, Jehan Balechou, is indeed our man, he had a third son, James, who lived at Hardwick until 9 February 1648 as publican of the Hardwick Inn.[81]

490 Adriaen Collaert after Maarten de Vos, the Task of the Church, from *The Divine Charge to the Three Estates*, *c*.1585–6. Kupferstichkabinett der Staatliche Kunstsammlungen, Dresden.

491 (*above left*) Philips Galle after Maarten van Heemskerck, the Pharos of Alexandria, from *The Eight Wonders of The World*, 1572. Rijksmuseum-Stichting, Amsterdam.

492 (*above right*) Bernard Salomon, Paul and the Viper, from the *Quadrins Historiques de la Bible*, printed by Jean de Tournes (Lyons, 1556). British Library, London (554.a.43(2)).

493 Detail of Fig. 491.

Now we have to indulge for a moment in some speculation. Supposing Balechouse to have been responsible for bringing with him some of the Flemish prints used at Hardwick, he might have spent some time in the Netherlands. But there is no record of him in Antwerp[82] so he may have crossed by sea to London or Southampton, to one of the Cinque Ports, or to Exeter or Plymouth – there was a French church in Exeter during the sixteenth century and Huguenot immigrants are mentioned in connection with Plymouth in 1569.[83] If he was in Exeter he clearly did not stay there long enough to become a freeman nor to have apprentices. He might have been employed on some important country house – Longleat is an obvious candidate – and Bess would then have come across him through her appeals for skilled craftsmen. When did Balechouse come into Bess's employ? His earliest mention in the Chatsworth accounts is 1578 but it is possible that he arrived several years before. By December 1589 at the latest he was staying at Hardwick on board-wages and no more than two years later had a room in the Old Hall.[84] Sometime around 1598 he designed for his own occupation the house at Hardwick then called the New Inn which survives somewhat altered as the Hardwick Inn at one of the southern entrances to the park.[85] He died around 1618. If he was the artist from Tours he would have been in his eighties.

How did Bess use his talents? Although never formally her clerk of works, he paid the skilled workers and acted as a kind of general foreman. Evidently a man whom Bess trusted implicitly, Balechouse was consulted on building matters and took the decision in Bess's absence to heighten the turret windows of the New Hall by five feet. He was responsible for the painted frieze in the gallery, with the stencilled arabesques and strapwork on panelling as well as the painted cloths in the chapel; he presumably executed the decorative paintings that survive behind the tapestries in the Withdrawing Chamber. At wages of £2 per year with frequent additional rewards, and perhaps enjoying the tenancy of a ninety-four-acre farm at Stoney Houghton,[86] Balechouse was better paid than any other craftsman at Hardwick. After Bess's death in February 1608, Balechouse continued working at

494 John Balechouse, painted cloth depicting Paul and the Viper, c.1600–01.

495 (*above*) Crispijn de Passe the elder after Maarten de Vos, *Visiting the Sick*, from *The Seven Acts of Mercy and the Last Judgement*. Graphische Sammlung, Albertina, Vienna.

496 (*right*) Detail of Fig. 495.

497 (*far right*) Detail of Fig. 494.

Hardwick for her son William Cavendish, receiving in all £75 19s. for unidentified building and decorating projects.

Knowing more, from the examination of the painted cloths in the chapel, about his artistic methods, which included combining two or more prints to form a new composition, it is probably safe to go beyond these facts and to suggest that it was Balechouse who painted *The Return of Ulysses to Penelope*, which is an example, albeit rudimentary, of this procedure. Assuming that the picture was painted in this country, his arrival in England took place no later than 1570, and his involvement perhaps as designer of other decorative work of that decade becomes possible, even probable – the Shrewsbury and its sibling hangings, the patchwork Virtuous Women, the Virtues and their Contraries. During the 1580s and 1590s, he was probably responsible for selecting with Bess source material for use on the painted or embroidered forepart given to Queen Elizabeth in 1599 (see above, p.275) and he is much the most likely designer of the plaster overmantels in the Old Hall in which a figure or figures are selected from prints. He is also the natural candidate for the designer of the frieze of the High Great Chamber in the New Hall, some of whose sources have yet to be identified. Indeed, he may well have co-ordinated the whole of this interior.

In short, it was probably Balechouse more than

anyone else who worked out for Bess – presumably under her direction and with her active participation – the various decorative progammes that run through the houses, marshalling for use in masonry and plasterwork, joinery, textiles and painting a range of German, French and Flemish printed source material. This range seems to have been kept to hand for further use when needed and augmented by up-to-date additions, either acquired through continuing contacts abroad or purchased from booksellers or print shops in London. One opportunity for the latter occurred on Bess's last visit to the court of Queen Elizabeth from November 1591 to July 1592, when she spent extravagantly on clothes, plate and tapestries.[87] Perhaps she bought prints too: Balechouse had been left in charge at Hardwick.

It is conceivable that Balechouse was assisted in some of the design work by Richard Hickes, the director of the Sheldon tapestry works. Bess paid '... Mr Sheldon's man for seventeen armses to set upon hangings ... and also ten shillings to hang tapestries' on 20 February 1592, presumably the thirteen panels of *The History of Gideon* which she had bought the previous year from Sir William Newport, the nephew and heir of Sir Christopher Hatton.[88] Hardwick and Sheldon tapestries share at least three print sources that were not commonly used elsewhere, the suite of hunting scenes engraved by Philips Galle after Johannes Stradanus, *The Five Senses* by Cornelis Cort after Frans Floris and *The Seasons* by Crispijn de Passe after Maarten de Vos.[89] Additionally, Bess read another book, 'Calvin uppon Jobe', whose woodblock titlepage design Richard Hickes had copied in the borders of the Sheldon tapestry maps woven for Ralph Sheldon in 1588 (although it should be remembered that Calvin's writings were amongst the books most often found in the libraries of commoners during the sixteenth century). Some interaction between Balechouse and Richard Hickes may therefore have taken place. If so, the community of country-house builders towards the end of Elizabeth's reign was even tighter-knit than has hitherto been apparent.

What did Bess intend her houses to tell her contemporaries? The distribution of decoration recorded in the 1601 inventory offers a clue. The fact that the windows of the New Hall increase in height towards the top of the house, expressing on the outside the different function of the storeys inside – the ground floor principally domestic, the first floor private, the second floor for state – is well known. What commentators have not (to my knowledge) remarked on before is that the subjects of decoration on these three storeys also differ somewhat in kind.

On the ground floor the Hall in 1601 was dominated by the armorial overmantel and by the 'Foure peeces of tapestrie hanginges with personages of forrest worke of fyftene foote and a half deep', possibly the fifteenth-century hunting tapestries now in the Victoria and Albert Museum.[90] Otherwise only 'Mr. William Cavendishe's Chamber' had notable decoration in the form of 'Fyve peeces of tapestrie hanginges of Forrest work'.

Armorials and decoration based on flowers and nature in general figure again in rooms on the first – private – floor, but biblical scenes predominated: tapestries telling the stories of Jacob, of Tobias and of David, along with scenes from the parable of the Prodigal Son; a 'Crucefixe of imbrodered worke' in the Low Chapel and 'too pictures of our Ladie the Virgin Marie and the three Kinges, the salutation of the Virgin Marie by the Angle'; a picture of the Virgin Mary also made a somewhat incongruous appearance amongst a number of identified portraits in the Low Great Chamber. From the gallery of the chapel the painted cloths depicting scenes from the life of St Paul would be seen shortly after the inventory was compiled. Two sets of tapestries with unidentified scenes, in the Countess of Shrewsbury's Withdrawing Chamber and Bedchamber, were probably mythological.

On the second floor, used for state occasions, came a different emphasis. Subjects drawn from nature and the Bible reappeared – from the Old Testament, the Sacrifice of Isaac, Joseph, David and Saul, Tobias, and the Judgement of Solomon; from the New Testament the parable of the Prodigal Son (and pictures of the Virgin Mary). But subjects taken from Classical history and mythology also achieved prominence. They include the stories of Ulysses and Penelope, Hercules, Diana and Actaeon, Phaethon, Europa, Atalanta.

The most obvious shift of emphasis, however, was the use in the grandest state rooms of the Virtues, Justice and Mercy in the overmantels of the Gallery and Charity in the Best Bed Chamber exemplifying the qualities that Bess perceived as directing her relations to those with whom she came into contact and, in Charity, her most fundamental attitude towards human relations. In addition to these, ten Virtues were depicted on the first set of hangings in the Withdrawing Chamber with Faith, Hope and Temperance on the hangings in the Best Bedchamber. There were also many panels embroidered with Virtues (and other subjects), some of which could, in the early years of the twentieth century, be seen on the canopy in the High Great Chamber[91] though they are now mostly framed up in screens. Only on the second floor of the New Hall were the Virtues explicitly mentioned in the 1601 Inventory. Elsewhere at Hardwick their presence was implicit in the many stories drawn from the Bible and Classical mythology, most obviously in the frieze of the High Great Chamber.

This cannot be a coincidence but must rather have been part of a deliberate iconological programme. Running like an almost invisible thread through the warp and weft of Hardwick is another virtue. Just as Bess had a special liking for the biblical story of Tobias – the Tobias prints were employed at least three times and Tobias was regarded as a pre-eminent *exemplum patientiae* – so the Classical characters with whom she identified most closely were Lucretia, the virtuous wife, and Penelope, whose twenty years' wait for her husband Ulysses made her the absolute personification of Patience.

One or the other appears in the painting generally known as *The Return of Ulysses to Penelope* (Figs 423, 498), and the possible circumstances of its commission should be considered here. It may, of course, have been simply an allegory of Patience, depicting Ulysses returning to Penelope (or Tarquinius Collatinus to Lucretia). However, depending on two continental woodcuts, and contrasting the pseudo-antique with the contemporary-modern, it resembles the group portrait of *Edward VI and the Pope*, which was also painted around 1570 possibly to persuade Queen Elizabeth to act more decisively to destroy idols or to dissuade the Duke of Norfolk from his plan to marry Mary Queen of Scots.[92] Might not *The Return of Ulysses to Penelope* have had some similar function in 1570?

What was happening in England about this time that might have triggered someone into commissioning it? Working backwards from the date of the painting, on 25 February 1570 Pope Pius V issued the 'mad and beastly bull', *Regnans in excelsis*, which excommunicated Elizabeth and released her subjects from their allegiance to her. This had been preceded, in November and December the previous year, 1569, by the rebellion in Durham and Yorkshire in support of the old faith. The most harassing event of that year for the Shrewsbury family, however, must have been the arrival, on 4 February, of the Catholic fugitive from north of the border. The Earl of Shrewsbury, then aged forty-two, had been given by Queen Elizabeth the dubious privilege of guarding Mary Queen of Scots, the very individual who was to bring the Duke of Norfolk to his death and became a focus for intrigue on a European scale until her own death in 1587. She had spent the previous eight months, since mid-May 1568 when she had crossed the border into England, at Carlisle Castle and Bolton Castle under the custody of Lord Scrope, Warden of the Western Marches; his wife Margaret was the sister of the Duke of Norfolk whom she may have encouraged (though he later denied this) in his ultimately fatal plans to marry the Queen of Scots.[93] Norfolk's ambition to marry Mary had been mooted several years earlier and by the time of the Queen's arrival at Tutbury must have been common knowledge.

It is not difficult, therefore, to imagine that, with her dangerous attraction for the opposite sex, the twenty-seven year old Mary Queen of Scots brought to the Shrewsbury household the seeds of marital tension, and began the rupture between them.[94] Their first serious row is said to have taken place in 1577, and by 1583 Bess and her sons, William and Charles Cavendish, were spreading rumours that the Earl had been too intimate with Mary, a charge that she passionately refuted. With the benefit of hindsight it seems possible that, even as early as 1570 (the date of one of many attempts to free Mary), *The Return of Ulysses to Penelope* had a very specific message, to warn the wealthy, powerful and still-young Earl against his dangerous prisoner by reminding him of his faithful and patient wife at Chatsworth.

Is there anything in the painting to suggest that this hypothesis was the actual motive behind the commission? Returning to the woodcut sources we notice that they originally illustrated scenes from the Book of Kings and from Esther, two texts that were eagerly seized upon by Protestants. 'It was', as Aston has said, 'the preoccupations of the reformers, with their fierce fidelity to the old law that gave new prominence to certain kings of the Old Testament.'[95] One of the Amman woodcuts used by the painter illustrated the dreams of Nebuchadnezzar, the autocratic conqueror of the ancient Middle East, who ostentatiously endowed Babylon with the celebrated hanging gardens and the great ziggurat which were amongst the Wonders of the World. The Jews regarded his eventual decline into madness as a punishment for worshipping the wrong gods and, in the sixteenth century, his monumental statue was represented as an object of idolatry in a painting by Pieter Aertsen.[96] Again, natural associations were made in the sixteenth century between Babylon and Babel, the tower 'whose top may reach unto heaven', and between the fall of Babylon and the decline of papal Rome; in fact, William Fulke preached *A Sermon*, proving Babylon to be Rome, in the same year, 1570, that *The Return of Ulysses to Penelope* was painted.[97] The other woodcut adapted for the painting depicted the return of Mordecai, the servant who, in the story of Esther, had overheard King Ahasuerus's courtiers plotting. This would have been in 1570 – the year after Mary's arrival at Tutbury – a highly topical subject, and it should be remembered that it was a print from Heemskerck's *Story of Esther* that was used for the bed-bound figure of Henry VIII in *Edward VI and the Pope*. Dealing as they did with idolatry and subversion, these woodcuts by Amman might have been no

mere coincidental choice for *The Return of Ulysses to Penelope*.[98]

Both Lucretia and Penelope are depicted in the embroidered hangings, which by 1601 were in the Withdrawing Chamber at Hardwick. Perhaps they too represent an after-shock of the Earl's possible association with his royal prisoner, although Bess had for many years previously been preoccupied enough with the figure of Lucretia to give the name to her last daughter who was born (and died) in 1557. In selecting for these hangings Lucretia as the virtuous wife who, raped by Tarquinius (as described by Livy, *Ab Urbe Condita*, I, chapters 57–8), took her life once she had lost her virtue, Bess was following the traditional view of Lucretia as 'the main prototype of chastity and faithfulness in marriage'. Not possessing, so far as is known, more up-to-date images of the heroine, Bess was presumably unaware of a shift of emphasis in the message conveyed by Lucretia that occurred by the end of the century.[99] It is demonstrated by the text accompanying Crispijn de Passe's engraving in the suite of *Nine Female Worthies* of 1601–2: 'I, Lucretia, complain to the gods of the infamous deed inflicted upon me: let no adultress cite my example.' Under the oval is a more general message: 'God has laid down the marriage laws for all time: a marriage may not simply be dissolved . . .'

In another suite by Crispijn de Passe, Lucretia is described as 'non pietas sed castitas' – not dutiful though chaste – while in a suite by Raphael Sadeler after Maarten de Vos her suicide is more sternly criticised: 'You try in vain to redeem Tarquin's act of violence with your blood: praise is due to chastity which stands firm without bloodshed.' Penelope seems to be free from any such taint. She appears in the Ulysses tapestries in the High Great Chamber. Patience figured in one of the de Vos prints used on the painted cloths and was also the subject of the Heemskerck suite that provided the figure of the man with the crazed eyes, deranged hair and manic gesture in the overmantel of the Hill Great Chamber in the Old Hall. He was abstracted from the first print, depicting the Triumph of Patience, from the suite of the same title. The print embodies many ideas which, though not expressed in the actual decoration of the houses, was implicit in their autocratic mien. The scheme of the allegorical triumph, which underwent a remarkable revival in the fifteeenth and sixteenth centuries, was based on the triumphs of classical times but, as Ilja Veldman has reminded us,[100] assumed in the Renaissance the added significance of personal triumph. What lies behind the figure of the overmantel relief, unseen by all but those who knew the Coornhert/Heemskerck source, is the figure of Patientia seated on a triumphal car, drawn by Spes and Desiderium, pulling behind her Fortuna, blindfold and shackled, with various symbols of her fickleness and unpredictability. The Latin text beneath the image explains the meaning; translated it reads: 'And just as a white rose burgeons among the dense thickets of thorns and is not shouldered aside by them, and as the lilies bloom in the spring, so Patience now rides forth on a splendid car. Mighty Fortune, whose powers are now broken, has had to yield honour to her and follows, shamed, in chains. Sweet Hope draws the car, accompanied by winged Desire.'[101]

It is surely not being over-sophisticated to suggest that Bess identified herself with Patience seated in triumph in a splendid car, but alluded to this virtue obliquely, choosing for the overmantel Desiderium, who personified mankind's longing for salvation and, with Hope, was one of the forces that make endurance possible. The device of the wild rose on the banner held by Patience not only corresponded precisely with the Hardwick emblem but also, shown flourishing amongst thorns, as explained in the caption, could be read as a symbol of the survival of her line against all the setbacks and difficulties of her turbulent life. The point is, that only by reading and understanding the text could Bess have realised that this one particular print neatly summarised everything she stood for; moreover, she seems to have expressed it in the form of a riddle that could be understood only by a tiny handful of initiates. Neither is the mark of someone uncultured.

As to Bess's attitude towards religion, no clear signals are received from her public life and activities. She was, and remained, a close friend of Elizabeth I, which suggests that publicly at least she probably supported the Elizabethan Settlement: one of the books in her bedchamber was 'Calvin uppon Jobe' whose reforming message was clear from the words of Calvin's Preface:

If ever men needed to learne what patience is: surely the state of this present time ought to leade yea and to drawe them to it. For if we looke well about us, we shall finde that there hath not bin almost any Realme or countrie, wherein God hath not uttered greate Scourges. If ye demand the cause: it is evident, so as even the blind . . . may see it. Let the old men that are now alyve consider the wicked things which they have seen committed commonly, since they were able first to remember, unto this day: and must they not needs say (as it was sayd of the time of the general flud) that all flesh hath corrupted his wayes upon earth, that all is full of extorcion, and outrage, and that such as beare the name of Christians do (as sayeth sainct Peter) fulfill the waye of the heathen, by livinge in shamefulnesse, pride, lecherie, drunkennesse, gluttonie, quaffing and abhominable idolatrie. But like as it is good to knowe the causes of the adversities that happen, to the intent that men may the better bethink themselves, to amend as well publickly as privately: so is it ryght necessarie to be sensed with true patience, that we sink not under the burthen when Gods scourges continue long vpon us, for even that also is one of the points of the amendment which he requireth of us. Nevertheless, it is a thing that cannot be learned elsewhere than in Gods woord . . . He is willing to have pitie upon his creatures, and by word he giveth comfort and patience to all such as are pinched: but specially he comforteth those that are already under his banner, graunting them to have peace in him, although they will have none in the world.

On the other hand, Bess had objects at Hardwick which would have been regarded as idolatrous – a 'Crucefixe of imbrodered worke' in the Low Chapel as well as 'too pictures of our Ladie the Virgin Marie and the three Kinges [the Adoration of the Magi], the salutation of the Virgin Marie by the Angle [the Annunciation]'. There was also a picture of the Virgin Mary amongst a number of identified portraits in the Low Great Chamber.

It should be easier to comment on Bess's religious position after an examination of the prints used in the composition of the painted cloths. Recent research, however, suggests there is little evidence that prints – even depicting subjects which might seem to offer the possibility of it – were actually used for sectarian propaganda. In fact rather the opposite seems to be true. The parable of the Prodigal Son is a subject that appears at Hardwick and elsewhere in Elizabethan decoration: Barbara Haeger[102] has written that, despite the fact that the biblical text is interpreted differently by Catholics and Protestants,

Sixteenth and seventeenth-century Netherlandish representations of the parable of the prodigal son, with one exception [the six woodcuts of the 1540s by the Amsterdam artist Cornelis Anthonisz. which express strongly Protestant sympathies], do not convey sectarian interpretations of the biblical text. They simply stress the father's love and compassion, thereby communicating the meaning accepted by Protestants and Catholics alike – the message that God is merciful and willing to forgive repentant sinners. The disputed points of interpretation are too complex to communicate within relatively accurate and naturalistic renditions of the scriptural account.

Haeger concluded: 'It seems not unreasonable to suggest that, like the parable of the prodigal son, the vast majority of biblical subjects depicted in the Netherlands during the sixteenth and sevententh centuries can be considered neither specifically Catholic nor Protestant in nature.'

Ilja Veldman, discussing prints illustrating the work ethic, has clearly set out the difficulties of using prints to determine an individual's religious views: 'The religious beliefs of artists working in the sixteenth century are often hard to ascertain partly because denominational dividing lines were not yet sharply drawn. The problems are even greater when it comes to discovering the denomination of those who purchased the prints.'[103] Emphasising the different religious upbringings of Netherlandish artists she continues:

Cornelis Anthonisz. of Amsterdam (1507–53) originally came from a Catholic background, but he exhibits clear reformist and humanist influence, and his work was largely concerned with moral edification. This is also true of Maarten van Heemskerck (1490–1574), a Catholic from Haarlem, who specialized in ethical teachings during his long period of collaboration with Coornhert. Of the artists dealt with here, Heemskerck expresses in his prints the most old-fashioned views with regards to the work ethic (seeing labor as a task assigned by God, without any material ends), but this is because his work is the earliest. Hadrianus Junius (1511–75), who wrote the captions for the engravings of Heemskerck and Philips Galle, was first and foremost a humanist; though a Catholic, his views were unorthodox. Cornelis Bos (1506/10–1556) and Cornelis Massijs (1510/11–1556/57) were permanently banished from Antwerp for their sympathies with the 'Loists' of Eloy Pruystinck, a sect related to the Lutherans. Another Antwerp artist, Willem van Haecht, also inclined toward the reformists; of his fellow townsman, Gerard de Jode (d.1591) nothing is known on that score. Philips Galle (1537–1612) was a Catholic profoundly interested in ethical questions, who appears to have had sympathy also for the Family of Love. Maarten de Vos (1532–1603) was a Lutheran, but agreed to convert to Catholicism after the fall of Antwerp . . . Crispijn de Passe the Elder (1564–1637) was a Mennonite, and moved to Cologne after Antwerp was taken. From his new home, however, he stayed in close contact with de Vos, his maternal uncle, who carried on supplying him with preparatory drawings to be cut. Despite his beliefs, no characteristically Mennonite standpoint is discernible in the prints he designed, with the exception of a strong emphasis on morality and devoutness. Hendrick Goltzius (1558–1617) was greatly influenced in his youth by the ideas of Coornhert, who believed that all human endeavor should be based on the Bible.

These differences in denominational background typify the situation in the Netherlands in the latter half of the sixteenth century. None of these artists was a Calvinist, or at any rate registered as such; nor is there a trace of Calvin's ideas in any of the prints.

Particularly notable in this list of artists are the two who so influenced Hardwick, Maarten van Heemskerck and Maarten de Vos: their position was diametrically opposite, the one a Catholic befriending humanists, the other a Lutheran outwardly professing Catholicism.

Heemskerck's Tobias (1556) and Prodigal Son illustrations were two of the many suites he designed to provide visual reminders of the great moralising stories of the Old and New Testaments. Both represent narrative treatments of biblical subjects and, as noted in the concluding chapter, were thus acceptable even after the Reformation. The unusual aspect of Heemskerck's treatment of the Prodigal Son parable is his faithfulness to the biblical story, which ends by emphasising the response of the Prodigal's envious brother as an admonition to eschew envy and be charitable towards others.[104]

Heemskerck's set of *The Twelve Patriarchs* was similarly uncontroversial as subject matter for these figures were the sons of Jacob, described in various books of the Old Testament. His iconography, however, is particularly obscure – for the fact is that the identity of the figures on the dependent overmantels was lost sooner or later and has only now been recovered. As Veldman and de Jonge discovered, Heemskerck based his illustrations partly on the text of Genesis and partly on the woodcuts accompanying each chapter of *De testamenten der twalf patriarchen Jacobs kinderen*, woodcuts perhaps designed by Joos Lambrecht around 1541;[105] the foreword of the *Testamenten*, paraphrased, announces that the book contains 'Christian warnings, teaching, and most lively admonitions, not only for the children of Jacob, but also for all faithful and true children of God who, by means of a good life, testify to their spiritual perfection, fixity of heart and purity of faith. For Holy Scripture has revealed that those who are descended from Isaac and Jacob have struggled piously and valiantly against fleshly desire'.[106] In the Netherlands the book was placed on the index of books prohibited by the Spanish in 1570.

In the two prints selected for overmantels in the Old Hall, Heemskerck included, besides the patriarchs themselves, creatures indicative of the character's particular virtue or vice, and mythological or allegorical figures who relate in one way or another to the activities represented in the background of the designs, but when the prints were adapted in plaster these were omitted, perhaps as being too obscure for the moral edification of the rooms' occupants, Bess's favourite son William Cavendish and her receiver of rents, William Reason.

Heemskerck's was one of the two sets of the Nine Worthies used at Hardwick, adapted for biblical figures in the painted cloths in the chapel (the other was Galle's, which seems to have been particularly well known in England, see pp.115–16). They were presumably purchased because they provided a serviceable series of figures (three of them specifically Christian) to replace the saints and apostles banned in Protestant countries. As Tessa Watt has said: 'The great appeal of the worthies can be explained by the way they integrated various cultural strands of the period: the medieval chivalry of the popular printed romances, the "Renaissance" interest in classicising mythology and the Protestant focus on the historical figures of the Old Testament and Judaic history. They were entertaining and heroic, while at the same time permeated with a nationalistic sort of religiosity.'[107]

However, Veldman has related the Heemskerck set, whose preliminary drawings date from 1567, the year after the *Beeldenstorm*, to current political events in the Netherlands, suggesting that these militaristic images were perhaps intended to encourage the diffident and self-effacing Phillip II by their example.

The four other suites after Heemskerck used at Hardwick – *The Triumphs of Petrarch*, *The Triumph of Patience*, *The Four Temperaments* and *The Eight Wonders of the World* – are all elaborately allegorical. *The Triumph of Patience* (1559), from constituent prints of which were derived the winged figure in the overmantel of the Hill Great Chamber of the Old Hall and the oxen in one of the painted cloths in the chapel, in Veldman's words 'can be read from the first print to the last as a succession of stages through which man passes on his way to the ultimate goal of divine mercy'.[108] The innovative feature of the suite (in which Heemskerck collaborated with the eminent Haarlem humanist Dirck Coornhert, who also engraved the set) was the combination of allegorical and biblical figures with Christ in order to 'point a moral which applies to all mankind',[109] the moral in this case being 'patience in adversity'.

The Triumphs of Petrarch (1565) provided John Balechouse with several figures used in the painted hangings. The prints, which were engraved by Philips Galle, represent another collaboration between Heemskerck and a leading humanist, this time Hadrianus Junius, who supplied the Latin verses beneath the prints. Heemskerck's compositions were inspired by Petrarch's poetry and based on prints by Georg Pencz. Another suite by Heemskerck and Junius followed in 1566, *The Four Temperaments*, perhaps published by Philips Galle in Haarlem: one figure was copied for the painted cloth illustrating the Conversion of Saul. These prints treated a subject already defined in classical times and widely popular by the sixteenth century: under this system an individual's temperament was believed to derive from the balance of the fluids – blood, choler, black bile and phlegm – secreted by the body, these also being influenced by the planets and the seasons. The suite displays several features diverging from contemporary practice without breaking new ground iconographically.[110]

The prints after Maarten de Vos employed in decoration at Hardwick are of much the same kinds. The Elements, Seasons and Virtues are engravings which involve allegory but as subjects they were completely familiar to all educated Elizabethans.[111] Two suites, on the other hand, *The Divine Charge to the Three Estates* (c.1585–6) and *The Seven Acts of Mercy and the Last Judgement*, are certainly less familiar today. In the former, de Vos developed a subject which – rarely found in the visual arts before the fifteenth century – had previously been illustrated by Heemskerck.[112] The three estates were the fixed orders into which humanity was divided – the clergy, the ruler and the people – each having clearly defined responsibilities and answering directly to God. De Vos used a favourite device (learnt no doubt from Heemskerck), depicting the representatives of the three estates in triumphal cars, accompanied and drawn by figures or creatures personifying their appropriate virtues. The fourth print illustrates the reward for fulfilling the tasks and shows the three estates united by Faith, Hope and Charity; the Latin lines beneath carry the message: 'So long as all keep to this path and diligently perform the duties of their profession, trusting sincerely in the tranquility of a pious heart, Love will unite us with God most high, and Hope and Faith will bring us, all our trespasses atoned for, to exalted seats in heaven.'[113]

Some of these suites of prints, therefore, depicted subjects that were commonplace in the Elizabethan mentality, others were, as just seen, far more obscure: in Veldman's words, 'With their complex allegories and Latin texts, the prints [of this allegorical kind] . . . were distributed among the well-to-do class of burghers: fellow artists, scholars and teachers, merchants and superior artisans, people with a good education who were able to understand the Latin and the complicated allegories'.

Despite the fact that one and possibly two Protestant Bibles illustrated by Amman and Salomon had been employed for decoration that subsequently found its way to Hardwick, the Biblical prints used during the 1590s put no particular denominational message while the allegorical were suffused by humanist qualities whose meaning could only be fully comprehended by reading their accompanying texts. Assuming, as we have been obliged to, that Bess was personally involved in choosing these prints, we are led inexorably to the opinion that, far from being disinterested in religion, she both read and thought profoundly about it, publicly demonstrating her Protestantism but privately probably tending, like her queen, to be 'a follower of Erasmus, a Christian Believer, but undoctrinal, therefore tolerant'.[114]

Chapter 16

SOME CONCLUSIONS

The comparatively few sets of ornament prints used in the decoration of Bess of Hardwick's great country houses reinforce the picture of Netherlandish predominance that has already emerged for most of our period. Their purpose was principally the transmission of style and ensured that, for all its austerity outside, no one could doubt that internally the New Hall reflected the Mannerist style current in Antwerp. The subject prints employed in the decoration of Hardwick, by contrast, complicate what is already an uncertain picture of religious art in Elizabethan England. The effect of the Reformation on religious art in England had been generally to replace images that might be considered idolatrous with narrative treatments of biblical stories. As Tessa Watt has written:

> The tradition of visual 'stories' from the Scriptures had immaculate Protestant credentials. Luther expressed a wish for 'the whole Bible to be painted on houses, on the outside and inside, so that all can see it. That would be a Christian work.' . . . The Elizabethan homily against idolatry made a careful distinction between narrative pictures and static icons: 'And a process of a story, painted with the gestures and actions of many persons, and commonly the sum of the story written withal, hath another use in it, than one dumb idol or image standing by itself.' William Perkins [*A reformed Catholike*, 1598] was against biblical painting in churches, but not in domestic settings: 'We hold the historical use of images to be good and lawful: and that is, to represent to the eye the acts of histories, whether they be human or divine: and thus we think the histories of the Bible may be painted in private places.'[1]

To the narrative-type depictions of mainly Old Testament subjects, and the occasional survival at Hardwick of apparently devotional images of the Resurrection or the Virgin Mary, must now be added prints of a distinctly humanist nature. How had this ambivalence in the face of the reformation of images come about?

Queen Elizabeth characteristically sent no consistently clear signals, indeed rather the opposite. On the one hand, she publicly rebuked the Dean of the Chapel Royal for providing her, for a New Year's gift, with a prayerbook he had had bound with 'several fine cuts and pictures representing the stories and passions of the saints and martyrs' that he had bought from a German;[2] on the other hand, she appalled her hardline Protestant ministers by hanging a devotional picture of the Virgin Mary in her private chapel, and retaining the cross and candlesticks well into the 1560s: twice they were broken by iconoclasts and subsequently replaced, the second time, after October 1567, by a tapestry depicting the Crucifixion.[3] Elizabeth still had the cross on her altar in 1586. Margaret Aston has commented:

> There were particular moments when it is clear that she made the most of the seeming traditionalism of her chapel services, but the long-continued and vexatious display of the cross may seem to spell out some personal preference. Elizabeth combined a broad-minded interpretation of *adiaphora* with the belief that external dignity of worship might help without hindering true believers. Readiness to use a cross or crucifix did not make her doctrinally a Lutheran, nor, to her way of thinking, was that something worth disputing over. The end result of such an approach was confusing.[4]

Horrified by the orgy of iconoclastic destruction at the very outset of her reign, in 1559 Elizabeth had issued her visitors charged with removing various types of images in churches with articles and injunctions which differed significantly in their wording:[5] it was widely recognised, for example, that church images had found their way into private houses, but the injunctions pointedly refrained from ordering their defacement. Probate inventories dating between about 1480 and 1580 show that pictures of the Passion, the Virgin Mary and saints survived in private houses into the 1560s and 1570s, confirming that, as noted earlier, private chapels were regarded as to some extent outside normal ecclesiastical controls. Some objects that would undoubtedly have been considered idolatrous are still extant to this day, for instance a monument carved with representations

of the Resurrection and the Ascension, commemorating Sir Edward Saunders and his wife (1573) at
Weston-under-Wetherley in Warwickshire, or a
carved relief depicting the Crucifixion and dated 1577
at Rushton Hall, Northamptonshire.[6]

Crucifixion scenes were also commissioned anew
in painted glass in domestic chapels. In churches, glass
depicting scenes of the traditional kind had been
spared destruction despite being considered superstitious because the buildings were clearly unusable if
not weathertight. The injunctions of 1559 authorised
'preserving nevertheless or otherwise repairing the
walls and glass',[7] and nearly twenty years afterwards
William Harrison recorded in 1577 that 'stories in
glasse windows' still remained in most parts of
the country. As Archbishop Laud said at his trial in
1644 '. . . Contemporary Practice, (which is one of
the best Expounders of the meaning of any Law) did
neither destroy all coloured Windows, though Images
were in them, in the *Queens* time, nor abstain from
setting up of new, both in her, and *King* James his
Time.'[8]

Bess was not remarkable, therefore, in preserving
superstitious images in her houses, which should
perhaps be seen as signifying a desire for toleration in
religion. This was an attitude that accorded well with
her monarch's and was held by unorthodox religious
thinkers such as John Dee who, despite immersing
himself in astral magic, passionately longed for the
reunification of Protestants and Catholics in one
universal religion that would also embrace the Jews.[9]
But how far was Bess's apparent taste for humanist-
type prints paralleled in other houses? Exhaustive
study of country-house inventories may eventually
enable us to answer this question but, unfortunately,
surviving inventories vary greatly in detail: those of
Longleat – one house it would particularly interesting
to know about – are frustratingly uninformative about
subjects of decoration. Others are more specific. One
is the well-known Lumley Inventory of 1590 which
specifies the subjects of all the portraits and other
pictures in the collection of John, Lord Lumley;[10]
another is the inventory of the Earl of Leicester's
belongings at Kenilworth Castle at his death in 1588.
It gives a splendid picture of the richness of the
furnishings of the castle in its heyday but more impor-
tantly, in the section entitled 'Hanginges', specifies
many of the subjects. Here is the list:

[1] Eight peeces of flowers, beasts, and pillors,
arched . . .

[2] Eleaven peeces of fyne tapestrye of fforest
worke . . .

[3] Eight peeces of deepe hanginges, bought of
the Ladye Lennox, all quarter-lyned with
canvas.

[4] Eight peeces of historie, quarter-lyned with
canvas . . .

[5] Twelve peeces of historie . . .

[6] Eight peeces of hangings, fforest worke . . .

[7] Sixteene peeces of gilt leather hanginges,
having on the topp the picture of a man and
a woman . . .

[8] Three peeces of gilt leather hangings of the
storie of Susanna, paned gilt and blew . . .

[9] Three peeces of gilte leather hangings of the
storie of the Prodigall Childe, paned gilt and
blew . . .

[10] Two like peeces of the storie of Saule, paned
gilte and blew . . .

[12] Three peeces of gilt hangings of red leather,
paned gilt and blew . . .

[13] One pair of guilt leather hangings, gilt and
greene, of the story of Tobie . . .

[14] Fyve peeces of leather hangings, gilt and
black . . .

[15] Ffower peeces of the historie of Sawle, lyned
with canvas . . .

[16] Six peeces of the historie of Hercules . . .

[17] Six peeces of Lady Ffame, &c . . .

[18] Six peeces of flowers and beasts . . .

[19] Ffower peeces of fflowers and beasts . . .

[20] Nyne peeces of Hawking and Hunting . . .

[21] Seaven peeces of the storie of Jezabell . . .

[22] Eight peeces of the historie of Judith and
Holofernes . . .

[23] Fyve peeces of the storie of David . . .

[24] Six peeces of the storie of Abraham . . .

[25] Eight peeces of fflowers and beasts . . .

[26] Fyve peeces of the storie of Sampson, of oulde
stuffe . . .

[27] Six peeces of fflowers and beasts . . .

[28] Nyne fayre peeces of the storie of Hercules,
antiques . . .

[29] Six peeces of the storie Hippolitus . . .

[30] Eight peeces of the storie of Alexander the
Great . . .

[31] Six peeces of the storie of Naaman the
Assyrian . . .

[32] Eight peeces of the storie of Jacob . . .

[33] Eight peeces of fflowers and beasts pillard . . .

[34] Ffower peeces of leather hangings, gilte and
blacke . . .

[35] Six peeces of vardures, of very ould stuffe . . .

[36] A peece of hangings of red linsey wolsey, with
borders and pillars painted . . .

[37] Three peeces of stamell clothe, embrothered
all over with armes, beasts, fflowers, &c . . .[11]

In addition to these hangings, Leicester owned a good
many pictures, mostly portraits of contemporaries,
with a few exceptions:

The picture of St. Jerom naked . . .
The picture of the Baker's Daughter
The picture of Alexander Magnus . . .
Two pictures of Pompoea Sabina.
The picture of Occacion and Repentance.
A tabell of an historie of men, women, and chil-
dren, molden in wax.
Fyve of the Plannetts, painted in frames.
Twentie-three cards or maps of Countries.[12]

There is a very familiar ring to these subjects: we have met many of them at Hardwick. The first item on Leicester's list, the 'Eight peeces of flowers, beasts, and pillors, arched . . .' is very reminiscent of Bess's 'nyne peeces of hanginges . . . with petestalls and portalls . . . and with portalls and pavementes rownde about . . .', or her 'one long quition for the Chare . . . imbrodered . . . with a portall and beastes, birdes and flowers . . .' Both Kenilworth and Hardwick — particularly Hardwick Old Hall — had several sets of hangings of 'forrest work'. Leicester owned several sets of unidentified 'historie' along with others specifi-cally identified, Hercules, Hyppolitus, Alexander the Great. Leicester's Old Testament stories — Abraham, David, Jezebel, Judith and Holofernes, Sampson, Saul, Susannah, Tobie — had their counterparts at Hardwick, albeit some in needlework rather than in tapestry. Bess's 'Fyve peeces of hanginges called the planetes' matched his 'Fyve of the Plannetts, painted in frames'. He had a set illustrating the story of Susanna, she concentrated on the example set by Penelope.

So the subjects corresponded closely. They may — although there is now no way of verifying this — in some instances have derived from the same suites of prints. Leicester's 'pair of guilt leather hangings, gilt and greene, of the story of Tobie . . .' and his 'Three peeces of gilte leather hangings of the storie of the Prodigall Childe, paned gilt and blew . . .' might well have derived from the Heemskerck sets, particularly as the Heemskerck prints of the story of Esther and Ahasuerus were copied by the anonymous maker of the Walsingham set of leather hangings (p.97). Even his 'Seaven peeces of the storie of Jezabell . . .' may also have derived from Heemskerck.[13] In fact, there is usually one or more Heemskerck suite for almost all the hangings listed at Kenilworth in 1588.[14] One of the most interesting and suggestive descriptions is the 'Six peeces of Lady Ffame, &c . . .' This sounds remarkably like Heemskerck's suite, *The Triumphs of Petrarch*, used extensively at Hardwick by John Balechouse in the hangings he painted for the chapel.

The case is, of course, not proven, but it may be that there was a taste for the kind of prints we have seen adapted for decoration at Hardwick in aristo-

cratic, well-educated circles, people who enjoyed the challenge of deciphering elaborate allegories. Inciden-tally, it is comforting to learn that allegories were so complicated that they sometimes defeated contem-poraries: on one occasion, a member of the Vane family sent 'the poet Waller, in 1639, a handkerchief so curiously embroidered that he could not discover the meaning of its riddling conceits, and proposed sending it to Oxford, to the astrologer, and calls for the help of Sacharissa in his perplexity'.[15] By the 1760s, Horace Walpole experienced great difficulty with the 'Rainbow' portrait of Queen Elizabeth:

. . . a very extraordinary picture, finished with great labour, & in the highest preservation. It is the handsomest I have ever seen of Her. The Dress is most magnificent, her head attire is in the Persian manner & wondrously lofty. her robe of yellow Satten is powdered with eyes & ears, & in her hand She holds a rainbow, with these words above it, 'Non sine Sole Iris'. Her Majesty's Devices are not often very Intelligible; I suppose this piece was a present to Lord Burghleigh, & implied that She heard & saw every thing herself, & that all his greatness was only by reflection from her.[16]

We cannot expect to find much evidence that the taste for prints depicting humanist allegories spread lower down the social scale, given that it was rare even for a member of the most prosperous section of Tudor society to possess pictures or sculpture. Analysing Tudor inventories of London aldermen and merchants, landed gentry and courtiers (and in one instance Henry VIII's goldsmith), Susan Foister con-cluded that 'roughly one in ten of the people named in the inventories over the period c.1480–c.1580 owned some kind of work of art; nine out of ten did not . . . But it is clear that the majority of even the most prosperous class in Tudor England did not own any paintings or sculpture at all, though they did frequently own painted hangings.'[17] Many painted cloths, as the Painter-Stainers complained, were 'wrought with stencil pattern or otherwise as painted and printed sleight upon cloth, silk, leather or other things . . . with work of sundry colours or with gold foil or silver foil that is deceitful' and prints may well have been used in their design.[18] Unfortunately pre-cious few have survived even at the higher levels of society let alone the lower.[19] However, the wall-paintings in 61 High Street, Amersham, Buckingham-shire, mentioned earlier, may represent the deplorable quality achieved by the artists working on painted cloths and their subject — the Nine Worthies — was popular throughout English society during the twenty-five years either side of 1600.

Though of medieval French origin, the Worthies became increasingly common after the Reformation, appearing more and more frequently in Flemish and German prints as the century progressed.[20] The full set of nine, according to Caxton's introduction to *Morte d'Arthur*,[21] consisted of three Pagans, three Jews and three Christians: Hector, Alexander of Macedon and Julius Caesar; Joshua, King David and Judas Maccabeus; King Arthur, Charlemagne and Godfrey of Bouillon (Boulogne). In England Godfrey was some times replaced by Guy of Warwick, while the whole set could be amplified by the addition, for instance, of Henry VIII as in George Cavendish's *The Metrical Visions* of 1558 – 'Victoryously didest rayn/ The viij Herrye/Worthy most souerayn/Tenth worthy worthy'[22] – or Elizabeth I, with Christ and St Peter, on the set of spoons called the Tichborne Worthies in the British Museum.

The Nine Worthies appear in popular as well as more specialised literature,[23] but the most intriguing reference is an exchange in *Love's Labours Lost*, Act V, written about 1594–5, where Shakespeare has Costard interrupt Sir Nathaniel (playing the part of Alexander) thus: 'O sir, you have ouerthrowne Alisander the Conquerour: you will be scrapt out of the painted cloth for this. Your Lion that holds his Polax sitting on a close stool, will be given to Aiax. He wilbe the ninth Worthie . . .' It was John Nevinson who pointed out the similarity between this passage and Alexander's banner in the Amersham merchant's wallpainting: the banner has a lion seated on a backstool which could jocularly be described as a close-stool,[24] while Julius Caesar, who was replaced by Pompey in the play, has leg-armour with what could easily be described as 'libbard's head on knee'. Shakespeare must have been describing the very Philips Galle suite used not only by the painter of lowly ability at Amersham but by altogether more accomplished craftsmen working in aristocratic or at least genteel circles – even Thomas Trevelyon's drawings in his Miscellanies of 1608 and 1616 were made for the instruction of gentle ladies.

This is a rare instance where it is possible to show that some continental prints achieved a widespread appeal.[25] There are plenty of other subjects found in aristocratic houses such as Kenilworth or Hardwick that were common lower down the social scale – Tessa Watt has found (from survivals of wall painting and contemporary remarks) that the four most popular biblical subjects of the late sixteenth century were the stories of Susanna and of Tobias, and the parables of the Prodigal Son and Dives and Lazarus[26] – but it is not possible to identify for certain the prints that must have been used at this level. The Prodigal Son wallpaintings at Knightsland Farm near South Mymms in Hertfordshire have been compared by Watt to Rue de Montorgueil woodcuts 'or a similar series on the same theme', and by Muriel Carrick to engravings after David Vingboons, neither to my complete satisfaction; likewise, I have found no obvious source for the painting of Dives and Lazarus at Pittleworth Manor in Hampshire.

So it must remain uncertain how often relatively costly foreign prints actually influenced contemporary popular culture. Inexpensive single-sheet woodcuts were far more readily available – being sold throughout urban and rural England by chapmen and vagrants – than costly foreign books and prints. The latter had to be sought either from specialised booksellers in London (like John Scott who travelled abroad in search of books for Bishop Cosin),[27] or direct from the Continent. Otherwise patrons could employ a foreign craftsman who himself owned a stock of prints or imported them specially, as must have happened in Newcastle, where wealthy merchants commissioned elaborate Mannerist overmantels from an accomplished carver.

The concentration of continental-type decoration in the major ports of England suggests that these towns, which often had substantial immigrant communities, were significant points of entry for foreign prints. They included Newcastle, Lynn, Yarmouth, Ipswich, Southampton, Exeter, Plymouth, Barnstaple and Bristol. All were river ports, a fact that explains the dissemination of continental influence into their hinterland. Besides such internal commerce, other factors contributed to the spreading awareness of continental prints: the intellectual community, the growth of professions and trades, the linking of families in marriage, contacts and friendships forged at university and the Inns of Court.[28]

In fact, any communities, whether of merchants as members of a company, of lawyers as benchers of an Inn, or of immigrants as congregations of a foreign church, were potentially channels through which continental ideas might flow. One of the most tantalising of such communities, because so secret, was the Family of Love, a fellowship of men and women founded by the Netherlandish mystic Hendrick Niclaes in Emden in 1540, which had a substantial following in England. Members believed that 'commitment to any definite religious confession was unimportant. What mattered was an intense inner mysticism centred on charity'[29] – tenets that resulted in the Fellowship becoming well-nigh invisible, preserving no records of membership and deliberately destroying documents that might prove useful to its enemies. In that members' conscience 'allowed them to observe outwardly the rites of any Church that happened to be in power, for they denied – and were always persecuted for denying – that the visible Church had any significance . . .',[30] the fellowship shared the outward conformity but inward dissention of humanists.

Members or sympathisers on the Continent included many of the leading intellectuals, men like Christopher Plantin, who printed numerous Familist treatises, probably enjoying financial support of other Familists and owed his own survival during the pendulum-swings of religious change to his outward flexibility of religious observance. His printing houses became a centre of Familism and many of his friends, artists, authors and assistants were also sympathetic to Familist ideas, the cartographer Abraham Ortelius (who had English contacts, for example the Queen's mathematician John Dee), the humanist scholar Justus Lipsius and the printer, artist and publisher who succeeded Dirck Coornhert as Heemskerck's reproductive printmaker, Philips Galle. Familist books and publications would have been available in London at the bookshop owned by Arnold Birkmann of Cologne[31] and membership in England embraced villagers, foreign merchants such as Emmanuel van Meteren and guardsmen to the Queen alike. It was even suggested that Elizabeth was herself receptive to some of their ideas: no more than three years after her death a critic argued that 'she had always about her some Familistes, or favourers of that Sect'.[32] Could it be that where we have seen the use of Philips Galle's prints in England a sympathy with Familism is indicated?[33]

It is almost certainly unsafe to go so far, and it is significant that there is no suggestion of sympathy with Familists in Patrick Collinson's recent essay on the religion of Queen Elizabeth.[34] But, if we are correct in our speculations at Hardwick, the sophistication of the intellectual (and perhaps the social) élite of England should not be underestimated. What does seem clear is that there is little evidence in these circles for substantial iconophobia – 'the total repudiation of all images' – attributed to Protestants in the years around 1580.[35] Indeed, judging only by the surviving decoration that has yielded up the secret of its creation, prints of all kinds – ornamental and subject prints, biblical, historical, allegorical – were very much part of contemporary life. If there was an overwhelming preference for Flemish and Dutch prints (as there was), it may be that the moralising overtones of many of them struck a sympathetic chord in English society. For after the abolition of the confessional at the Reformation there was what has been described as a 'widespread conviction that the unaided Protestant conscience was an inadequate sanction for morality . . .'[36] Although some of the mechanisms by which they were introduced into this country, and moved between patron and patron, craftsman and craftsman, need to be explored further, the role of continental prints in Elizabethan and Jacobean art and decoration is assured.

Abbreviations

BE	*Buildings of England* (Harmondsworth, 1951–)
Burl. Mag.	*Burlington Magazine*
CL	*Country Life*
H.	F.W.H. Hollstein, *Dutch and Flemish Etchings, Engravings and Woodcuts, c.1450–1700*, vols I-XXXI (Amsterdam, 1949–87), vols XXXII–XLIII (Roosendaal, 1988–93), vols XLIV– (Rotterdam, 1995–)
H. *Ger.*	F.W.H. Hollstein, *German Engravings, Etchings and Woodcuts, c.1400–1700* (Amsterdam, 1954–)
M.-H.	Marie Mauquoy-Hendrickx, *Les Estampes des Wierix* (Brussels, 1978)
M.	Hans Mielke, *Hans Vredeman de Vries* (Berlin, 1967)
NH, Heemskerck	Ilja M. Veldman, *Maarten van Heemskerck, 1498–1574*, 2 vols, *The New Hollstein Dutch and Flemish Etchings, Engravings and Woodcuts, 1450–1700*, Part I (Roosendaal, 1993), Part II (Roosendaal, 1994)
RCHM	Royal Commission on the Historic Monuments of England
RIBA	Royal Institute of British Architects
S.	Sune Schele, *Cornelis Bos: A Study of the Origins of the Netherlands Grotesque* (Stockholm, 1965)
T.	John Summerson, 'The Book of Architecture of John Thorpe in Sir John Soane's Museum', *Walpole Society*, XL (1964–6)
TIB	*The Illustrated Bartsch*, ed. W. Strauss (New York, 1978–)
V&A	Victoria and Albert Museum, London

Notes

Preface

1 Eisenstein 1993, p.xv.

2 Peter Daly (ed.), *The English Emblem Tradition*, I, (New York, 1988), p.ix.

3 The use made of costume books by artists has been little explored: however, Bianca M. du Mortier has made an interesting start in her article '. . . Hier sietmen Vrouwen van alderley Natien . . . ; Kostuumboeken bron voor de schilderkunst?', *Bulletin van het Rijksmuseum*, 39, no. 4 (1991), pp.401–13.

4 *The Geneva Bible: A facsimile of the 1560 edition* (Madison, Wisconsin, and London, 1969); see Hill 1994, pp. 18, 56–66; and David Daniell (ed.), *Tyndale's New Testament: Translated from the Greek by William Tyndale in 1534* (New Haven and London, 1995 edn), pp. xi–xiii. The last known edition of the Geneva Bible was pablished in 1640.

1 Introduction

1 Quoted in Davies 1964, p.5, from John Leake's treatise on the cloth industry, published in London (1577). I have been unable to find another reference to this work.

2 Cambridge 1979, most recently reprinted in 1993.

3 Francis Bacon, *Novum Organum*, Aphorism 129.

4 Eisenstein 1993, p.46.

5 Yates 1984, p.185.

6 Dickens 1968, p.51, cited in Eisenstein 1993, p.303.

7 Saxl and Wittkower 1948.

8 Watt 1994, p.192, citing W.J. Ivins, junr., *Prints and visual communication* (New York, 1969 edn).

9 Landau and Parshall 1994.

10 Ibid., p.104.

11 Ibid., p.221.

12 Thurley 1993, p.88, citing Elizabeth Armstrong, 'English Purchases of Printed Books from the Continent, 1465–1526', *English Historical Review* (1979), pp.268–90.

13 Hartley 1984, p.82.

14 Ward-Jackson 1969, p.3; Byrne 1981, p.19, and Landau and Parshall 1994, pp.359–60, list some of the uses of prints.

15 In addition to the *Codex Escurialensis*: Byrne 1981, p.13.

16 Van Uchelen 1987, pp.15–18.

17 Landau and Parshall 1994, p.31. According to Nicolas Barker, the output from a woodblock may have run into millions.

18 Watt 1994, p.141.

19 Landau and Parshall 1994, Appendix, pp.369–71.

20 Ibid., pp.236–7, 350–54.

21 Multiplying Elizabethan prices by a factor of 500 is suggested by Charles Nicholl, in Nicholl 1993: 'Thus a pint of ale cost a halfpenny (£1), a cheap dinner at a London "ordinary" 6d. (£12), a serviceable dagger 12d. (£25). A jobbing stonemason earned 10d. (£20); a writer sold a pamphlet to his publisher for 40s. (£1,000) and perhaps got the same again for a "dedication fee".'

22 Watt 1994, p.142.

23 Gent 1981, Appendix, pp.66–86.

24 They are: Hans van Schille, *Form und weis zu bauwen* (1580); Vredeman's *Architectura* (1581, M.XXII); Vredeman's *[Architectura] Das Erst Büch* (presumably 1578, M.XII; Vredeman's *Architectura . . . de Oorden Tuschana* (1578, M.XXIV); Vredeman's *[Architectura] Das Ander Buech* (1578, M.XIII); Cornelis Floris's *Veelderley niewe inventien . . .* (1557); Philips Galle's *Instruction et Fondements de bien pourtraire* (1589); Vredeman's *Differents pourtraicts de menuiserie*. I am indebted to Jane Fowles, former Librarian at Longleat, for this information. Miss Fowles was of the opinion that this volume, along with the other surviving books on art and architecture at Longleat, came into the library during the time of the first Viscount Weymouth, who owned the house between 1682 and 1714.

25 Karl Gustav Wrangel (1613–76), the builder of Skokloster, had around 2,400 volumes in his library, which was founded in 1665. After his death, the collection was split into four, although each quarter was representative of the whole in content. Approximately 800 of his books still survive in the library, along with books belonging to the Brahe and Bielke families.

There is, in Nottingham University Library, Dept. of Manuscripts (Press-mark Mi.I17/1), a list of books belonging to Francis Willoughby (died 1672) some of which might have come to him from his grandfather Sir Francis, the builder of Wollaton Hall near Nottingham. These books were largely dispersed by sale at Christie's on 13 June 1925. I am indebted to Mark Girouard for this information and for supplying a partial transcription of this list. I have been unable to trace any books belonging to Bess of Hardwick.

26 For a list of London booksellers with whom Plantin traded, see Clair 1960, p.210.

27 For Pepys's purchases of prints see P.A. Hulton's introduction to Latham 1980, p.xixff.

28 *The Gentleman's Exercise* (London, 1612), p.47, cited in Gent 1981, p.32n.

29 Gent 1981, p.10.

30 See p.218.

31 Gent 1981, p.32 and n.120.

32 Eisenstein 1993, p.33; see also Arthur M. Hind, *An Introduction to a History of Woodcut* (New York, 1963 edn), p.230ff; Allan Stevenson, 'The Quincentennial of Netherlandish Block-books', *The British Museum Quarterly*, XXXI (1966–7), pp.83–7.

33 Stevenson, op.cit., pp.86–7.

34 Purvis 1935, pp.107–28; C. Grössinger, *Ripon Cathedral Misericords* (Ripon, 1989).

35 Purvis 1935, pp.124–5. For recent work on the influence of Continental prints on misericords, see Malcolm Jones, 'The Misericords of Beverley Minster: a Corpus of Folk-loric Imagery and its Cultural Milieu, with special reference to the influence of Northern European iconography on Late Medieval and Early Modern English Woodwork', unpublished Ph.D. dissertation, Polytechnic South West (1991).

36 Croft-Murray 1962, p.17.

37 Moore 1988, pp.xii, 2–3, 81–3.

38 The books were Thomas Linacre, *Galeni Pergameni de symptomatum differentiis liber unus* (1519), and R. Pace, *Oratio . . . in pace* (1518): McKerrow and Ferguson 1932, nos 7, 8; also Thurley 1994, p.89.

39 McKerrow and Ferguson 1932, p.xvi.

40 These have been brilliantly identified by H.G. Wayment, in Wayment 1958, pp.378–88.

41 Ibid., pp.386–7, gives a full list of sources used.

42 Ibid., p.386.

43 Baggs 1969, pp.295–301.

44 Strong 1967, pls 25, 41, 43–4; another notable instance is that of Girolamo da Treviso who based his painting *The Four Evangelists Stoning the Pope* on a woodcut by an anonymous artist in the 1536 translation of the Bible into English (ibid., pls 4–5).

45 Saxl and Wittkower 1948, 38, *4*, *a*, *b*, *c*. For Holbein's *Erasmus* compare Cesariano's 1523 edition of Vitruvius, Book IV, folio LXIIIr.

46 Hackenbroch 1979, ill.743; the same Holbein print, or another inspired by it, seems also to have been used as the basis of a carved oak panel perhaps of early seventeenth-century date in the church of St Leonard, Hereford.

47 Thurley 1993, p.208, fig.274.

48 Croft-Murray 1962, p.21.

49 V&A, W. 29–1932.

50 Thurley 1993, p.89. Thurley also illustrates (figs 123–4) the cover and five plates of the classical orders from a French treatise on geometry owned by Henry VIII.

51 This information was presented to a conference on the Tudor and Jacobean Great House in January 1994 by Robert Bell and Kirsty Rodwell, in Malcolm Airs (ed.), *The Tudor and Jacobean Great House* (Oxford, 1994), p.56. Other exam-

ples occur at Bunbury in Cheshire, and at Chivelstone, South Pool and Black Awton (all in Devon) during the 1520s.

52 See Wilson 1987, especially pp.112–14.

53 James Lees Milne, *Tudor Renaissance*, 1951, p.71 (cited in Chaney 1991, p.237).

54 Dinsmoor 1942, p.65.

55 Dinsmoor (ibid., p.68, n.66) gives the following list: 'The fourth book was reprinted in Venice in 1540, 1544, 1551, and about 1562, besides appearing in the collected quarto editions of 1566, 1584, 1600, 1618, and 1619, and in the Italian-Latin folio editions of 1568/69 and 1663. Flemish translations were published in Antwerp in 1539, 1549: French translations at Antwerp in 1542, 1545, 1550: German translations at Antwerp in 1542, 1558, and at Basle in 1609: Spanish translations at Toledo in 1552, 1563, 1573; Dutch translations at Amsterdam in 1606, 1616; and an English translation at London in 1611.'

56 Book IV, fols 67v, 68r, 68v, 69r, 70v in Peake's 1611 English edition (Dover repr., New York, 1982).

57 Lord Sandys had earlier commissioned Flemish glass painters to design and execute windows for his Guild Chapel of Holy Trinity in Basingstoke, and these were perhaps complete by 1524; Wayment 1982, pp.141–52.

58 Puloy 1983 dates this ceiling c.1520, but Pevsner implies that the church may have been furnished around 1540 (N. Pevsner and B. Cherry, *The Buildings of England: Hertfordshire* (Harmondsworth, 1978), p.400).

59 Comparably early examples of the use of Serlio on the mainland are the ceilings of the Rittersaal of the Schloss at Neuburg-an-der-Donau (c.1537), of a room in Gripsholm Castle, Stockholm (between 1537 and 1544), and of the Library at Chenonceau, perhaps in the 1540s. The Galerie Henri II at Fontainebleau also has a coffered wooden ceiling which might derive from Serlio; it dates from the early 1540s.

60 Thurley 1993, p.108.

61 Summerson 1977, figs 11, 12.

62 Gould 1962, pp.56–64; and Moxey 1976, pp.109–87.

63 The design was later popularised for paving by C.A. d'Aviler's architectural treatise *Cours complet d'architecture* (Paris, 1691), plate 203t, Anthony Wells-Cole, 'Designs for Decorated Floors', in C.G. Gilbert, J.R. Lomax and A.D.P. Wells-Cole, *Country House Floors* (Leeds, 1987), fig.7.

64 Howard 1990, pp.209–11.

2 THE INFLUENCE OF ITALIAN PRINTS

1 The Stuebchen, now in the Bayerische Nationalmuseum in Munich, was illustrated in H.R. Hitchcock's masterly *German Renaissance Architecture* (Princeton, 1981); Hitchcock remained unaware of the derivations from Serlio.

2 He is amongst those portrayed in the painting begun by Holbein but left unfinished at his death; it is illustrated, for example, in Strong 1967, pl.55.

3 Raphael's lost drawing of the statue discovered in Rome c.1500 was engraved by Marcantonio Raimondi, *TIB*, XIV, p.155, no.192; see also R.M. Mason and M. Natale (eds), *Raphael et la seconde main* (Geneva, 1984), no.53, and Bober and Rubinstein 1986, no.1, p.51.

4 Book IV, fol.60v.

5 John Cornforth, *English Interiors, 1790–1848: The Quest for Comfort* (London, 1978), fig.49.

6 Tipping 1929, fig.xxxix. Another chimneypiece derived from this design is at Elmore in Gloucestershire, *CL* (26 Dec. 1914), p.852.

7 Reproduced in Colum Giles, *Rural Houses of West Yorkshire, 1400–1830*, RCHME (London, 1986), p.159.

8 In France, the ceiling of the Galerie Henri II at Fontainebleau of the 1540s; in Germany the ceiling of the entrance to the Schloss Neuburg-an-der-Donau, of the same decade.

9 Puloy 1983, p.149, pl.vi.

10 Amongst numerous later examples are ceilings at Kalmar Castle (1590s) in Sweden, a floor at Count Wrangel's mid-seventeenth-century Skoklosters Slott, near Uppsala, Sweden, and the sounding-board of the pulpit at Ribe in Denmark (dated 1596).

11 Others occur, for instance, at Lees Hall, Thornhill and Barkisland Hall, c.1638.

12 Ceilings in the Palazzi Conservatori, Farnese and Spada in Rome are of this pattern, while the ceiling of the Scala Regia in the Vatican is an adaptation. In France, it appears in the vault of the church of St Jean at Joigny from 1557. Decorative tiling on a dado in the new cathedral at Salamanca in Spain, of the mid-century, follows the pattern, as do the panels of a Flemish cabinet now in the museum in Utrecht. In Germany, too, the pattern was popular, appearing on the ceilings of the hall in the Rathaus at Poznan after 1553, the Festsaal of Schloss Ortenburg, c.1600, as well as on a cupboard in the Museum für Kunsthandwerk in Frankfurt. One of the ceilings in Rosenborg Slot in Copenhagen is also of this pattern.

13 Also a ceiling at Church Farm, Barton, Cumberland (1628); further south, similar ceilings occur in the now demolished Red Hall, Leeds, and at Marsh Hall, Northowram, near Halifax.

14 Curiously, this is almost exactly contemporary with a distinguished example of the use of the pattern in Italy, where Borromini used it for his vault in the Church of San Carlo alle Quattro Fontane, from 1638.

15 Otherwise the instances belong to the seventeenth and the eighteenth centuries: they include one pattern of parquetry flooring 'lately made at Somerset House', and published in the 1670 English translation of Le Muet's Palladio; a painted floor in a house at 12 North Street, Wisbech, Cambridgeshire, and James Gibbs's coffered dome of the Radcliffe Camera, Oxford, of the 1730s.

16 This is now thought to be eighteenth-century.

17 The last now in the V&A. Ceilings of the same pattern also occur in Wales, at Gwydir and Powis Castles, and from a house in Raglan, now at Badminton House, Gloucestershire. Further examples are at Birtsmorton Court (Worcestershire), Melbury Court and Forde House (Dorset), Stockton House (Wiltshire), Dunsland House (Devon), Bramshill (Hampshire) and Knole (Kent). A particularly ingenious modification of the pattern occurs on the ceiling of the Chapel Room at Danny in Sussex, c.1595: the cruciform shapes have overlapped tips but are also elaborated with smaller cruciform shapes at their centres, which produces a richly varied pattern. In London itself, two examples were to be found in houses in Lime Street, while the

Queen's Boudoir at Kew Palace has another of c.1631.

18 Summerson 1990, p.25, figs 8, 9.

19 Perhaps the most surprising eighteenth-century borrowings from Serlio were those made by Robert Adam, an architect not usually associated with dependence on pattern-book sources, as his style is generally believed to have derived from first-hand experience of the classical buildings in Italy and Dalmatia. In *The Works in Architecture of Robert and James Adam*, the pattern of the ceiling of the tribune around the Ballroom erected in the garden of the Earl of Derby at the Oaks in Surrey derives from Serlio's interlocking circles (Book IV, folio 70v lower right), and it is difficult not to accept Serlio as the source of two of Adam's ceilings at Syon: the Ante Room has an octagon in the centre with hexagons at the corners – in effect, the greek-cross pattern without the crosses – and the Gallery has the overlapping octagons, subtly subdivided in exactly the way in which they were a century and a half earlier but treated, of course, in a different, far more classical manner.

20 Wells-Cole 1990a, pp.1–41.

21 Wittkower 1984, p.74.

22 Gent 1981, p.84; Gent found evidence of four copies of the 1601 Venice edition, too.

23 William Cecil's comment on Palladio was quoted by Strong 1986, p.45; for the Haynes Grange Room, which belongs to the Victoria and Albert Museum but has not been on display for many years, see Girouard 1992, pp.171–86.

24 Gent 1981, p.81.

25 The suite consists of 28 plates by an unknown engraver, Riggs 1977, p.165 and List no.1, p.311.

26 One of the earliest is Virgil Solis's Lutheran Bible printed in Frankfurt in 1563 where the highly elaborate titlepage, *The Prophets,* which may mostly be his own design, has a cartouche at the foot of the page copied direct from Battini's *Vigilate* with minimal alteration. Solis also copied Battini's cartouche with the inscription 'ne quid nimis . . .' for the left-hand element of his own plate inscribed 'WILTV DIR SELBST . . .' The plates also served cartographers well. Abraham Ortelius used one for the title cartouche on his map of the Pacific, published in 1589, see Hugh Cortazzi, *Isles of Gold: Antique Maps of Japan* (New York, 1984); another appears on his map of the British Isles the following year. Similarly, Gerard Mercator borrowed three for his maps of Marca Brandeburgensis, Walachia and Abruzzo, published in the *Atlas* in 1613. On one occasion a plate by Battini was put to use by a tapestry designer, for the cartouches in the centre top and bottom of a Flemish grotesque tapestry now in the V&A, Wingfield Digby 1980, cat. no.47.

27 See *CL*, 7 Oct. 1905, pp.486–91.

28 Saxl and Wittkower 1948, 41, 6, 7.

3 THE INFLUENCE OF GERMAN PRINTS

1 Hayward 1976, p.201.

2 Ramsay 1986, pp.116–52.

3 For the miniaturists see Carl Winter, *Elizabethan Miniatures* (Harmondsworth, 1948), pp.25, 26 (cited in Gent 1981, p.32n.); for the trunk see James Yorke, 'A Chest from Cockfield Hall', *Burl. Mag.* (Feb. 1986), pp.85–91.

4 For detailed discussion see pp.201–5.

5 Oman 1978, fig.32; they are said to have belonged to the antiquary Sir Robert Bruce Cotton (1571–1631).

6 Jervis 1984, p.375.

7 In the V&A; see Jourdain 1924, p.95, fig.120; from the same suite of the Planets (*TIB* 163–9) a carver copied the figure of Mars, symbolising War, for one of the entrance doors at Audley End in Essex.

8 O'Dell-Franke 1977, pl.21, c1–9. Marcus Binney, 'Loseley Park, Surrey', *CL* (2 Oct. 1969), pp.802–5; (9 Oct. 1969), pp.894–7.

9 Binney, *ibid.*, pp.894–5.

10 *TIB*, vol.19, part I, 177.

11 Bankart 1908, fig.272.

12 *CL* (30 July 1904), p.163.

13 I am indebted to Peter Brears for consulting me about possible print sources for these trenchers (which are in Strangers Hall, Norwich), thus bringing them to my attention. Although Virgil Solis's woodcuts had first appeared in 1560, the earliest publication in which they were combined with the elaborate ornamental frames was the 1562 edition of the *Biblische Figuren*. An alternative source for Solis's biblical illustrations in England was the first, 1568, edition of the *Bishop's Bible* which used copies of the Solis woodcuts, printed from blocks perhaps borrowed or rented from the Cologne publishing house of Quentell. For the complex history of Solis's illustrations see Margaret Aston, 'The *Bishops' Bible* Illustrations', *Studies in Church History*, 28 (1992), pp.267–85.

14 Some of the woodcuts were later used in the edition of Josephus Flavius's history of the Jews which appeared under the title *Opera Josephi viri inter Judaeos doctissimi ac disertissimi, quae ad nostram Ætatem pervenerunt, omnia, nimirum . . .* in 1580.

15 For instance, Heemskerck's illustrations of the Story of Esther, engraved by Philips Galle (*TIB* 5601.017), appear virtually unchanged in Amman's woodcuts for the 1564 Frankfurt *Biblia Sacra*. Amman's woodcut was used, with his depiction of the Triumph of Mordecai on the genuinely old panel of an otherwise 'antiquarian' sideboard made for Speke Hall, Liverpool, in the second half of the nineteenth century, which incorporates a genuinely old relief depicting Esther before Ahasuerus and The Triumph of Mordecai, both from the *Biblia*. For similar German panels see Heinrich Kreisel and Georg Himmelheber, *Die Kunst des deutschen Möbels* (Munich, 1981), I, figs 341, 342.

16 Archer 1976, p.1452, figs 3, 4.

17 Cabot 1946, figs 16a–b, 17a–b.

18 Ibid., pp.25, 32, fig.20; for the Death of Jezebel see Brooke 1987, p.9.

19 A monument in St Thomas, Salisbury, carved by Humphrey Beckham to commemorate himself before his death in 1671, has the Sacrifice of Isaac: the figures appear to have been adapted from Amman, the background from Gerard de Iode's *Thesaurus* (1579, 1585). The monument is illustrated in RCHM *Salisbury*, I, (1980), pl.47.

20 One of Dietterlin's designs for the Tuscan order was employed for the titlepage of Julius Guglielmus Zinegraff's *Emblematum Ethico-Politicorum Centuria*, printed by Johann Theodor de Bry in Frankfurt in 1619; see Yates 1986, pl.17.

21 Tipping 1929, p.329.

22 Kerry Downes, *Hawksmoor* (London, 1959), letter 147; I am indebted to Dr Terry Friedman for this reference.

23 Helen Hills, 'Bramshill House, Hampshire – II', *CL* (17 Oct. 1985), figs 2, 3.

24 RIBA Smythson drawings (III/28), see Girouard 1983, p.269.

25 The relationship is so close that Girouard discounts the possibility of Smythson's involvement here, on the grounds that his proven uses of Dietterlin originals always altered the source more radically. On the other hand, it will be shown (p.64) that Huntingdon Smythson slavishly copied a print source to the extent of reproducing side-by-side two designs that were intended to be alternatives. So it was perhaps he who designed the Wentworth Woodhouse gate, particularly as the entrance to the contemporary Bear Pit there was derived from a source that must have been known to Smythson's grandfather, Robert, when used at Hardwick (see p.16). The correspondence between the Dietterlin design and the gate was noted independently by Marcus Binney, 'Wentworth Woodhouse revisited', *CL* (17 March 1988), p. 627, figs 14, 15.

26 Oliver Hill and John Conforth, *English Country Houses, Caroline, 1625–85* (London, 1966), figs 172, 173, p.113. Aldenham Place in Buckinghamshire also has some architectural decor-ation that recalls Dietterlin, ibid., p.218.

27 Krammer, *Schweiff Buchlein* (Cologne, 1611); Kasemann, *Architectura lehr-seivlen Bochg* (1615); Altzenbach, *Architectur* (Cologne, 1653–9). Incidentally, in a rare error, Margaret Jourdain attributed one of Altzenbach's designs to Vredeman de Vries, see Jourdain 1924, fig.16A.

28 Jervis 1974, pp.36–7 and nos 180–242; also Jervis 1984, p.169. A copy of Ebelmann's *Seilenbuch* of 1600, in which he collaborated with Guckheisen, was included in the first catalogue of the Bodleian Library in Oxford; I am indebted to Lady Bullard for this information.

29 This discovery was made independently by Victor Chinnery: the cabinet passed through the hands of the London dealer, Ronald Lee, but its present whereabouts are unknown.

30 See Wells-Cole 1990, p.37.

31 Spectacular examples may be seen in Denmark, in the cathedrals of Roskilde and Århus, and the Annakerck in Helsingør.

32 E.F. Strange, 'Furniture at Hatfield House', *Old Furniture*, Nov. 1928, pp.136–7.

33 Croft-Murray 1962, pp.194–5; Auerbach and Adams 1971, p.103.

34 The suite consists of the title cartouche and twenty-four plates with cartouches, Collijn 1933, no.83.

4 THE INFLUENCE OF FRENCH PRINTS

1 This had been founded at Douai in the Spanish Netherlands in 1568, but after the Protestants took over the town ten years later, the seminarists were obliged to move out, eventually settling in Rheims where they were protected by the Duke of Guise and partly financed by the Vatican. In the words of Charles Nicoll, the seminary was 'a centre for the printing of anti-government tracts and banned devotional works . . . and it was a training-ground for militant Catholic missionaries who returned to succour or subvert, according to

your view, the people of England'; Nicoll 1992, p.121ff.

2 Elton 1974, p.295ff.

3 Selections can be seen in Zerner 1969, and in *TIB*, 33. The most comprehensive modern survey of printmaking in sixteenth-century France is Los Angeles 1994.

4 Blunt 1980, figs 38, 39, 77; the debate whether this style of decoration should be attributed to Francesco Primaticcio, as Vasari asserted, or to the older artist, Antonio Rosso, who had preceeded him to Fontainebleau, is hardly relevant here: Blunt (p.62) accepted Primaticcio as the inventor.

5 Inigo Jones owned a copy and used it for masque designs, see p.157.

6 The ewers survive in Seville Cathedral, see Hernmarkt 1977, pl.607.

7 Jessen 1920, pp.72–3.

8 Marcus Binney, *CL*, 2, 9, 16 Dec. 1976.

9 Biddle 1970.

10 Binney, op.cit., p.1761: the suggestion was first made by Gordon Slade.

11 Saxl and Wittkower 1948, p.39, fig.6; Frances Yates, 'The Allegorical Portraits of Sir John Luttrell', *Ideas and Ideals in the North European Renaissance: Collected Essays Vol. 3* (London, 1984).

12 Strong 1969a, p.86.

13 National Portrait Gallery, London, no.535.

14 Roy Strong 1969a, p.8.

15 Zerner 1969, IM60; Los Angeles 1994, no.62; it looks as though Maarten van Heemskerck might have been inspired by the same mask for his portrait of Machteld Suijs, now in the Cleveland Museum of Art, *Burl. Mag.*, CXXXIV, no.1076 (1992), p.699, fig.1.

16 Zerner 1969, IM56.

17 Waterhouse, 1983, pp.13–14, and Auerbach, 1954, p.163.

18 Auerbach 1954, p.187.

19 These are at Parham in Sussex (Mercer 1962, pl.50), and at Knole in Kent.

20 This is now the property of the National Portrait Gallery but remains *in situ* at Arundel Castle. Roy Strong considered even this elaborate version (like the two others at Parham and Knole) to be a copy of a lost original by the artist: Strong 1969, p.72 no.7.

21 *TIB*, 33, 121 (425); this print may also have provided Scrots with the incidental figure supporting a shield in the simpler versions of the Surrey portrait. For a recent discussion of the Arundel version, including mention of the source, see Hearn 1995, no.14, pp.50–52. Luca Penni's brother 'Bartholomew Penn' worked as a painter in England and could have been the agent through whom Guillim Scrots (or whoever painted this version) employed the print. G.B. Pittoni has been suggested as its author by implication (Amsterdam 1988, no.542.1).

22 A convenient list is given in Jervis 1984.

23 The latter copied from Enea Vico, Agostino Veneziano, Antonio da Brescia, Nicoletto da Modena and others.

24 Ten and thirty-two plates, respectively.

25 The former expanded from the 1550 edition.

26 One of the plates incorporates a strapwork design copied from Vredeman de Vries's *[Architectura] Das Erst Büch*, first published in 1565.

27 Saxl and Wittkower 1948, 40: 7 and b.

28 Summerson 1966, T50, T71–2, T75–8, T160, T165.

29 White 1982, figs 6–7; Ladd 1978, pp.7–20, pl.15.
30 Sir William was a staunch religious reformer, entirely in tune with Queen Elizabeth, whom he served as unofficial adviser for most of her reign. A member of every Elizabethan parliament until his death in 1600 he knew all the most powerful men in England; he must also have been in touch with leading Protestant refugees as he had his portrait painted by Lucas de Heere. He seems to have been his own architect at Loseley.
31 This, incidentally, has a pattern of coffering in the canopy which resembles that of one of Ducerceau's triumphal arch designs of 1549.
32 The two were issued in a combined edition in 1568, with *Le Premier Tome de l'Architecture* forming the first nine books and the *Nouvelles inventions* books ten and eleven.
33 Tipping 1927, p.316. Tipping gives the date of the publication as 1576 which must be a typographical error.
34 Drury 1983, p.120.
35 De L'Orme, 1648 edn, fol.269r. De L'Orme devoted several pages to patent solutions for smoking chimneys.
36 De L'Orme, 1648 edn, fol.254r.
37 Smythson drawings, III/1(2); de L'Orme, 1648 edn, fol.111r.
38 Harris and Higgott 1989, pp.48–9.
39 For Delaune see Los Angeles 1994, p.469.
40 Hayward 1976, pls 380–84.
41 Hackenbroch 1960a, figs 182–4 (French) and 218–20 (probably Swiss); other examples are cited by Margaret Swain (Swain 1980, pp.41–4).
42 See *Burl. Mag.* (March 1992), p.xxxv.
43 See pp.240, 210 and 275 respectively.
44 For discussion of the engraver P over M (and accession details and marks) see Hackenbroch, 1960b, pp.18–24, Oman 1978, Appendix 1, pp.141–6, Glanville 1990, pp.91–2, and Alcorn 1993, pp.48–52.
45 Watt 1994, pp.183–93.
46 Swain 1980, pp.53–5 cites examples.
47 McKerrow and Ferguson 1932, no.157.
48 Swain 1973, p.18.
49 Wardle 1981, no.29, and Glanville 1990, no.91, pp.458–9; could there be some connection between this salt and the 'great guilt salt with a Cover & pictures waying threescore too ounces' recorded in the 1601 inventory of Hardwick Hall? Certainly the use of Paradin, and of the Nine Worthies, perhaps based on prints after Heemskerck (which were also used at Hardwick), suggests there may have been.
50 Farmer 1984, pp.80, 85, 99. For Scotland, see Michael Bath, 'Alexander Seton's Painted Gallery', in Gent 1995, pp.101–2.

5 THE INFLUENCE OF NETHERLANDISH PRINTS: I

1 The area of the Netherlands, at 34,000 square miles, was roughly three-quarters that of England (51,000) and, including Wales, their populations were not dissimilar at approximately 3,000,000. In the Netherlands an unusually high proportion of the population lived in towns: by mid-century, there were no fewer than nineteen with a population of over 10,000: in the whole of the British Isles there were only four. For statistical information see Parker 1979, pp.19–29.
2 For the vicissitudes of trade relations between England and Antwerp see Ramsay 1975 and 1986.

3 The English monarchy borrowed heavily on the Antwerp money-market, £1,840,000 between 1552 and 1554, with substantial sums during the reign of Elizabeth.
4 Their designer was a military engineer from Bergamo, Donato Pellizuoli. After the outburst of iconoclasm in 1566, the Duke of Alba had a new Italianate citadel built to the south of the city in 1567–8; much hated as a symbol of oppressive Spanish rule, it was partially demolished by the citizens of Antwerp in 1577.
5 Girouard 1985, p.142.
6 Antwerp was nearly twice the size of any other city in the Netherlands. The figures given in Voet 1973, p.154, show that it compared with towns like Leiden (14,300 inhabitants in 1514), Haarlem and Amsterdam (each 13,500), Delft (11,700), Dordrecht (11,200) and Rotterdam (5,300). Further south, in 1526, when the population of Antwerp was 55,000, Louvain had 17,000 inhabitants, Brussels 20,000, Bruges 25,000 and Ghent about 35,000. Population was rising in the sixteenth century: that of Amsterdam increased from the 13,500 of 1514 to more like 30,000 by 1550s, but Antwerp had expanded even faster, to 100,000 by 1560, so that in Europe only Paris, Venice and Naples were larger. Significantly, of Antwerp's total population of 104,981 recorded in the census taken in October 1568, almost ten per cent (10,263) were temporary residents, either merchants or visitors.
7 The first printing had actually been started at Cologne in 1525 and was finished at Worms the following year. Tyndale had several books published in Antwerp from 1528 onwards, including his translation of the Pentateuch (1530). He was only the first of many Protestant scholars to work under the patronage of the Merchant Adventurers but the effectiveness of the immunity enjoyed by them was tragically demonstrated in May 1535 when Tyndale was lured from the gates by a man named Henry Phillips (posing as a convert) and seized by agents of the Council in Brussels: the following year he was strangled. See David Daniell (ed.), *Tyndale's New Testament, Translated from the Greek by William Tyndale in 1534* (New Haven and London, 1995 edn), pp. viii–ix.
8 Dickens 1989, p.94.
9 Denization of foreigners engaged in the woodworking trades, for instance, averaged fewer than ten craftsmen per annum during the early 1560s but rose to thirty-five in 1567 and to eighty-one in 1568, thereafter settling down to the former pattern until the early 1580s – see Forman 1971, pp.94–120. For the immigration of Netherlandish sculptors, see the Appendix to White 1992, pp.34–74.
10 Summerson, 1977, p.53.
11 Aston 1988, p.234.
12 Ibid., p.267.
13 During the reign of Elizabeth, van Meteren, who was a cousin of the cosmopolitan Antwerp humanist Abraham Ortelius, travelled back and forth on business between London and Antwerp, maintaining links with many artists in the Netherlands: Hodnett 1971, pp.17–18.
14 Dickens 1989, pp.301–7, 339–44.
15 In 1582–3, with the Spanish threat creeping ever closer to Antwerp, eighty-one foreigners involved in the woodworking trades came to London (not all from the Netherlands): Forman 1971, pp.94–120.

16 The Registers were opened in 1453 with 35 names. A further 303 masters were entered between 1454 and 1500 and thereafter an increasing number were registered, 135 in the decade 1501–10, 158 in 1511–20, 156 in 1521–30, 218 in 1531–40, 171 in 1541–50, 346 in 1551–60, 147 in 1561–70, 233 in 1571–80, 160 in 1581–90 and 201 in 1591–1600. Average membership must have been between two and three hundred at any one time.
17 *Schilder-Boeck*, quoted in Voet 1973, p.351. For a modern account of printmaking in the Netherlands during the century after 1540, and of van Mander's view of prints, see Riggs and Silver 1993.
18 Riggs 1977, p.17; van den Coelen 1995.
19 Riggs 1977, p.218.
20 Ibid., p.218; M.I, II, XIV–XIX.
21 Riggs 1977, Handlist no.206; M.II.
22 Riggs 1977, Handlist no.101, *Compertimentorum quod vocant multiplex genus* . . .
23 Ibid., p.135: Bol and Bruegel each produced only one etching for Cock, Frans Floris fewer then a dozen, some of these in collaboration with Cock; ibid., pp.327–8.
24 Ibid., p.21.
25 The literature on Galle is increasing fast; the most recent studies are those of Veldman 1991, and Sellink 1992, 1992a and 1993. Manfred Sellink also plans a major article on the *Prosopographia* (see pp.116–19).
26 Sellink 1993, p.154.
27 Manfred Sellink has estimated that his published prints numbered around 3,600 (Sellink 1992, p.13).
28 Christopher Plantin – a Frenchman – was a bookbinder by trade, but turned to printing and publishing in 1555. As Voet has written: 'In the troubled years after the Spanish Fury (1576), Christopher Plantin was often constrained to print and publish works that might displease the Spanish authorities and their supporters. To cover himself, he devised a means of distinguishing between books which he freely undertook to produce, or at least found not to be irreconcilable with his personal position, and those that were forced upon him or were likely to have unpleasant consequences for him . . . Sometimes, however, he preferred to publish potentially dangerous works anonymously or under the name of one of his sons-in-law, or even one of his journeymen.' Voet 1972, II, p.8. For references to Plantin's possible membership of the Family of Love, see n.31 on p.320.
29 Voet 1973, p.334.
30 I am indebted to Christiaan Schuckman for drawing my attention to the influence of Flemish prints on Russian icons; for their influence on Indian miniatures, see the *Bulletin van het Rijksmuseum*, no.1 (1993), pp.39–40, for two miniatures (one reproduced, ill.9) based on prints of Mucius Scaevola and Titus Manlius by Hendrick Goltzius, 1596 (*TIB*.98 & 100). Further references to the influence of Flemish and Dutch prints in distant countries can be found in Amsterdam 1993, p.196, n.26.
31 Ward-Jackson 1979, p.14. Ward-Jackson's brief account of ornament during this period remains one of the most accessible in English, with Byrne 1981.
32 For Zoutleeuw and Roskilde see von der Osten and Vey 1969, pls 249–50; for Tournai see Avery 1969, fig.7.

33 For Cornelis Floris see Hedicke 1913, and Schele 1965.

34 Nineteen plates with titlepage and colophon, engraved by Balthasar Bos and published by Hieronymus Cock; Riggs 1977, list no.63. Some of the designs were copied from Enea Vico.

35 One plate was copied by a Spanish goldsmith, Gomes Alonso of Barcelona, for his masterpiece in 1556.

36 Summerson 1977, pp.175, 559 n.2. *re Cåves*

37 Eighteen plates, undated, engraved by Frans Huys.

38 The titlepage of the new edition bears the signature RENATUS B. FECIT. which has led to the whole suite being attributed incorrectly to René Boyvin: Byrne 1981, pp.44–5.

39 I am indebted to Dr David Bostwick, who has made a study of the plasterwork of this region, for passing on this information, from his unpublished Sheffield University PhD dissertation, 1993.

40 A Floris mask also appears on the ceiling of the Great Dining Room at Aston Hall, Birmingham, built by John Thorpe for Sir Thomas Holte in the 1620s.

41 They include the tombs of Mary Queen of Scots and of Winifred Paulet in Westminster Abbey; of Sir Richard and Sir Michael Blount in the chapel of St Peter ad Vincula in the Tower of London; and the tomb of Sir Christopher Wray, at Glentworth in Lincolnshire.

42 One of the other masks derives from a set engraved by Adam Scultori, which includes a copy of the Floris mask, so the later suite was probably the one used by the anonymous painter.

43 Riggs 1977, list nos 64–6.

44 This panelling is now *ex situ* but preserved in the V&A, 4870–81-1856.

45 Mann 1933, p.22 and pl.XIV.

46 International Society for the Study of Church Monuments (now The Church Monuments Society), *Bulletin*, 7 (1982), pp.127–8.

47 Mark Girouard, 'Burghley House, Lincolnshire – II', *CL* (30 April 1992), p.60. See also Jon Bayliss, 'Thomas Kirby Again', *Church Monuments Society Newsletter*, II, no.1 (1995), pp.6–7, and Jonathan Edis, '"Thomas Kirby" – A Royal Connection?', *idem*, II (1995/6), pp.42–3. Edis suggests that this carver was also responsible for two tombs erected in 1573 at Fotheringhay, Northamptonshire, in memory of two fifteenth-century Dukes of York, and for the mural monument to Sir Oliver Boteler (d. 1618) at Sharnbrook, Bedfordshire.

48 Bayliss 1993, pp.45–56.

49 Amsterdam 1986, pp.240–42. The most detailed discussion of Cornelis Bos is Schele 1965, but new light has recently been thrown on Bos's movements after 1544 in van den Coelen 1995.

50 The French edition was published in Paris in 1546.

51 For instance, a pyx now in the V&A, M.41–1952, Amsterdam 1986, no.262.

52 Elements on the drum, which dates from shortly before 1566, derive from Bos's engravings, S.132 and 129; probably of Flemish or Dutch origin is a decorative panel, in the V&A, derived from S.130. Pilasters from a monument in Uppsala Cathedral in Sweden also derive from Bos, S.1965, p.100, fig.55.

53 Untitled suite of sixteen plates, three signed with a monogram, S.71–86.

54 Ten plates of grotesques in the style of the Vatican, S.133–43.

55 North Mymms Park was built between 1582 and 1603. The wall paintings were brought to my notice by Muriel Carrick: my identification of the grotesques as from a print by Bos was noted by her in 'More Hertfordshire Wall Paintings – a connection with those in Essex and possible attributions to printed sources', *Archaeological Journal*, 148 (1991), pp.296–7, and published in full in Ann Ballantyne, Muriel Carrick and Patricia Ryan, 'Wall-Paintings at North Mymms Park, Hertfordshire', *Archaeological Journal*, 151 (1994), pp.369–99.

56 Three plates dated 1554, three signed by the engraver, Jacob Honnervogt. In one of the plates Bos borrowed figures from a print by the Fontainebleau artist, Antonio Fantuzzi, in turn providing two models for the Italian engraver, Giovanni Battista Pittoni, for his *Imprese di diversi principi* (1562). The German maker of a box inlaid with ivory and dating from the late sixteenth century, in the V&A, copied one for the decoration on the lid (S.200). The quotations from Seneca were borrowed from a translation published in Strasbourg in 1536, see van den Coelen 1995.

57 The date of publication is uncertain, Hedicke (1913) suggested 1540, Collijn (1933) 1550.

58 Cartouches framing proverbs in French, and vases with fruit, twenty plates, S.177–96. There is a related suite with landscapes by an unknown designer, plates from which survive in Vienna and Amsterdam: Schele believed that Bos copied the plates from the set with the landscapes, but more recently Bos has been credited with the design of these too.

59 S.177, 179 and 187.

60 S.189.

61 S.184. Vredeman de Vries borrowed two birds from S.180 for a cartouche in his first suite of cartouches, *Variarum protractionum libellus*, published in 1555; and Jacob Floris used a plate (S.187) for his suite of cartouches entitled *Compertimentorum quod vocant multiplex genus*, published in 1567.

62 In a presumably unrelated instance, another plate from the same suite (S.180) was used for a panel in the balustrade of the west stair at Castle Ashby in Northamptonshire.

63 Collijn 1933, pp.50–52, Amsterdam 1988, no.83.

64 Some of Cornelis Floris's two sets of independent cartouches published in 1556 and 1557 have much the same quality (pp.48–9).

65 Thirteen plates, H.XI, p.2, nos.42–54, and H.XIV, p.104, nos 42–54. These plates were much copied, see Fuhring 1989, p.328.

66 F.P. Jensen, '"Hercules-harnisken" og dens skaber Eliseus Libaerts', *Vaabenhistoriske Aarboger*, XXVIII (1982), p.50, figs 1, 6. The attribution of these parade armours to Libaerts, first made by Rudolf Cederstrom and Karl Eric Steneberg, *Skokloster Skolden* (Stockholm, 1945), and accepted by John Hayward in his book review, 'A Triumph of the Metal Worker's Craft', *Apollo* (April 1946), pp.84–6, has been very controversial, and an attribution of related armours and shields to Etienne Delaune as designer, and to the French royal armourers working for Henri II, has often been preferred; see Stephen V. Grancsay, 'The Armor of Henry II of France from the Louvre Museum', *The Metropolitan Museum of Art Bulletin*, n.s., XI (1952), pp.68–80; *idem*, 'Royal Armorers: Antwerp or Paris?', *MMA Bulletin*, n.s., XVIII (1959), pp.1–7 (p.7: 'Perhaps both Libaerts and Lochorst, though Flemish themselves, were employed in the French royal armory.'); Helmut Nickel, 'The Battle of the Crescent', *MMA Bulletin* (Nov. 1965), pp.111–27; *idem*, 'Arms and Armor from the permanent collection', *MMA Bulletin* (Summer 1991), pp.26–7.

Nevertheless, it is probable that at least some of the armours were decorated (if not made) in Antwerp where Libaerts was established as a freeman of the Corporation of Goud- en Zilver Smeden by September 1557: he was employed both by Erik XIV of Sweden and Frederick II of Denmark, and made unsuccessful overtures to Robert Dudley, Earl of Leicester, in March 1565; for a convenient picture of his peregrinations in search of patronage see Jane Clark, 'Eliseus Libaerts and his English connections', *The Journal of the Arms and Armour Society*, XI, no.2 (Dec. 1983), pp.41–6. It is clear that the relationship between Eliseus Libaerts and three designers (all of whom were at times derivative), Etienne Delaune, Jacob Floris and Vredeman de Vries needs to be explored further.

67 The suite was evidently known to contemporary Flemish tapestry designers too, for a late sixteenth-century tapestry hanging on the staircase at Hardwick Hall in Derbyshire has one of the cartouches in the middle of its upper border.

68 Gerard Mercator, on Militaria Italica and Insulae Caelan; Abraham Ortelius, Tartary, Turcici, Asiae, Americae and Gelriae and Cliviae, published in his *Theatrum Orbis Terrarum* in Antwerp in 1570, and Culiacanae, Andegavensis, Veronae Urbis and Romanae, in the *Additamentum* of 1579.

69 Engraved by Petrus a Merica (Pieter van der Heyden) and published in Antwerp by Hieronymus Cock (seventeen plates); Hollstein combined this suite with the next, titled *Compertimenta pictoriis flosculis manubiisque*, H.VI, p.256, nos 1–35 and H.IX, p.31, nos 70–104.

70 Or perhaps Antonio Fantuzzi's reproduction in print of the cartouche in the Galerie François I at Fontainebleau.

71 Cartouches after Floris designs occur on the façade of the late sixteenth-century Gewandhaus at Brunswick, and in the decoration of the early seventeenth-century chapel of Fredericksborg Slot at Hillerød in Denmark, this by a Flemish architect, Hans van Steenwinckel. In Spain, the *coro* of the Cathedral at Burgos in northern Spain has stalls that are one of the masterpieces of the sculptor, Felipe Vigarny, but the Bishop's stall, in the very centre, has the two cartouches from Floris, one on the back panel, the other beneath the seat: Flemish Mannerism here makes an odd bedfellow for the pure early Renaissance of Vigarny's carving. The adaptation of another cartouche for the titlepage of Giovanni Battista de' Rossi's *Virtues . . .* is geographically the most distant example of plagiarism.

In the Netherlands the set proved useful to Abraham Ortelius for his *Theatrum Orbis Terrarum* of 1570 (on his map of the British Isles) and the *Additamentum* of nine years later (Hispaniae Novae). Mercator also made use of the set in his *Atlas* (on Poictou, Helvetiae, Zelandia, Artesia, China and Terra Sancta). One plate also provided the inspiration for the design of a late sixteenth-century tapestry decorated with a scene of a boar-hunt.

72 Prinknash Priory in Gloucestershire was remodelled during the first decade of the seventeenth century, acquiring another overmantel cartouche copied from Floris's *Compertimentorum*.

73 It is difficult to know what to make of six panels of painted glass surviving at Temple Newsam near Leeds. They depict angels holding instruments of the Passion with, below each figure, one of two cartouche designs derived from Floris's *Compertimentorum*. They have generally been taken to be Victorian, the work of Burlison and Grylls for the chapel designed by G.F. Bodley for Mrs Meynell Ingram in 1877, but it is possible that one panel is seventeenth century and is the sole survivor of a set made for the chapel built in the house by Sir Arthur Ingram during the 1630s – the remaining five would then be Victorian replacements, see Anthony Wells-Cole, 'The Dining Room at Temple Newsam', *Leeds Arts Calendar*, no.100 (1992), pp.16–24.

74 Twelve plates, engraved by Petrus a Merica (Pieter van der Heyden) and published by Hieronymus Cock; Hollstein combined this suite with the previous set titled *Compertimentorum quod vocant multiplex genus . . .*, H.VI, p.256, nos.1–35 and H.IX, p.31, nos.70–104.

75 One Floris plate was elaborated by Peter Hille for the titlepage of the *Historia* published in Berlin in 1578 – see Busch 1969, pl.190 – and Mercator used another of the cartouches for the map of Anjou and Hollandt.

76 The main study of Vredeman's designs is Hans Mielke, *Hans Vredeman de Vries* (Berlin, 1967); some illustrations have appeared in anthologies by Jessen 1920, Warncke 1979, Berliner and Egger 1981 and Amsterdam 1988. Peter Fuhring's fully illustrated Hollstein volumes, including many new discoveries, will appear in 1997.

77 Forssmann 1956, pp.86–7.

78 For the citadel see Voet 1973, pp.176–7, 205; some of Vredeman's designs for the fortifications survive in the Stadsarchief in Antwerp, see F. Blockmans, 'Een krijgstekening, een muurschildering en een schilderij van Hans Vredeman de Vries te Antwerpen (1577–1586)', *Antwerpen: Tijdschrift der Stad Antwerpen* (April 1962), pp.20–42, figs 16–21.

79 J. Van Roey, 'De Antwerpse schilders in 1584–1585. Poging tot sociaal-religieus onderzoek', *Jaarboek van het Koninklijk Museum voor Schone Kunsten te Antwerpen* (1966), p.119.

80 M.I, II, III, VI, VIII.

81 M.XII, XIII.

82 M.XIX, XX, XXI.

83 A recent culprit in this respect, alas, is Mowl 1993, whose handsomely illustrated book regrettably undoes the work done for Vredeman in Girouard 1983.

84 They consist of a title and eighteen plates, paginated A–S, and a title and twenty-two plates, numbered 1–22, M.XII and M.XIII.

85 Antwerp 1578; it consists of a title and twelve plates, M.XXIV.

86 The decoration of the pedestals on the outer face derives from the Doric pedestal in plate G of *Das Erst Büch*. There is a remote possibility that Vredeman himself designed the Oosterpoort, for he was on the run from religious persecution during the first years of the 1570s and the gate bears some resemblance to his design for the gate on the east face of the Kaisertors in Wolfenbüttel, dating from 1589, see Irmscher 1985, pl.15.

87 The door from the courtyard to the chapel in the north wing, for instance, has a pilaster carved with ornament taken from the Doric pedestal in plate G of *Das Erst Büch*. Moreover, this influence was felt in the field of movable furniture, for an early seventeenth-century table in the equally remarkable castle of Kronborg at Helsingør has a frieze copied from one in *Das Ander Buech*.

88 In Germany two instances have come to light and there must be many more: the earlier is a funerary monument in the church at Coburg, dating from the 1580s, the later the decoration of an oriel window of the dispensary at Lemgo. In France, where architects never gave themselves over whole-heartedly to the influence of Ant-werp, both instances noted belong to the 1580s: in Strasbourg the Hôtel du Commerce has a frieze and pediment that are copied precisely from plates in *Das Erst Büch*; and at Hesdin, the frieze over the west door of the church of Notre-Dame was taken from a frieze in the same series.

89 For Condover see Malcolm Airs, 'Lawrence Shipway, freemason', *Architectural History*, 27 (1984), pp.368–75. A plate in *Das Ander Buech* was copied for the strapwork cresting of the overmantel in the hall at Benthall Hall, also in Shropshire: perhaps a Condover joiner was employed at Benthall around 1583. The same joiner's shop may have been responsible for two instances of the use of plate 14 from *Das Ander Buech* in the neighbouring county of Herefordshire in the 1620s: on the lower frieze of the pulpit at Allensmore and on the lower frieze of a chimneypiece in the Old House in Hereford itself, dated 1621. The same plate provided the source for the frieze of an overmantel in Postlip Manor, near Winchcombe in Gloucestershire, and the house may just belong to this west-Midland group of houses, rather than to another group, further south, where considerable dependence on Vredeman's *Architectura* has also been discovered.

90 When Arnold moved to Oxford to build Wadham College for Dorothy Wadham from 1610 onwards, he used precisely the same method for the central taffril of the hall screen – indeed all the crestings in the hall and chapel, and in the exactly contemporary Spencer Chapel in Yarnton Church, were copied from *Das Erst Büch*.

91 C.J. Richardson's drawing (in the V&A) shows this polychromy; Richardson illustrated another wind-porch at Montacute with an ornamental cresting related to what Mark Girouard has dubbed the Longleat motif.

92 These houses, with several more, have been associated with Arnold on stylistic grounds, see Oswald 1959, pp.23–30.

93 Girouard 1983, pp.197–9.

94 The fascinating architectural decoration of this house is considered in more detail on pp.142–4; the panelling and frieze in the Raleigh Room are illustrated before later alteration in *CL* (26 March 1904), p.450.

95 Aymer Vallance, *Art in England During the Elizabethan and Stuart Periods*, ed. Charles Holme (London, 1908), p.70.

96 Two other houses within ten miles of Bath have plaster ceilings derived from this Vredeman design though executed on a flat ground, Beckington Castle in Somerset and Cold Ashton Manor in Gloucestershire. Additionally, the barrel-vaulted ceiling of the dining room at Forty Hall in Enfield, a house built by Sir Nicholas Raynton in 1629 and therefore of almost exactly the same date. The Forty Hall ceiling is barrel-vaulted as at Beckington but there are enough differences in the way the pattern has been fitted to the field available to suggest that Arnold had nothing to do with this house; recent research has proved that the plasterwork at Forty Hall fits into a group of London-made ceilings of the early seventeenth century; see Gapper 1990, p.39 and pl.58.

97 I missed this derivation which was pointed out by John and Jane Penoyre (Penoyre 1994, fig.7).

98 Now in the V&A, 4870–81-1856; Wells-Cole 1981, pls 28A, 28B, 29A, 29B.

99 It is now in the Burrell Collection in Glasgow.

100 It is interesting and perhaps significant that Smythson's ingenious adaptation here is paralleled by that of William Arnold's in the strapwork decoration of Beckington Abbey ceiling, pp.61–3.

101 Is there any connection between the Smythsons (or tradesmen with whom they had worked) and the exceptional Carolean church of St John, Briggate, in Leeds, consecrated in 1634? This has several panels carved with a frieze copied from plate K of *Das Erst Büch*, as on the chimneypiece at Hardwick. It is difficult otherwise to explain this apparently isolated instance in Yorkshire. The remarkable screen across the twin-aisled chancel has taffrils that show an obvious stylistic affinity with the designs for scrolled gables in *Das Erst Büch*, though without copying any of them precisely. The joiner probably responsible for the screen at St John's was Francis Gunby, who also worked at Wakefield Parish Church (now the Cathedral), at the Palace of Bishopthorpe for the Archbishop of York (where he made the pulpit, now at Rotherfield in Sussex) and at Temple Newsam near Leeds for Sir Arthur Ingram; but it is not known to whom he was apprenticed.

102 The caryatids of the overmantel and panelling in the oak room at Holywell in Ipswich derive from plate H in *Das Erst Büch* (or perhaps from the almost identical term in Vredeman's *Caryatidum*, plate 2, left-hand design) and so does some panelling in a farmhouse at Ashdon in Essex, which is painted with a design from plate G. The pierced taffrils of the fountain in the Great Court of Trinity College, Cambridge, along with those of the hall screen, were clearly adapted from Vredeman types.

103 There is one other example of the use of Vredeman's *Das Erst Büch* in Kent: the early seventeenth-century Cale Hill farmhouse, Little Chart, has a pattern of strapwork copied from plate K carved on the lintel of the porch.

104 Nikolaus Pevsner and Edward Hubbard, *Cheshire*, *BE* (Harmondsworth, 1971), p.114.

105 The frieze from *Das Erst Büch*, pl.C; the metope from *Das Ander Buech*, pl.4; the gable and cartouche below, from *Das Ander Buech*, pl.5.

106 The book consists of a titlepage, text pages and twenty-three plates numbered ff.1–23, M.XXII. Subsequent editions appeared in 1581, 1587, 1597, 1598, 1615, undated, and 1709.

107 The chimneypiece of a house at Enfield in Middlesex, mentioned earlier, has pilasters derived from folio 1.

108 The book consists of the titlepage, text pages and thirty plates, M.XXXII.

109 Each consists of thirteen plates including the title, M.I and M.II.

NOTES TO PAGES 69–79

110 The earliest example is a single map, of Bavaria, in Abraham Ortelius's *Theatrum Orbis Terrarum* of 1570, followed by five maps in the *Additamentum* of 1573. All these, and five cartouches used on three separate maps of Mercator's, which were finally brought together in the *Atlas* in 1613, were derived from *Multarum variarum'que*. The second set was apparently copied only by Virgil Solis for the frame of a portrait in a substantial suite entitled *Imagines Quondam Principum* 1568: Virgil Solis was a noted plagiarist of Vredeman and his contemporaries.

111 A plate in the first set was clearly the model for a cartouche on another tomb in Westminster Abbey illustrated by Alexander Speltz, *The Styles of Ornament* (London, 1910), pl.267, no.1, pp.437, 437; but the tomb in question has not been identified and may have disappeared.

112 I am indebted to the Hon. Richard Hewlett for drawing it to my attention and for sending me a copy of his research findings, some of which I have incorporated here.

113 Girouard 1992, p.180. The connection between Grafton Manor and the Sheldon factory is documented by an entry in the Grafton Estate Book which records a payment to Richard Hyke (Hickes) for hangings in 1568; see Kendrick 1926, p.35.

114 In addition, a plate from the first set may have inspired the frame of an unusual creed board, dated 1635, at Terrington St Clement in Norfolk, while during the Elizabethan and Jacobean revival of the early nineteenth century another was copied by the celebrated carver, W.G. Rogers, for his trade-card in 1831 (illustrated by Rosamond Allwood, 'Wood Carving: The "high art" of Victorian furniture-making', *Antique Collecting*, March 1988, fig.2, p.49).

115 In conversation, 1992; the workshop produced tombs until *c.*1610–15 and by the 1640s was in the hands of Richard Hall, a Nottingham tombmaker who died in 1680, see Jon Bayliss, 'A Dutch carver: Garrett Hollemans I in England', *Church Monuments*, VIII (1993), p.56, n.17.

116 A new edition was published by Paul de la Houe in Paris in 1601, Mielke 1967, M.III.

117 Although unsigned, these have been ascribed to him by Hedicke 1913 and Jessen 1920, and all subsequent authors; they consist respectively of twenty plates, numbered I–XX, and sixteen plates, paginated A–Q, M.VII and M.VIII.

118 Mercator's engravers made use of eleven cartouches on as many maps, and both suites of cartouches were avidly plundered by Abraham Ortelius for the title cartouches on twenty maps in his *Theatrum Orbis Terrarum* of 1570, with three more in the *Additamentum* of 1573.

119 V&A, Prints, Drawings and Paintings Collection, volume with pressmark 93 B 136.

120 The frieze incorporates the arms of the founder, the University and the fifteen colleges founded before 1571, see RCHM, *An Inventory of the Historical Monuments in the City of Oxford* (London, 1939/1966), p.50.

121 This survives in the Devon Record Office (see pp.160–62).

122 It consists of a title (probably by Nicolaes de Bruyn) and thirteen plates, Mielke 1967, M.XVI.

123 This technical device also occurs in the titlepage of Vredeman's suite of designs for fountains published in 1568, Mielke 1967, M.XVII.

124 Hedicke 1913, and Amsterdam 1988, p.117. However, this by now traditional attribution has recently been challenged and their design ascribed to the author of the book himself, see van Uchelen 1987, pp.3–44, particularly pp.21–2. The argument briefly is this: Vredeman's name does not appear on the titlepage, where the exercises are said to be 'resplendent in rare ornamentation, shadings and perspectives derived from imagery and architecture: never previously published. The work of Clemens Perret of Brussels, still in his eighteenth year'. So Perret is envisaged as having designed the cartouches, modelling them on 'existing examples by Hans Vredeman de Vries, Cornelis Floris, Cornelis Bos or Italians such as Vico and Veneziano'. The problem with this is, however, that these cartouches fit in quite naturally with Vredeman's development as a designer of the type, while they are far too accomplished to be the first known attempts by an eighteen year old calligrapher, however talented. Additionally, the fact that a copy of the book survives in the Herzog August Bibliothek, Wolfenbüttel, lends weight to Vredeman's being the designer, for he was employed by Prince Julius from 1586 to 1589. All in all, Vredeman still seems by far the most likely author of these cartouches.

125 The suite consists of thirty-five plates, M.XVIII. This is the only dated edition but there is plenty of evidence to suggest that the plates were printed until they were worn out, perhaps even as late as 1640.

126 For instance, Gerard Mercator used two for maps of Latium and Insulae India Orientalis in his *Atlas*, and the Italian, Giacomo Franco, adapted one plate for the titlepage of his book of designs for lace, *Nuova Inventione de diverse mostre* (Venice, 1596). The set was certainly known in Sweden, for the painted ceiling of a room at Sjösa, a country house in Sodermanland, has a cartouche copied directly from one of Vredeman's plates.

127 See p.5.

128 It is one of the two copies surviving in the V&A, pressmark 86 G 46, see van Uchelen 1987, pp.11–12, and n.17; the four other copies are in the British Library, the Bodleian Library in Oxford, Cambridge University Library and the Pepys Library at Magdalene College, Cambridge.

129 One noteworthy feature of the cartouches in Speed's maps is that they have a somewhat second-hand appearance, as if they were copied from some intermediate publication. Speed based his maps on those of John Norden but the latter does not seem to have copied cartouches from Vredeman. Thomas Clerke's manuscript map of Borrowhall in Holkham, Norfolk, is illustrated in S. Tyacke (ed.), *English Map-Making 1500–1650* (London, 1983), fig.34.

130 V&A, W.35–1914.

131 V&A, 404–1872.

132 Thomas Dingley, 'History from Marble', *Camden Society*, no.94 (1867), pl.CXXXVII; a description of the monument, together with the inscriptions, is given in F.T. Havergal, *Monumental Inscriptions in the Cathedral Church of Hereford* (1881), p.6. I am indebted to Penelope E. Morgan, Hon. Librarian in the Cathedral Library, Hereford, for these references.

133 Since 1924 it has been in the church at Tawstock in north Devon, a church that is remarkable for the number and quality of its funerary monuments.

134 A.C. Bisley, *The Slate Figures of Cornwall*, p.3; I have been unable to trace this publication, which is referred to in Rowse 1972, p.359, n.37.

135 No more than six copies survive in public collections, see van Uchelen 1987, pp.26, 38; the titlepage is illustrated on plate 2.

136 The prints were engraved by Dirck Coornhert; the attribution of the cartouches was not made by Mielke but by Peter Fuhring (1989), p.328, no.72; see also Amsterdam 1988, cat. no.72.1–4. Ilja Veldman says that Heemskerck was not the author of these subject prints.

137 M.XX. Five cartouches attributed to Marc Geerarts the elder were added to a later edition, Hodnett 1971, pp.16, 71.

138 Ortelius's *Album Amicorum* was first published by Jean Puraye, 'Abraham Ortelius Album Amicorum', *De Gulden Passer* (Antwerp, 1968), but Vredeman's authorship of the drawings went unrecognised, although Hans Mielke had examined them after he had completed his thesis; they were finally published by Gunther Irmscher (1985–6); only one drawing was illustrated, pl.10; I am grateful to Dr Irmscher for supplying offprints of his two articles.

139 Ortelius: 'Junonis' on his map entitled Graeciae, 'Herculis' on Namurcum, 'Cybelis' and 'Solis Invicti' on Romani Imperii. Saxton: 'Dianae' on Somerset, 'Canopi' on Denbigh and Flint, 'Isis' and 'Pacis' on Hereford, and 'Spei' on Essex. Mercator: 'Penatium' on Tuscia, 'Pietatis' on Corsica.

140 One belonged to John Selden (1584–1654), who bequeathed it to the Bodleian Library in Oxford. Samuel Pepys's is in his library at Magdalene College, Cambridge. A third, bearing the autograph of Ortelius himself, is in the British Library. Ortelius gave his nephew, Jacob Cools, a copy of the 1582 reprint, and this survives in Cambridge University Library. William Camden records in a letter to Ortelius that William Cecil, Lord Burghley, was given a copy by Dean Goodman.

141 If Smythson had owned the book, his drawings might have revealed more evidence of it. So the book probably belonged to Sir Francis Willoughby, but neither the 1573 nor the 1582 edition can be traced in the manuscript list of Willoughby's books which survives in Nottingham University Library, Mi.117/1.

142 Titlepage and six plates, M.XXIII.

143 M.IV; it consists of a titlepage, dedication page (to Antonio Perrenot) and twenty plates numbered 1–20.

144 M.V; the dedication is to Cardinal Granvelle.

145 See Mielke 1967, M.IV, M.V, and M.VI.

146 At least two tapestries show details derived from its plates: one is in the Metropolitan Museum of Art in New York, another in the V&A (T.130–1869), which belongs to a set depicting landscapes and gardens woven in Brussels for the Contarini family in Venice and bearing their arms – it depicts boats on a canal in front of a pavilion with a tower, architectural features that appear to have been copied from this suite.

147 Summerson 1966, T.216.

148 M.VI; the suite consists of twenty plates with a dedication page. For van Mander's description of them in his *Schilder-Boeck* ('Ovalen, Perspecten, met de Puncten in't midden, voor de Inlegghers'), see Hanns Loerke, *Das Leben der niederlandischen und deutschen Maler des Carel van Mander . . . nach der Ausgabe von 1617* (Munich and Leipzig, 1906), p.108. The whole series was reproduced in Jervis 1974, nos 122–41.

149 Seventeen plates with a title, Mielke 1967, M.XVII.

150 Twenty-four plates, Mielke 1967, M.XXI.

151 This correspondence was noted independently by Graham Reynolds, in his review of the exhibition *Artists of the Tudor Court*, V&A, 1983; see Reynolds, 'The English Miniature of the Renaissance: A "Rediscovery" Examined', *Apollo* (Oct. 1983), pp.308–11, figs 4, 5.

152 M.XXVI, consisting of a title and twenty plates numbered 1–20.

153 M.XXVIII.

154 However, it has been suggested that the design of an overmantel at Bramshill in Hampshire is a simplification of a garden design in the *Hortorum Viridariorumque*, see Helen Hills, 'Bramshill House, Hampshire – II', *CL* (17 Oct. 1985), p.1099.

155 M.XXXI; vol.I consists of a title, text and forty-eight plates, vol.II has a title, text and twenty-four plates numbered 1–24.

156 Mielke, XIV; it consists of a titlepage and sixteen numbered 1–16.

157 One instance of borrowing from the suite occurs in a dedication-plate designed by Georg Hass and printed in Vienna in 1583. The celebrated carillon clock made in 1589 by Isaac Habrecht of Strasbourg, which is now in the British Museum, is another example, see Hugh Tait, *Clocks and Watches* (London 1983), fig.14. The clock is a reduced version of the monumental clock made by Habrecht for Strasbourg Cathedral between 1571 and 1574, the latter being decorated with paintings known to be by Tobias Stimmer. It is thought that Stimmer might have collaborated with Habrecht in decorating the smaller clock, too, but the many caryatid figures on the sides and back, together with those on the penultimate storey of the front, all derive from Vredeman's *Caryatidum*, with the bare minimum of adaptation. It may well be that much of the remaining decoration also derives from printed sources available to any craftsman. A further instance of the use of a plate in the *Caryatidum* occurs on a Spanish or Portuguese silver-gilt dish of *c*.1565–75. Here the embossed Old Testament scenes (after prints by Etienne Delaune) on the inner frieze are separated by paired terms adapted from those on the right-hand side of Vredeman's plate 11. The dish, which survives in the Cathedral Treasury at Seville, is illustrated in Hayward 1976, pl.407.

158 Christie's, 30 Nov.1983, lot 80.

159 I am indebted to Nigel Bartlett for drawing this example to my attention.

160 The sorry remains were illustrated in an undated Raglan Castle guide-book.

161 McKerrow and Ferguson 1932, no.198.

162 *CL* (13 Feb. 1992), p.45, fig.4.

163 The virtually identical terms in Vredeman's 1565 [*Architectura*] *Das Erst Büch*, plate H (l.h.) could have been used instead.

164 M.XI.

165 This is discussed in some detail on pp.52–3; see also note 66 on p.306.

166 M.XV; it consists of a titlepage and sixteen unnumbered plates perhaps by Lucas or Johannes Duetechum: a second edition appeared in 1612.

167 V&A, on loan to Oxburgh Hall in Norfolk.

168 This tapestry is in the V&A (T.213-1911); for the early dating see Wingfield Digby 1980, cat. no.46.

169 Kendrick 1924, pp.10–11.

170 M.IX: it consists of the titlepage and twenty-six plates, numbered 1–27. The suite went into two further undated editions.

171 There are generic similarities between Vredeman's plate 25 left and the Southwark School monument to Lady Jane Seymour (d. 1560), daughter of Edward Seymour, Duke of Somerset, in Westminster Abbey.

172 M.XXVII. Hedicke 1913 and Delen 1934–5 suggested that the suite was published in 1583, Thieme–Becker suggested 1588. Galle's first Vredeman publication, according to Karel van Mander, was the *Hortorum Viridariorumque Elegantes & Multiplicis Formae*, which is dated 1583 on the titlepage, so a date in the later 1580s is certainly possible for the *Differents Pourtraicts*. The entire suite of plates, less the titlepage, was reproduced in Jervis 1974, nos 142–57.

173 A considerable amount of somewhat Flemish-looking furniture survives in East Anglia, some of which was probably made in this country by immigrant Flemings; see Wells-Cole 1990a, pp.1–41, fig.41. On the other hand, a table in St Margaret, King's Lynn, though unmistakably English in feel, resembles an example in one of Vredeman's plates, having tapered baluster supports beneath a vestigial Ionic capital. It should be noted, however, that this form of support is also a feature of designs in a later Flemish pattern-book, the *Verscheyden Schrynwerck*, published in 1630 after designs by Jan Vredeman de Vries's son, Paul; Jervis 1974, also reprinted all the plates of the two parts of this later publication, less their titlepages, nos 322–59.

174 *Differents Pourtraicts de Menuiserie*, plate 10, left-hand design, upper right-hand baluster. The screen at St John was probably made by Francis Gunby, a Leeds man, who was paid £15. 14s. 8d. for making the very similar screen in what is now Wakefield Cathedral.

175 I am indebted to Jon Bayliss for the attribution of these monuments to Garrett Hollemans I, and for showing me the photographs that led to this comparison; Bayliss's research on Hollemans was subsequently published; see Bayliss 1993, pp.45–56, pls 4, 5.

176 Two other instances of such brackets should also be noted, on the porch of Lord Leicester's gate-house at Kenilworth Castle, which was presumably built between *c*.1563 and *c*.1570 (N. Pevsner, *Warwickshire*, BE, Harmondsworth, 1974, p.323), so must pre-date the Vredeman plate; and on the engraved titlepage of *The Workes of the Most High and Mighty Prince, James . . .*, printed by Robert Barker and John Bill in London in 1616 (Corbett and Lightbown 1979, p.136): this might well have been derived from the Vredeman design.

177 It may be worth touching on the interesting though improbable suggestion made by Giles Worsley (*CL* (16 Feb. 1984), p.401) that Vredeman's two-tier sideboard, on his plate 9, was the inspiration for the chimneypiece and overmantel in the great chamber at Stockton House in Wiltshire: both are of two superimposed storeys framed by paired columns, the upper enclosing niches. However, Stockton, which was built by Sir John Toppe about 1600, belongs to a group which includes Montacute where there are chimneypieces and overmantels of the same kind and it is more likely that the inspiration came from an engraving of a triumphal arch.

178 Hodnett 1971.

179 Aston 1993, pp.167–75.

180 Van Dorsten 1970, pp.26, 32.

181 Hodnett 1971, pp.23–4; the portrait is illustrated and discussed in Hearn 1995, no.41, pp.86–7.

182 Hodnett 1971, pp.20–21.

183 For *Diversarum Protractationum* see Collijn 1933, no.64, pp.56–7, fig.51. Ilja Veldman tells me that the discovery that these title cartouches (which were unknown to Mielke in 1975) form a contents-list to the *Thesaurus* has been made independently at the Rijksprentenkabinet in Amsterdam, which has recently acquired another set of the plates. An article on their significance is being prepared by Ger Luijten, Chris Schuckman and others for publication in the Rijksmuseum *Bulletin* in 1997.

184 At Hardwick Hall, see p.271.

185 Wells-Cole 1981, pp.1–19. Less certainly derived from Geeraerts, because of its ruinous state, is a relief panel of Elizabethan date which survives on the east gate at Wilton near Salisbury in Wiltshire; one panel was copied from Vredeman de Vries, see pp.69–70.

186 Wells-Cole 1981, pp.8–11.

187 America contains a figure of an Eskimo, probably based on the engravings made from John White's drawings done in 1577, when White accompanied Sir John Frobisher on his second voyage in search of the north-west passage; *The Continents* must therefore date after 1577 and before Geeraerts's death, perhaps in 1590 and certainly before 1604. *The Elements* must be contemporary.

188 For this and other glass at Gorhambury see Archer 1976.

189 Jervis 1984, p.88.

190 A Frankfurt-made inkstand of *c*.1589 in the V&A (840–1182) reproduces ornament designed by de Bry, and Jervis 1984 (p.89) mentions the use of a panel of ornament after de Bry in the title of a book published in Frankfurt in 1627.

191 Jervis 1984, p.88.

192 Stanley-Millson and Newman 1986, p.28 [118].

193 See Wells-Cole 1981, pp.1–19.

194 Clifford Smith 1930, no.634, pl.40.

195 Archer 1976, p.1452.

6 THE INFLUENCE OF NETHERLANDISH PRINTS: II

1 See Gent 1981, p.10ff.

2 The process is well described by Glanville 1990, p.88.

3 Thomas Kerrich, *A catalogue of the prints which have been engraved after Martin Heemskerck* (Cambridge, 1829); the New Hollstein series illustrates all known prints after Heemskerck. For Floris see Carl de Velde, *Frans Floris (1519/20–1570)* (Ghent, 1975) and Riggs and Silver 1993, pp.8–12. The three volumes of the New Hollstein dealing with the prints after Maarten de Vos were published in 1995 and 1996.

4 For Maarten van Heemskerck's life and contacts with humanists in the northern Netherlands, I have relied heavily on Veldman 1977.

5 Hulsen and Egger 1975.

6 Freedberg 1987, pp.224–6.

7 Veldman 1987, pp.193–210; Saunders 1979, pp.59–83.

8 Veldman 1987, p.193, quoting Carel van Mander, *Schilder-Boeck* (Haarlem 1604; reprint Utrecht 1969), fol.247r.

9 Van Gelder 1964, p.7.

10 Item 227 in the 1656 inventory of Rembrandt's possessions, Clark 1966, p.203.

11 He twice adapted the same figure from Philips Galle's engraving of Jonadab Counselling Amnon; Gabriele Finaldi, 'Zurbaran's Jacob and his Twelve Sons', *Apollo* (Oct. 1994), pp.1–16.

12 See Cole 1980, pp 247–67, and Cole 1993, *passim*.

13 Mary Hervey, *The Life, Correspondence and Collections of Thomas Howard Earl of Arundel* (Cambridge, 1921), p.329; I am indebted to Margaret Aston for this reference. The early seventeenth-century picture Bible was offered for sale at Sotheby's, 30 June 1992 (lot 130).

14 Hayward 1976, p.381, pl.462.

15 Aston 1993.

16 Strong 1960, pp.311–13; Strong 1969, I, pp.344–5.

17 Aston 1993, pp.101–7.

18 Hall 1984, p.116.

19 Esther 3:10.

20 See Simon Jervis, 'Leather Hangings', *Furniture History Newsletter*, 93 (Feb. 1989), pp.8–9, repr. p.9. Jervis states that the Walsingham hangings 'cannot be pre-seventeenth century', without giving any reasons; John W. Waterer, 'Dunster Castle, Somerset, and its painted leather hangings', *Connoisseur*, 164 (March 1967), pp.142–7, argues that the comparable set there, painted with the story of Antony and Cleopatra, dates from the second half of the sixteenth century.

21 Aston 1993, pp.26, 31, 36.

22 See pp.294–5 for a summary.

23 See p.77 and note 136 on page 308.

24 Veldman 1977, pp.62–70, figs 39–46.

25 Veldman 1977, pp.133–41.

26 It inspired the decoration of a Spanish or Portuguese gilt dish dating from 1565–75, whose inner frieze has four embossed scenes of triumphs derived from Heemskerck's suite: the dish is in the Seville Cathedral Treasury, see Hayward 1976, p.376, pl.407.

27 Two of the preliminary drawings, belonging to the Duke of Devonshire at Chatsworth, are dated 1565, Veldman 1977, p.106, and Veldman 1986a, pp.58–66.

28 Veldman 1977, p.98, has Junius return to Haarlem in 1550 where he was rector of the Latin School in 1552 and 1553.

29 See W. Bok von Kammen, *Stradanus and the Hunt* (Ann Arbor, Mich., 1980); for a convenient summary of the publishing history of Johannes Stradanus's hunting designs see Peter Fuhring, *Design into Art: Drawings for Architecture and Ornament, The Lodewijk Houthakker Collection* (London, 1989), no.94; and Niall Hobhouse (ed.), *Drawings from the Houthakker Collection* (Hazlitt, Gooden & Fox, London, 1993), p.10.

30 See pp.182–4, 272, 275.

31 Von der Osten and Vey 1969, p.331.

32 I am extremely grateful to Chris Schuckman for letting me have a copy of his article (in Dutch) on Maarten de Vos for the forthcoming *Macmillan Dictionary of Art*.

33 See Veldman 1992, p.262.

34 For a discussion of the Heemskerck-album see A. de Bruin, F. van Daalen, J.P. Filedt-Kok, I. van Leeuwen and I.M. Veldman, 'Conservatie, restauratie en onderzoek van een zestiende-eeuws prentenboek, het *Heemskerck-album*', *Bulletin van het Rijksmuseum*, 38, no.3 (1990), pp.173–214 (summary pp.254–7). For a discussion of the *Thesaurus* see Mielke 1975. Chris Schuckman tells

me that there are only three copies of the first edition of 1579: the Rijksprentenkabinet in Amsterdam has acquired a copy with the Old Testament illustrations only, copies in Stuttgart and Wolfenbüttel have the New Testament plates as well.

35 Cabot 1946.

36 Swain 1980, p.44.

37 M.-H. 39.

38 See Archer 1990, p.309, fig.2.

39 N. Pevsner, *Northamptonshire*, BE (Harmondsworth, 1973), pp.369–70.

40 M.-H. 832–5.

41 For Gillis Coignet see Hessel Miedema, 'Nog een schilderij van Gillis Coignet: Judith toont het hoofd van Holofernes aan de inwoners van Bethulie, *Oud Holland*, 109, no.3 (1995), pp.143–51.

42 A date in the late 1630s is suggested by the similarity of the oak hall screen at Prideaux Place and the pulpit at St Eval, which is dated 1638 (I am indebted to John Shapland for this information).

43 The suite was also used as the basis for carved reliefs on the rood-screen from s-Hertogenbosch (Avery 1969, pp.12, 26 n.43, fig.15).

44 H. IV, nos 65–115; H.XLIV, nos 275–325.

45 A detailed family history is given in Sir H.C. Maxwell Lyte's *History of Dunster*, while the house is described in Tipping n.d., pp.313–20.

46 See p.163.

47 Samuel Pepys also owned a set of the prints of *Vita, Passio, et Resurrectio . . .* ; Latham 1980, Appendix I, Loose Prints, 348–87.

48 They are now at Hatfield House in Hertfordshire.

49 Rosalys Coope was responsible for identifying the source of these scenes.

50 The fact was noted on cards in the photographic library at the Warburg Institute in London. The prints are H.XLIV, nos 1282–4.

51 The print is illustrated in Zweite 1980, fig.222; the subject was not new – Thomas Cromwell had 'a border of arras work with a picture of Occupation and Idleness', listed in his inventory of 1527 (Brewer, *Letters and Papers of Henry VIII*, IV, pt.2, p.1454).

52 M.-H. 1470.

53 John Broome, 'Samuel Baldwin: Carver of Gloucester', *Church Monuments*, x (1995), pp.37–54.

54 See p.236.

55 G.W. Braikenridge recorded that this relief was made of white marble, which may suggest that it was not a locally-made piece, or indeed necessarily English; see Sheena Stoddard, *Mr Braikenridge's Brislington* (Bristol, 1981), no.40, repr. p.47. The relief was certainly based on the suite of separate prints engraved by Adriaen Collaert (Nordenfalk 1985, fig.14d), rather than on the panoramic conflation published by van Londerseel.

56 See, for instance, Nevinson 1964, pp.103–7, and 1968, pp.1–38; Horst Schroeder, *Der Topos der Nine Worthies in Literatur und bildender Kunst*, (Gottingen, 1971), and 'The Mural Paintings of the Nine Worthies at Amersham', *Archaeological Journal*, 138 (1981), pp.241–7; and Oliver Fairclough, *The Grand Old Mansion: The Holtes and Their Successors at Aston Hall, 1618–1864* (Birmingham Museums and Art Gallery 1984), p.68, and pl.38.

57 For Wiston see p.140, Hardwick p.247, Burton Agnes p.172.

58 Eight prints from this set published by Assuwerus van Londerseel survive in Antwerp, Stedelijk Prentenkabinet, F.II/B.505–512, inv. nos 6181–8.

59 Holbein, H. 31a; Kirmer, Warncke 1979, nos 499–500; Hillebrand, H.1–4; and Hauer, H.3–4.

60 Besides the incomplete set (lacking only King Arthur) in the Stedelijk Prentenkabinet in Antwerp, F.II/C.195–202, there are complete sets of the first edition in the Bibliothèque Nationale in Paris and the Albertina in Vienna; a second edition was published by Galle's grandson Johannes Galle. I am indebted to Manfred Sellink for this information and for the opinion that Galle simply acted here as publisher. I have not found a single print from the set surviving in England.

61 Veldman 1991, Sellink 1992, 1992a and 1993.

62 Veldman 1991, figs 4–9, 10–13.

63 Veldman 1991, p.285, figs 28–9; Sellink 1992, p.20; his forthcoming examination of the *Prosopographia* is eagerly awaited. Galle may have been inspired by the allegorical figures in a suite of prints he had engraved in Haarlem in 1563, *The Unhappy Lot of the Rich*, after designs by Maarten van Heemskerck (Veldman 1977, pp.85–90, figs 58–63), although their treatment as individual figures strongly recalls the work of Maarten de Vos – for instance, Virtus tramples a satyr under foot just as de Vos's Virtues engraved by the Sadelers do. Indeed, one of the latter, appended to the Antwerp copy of the *Prosopographia* led Knipping (1939) initially to attribute all the figures in this publication to Maarten de Vos.

64 Eisenstein 1993, pp.32–3: 'Insofar as the vernacular-translation movement was aimed at readers who were unlearned in Latin, it was often designed to appeal to pages as well as to apprentices; to landed gentry, cavaliers, and courtiers as well as to shopkeepers and clerks. In the Netherlands, a translation from Latin into French often pointed away from the urban laity, who knew only Lower Rhenish dialects, and toward relatively exclusive courtly circles.' However, Ilja Veldman has suggested (in correspondence with the author) that the use of French in Antwerp prints was connected with the possibility of their export to the south.

65 M.-H. 1350–51.

66 Anneke Tjan-Bakker has discovered that these two suites were also used for the decoration of a series of six English manuscripts dating between 1600 and 1607; Mrs Tjan-Bakker is researching these for a forthcoming dissertation and I am most grateful to her for drawing my attention to them. She has also pointed out that Michael Archer's attribution of *Florae Deae* to Jan (Johannes) Sadeler is problematical, for the plate he illustrates is signed 'Sadler excud.' (*i.e.* published), and the initial letter must refer to Justus Sadeler: the suite may actually have been the work of Adriaen Collaert.

67 Amsterdam 1993, p.116.

68 Through the figures of John Dee, Abraham van der Doort and Cornelis Drebbel: Yates 1986; Strong 1986, pp.198, 216.

69 I am indebted to Sarah Finch-Crisp for sending me a copy of her leaflet on this carved panel, and the paint analysis which indicates that the paint is probably original.

70 *TIB*, 3 (Commentary), pp.7–8; Nadine Orenstein, Huigen Leeflang, Ger Luijten and

Christiaan Schuckman, 'Print Publishers in the Netherlands, 1580–1620', Amsterdam 1993, pp.167–200.

71 See Swain 1980, pls 28–9.

72 More than a century later, in the 1740s – in what must be one of the most surprisingly retardataire instances of borrowing from a sixteenth-century print – two of Goltzius's Roman Heroes, Publius Horatius and Mucius Scaevola, were adapted for engraved brass decoration inlaid into a cabinet attributed to John Channon (1711–c.1783), an Exeter joiner who established his workshop in St Martin's Lane, London, in 1737. He clearly had Germanic origins, connections or training, presumably with access to a stock of continental engravings. It is also known that the Scottish painter Gawen Hamilton had access to Goltzius prints during the short period that he was working in the St Martin's Lane area of London.

73 T134-1929, described in Nevinson 1938, p.51 and pl.xxxiv.

74 Cabot 1946, figs 22–3; Mrs Cabot also mentioned a chair-back in the collection of Mrs W. Tudor Gardiner of Boston.

75 In the Untermyer Collection, Metropolitan Museum of Art, New York, (Hackenbroch 1960a, fig.14), and Fitzwilliam Museum, Cambridge; the eighteenth-century panel was in the Richmond Collection, see Therle Hughes, 'The English Embroiderer at Leisure', *Country Life Annual*, (1963), fig.4 lower, p.46.

76 Swain 1980, pls 20–21; she even demonstrated that the source was not the engraving by Schelte à Bolswert, which included extra figures at the left, but a later, more accurate reproduction by François Ragot (1638–70). Other scenes deriving from Rubens have have been recognised, see Marion Bolles, 'Bible Pictures in English Needlework', *Antiques Magazine* (March 1946).

77 The window was given by a Fellow of the college, Luke Skippon, in 1639, under Wren's successor, John Cosin, see Hartley 1984, p.64; and RCHM, *An Inventory of the Historical Monuments in the City of Cambridge* (London, 1959), II, p.158.

78 Huntington Antiques Ltd. (*Apollo*, May 1991, suppl. p.35), and Warwick Castle respectively.

79 The date of the Bolsover range is disputed, Patrick Faulkner preferring 1635–40, Mark Girouard 1663–6 and the Lincoln mason Samuel Marsh, see Faulkner, *Bolsover Castle* (guidebook, London, 1992), pp.52–3; for Nottingham Castle see N. Pevsner and E. Williamson, *Nottinghamshire, BE* (Harmondsworth, 1979), p.227.

7 THE INFLUENCE OF ENGLISH PRINTS

1 Both have been reprinted at least once since their first appearance.

2 Used by Inigo Jones, see p.157.

3 Summerson 1990, pp.24–5; Shute is the most likely of the many other publications, both earlier and later, for which the same compartment was used, McKerrow and Ferguson 1932, no.110.

4 Baty 1982, pp.21–6, figs 3.1, 3.2.

5 Information from David Bostwick.

6 Folger, fols 259v–264r, 265v; for a more detailed discussion of Trevelyon see pp.235–40.

7 This discussion of Gedde is a much-abbreviated version of Wells-Cole 1990b.

8 Copies of the original edition are extremely rare, but one reprint was published in 1848 by Henry Shaw as part of the Jacobean revival, and the Leadenhall Press published a facsimile of the Earl of Ashburnham's copy in 1898. The name of the author appears at the foot of a page addressed to 'the willing practisers of glazeing, and annealing in Glasse' in the form 'Wa: Gedde', but on two of the four woodcut titlepages (of three different designs, all in the current Antwerp manner) it is given as Walter Gidde.

9 Likely candidates are fols 1, 4, 5, 8, 9, 10, 21, 27, 28, 33, 34, 48, 49, 62 and 65.

10 Fols.2, 25 and 51; one of the three ornamental tailpieces is clearly adapted from that used on the page addressed by Robert Peake 'To the Lovers of Architecture' in his 1611 translation of Serlio.

11 From Gedde's fol.25 derive, by division, fols 8, 31, 45, 60 and 64.

12 Gedde's fol.86, for instance occurs in a variant form in Francesco Pellegrini's *La Fleur de la Science de Pourtraicture* published in Paris in 1530.

13 Among the many patterns at Bramall Hall in Cheshire (by no means all of whose windows, however, are early in date), at least one matches a plate in Gedde (fol.5). There are other instances at Little Moreton Hall in Cheshire (fol.65), at Whitehall in Shropshire (fol.25), in the hall at Rushton in Northamptonshire (fol.65); and at Gorhambury in Hertfordshire, see Archer 1976, p.1451. At Joyners' Hall in Salisbury and Weare Giffard in Devon the pattern is one which appears to derive from basketweaving (fol.57).

14 Perhaps Gedde actually worked at East Sutton Place and designed the leading pattern himself; or perhaps he simply made an accurate sketch of it and reproduced it in his book. Simon Jervis, however, has pointed out to the author in correspondence that C.J. Richardson had restored East Sutton Place during the early nineteenth century, which raises the possibility that he actually designed the window there, basing it on Gedde.

15 The same pattern was used much later for the paving of the Scagliola Hall at Burghley in 1801–3, though again Gedde was by no means necessarily the source here, for the pattern was readily available in William Chambers's *A Treatise on Civil Architecture*, 1768 (opp. p.84). Similarly, fictive blocks like those of Gedde's fol.5, which were used for paving in Classical times, were certainly employed by Hawksmoor in the choir of Beverley Minster, but C.A. d'Aviler's *Cours complet d'architecture* of 1691, pl.203, is a more immediate and likely source. On the other hand, Gedde may have been the source for G.F. Bodley's paving in the choir of Holy Angels, Hoar Cross in Staffordshire, which corresponds precisely with fol.7, a plate which, incidentally, may have inspired the pattern of an eighteenth-century wallpaper hung at Aston Hall, Birmingham.

16 Penoyre 1994, figs 61, 62.

17 Fol.63 with that in the ballroom, where two broad contra-acting serpentine ribs are intersected by circles and squares; fol.71 with the ceiling of the Great Staircase, where circles and quatrefoils intersect (this pattern is also found on ceilings at Canonbury House, Islington, and Pinkie House, Midlothian), and fol.48 (with the addition of only one line) with the narrow ribs on the ceiling of the Spangle Room.

18 The astonishing complexity of the ideas embodied in titlepages is fully demonstrated in Corbett and Lightbown 1979. One of their most interesting discoveries, from the point of view of the present study, is that three figures on the titlepage of Sir Walter Raleigh's *History of the World* (London, 1614) derive more or less unchanged from Philips Galle's rarely used *Prosopographia* of c.1590; ibid., pp.128–35. See also pp.116–19, above.

19 For one example, now in the Bibliothèque Royale Albert I in Brussels (VB 5335), see Simon Jervis, 'A seventeenth-century book of engraved ornament', *Burl. Mag.* (Dec. 1986), pp.893–903.

20 P.A. Hulton, 'Introduction' (p.xix) in Latham 1980.

21 See Auerbach 1954, pp.128–9 and pl.38; this frame could have been adapted from the lower edge of pl.xxx of Clemens Perret's *Exercitatio Alphabetica* published in 1569. For the titlepage see McKerrow and Ferguson 1932, no.127a. David Bostwick discovered that a printer's ornament used, for instance, in Robert Barker's 1619 edition of the King James Bible was copied for a plasterwork frieze at Cartledge Hall, Derbyshire, see Bostwick 1993, pls 5.22, 5.23.

22 Auerbach 1954, pp.127–8 and pl.43; she also mentions the use of a woodcut in 1518–20, pp.33ff. I am most grateful to Malcolm Jones, of the Centre for English Cultural Tradition and Language at Sheffield University, for pointing out to me (in correspondence) that several sets of banqueting trenchers dating from the middle of the seventeenth century onwards have circular engravings pasted on them. The London printseller Peter Stent advertised two sets of plates specifically for this purpose in 1653, and Dr Jones has recorded sets of trenchers pasted with engravings copied from originals by Crispijn de Passe the elder and Marc Geerarts the elder.

23 Both these bindings are in the Untermyer Collection in the Metropolitan Museum of Art in New York, Hackenbroch 1960a, figs 53, 57.

24 McKerrow and Ferguson 1932, no.199; the format of the page-border is not precisely the same as that of the carving and a number of other differences are visible; the needlework binding is in the Untermyer Collection, Hackenbroch 1960a, fig.53. The same woodcut seems to have been modified for the overmantel relief in the hall at Great Fulford in Devon. Deborah Howard has discovered that the monument to Sir George Hay, 1st Earl of Kinnoull (died 1634), at Kinoull, Perthshire, was inspired by the frontispiece of Sir Walter Raleigh's *History of the World* (London, 1614); see D. Howard, 'The Kinoull Aisle and Monument', *Architectural History* 39 (1996), pp.36–53.

25 Trevelyon and the Abbott family of Devon plasterers also made use of Edward Topsell's *The History of Foor-footed Beasts and Serpents* which appeared in 1607 and 1608.

26 McKerrow and Ferguson 1932, no.142; both the English and the original French titlepages are reproduced in Gottfried S. Fraenkel, *Pictorial and Decorative Title Pages from Music Sources* (New York, 1968), nos 54 and 32 respectively.

27 B. Cherry and N. Pevsner, *Devon, BE* (1989 edn), p.269.

28 McKerrow and Ferguson 1932, nos 157, 158.

29 John Milsom, 'Music and Worship in Tudor England', in Ford 1989, pp.179–92.

30 A print 'Invented by Samuell Ward preacher of Ipswich' but printed in Amsterdam in 1621 was copied for at least two needlework pictures, details from Richard Shorleyker's *Schole-house for the needle* (1624) were copied on a sampler in the V&A, Circ.279-1923, while William Marshall's

frontispiece design for *Eikon Basilike* (1649) was adapted for an embroidery in the same museum, T.117-1936 (Nevinson 1940, pp.9–10).

31 Nevinson 1950, pp.138–40.

32 Alexander Globe has estimated that at one time or another 'Peter Stent sold at least 465 single sheets . . . and 101 sets and books printed from 1288 engravings, giving a total of 1753 copper plates. No earlier printseller owned even an eighth as many'. A. Globe, *Peter Stent, London Printseller circa 1642–65* (Vancouver, 1985), p.7.

8 Masonry

1 Adrian Woodhouse, 'In Search of Smythson', *CL* (19 Dec. 1991), pp.56–8; ibid. (26 Dec. 1991), pp.36–9.

2 Girouard 1962.

3 Girouard 1962 (I/16). Similar numerical references in the text are to this publication.

4 See Schele 1965, pp.144–8; the Smythson chimneypiece is Girouard 1962 (IV, 10). My discovery of these sources has led Mark Girouard to re-attribute this sheet, formerly given to John Smythson the younger, to Robert.

5 This suite supplied the idea for the tomb, dated 1627, of the first Countess of Devonshire in the small church of Ault Hucknall in Derbyshire, Girouard 1962 (III/27).

6 Girouard 1983, pp.272–3.

7 See Simon Jervis, 'A Seventeenth-century Book of Engraved Ornament', *Burl. Mag.* (Dec. 1986), p.894.

8 Summerson 1966.

9 T.75–T.78, T.165, T.166, from the former; T.50 from the latter. For Thorpe's translation of Ducerceau's *Leçons* see Karl-Josef Holtgen, 'An Unknown Manuscript Translation by John Thorpe of du Cerceau's *Perspective*', in Chaney and Mack 1990, pp.215–28; John Thorpe also translated Blum, a work which his father Thomas Thorpe had consulted for Ionic capitals at Kirby. Holtgen investigated the sources of Richard Haydock's illustrations in his translation of Lomazzo's *Trattato dell'arte*, discovering the models in Dürer, Beham, Serlio, Vitruvius, Ducerceau and various anatomical writers (p.215).

10 David L. Roberts was the first to suggest that Thorpe might have known Perret's publication, see note 12, below.

11 Summerson, 1966, p.27.

12 Girouard 1992, pp.194–5, pl.177. I wonder whether T.85 should be associated with Thornton College, the Lincolnshire house built by John Thorpe between 1607 and 1611? That house was built on a plan adapted from this same Protestant Temple design but 'when it was finished, fell quite down to the bare ground without any visible cause and broke in pieces all the rich furniture that was therein' and it was rebuilt 'on the east side of the court of the abby [Thornton Abbey], and is all built on arches of the old [abbey] building' (*The Diary of Abraham de la Pryme* [1697], *Surtees Society*, LIV, pp.145–6, cited in David L. Roberts, 'John Thorpe's drawings for Thornton College, the house of Sir Vincent Skinner', *Lincolnshire History and Archaeology*, 19 (1984)). T.85, like the accredited Thornton plans T.67 and T.68 (but unlike any other of the Thorpe drawings), has what appear to be buttresses but must have been pilasters applied to each storey.

13 Pure classical details survive at Sir William Sharington's Lacock Abbey, converted during the 1540s from a suppressed nunnery. There is a handful of buildings that are similar to Longleat in character including Chalcot House in Wiltshire, owned by Sir Henry Vere, and Sherborne House in Gloucestershire which was built between 1551 and 1574 by the bailiff of Sir John Thynne's manor at Buckland.

14 Maurice Howard has written: 'The "meanings" which particular architectural patrons understood and contested in relation to their political self-identity can be grouped under three headings: Protestantism, a sense of nationhood and the idea of "Commonwealth"'. Maurice Howard, 'Self-Fashioning and the Classical Moment in Mid-Sixteenth-Century English Architecture', in Gent and Llewellyn 1990, pp.198–217, especially p.208ff.

15 Mark Girouard, 'New Light on Longleat. Allen Maynard: A French Sculptor in England in the 16th Century', *CL* (20 Sept. 1956), p.595.

16 Jervis 1974, no.92, and Blunt 1969, fig.27.

17 The classical porch at Grafton may just have been influenced by a Classical triumphal arch at Pola in Dalmatia illustrated by Serlio (III, fol.59): although this is Corinthian not Doric as at Grafton, it appears to give a Classical authority for the first-floor column placed centrally over the arch below, a conceit popular in early classical porches in England. Grafton has, above the window at first-floor level, a band of Vitruvian scroll probably copied from elsewhere in Serlio.

18 The fact that the second, untitled suite of Vredeman's cartouche designs was used at Wilton is no obstacle, for the sets were absolutely contemporary, virtually indistinguishable in style, and were very likely bound up together.

19 Mark Girouard, 'New Light on Longleat. Allen Maynard: A French Sculptor in England in the 16th Century', *CL* (20 Sept. 1956), p.597.

20 Here the frieze occurs on the central section which represents material reused from elsewhere; I am grateful to Mark Girouard for drawing this monument to my attention.

21 Further examples, in order of date of death, commemorate Sir William Uvedale (d.1569) at Wickham, commemorating Sir Robert Oxenbridge (d.1574) at Hurstbourne Priors, and an unknown family at Mottisfont, where the monument is dated 1584.

22 These are illustrated in Blunt 1969, figs 29–30.

23 Schele 1965, no.70. For a full discussion of the Mason monument see Martin Biddle, 'Early Renaissance at Winchester' in John Crook (ed.), *Winchester Cathedral, Nine Hundred Years, 1093–1993* (Chichester, 1993), pp.286–94.

24 The watercolours of the tomb itself and the armorials and inscription are in the collection of Bristol City Art Gallery. The inscription seems to contradict the opinion recorded in J.F. Nicholls and J. Taylor, *Bristol: Past and Present*, II (1881), p.130, that the individual commemorated was 'Athalin, wife of John Newton, brother to Sir Henry Newton, who died in 1599'. I am indebted to Karin-M. Walton for this information.

25 L.A. Shuffrey, *The English Fireplace and its Accessories* (London, 1912), pl.XXVI.

26 The date on the panelling of the Brown Parlour, formerly on the ground floor, see Roger White, 'Wiston House Remodelled', *Architectural History*, 27 (1984), pp.241–54, citing *The Victoria County History: Sussex* (1980), VI, part I, pp.261–2.

27 All three roofs, incidentally, show some stylistic affinities with that of Burghley, which, Mark Girouard now dates to the rebuilding of 1572–87: see Girouard, 'Burghley House, Lincolnshire – I', *CL* (23 April 1992), p.58.

28 Once thought to have been 'a single unified Elizabethan overmantel removed by Blore from the great hall in 1840', Roger White pointed out that the elements are made of different stone and assigned a later, 1620s, date to the upper portions of the composition (White, op.cit., p.244); he believes the lower portion may have come from the Great Chamber. I see no need to distinguish between the components in date.

29 The translation is from the 1611 English edition.

30 From Isaac Ware's 1738 English edition, Book IV, p.92; the frieze is illustrated on plate XXX. In the original 1570 Venice edition, the frieze appears on fol.47r of Libro Quarto.

31 In the 1981 Brussels reprint of the 1641 edition.

32 See pp.115–16, above. Elsewhere at Wiston other Flemish designers were recalled, Cornelis Floris in a mask on a doorcase in the east wing, and Vredeman de Vries in the decorated timber columns of the hall screen which have low-relief strapwork copied from his *[Architectura] Das Erst Büch* of 1565.

33 The full title is *Icones Livianae: Praecipuas Romanorum Historias Magno Artificio ad Vivum Expressas oculis repraesentantes, succinctis Versibus illustratae: per Philippum Lonicerum. Cum gratia & priuilegio Caesareae Maiest. MDLXXII.*

34 The prints are *TIB*, 20, I, 3.12 and 3.13, respectively.

35 H. 517–23 (de Passe the elder).

36 Girouard 1983, p.146.

37 N. Pevsner, *Wiltshire*, BE (Harmondsworth, 1975), pp.303–4; Summerson 1966, pp.87–8.

38 The original arrangement is shown in a drawing by C.J. Richardson, V&A Print Room, 93.H.15.

39 They are not in Hollstein's catalogue. The Orpheus print is inscribed HCF, for *Hans Collaert fecit* and the central scene is surrounded by seven compartments enclosing figures of the Nine Muses. The two other prints at Antwerp are additionally inscribed with the name of the publisher, Eduwaert van Hoeswinckel, and depict Sedulitas, with the Seven Liberal Arts, and the Four Elements, with the seven Planets (Antwerp, Stedelijk Prentenkabinet, III./C.245–7); the attribution to Jan Snellinck was Hans Mielke's (Mielke 1975, pp.36–7, fig.8); see also Veldman 1992, p.255, fig.40.

40 For William Arnold's life and work see Oswald 1959, pp.25–30, and Colvin 1978, pp.70–71. A man named Arnold Gouerson or Goverson was employed by Thynne as a joiner between 1555 and 1558 but had left Longleat by the summer of 1563 (perhaps even before William was born), as a letter from Thynne's steward, George Walker, records (12 May 1563): 'The Joyner that went away doth work wt Sr Hary Asheley in Dorsettshire. The other hath wrought his Collumes & now is in hand wt the fryse.' That the joiner was Gouerson is made more probable by the fact that William Arnold, his presumed son, had settled at Charlton Musgrove, not far from the Ashley's house at Wimborne St Giles, by 1600 at the latest.

41 Giles Worsley, 'On the Ruins of Ruperra', *CL* (23 Oct. 1993), pp.1277–9.

42 Letter from the Petre archives from Ingatestone Hall, quoted in Oswald 1959, p.26.

43 Serlio, Book III, fols.19r, 48r.

44 The gatehouse was illustrated in Hutchins's *History of Dorset* in 1774 and is said to have been moved to Hinton St George in 1800 (Oswald 1959, pl.66); however, there is no trace of it there and Professor Michael Jaffé is certain that it was never moved.

45 The basket arch is an interesting feature: it is paralleled on the tomb of Sir William Sharington (d.1566) at Lacock and on that of Sir Anthony Poulett (d.1600) and wife (d.1601) at Hinton St George in Somerset. From its similarity to the Montacute monument, the latter must have been designed by Arnold.

46 Mielke 1967, M.XXIII.

47 Nevinson 1964, p.104: 'They came to Graciousstrete where in their waye the conduit thereof was finely trimmed whereon was painted verye ingeniouslye the nine Worthies with many notable proverbes and adages, written with fayre Roman letters on every side thereof...' (John Elder, *Camden Society*, 48 (1850), p.147).

48 The house has a plaster ceiling based on a print in Arnold's favourite set of designs by Jacob Floris, and a frieze copied straight from Vredeman's *[Architectura] Das Erst Büch* (1565).

49 Vredeman's *[Architectura] Das Erst Büch* of 1565 was quarried for the ornamented lower column of Deymond's monument commemorating Sir John Jefferey (d.1611) at Whitchurch Canonicorum in Dorset; the anonymous cartouches appear on his monuments to Sir Thomas Fulford (d.1610) at Dunsford and Sir John Acland (d.1620, monument erected 1613–14) at Broadclyst, both in Devon.

50 The pierced taffril of the monument commemorating William, Earl of Pembroke (d.1569), and family (formerly in Old St Paul's Cathedral, London, see White 1992, fig.14) possibly derives from Vredeman's *[Architectura] Das Erst Büch* and *Das Ander Buech* of 1565; Floris masks appear on the tomb of Sir Richard Blount (d.1564) and family in the church of St Peter ad Vincula in the Tower of London.

51 W. Douglas Simpson, *Edzell Castle* (Edinburgh, 1994), p.10.

52 H.XXII, 546–52; reversed copies by Pieter de Iode are in the Print Room of the British Museum, 1868.6.12.(456–462).

53 John Newman, 'An Early Drawing by Inigo Jones and a Monument in Shropshire', *Burl. Mag.* (June 1973), pp.360–67, and Harris and Higgott 1989, cat.6, pp.42–4. The latter suggest carvings on Roman sarcophagi in the necropolis at Arles (which Jones would have seen in 1609) as a possible source for the harpy and heavy swags on the tomb-chest, and an engraving by Angelo Falcone of the *Tomb of a Young Man*, after a design by Parmigianino, for Jones's composition of a reclining figure beneath a pair of cupids holding a plaque. However, winged eagles with swags appear in engravings after Cornelis Floris and Vredeman de Vries, and winged harpies (though not very similar to Jones's) in the latter's designs.

54 Research has proved that Jones owned all the obvious Italian architectural treatises, Alberti, Cataneo, Rusconi, Scamozzi, Vignola and Viola Zanini, all specifically mentioned amongst the books from the library of Jones at Worcester College, Oxford, see Harris, Orgel and Strong 1973, pp.217–18. Jones also owned many books on fortification, Italian history and topography, classical philosophy and so on. He was also familiar with Barbaro, Lomazzo, Labacco, Fontana, besides Vasari's *Vite* and drawing manuals by Fialetti, Palma Giovane and Guercino. For scenery and costume design Jones consulted engravings and woodcuts by Adam Scultori and Martino Rota after Michelangelo's Sistine Chapel paintings, by Marcantonio Raimondi after Raphael and Agostino Veneziano's prints of Classical sculpture, together with etchings by Parmigianino and Schiavone. For information on Jones's use of continental books and prints I have relied heavily on Harris and Higgott 1989; and on John Peacock, 'Inigo Jones as a Figurative Artist', in Gent and Llewellyn 1990, pp.154–79.

55 Somerset House had been granted to Queen Henrietta Maria by Prince Charles in 1626, see Harris and Higgott 1989, p.193.

56 For a discussion of the *Architectura Moderna* see Kuyper 1980, pp.28–33.

57 In hands other than Jones's *I Palazzi di Genova* seems to have inspired the window-surrounds of the 1630s block attached to the hall at Bolsover Castle and of Nottingham Castle.

58 Jones based his mannered substitution of brackets for triglyphs on his design for the screen in the chapel of Somerset House (1632) on an antique marble at Arundel House: Summerson 1986, pp.76–8; Harris and Higgott 1989, pp.198, 200.

9 PLASTERWORK

1 Claire Gapper very kindly lent me a copy of her unpublished London University MA Report, which she is expanding into a PhD dissertation. Other regional studies include French 1957, pp.124–44; Puloy 1983, pp.144–99; Bostwick 1990; Penoyre 1994.

2 For the Gunby brothers and their work in the north, see Bostwick 1994, pp.24–8.

3 Wells-Cole 1981; Claire Gapper, 'Chastleton House: the decorative plasterwork in context', in Airs 1994, pp.101–16.

4 I owe this reference to Claire Gapper.

5 Gapper, op.cit., p.115.

6 The sketchbook is one of the treasures of the Devon Record Office, 404M/B1: I am most grateful to Kathleen French for lending me her photostat copy many years ago. The Abbotts were by no means the only plasterers working in the West Country at this date: another was Robert Eaton, to whom has been attributed an overmantel of 1593 in the Gatehouse at Combe Florey, with several more on stylistic grounds (Penoyre 1994, pp.41–3).

7 Rosemary Verey (ed.), London 1983, pp.16–20.

8 French 1957, p.132.

9 Hackenbroch 1960a, p.xxvii and fig.57. It was also adapted for plasterwork at Gaulden Manor, Tolland, Somerset, see Penoyre 1994, fig.13.

10 John and Jane Penoyre have attributed at least one heraldric overmantel at Montacute to Robert Eaton of Stogersey, on stylistic grounds (Penoyre 1994, figs 48, 114).

11 Jervis 1974, nos 204–28.

12 Pp.92–3; H.IV, 102–7.

13 Gapper 1990, p.54.

14 Christopher Hussey, *CL* XCI (16 Jan. 1942), p.114.

15 Peacham, *Minerva Britanna*, p.26.

16 H. [Hans (Jan Baptist I) Collaert] 209–18; the actual print is reproduced in Amsterdam 1988, no.68.4.

17 Warncke 1979, II, no.556.

10 JOINERY AND CARVING

1 MacCaffrey 1975, p.269; it is very difficult to assess these values in present-day terms but a recent writer (Nicholl 1993, in the unpaginated preliminary pages) has suggested that the Elizabethan figures should, as a rule of thumb, be multiplied by 500, giving values of £2,000 and £45,000 for the joiner and weaver respectively.

2 Both these figures should be seen in the light of Exeter merchants' estates, a third of which were worth less than £1,000, a third between £1,000 and £2,000, and another third more than £2,000; one alderman, Thomas Walker, may have had as much as £25,000. The contents of one room in the house of an Exeter merchant, William Chappell, in 1580 were worth more than £100, 'of which the furniture represented less than ten per cent in value (two bedsteads, a cupboard, a table, four stools, and various chests and boxes). The hangings alone, of 'Painted Canvas of the Storie of Joseph, and Courtaines of redd and grene saie before the windowe' and the two sets of bed-hangings of red and green with a fringe and blue and yellow sarcenet with a silk fringe were worth far more. His set of gilt crewelwork chair and stool with silk fringes, and the wroughtwork cupboard cloths, damask towels and blackwork drinking cloths, plus the six yards of wroughtwork fringe to set about a cupboard, added up to an extremely richly textured interior, in which most of the richness and almost all the value lay in the imported textiles. See Philippa Glanville, 'The Crafts and Decorative Arts', in Ford 1989, p.296.

3 The Haynes Grange Room now belongs to the Victoria and Albert Museum in London. It was published by H. Clifford Smith, *The Haynes Grange Room* (London, 1935), and has been reinterpreted by Mark Girouard (1992), who associates it with Chicksands Priory, pp.171–86.

4 The Middle Temple screen has never aroused much interest: it was illustrated in two superb *CL* photographs taken *c.*1900, mentioned in Gotch 1914 and Mercer 1962, but has not been examined seriously before now.

5 Girouard 1992, pp.197–210.

6 According to the Minutes of Parliament, the hall was begun *c.*1562 and completed in 1571 or 1572, although some of the heraldic glass is dated 1570.

7 The pattern may have been part of the decorative stock-in-trade of a French carver, for similar patterns are relatively common on mid-century French furniture.

8 Floris's Tournai screen was itself based on a Flemish tradition which begins with the rood screen at Ste Waudru at Mons (1545–8) and continues with that in St Cunera at Rhenen, constructed between 1550 and 1560, see Avery 1969, fig.8.

9 The Floris cartouche framing the cypher of Elizabeth I on the Apollo overmantel from Chatsworth (now at Hardwick, see p.254) derives not from the same set as at Middle Temple but from a second set published the next year, 1567,

313

but the two suites were likely to have been bound together and plundered indiscriminately. The Canonbury House overmantels are now at Castle Ashby in Northamptonshire (see fig.65). The French-looking strapwork pattern also appears on a remarkable series of early seventeenth-century funerary monuments in West Country churches, see Wells-Cole 1981.

10 Adrian Gaunt, Thynne's joiner at Longleat from 1563 until at least the late 1570s, fitted up the interiors of the pre-fire house – it was burnt in 1567 – with joinery of a very classical character, including an wind-porch decorated with columns and terms, doors of marquetry, and doorcases framed with pilasters. In November 1568 he was paid £13. 6s. 8d. for work on the screen in the hall at Longleat, perhaps the screen that survives to this day.

11 Also the similar overmantel, depicting the same scene but from a different source, made for Toddington Manor in Bedfordshire (now in the V&A).

12 Serlio's folio 32v was copied for the chimneypiece in the hall at Wollaton at just the same date. The key-fret ornament under the top rail of the gallery front at Gray's Inn may come from Serlio, too.

13 The terminal crestings at Knole were adapted from Vredeman's *[Architectura] Das Erst Büch* and the term figures from another of his suites. The Audley screen seems to be particularly old-fashioned but has perspective arches that belong to the most up-to-date style of the late 1620s, see Mercer 1962, p.121.

14 The latter was moved to Badminton House, Gloucestershire – see N. Pevsner and D. Verey, *Gloucestershire: The Cotswolds*, BE (Harmondsworth, 1974), p.257 – along with a second chimneypiece and overmantel now in the Billiard Room.

15 For a more detailed discussion of their output see Wells-Cole 1981, pp.1–19.

16 Now in the V&A, 4870–81-1856.

17 For richly-carved panelling from houses in Ipswich and Great Yarmouth see Cescinsky and Gribble 1922, I, figs 283–91 (Ipswich, now at Christchurch Mansion), figs 317–26 (Great Yarmouth).

18 A panel over the entrance doorway bears the date 1601, and 1610 is the date in the frieze of the south-east bedchamber on the first floor and on the royal arms on the detached gatehouse. For a history and detailed description of the decoration at Burton Agnes, see Arthur Oswald's articles in *CL* (4, 11 and 18 June 1953). See also Imrie 1993. The house is likely to have been fitted out internally during the second decade of the seventeenth century.

19 RIBA, Smythson drawings, I/2.

20 Quoted in E.H. Gombrich, 'Icones Symbolicae: Philosophies of Symbolism and their Bearing on Art', *Symbolic Images: Studies in the Art of the Renaissance*, II (London 1978), p.144.

21 Imrie 1993, pp.57–61.

22 In her catalogue Mauquoy-Hendrickx (II, nos.848–51) attributes their design to Adrian van der Weert but the prints are clearly signed 'Martin de Vos inventor'.

23 The illustrations may in fact date from c.1541, the date on the woodcut of Nephthali, see Veldman and de Jonge 1985, no.3–4, pp.176–96.

24 Veldman and de Jonge 1985, p.178, n.9, and R. Sinker, *A Descriptive Catalogue of the Editions of*

the Printed Text of the Versions of the 'Testamenta XII patriarchum' (Cambridge and London, 1910).

25 The copy in the Print Room of the British Museum is undated but Knipping 1939, I, p.307, suggests 1579 as the date of publication; when the second, English-language, edition of Knipping's book appeared in 1974 the date was amended to c.1600 (II, p.499). Corbett and Lightbown 1979, p.132, however, give the date of publication as between 1585 (when the dedicatee Marie de Melun, Comtesse de Ligne, inherited the titles listed in the dedication from Robert de Melun who died that year) and January 1601 (when her husband inherited one of these titles, the Marquis de Roubaix, presumably on her death). Manfred Sellink, the modern authority on Philips Galle, says c.1590.

26 See Erwin Panofsky, 'Titian's *Allegory of Prudence*', in Panofsky 1970, pp.181–205. The monster originated in Hellenistic Egypt as the companion of Serapis (originally a god of the nether world) and may have been the equivalent of Pluto's three-headed Cerberus. In the Latinised West it came to represent the past, present and future, and from the fifteenth century onwards was associated with Apollo instead of Serapis; in the sixteenth, the three heads, divorced from any body, also came to be the symbol of Prudence, which 'not only investigates the present but also reflects about the past and the future' (ibid., p.197, quoting from Piero Valeriano's *Hieroglyphica* of 1556). Panofsky also pointed out that Stradanus's 'Apollonian sun-god was patterned after Michelangelo's *Risen Christ* in Sta Maria sopra Minerva' (ibid., p.194).

27 *TIB*, 269, 270; Fortitude and Temperance appear in the frieze with Hope and Charity lower down, between the blocks over the columns.

28 This description is Arthur Oswald's.

29 McKerrow and Ferguson 1932, no.120.

30 *TIB* 33, 109 and 108 respectively.

31 M.-H. 1372–79.

32 The identification is Arthur Oswald's.

33 *TIB*, 5601:038; Riggs 1977, List no.31, p.319.

34 For the other see pp.271, 275.

35 Thomas Wake, 'Some Early Furniture in the Keep and Black Gate, Newcastle upon Tyne', *Archaeologia Aeliana*, 4th ser., VIII (1931), pp.179–81 and pl.xxv; I am indebted to Rosemary Allan, Senior Keeper at Beamish, for this reference. The overmantel is also illustrated by Bruce Allsop, *Historic Architecture of Newcastle upon Tyne* (Newcastle-upon-Tyne, 1967), p.22.

36 For Newcastle trade see F.W. Dendy (ed.), 'Records of the Merchant Adventurers of Newcastle', *Surtees Society*, 93 (1893), and 'Records of the Company of Hostmen of Newcastle', *Surtees Society*, 105 (1901). A convenient summary of her trade can be found in Williams 1988, especially pp.259–60: customs documents record that 160,000 chauldrons of coal were exported abroad each year, but this was a clear understatement of the actual position, for the local hostmen recorded that they exported some 500,000 chauldrons: clearly, twice as much went undeclared as declared.

37 The *Chorographia* was reprinted by the Newcastle Typographical Society in 1818 and this account comes from that edition, pp.22ff.

38 Although at a later point in its history it adorned a chimneypiece carved with the date 1599, Thomas Wake, op.cit., p.181.

39 For Hunwick Hall see N. Pevsner and E. Williamson, *Durham, BE* (Harmondsworth, 1983), p.335; the photograph was kindly sent me by Rosemary Allan.

40 H.532–3.

41 Waterson and Meadows 1990, pp.36–7; this overmantel was sold by Mr W.D. Chaytor of Croft Hall near Darlington about 1980 and is now in the USA.

42 Arion actually resembles very closely the figure in a printer's mark designed for Sigmund Feyerabend and Johann Herbst of Basle by Jost Amman (illustrated in Busch 1969, pl.175), but I cannot bring myself to believe that this in fact provided the source.

43 Like the first Clervaux overmantel this was sold c.1980, but survives divided between two private collections at Taddington Manor and Prestbury in Gloucestershire. I am grateful to Peter Meadows, William Chaytor and Adrian Puddy for help in tracing them.

44 H.IV, 65–115, H.XLIV, 275–325.

45 *Northumberland County History* XV, p.218; I am indebted to Anna Eavis for this reference.

46 The carving of this overmantel relief was erroneously attributed to a nineteenth-century Italian woodcarver, Anton Leone Bulletti, who came to England in 1855 and worked at Chipchase Castle in the 1870s, see Rosamond Allwood, '"The Eminent Italian Artist, Signor Bulletti"', *Furniture History*, XXV (1989), pp.250–55. However, Allwood now agrees that the relief is genuinely seventeenth century, having subsequently discovered a reference which makes it clear that the chimneypiece pre-dates Bulletti's work at Chipchase: Rev. George Rome Hall, *Memoir of the History and Architecture of Chipchase Castle*, reprinted from *The Natural History Transactions of Northumberland and Durham*, 1877.

47 Veldman 1977, p.133, n.1.

48 *Ordinancie, inhoudende de poincten vanden Heylighen Besnijdenis ommeganck der stadt van Antwerpen, gheschiet inden iare M.D.LXI* (Antwerp), Veldman 1977, p.135.

49 Veldman 1977, p.141.

50 Nordenfalk 1985, fig.12, p.143, illustrates the whole suite.

51 N. Pevsner, *Northumberland, BE* (Harmondsworth 1974), p.234; Allsop, op.cit. (at n.35, above), p.27, gives the date as 1635, in error. The Merchant Adventurers' Court was above the Maison Dieu, not a separate building, as a correspondent to *CL* suggested (12 Jan. 1945).

52 M. Ross, *Architectural and Picturesque Views in Newcastle upon Tyne* (Newcastle, 1842), pp.31–2.

53 For a discussion of the relationship between the Beham/Pencz and Heemskerck suites see Veldman 1980.

54 See Veldman 1983, no.1, pls 1–8.

55 Ibid., p.24.

56 Figures representing industries are nineteenth-century and were presumably carved when the staircase was installed in Lewes Town Hall.

57 Constantia and Experientia, together with the Five Senses, were copied in 1894 (at precisely the same time as the Slaugham staircase was installed in Lewes Town Hall) on the staircase newels at Temple Newsam in Yorkshire in a scheme designed by C.E. Kempe with joinery by the Burgess Hill, Sussex, firm of Norman & Burt. Plaster squeezes from the Slaugham newel posts were used at Temple Newsam and survive in the house, see C.G. Gilbert, 'C.E. Kempe's Staircase

58 Or at any rate between 1585 and 1601, note 25, above.

59 For Slaugham Place see Mark Girouard, 'Renaissance Splendour in Decay', *CL* (9 Jan. 1964), pp.70–73, and Summerson 1966, p.104, pls 109–11.

60 The house is numbered 28–30 The Close and now belongs to the Tyne and Wear Building Preservation Trust.

61 N. Pevsner, I. Richmond, J. Grundy, G. McCombie, P. Ryder and H. Welfare N., *Northumberland, BE* (Harmondsworth, 1992), p.468.

62 Berliner and Egger 1981, 1, p.78, nos 840–45.

63 J.S. Robinson, 'Some Account of the Incorporated Company of Free Joiners of Newcastle-upon-Tyne', *Archaeologia Aeliana*, 3rd ser., v (1909), pp.170–96.

64 In case it should prove useful, here is the list, for which I am indebted to B. Jackson, Chief Archivist at Tyne and Wear Archives Service: 1617: Thomas Wilkinson, Thomas Taylor, Thomas Thompson, Cuthbert Green, John Robson. 1619: John Carnaby, Cuthbert Carnaby, Richard Dawson, William Hearon, Jonathon Haysoile, Geo [name illegible], Lawrence Serjeant, John Swaddle. 1621: Luke Cofer, John Foster, Richard Hudspeth, Thomas Hills, William Johnson, Thomas Wallas. 1629: John Hutchinson, William Milbourne, Richard Newton, William Wilkinson 1630: John Dod, John Fairland 1631: William Dobson. There is no means of assessing their relative importance and the list may start too late.

65 This leads us on to speculate whether the high-quality decoration of the inlaid room at Sizergh (in the V&A, 3–1891) was not also produced in Newcastle, even if by foreign craftsmen; the same applies to similar panelling in the Great Chamber at Gilling Castle near Coxwold in the North Riding of Yorkshire, where the 'architect' may have been the German Bernard Dinninghof who signed the glass in 1585.

66 With a similar example from Lanercost Priory now in the Bowes Museum.

67 By far the best account of Cosin's furnishing schemes is Hartley 1984. Hartley (pp.104–8) mentioned Dietterlin, Johannes Jakob Ebelmann and Paul Vredeman de Vries but concluded that no direct direct parallels could be found.

68 He is named in correspondence and in bills, see N. Pevsner, *County Durham, BE* (Harmondsworth, 2nd edn, 1983), pp.33, 115, 403. Robert Barker constructed the wooden ceiling at Brancepeth and made new seats at Sedgefield, see John Cosin to William Milbourne (20 April 1638), G. Ornsby (ed.), 'The Correspondence of Bishop John Cosin', I, *Surtees Society Publications*, 52 (London, 1869).

69 Hartley 1984, pp.58, 96.

70 B. Cherry and N. Pevsner, *London 2: South, BE* (Harmondsworth, 1984), p.344.

71 Wells-Cole 1990, pp.1–41.

11 METALWORK

1 The most substantial collections of Elizabethan and Jacobean plate are those of the V&A and the British Museum in London, and the Hermitage in St Petersburg, whence it found its way as the result of ambassadorial gifts; there are also fine pieces in the possession of Oxford and Cambridge colleges, the London livery companies and museums in the USA.

2 J. Evans, 'Huguenot Goldsmiths in England and Ireland', *Proceedings of the Huguenot Society of London*, XIV (1933).

3 Glanville 1990; see also Hayward 1976.

4 Glanville 1990, pp.147–77; for Beham see p.150.

5 Ibid., p.154.

6 Ibid., p.162; one example, the Vintners' Salt, London 1569–70 is illustrated, fig.169.

7 V&A, M.273–1925, Glanville 1990, no.91, pp.458–9.

8 Glanville 1990, figs 171, 186.

9 Hayward 1976, no.652, Glanville 1990, fig.193.

10 In the British Museum, Glanville 1990, fig.136; this replacement body was made *c.*1600 but it is impossible to know whether its engraving simply replicated the decoration of the original ostrich egg or coconut.

11 Hackenbroch 1960b, pp.18–24; Oman 1978; Allcorn 1993, pp.48–52.

12 Now in the Fowler Collection.

13 Now in the Museum of Fine Arts in Boston, Mass.

14 In the collection of the Duke of Buccleuch.

15 Now in the Toledo Museum of Art; John Hayward ascribed then to Nuremberg, Hayward 1976, no.519.

16 In the V&A, M.55a-f-1946.

17 P over M was not alone in adapting the Delaune print for the latter: Gyles Godet did the same for the woodcut he printed in Blackfriars, London, in 1566 (Watt 1994, pl.32b).

18 The book-binding is in the Museum of Fine Arts in Boston and Ellenor Alcorn argues for a date of *c.*1640–55 (Allcorn 1993, pp.108–10); as most of the similar silver-mounted bindings are associated with books printed in the mid-1630s to 1640s, her date seems unduly late.

12 PAINTING

1 Foister 1981, pp.274–5.

2 For Holbein's use of Italian prints for details of his paintings in the Privy Chamber at Whitehall Palace in London, see p.8.

3 Oliver, born into a French Huguenot family sometime before 1568, depended heavily on continental prints, of which he probably had a substantial collection: Finsten 1981, especially pp.140–95.

4 Strong 1969, p.157.

5 Strong 1986, p.114, figs 42–3. It seems probable that, in his equestrian portrait of the Prince at Parham Park in Sussex, Peake derived the horse from Dürer's engraving, *Knight, Death and Devil*, and that another print source lies behind the figure of Opportunity, Strong 1986, fig.45.

6 See van Dorsten 1970, pp.60–61 and frontispiece; in n.43 on p.61 van Dorsten points out that the Roman ruins in the background of this painting were copied from accurate drawings, see *Triomf van het Manierism* (Amsterdam, 1955), p.68. The same is true of the anonymous morality painting inscribed *O Man Thow Wretched Creature . . .*, now in the Tate Gallery, Hearn 1995, no.30, pp.74–5.

7 For the *Procession Portrait* now at Sherborne Castle in Dorset, see David Armitage, 'The *Procession Portrait* of Queen Elizabeth: A note on a tradition', *Journal of the Warburg and Courtauld Institutes*, 53 (1990), pp.301–7. The print after de Vos is H.XLIV, no.883. Richard Williams has recently discovered that the narrative painting *Jephthah's Daughter*, in the Royal Collection, depends on three from a set of four engravings by Gerard de Iode after Hans Bol (Hearn 1995, p.115). Clearly there is scope for more work on the print sources for allegorical and narrative paintings.

8 The main publications on the Hill Hall paintings are Roberts 1941, pp.86–92; Simpson 1977, pp.1–20; Drury 1983, pp.98–123; and Carrick 1989, pp.12–18.

9 Some architectural details derive from Hans Blum's *Quinque Columnarum* (Zurich, 1550); Drury 1983, pp.108, 110 and fig.7.

10 Simpson 1977, pl.v, fig.3. Although the compositions seem to derive from French prints, the style of the figure painting is Flemish: the involvement of Lucas de Heere has been suggested but not proved.

11 These manuscripts were explored by Lucy Gent (Gent 1981, pp.10, 31), and have been discussed more fully by David Evett, 'Some Elizabethan Allegorical Paintings: a Preliminary Enquiry', *Journal of the Warburg and Courtauld Institutes*, LII (1989), p.140–66.

12 Evett, op.cit., p.145.

13 Reginald Pecock, *The Reule of Crysten Religioun*, quoted in Aston 1988, p.305, n.46.

14 For another example see pp.174–5.

15 The earliest extant edition appeared in Ghent in 1552 but it may have been published first in the 1540s as one of the woodcut borders is dated 1541, and the book was popular in the Netherlands, with twenty-five Dutch editions during the sixteenth century, and in England, where forty-seven editions were printed from 1576 onwards. For the history of the editions of Lambrecht's *Testamenten* see Veldman and de Jonge 1985, pp.178–9.

16 *Index Librorum Prohibitarum* (Antwerp 1570), p.93: Veldman and de Jonge 1985, p.179, n.14.

17 I am grateful to Nicholas Smith, Under-Librarian in the Rare Books Department of Cambridge University Library, for checking the 1552 Ypres edition, and several English editions, for woodcut borders.

18 These and the other paintings at North Mymms Park were brought to my attention by Muriel Carrick, see n.55 on p.306.

19 David Watkin, 'Childerley Hall, Cambridge', *CL* (6 Nov. 1969), pp.1170–73.

20 Farmer 1984, pp.77–105.

21 Mrs Coope's researches are incorporated in P.A. Faulkner, *Bolsover Castle, Derbyshire* (English Heritage, London, 1992).

22 It is not known who executed these decorative paintings. I wonder whether some could be the work of John Balechouse, Bess of Hardwick's painter: after her death in 1608 he was employed in mysterious building and decorative work at Hardwick by her son William Cavendish, the builder of Bolsover, although he may have died around 1618 while the dates 1619 and 1621 appear in the paintings, as we have seen. Balechouse was paid in all £75. 19s., see Kettle 1992, p.11.

23 Croft-Murray 1962, pp.194–5.

24 Auerbach and Adams 1971, p.103. Buckett was also employed by Robert Cecil at the New Exchange in London, by Edward Alleyn at

Dulwich College and by the Painter-Stainers' Company.

25 For Pinkie Castle, see Michael Bath, 'Alexander Seton's Painted Gallery' in Gent 1995, pp.79–108. I am most grateful to Lady Bullard for letting me see an early draft of her article 'Talking Heads', which was subsequently published in the *Bodleian Library Record*, XIV, no.6 (1994), pp.461–500.

26 Hartley 1984, p.82.

27 For the first, see John D. Waterer, 'Dunster Castle, Somerset, and its Painted Leather Hangings', *Connoisseur*, vol.164 (March 1967), and Dudley Dodd, *Dunster Castle* (London, 1985), p.23. For the Walsingham set see Simon Jervis, Furniture History Society *Newsletter*, 93 (1989), pp.8–9.

28 The Stoneleigh panels depict the Saxon Earls of Mercia and the Norman Earls of Chester: they were made for Brereton Hall in Cheshire but were subsequently moved to Aston Hall near Birmingham and then to Atherstone Hall: Fairclough 1984, pp.73–4.

29 Archer 1990, pp.311, 313; Aston 1993, p.97.

30 M.-H. 39 and 40.

31 Archer 1990, p.309. The discovery of the Heemskerck source is mine: the print is NH, Heemskerck 89.

32 *TIB*, vol.4, nos 125–31.

33 For a discussion of Laud's defence see Aston 1988, pp.338–40.

34 Laud's defence continued: 'Nor do the *Homilies* in this particular differ much from *Calvin*. But here the Statute of *Ed. 6.* was charged against me, *which requires the Destruction of all Images, as well in Glass-Windows, as elsewhere*. And this was also earnestly pressed by Mr *Brown*, when he repeated the Summ of the Charge against me in the House of Commons. To which I answered at both times; First, that the Statute of *Ed. 6.* spake of other Images: and that Images in Glass-Windows, were neither mentioned, nor meant in that Law: The Words of the Statute are, *Any graven Images of Stone, Timber, Alabaster or Earth; Graven, Carved or Painted, taken out of any Church, etc. shall be Destroyed, etc.* and not reserved to any Superstitious Use. So there's not a Word of Glass-Windows, nor the Images that are in them. Secondly, that the Contemporary Practice, (which is one of the best Expounders of the meaning of any Law) did neither destroy all coloured Windows, though Images were in them, in the *Queens* time, nor abstain from setting up of new, both in her, and *King* James his Time.' W. Prynne, *Canterburies Doom* (London, 1646), p.59, cited in Archer 1990, pp.314–15.

35 Michael Archer, *The Painted Glass of Lydiard Tregoze* (Swindon, n.d.).

36 *TIB* 32 (277), Archer, *The Painted Glass of Lydiard Tregose*, fig.10; I am indebted to Michael Archer himself for pointing out this source, which he discovered after his article went into print.

37 Sir John St John of Lydiard Tregoze and Sir John Grandison of Battersea, who gave a window painted by Abraham van Linge to the parish church in 1631, were both members of Lincoln's Inn where van Linge had recently painted glass.

13 TAPESTRY

1 Ralph Edwards (ed.), *The Dictionary of English Furniture* (London, 1954), III, p.327.

2 Barnard and Wace 1928, p.287.

3 The inscription on his tomb reads: 'post-quam primam adolescentiam in bonit litteris Oxoniae exegisset, Galliam caeterasque regioned perlustrasset . . .', Nash, *History of Worcestershire*, I, p.71, cited in Barnard and Wace 1928, p.259.

4 Bodleian Library, MS Rawlinson D.807, fol.15.

5 He returned perhaps bringing his servant, Peter the Dutchman, who had worked in London and may be identical with Peter van Dort whose name occurs for many years in the Lord Chamberlain's accounts; Peter was apparently the only foreigner associated with the Sheldon workshops (Barnard and Wace 1928, p.272).

6 Kendrick 1926, pp.27–42 includes them and quotes the story of the town clerk of Warwick who travelled to Greenwich to seek the Earl's advice on poverty in the town, Leicester replied 'I marvaile you do not devise some way amongs you to have some speciall trade to keepe your poore on woork such as Sheldon of Beolye devised'. Barnard and Wace (pp.304–5) reject them as Sheldon products, citing stylistic similarities with the Armada tapestries woven by Spierinx at Delft.

7 Clark 1983, pp.283–4; see also Wells-Cole 1983, pp.284–5.

8 Humphreys 1925, p.197.

9 The circular strapwork cartouches that frame the fountains appear to have been adapted from a plate inscribed 'Clebolus Dum secunda fortuna arridet . . .', designed by Cornelis Floris in 1554 and published three years later in his collection *Veelderleij niewe inventien*.

10 McKerrow and Ferguson 1932, no.196; this titlepage was itself adapted from an ornamental page-border designed by Bernard Salomon and used, for instance, in the celebrated Lyons edition of Ovid's *Metamorphoses* published in 1557. The use on Lord Leicester's tapestries of a pattern derived from a Prognostication is interesting in view of the Earl's enthusiasm for astrology and horoscopes; see Thomas 1991, p.343.

11 As we shall see below, it is significant that the block was not used in another book which has the same titlepage compartment, the *Sermons of Master Iohn Calvin, vpon the Booke of Iob*.

12 For a convenient summary of Sheldon's tapestry works, together with catalogue entries on the museum's collection, see Wingfield Digby 1980, pp.71–83.

13 The V&A has had fragments of Worcestershire (Fig.375) and of Oxfordshire on loan from the Bodleian Library since 1913. The Museum also owns the lower right-hand corner of Oxfordshire, which had been cut and mounted as a two-fold firescreen by the time of the Weston Park sale (Fig.379). The lower right-hand corner of Gloucestershire, which was exhibited at the Vigo Sternberg Galleries in 1971, is still in private hands (Fig.376), and further pieces belong to the Bodleian. A fourth map, depicting Warwickshire and presumed to have borne the date 1588, has been lost, but its general appearance is known from the mid-seventeenth-century replacement belonging to Warwickshire Museums.

14 Wells-Cole 1990c, pp.392–401. I am grateful to the editor, Caroline Elam, for allowing me to adapt the article for this book.

15 The account of Oxfordshire in Camden's *Britannia* (1586) was paraphrased for the tapestry map.

16 H.v, 172–181; according to van Mander, these prints were made from drawings copied from Floris's paintings which were executed *c.*1554–5, see Carl van de Velde 'The Labours of Hercules, a lost series of paintings by Frans Floris', *Burl. Mag.*, CVII (March 1965), pp.114–23; Riggs and Silver 1993, p.9.

17 Vredeman's *Grottesco* of 1575 was used for the design of a tapestry with the Arms of Herbert in the V&A (see Fig.111); Wingfield Digby 1980, no.46, pp.52–3, pl.66; it was bought as Sheldon, but Wingfield Digby considered it to be Flemish.

18 *TIB* 177 (266), O'Dell-Franke 1977, e65-B.

19 M.XXI.

20 Peter Martyr is the Anglicised name of Pietro Martire Vermigli (1500–62), an Augustinian monk who fled from Italy as a suspected heretic in 1542, becoming Professor of Divinity at Strasbourg; he was in England, 1547–53, and when he left he continued to correspond with English Protestants. He published many theological treatises and commentaries from 1543 onwards (see *The Dictionary of National Biography*, XX, pp.253–6). McKerrow and Ferguson 1932, p.127, tentatively ascribed the design of this woodblock to Nicholas Hilliard on the basis of the initials NH on the central cartouche. Comparing details of the titlepage border and the tapestries leaves no doubt that it was this woodblock and not the somewhat simplified version used for the titlepage of Hugh Broughton's *Concent of Scripture*, 1590, that supplied the source; this obviates the need to move the weaving of the maps (despite their presumed date, 1588) to 1590 or later.

21 M.IV and XVII.

22 The source may conceivably be a suite by Hubert Goltzius which I have not yet located.

23 Not after Johannes Stradanus as I mistakenly said in 1983, following the catalogue entry in the V&A; see Amsterdam 1988, no.72.1. Ilja Veldman, in correspondence with the author, states that Heemskerck was not the author of these subjects.

24 S.197.

25 M.-H. 665, 667, 669, 671.

26 Now at Hatfield House, Hertfordshire.

27 Barnard and Wace 1928, p.303, n.1.

28 And possibly later, as records for the years 1603–4 and 1604–5 are missing; the first year that Francis Hyckes actually disappeared from the list as a worker is 1605–6, see Barnard and Wace 1928, pp.285–6.

29 Two had earlier been used in the decoration of the plaster frieze in the High Great Chamber at Hardwick, see pp.112, 270.

30 Kendrick 1912, pp.89–97.

31 At Sudeley Castle, Barnard and Wace 1928, pl.LV, fig.2.

32 In the Untermyer Collection at the Metropolitan Museum of Art, New York (Hackenbroch 1960a, fig.31).

33 Christie's, 28 May 1964, lot 61.

34 Much more closely than did the designer of the only other derivation from the print known to me, the overmantel in the London Charterhouse (see p.166).

35 Recent research is tending to suggest that the Raphael cartoons were actually intended to hang on the walls of the Sistine Chapel, see *The Art Newspaper*, 52 (October 1995), p.29. For Mortlake tapestries, see Wendy Hefford, 'Prince Behind the Scenes', *CL* (4 Oct. 1990), pp.132–5.

14 EMBROIDERY

1 Nevinson 1968, pp.1–38, pls 1–36.

2 Nevinson 1968, pp.1–2. A. Boissard, *Icones Quinquaginta virorum* (1585). J. Verheiden, *Praestantium aliquot theologorum effigies* (1602). H. Holland, *Herwologia* (Arnhem 1620).

3 *A Book containing divers sortes of hands* (1571). I am indebted to Nicolas Barker for factual information. His study of the Getty manuscript, provisionally titled *Thomas Trevilian's Great Book*, is to be published in 1997–8.

4 Nevinson 1968, p.6.

5 Nevinson 1968, pp.1–2.

6 1608 Miscellany, fol.20r; McKerrow and Ferguson 1932, no.76. who give the date 1551. Nicolas Barker says the compartment first appeared in 1550. A second compartment (Folger, fol.20v, Getty, p.596) probably derives from a lost titlepage upon which McKerrow and Ferguson 1932, no.306, dated 1642, also depends.

7 Folger, fols.259v–264r, 265v.

8 H.III, (Beham) p.76.

9 Folger fol.161v, from M.-H. 1475, 1476. Related prints of the *Miles Christianus* and the *Speculum Peccatoris* (published in a 1673 edition of Ignatius Loyola's *De Geestlijke Oefeningen*) are discussed in Knipping 1974, pp.69, 92.

10 Folger, fol.177v; Getty, p.413.

11 Folger, fols 63r–68v; Getty, pp.457–68; for the Jan Sadeler/Crispijn van der Broeck prints see Veldman and de Jonge 1985, nos 3–4, pp.176–98, figs 27–30.

12 Nevinson 1964, pp.103–7.

13 See above, pp.115–16, and n.60 on p.310.

14 Trevelyon even copied the signatures of Maarten de Vos and Philips Galle from the print of Polymneia, H.XVLI, no.1306.

15 For Breau/Matham, see *TIB*, 4:1 (210). For the Savery print, see Pieter J.J. van Thiel, 'Poor parents, rich children and Family saying grace . . .', *Simiolus*, 17, no.2/3 (1987), pp.90–149, fig.28. Chris Schuckman kindly informed me that two of the four original Pieter van der Borcht *Dives and Lazarus* etchings are in Brussels, and Ger Luijten gave me his attribution of the copies to Barra. For Jan Thiel, see H.xxx, nos 2–5.

16 Hackenbroch 1965, fig.29.

17 Hackenbroch 1960a, fig.26.

18 C.E.C. Tattersall, 'Mrs E.L. Franklin's Petit point Panel', *Burl. Mag.*, XXXIV (1918), p.41.

19 For instance, Hackenbroch 1960a, figs 50, 51, 56–8, 66, 73, 76, 83, 85, 88.

20 Hackenbroch 1960a, fig.44; Swain 1977, figs 42–3.

21 Solomon, on several panels of embroidery (Hackenbroch 1960a, fig.14, and elsewhere); Tomyris panel, in a needlework picture formerly in the collection of Sir William Plender; Herod (Hackenbroch 1960a, fig.57).

22 A cushion-cover in St John's College, Oxford, was based on a de Vos design in M. Baccius, *Den Schadt der Catholicken Sermoonen* (Antwerp, 1597), *Connoisseur* (Jan. 1916), p.31.

23 T.134-1928; besides the fisherman from the left of Galle's engraving, the designer included a deer from the same suite, *TIB*, 5601.104:12.

15 CHATSWORTH AND HARDWICK

1 Girouard 1989, p.6.

2 *Furniture History*, VII (1971), p.32.

3 For 'Calvin uppon Jobe' see McKerrow and Ferguson 1932, no.148, pp.127–8; a British Library copy is at 3165.f.14. The first French edition was published in Geneva in 1565. For 'the resolution' see Peter Milward, *Religious Controversies of the Elizabethan Age* (London, 1977), pp.73–6; I am indebted to Margaret Aston for this reference.

4 Watt, 1991, p.100, n.102, citing STC 2757–9.

5 Bess demonstrated an apparently impartial attitude to religion in her selection of portraits at Hardwick which included – besides the 'Quene of Scottes' – 'King Henry the Eight, Quene Elizabeth, Quene Marie, Edward the sixt, Duke Dolva [Alba], Charles the Emporer, Cardinal Woolsey, Cardinall Poole, Stephen Gardenner'; Boynton 1971, p.27.

6 The accounts are in the Folger Shakespeare Library in Washington, see J.L. Nevinson, 'Embroidered by Queen and Countess', *CL* (22 Jan. 1976), p.194.

7 A very similar table decorated with elaborate Mannerist cartouches and possibly by the same maker survives in the Burrell Collection in Glasgow.

8 The Four Continents, which have disappeared, were the only others.

9 Roy Strong's opinion, for instance, was that the artist 'is unknown, but probably Flemish, although there is a touch of Fontainebleau in the armoured knights and cavorting horse'. Strong 1969, p.41. Girouard hedged his bets, attributing it to a Flemish or English artist. Various guesses have been made as to the subject: Horace Walpole commented, 'This is said to be the Earl of Shrewsbury coming to court Elizabeth of Hardwicke' (Paget Toynbee (ed.), 'Horace Walpole's Journals of Visits to Country Seats, etc.', *Walpole Society*, 16 (1927–8), p.30); the 1792 Hardwick inventory listed it as 'A painting of an Historical Subject not known – date upon it 1570 . . .'; the Duke of Devonshire's comment was that 'The old picture in a black frame was always supposed to represent Mary informed at Fotheringay of her execution', *Handbook of Chatsworth and Hardwick* (1845), p.213. I am most grateful to Alastair Laing for this information, drawn from the files of The National Trust.

10 In correspondence with the author, Oct. 1994; the painting is discussed in some detail in Hearn 1995, p.101.

11 This list comes from Mark Girouard, 'Elizabethan Chatsworth', *CL* (22 Nov. 1973), p.1672.

12 The relief is now in the Withdrawing Chamber at Hardwick, having been brought by the 6th Duke from Chatsworth where, as he himself said, it had been 'for many years buried in the wooden packing case on the way to, and stumbled over by, all who approached the offices and kitchen'.

13 Because of the subject, the Chatsworth relief has been compared with another (now in the V&A) carved in wood and made for Toddington Manor in Bedfordshire, but if this depends on some printed source it is clearly not the same one, and its gadrooned frame is very much simpler.

14 *TIB*, xv, 58 (406); it was copied for instance in the decoration of a sixteenth century Milanese shield formerly in the collection of the Hon. Mrs Baillie Hamilton (exhibited BFAC exhibition 1900, cat. p.41, pl.LV); and in the decoration of the magnificent overmantel from the Maison de la Prévoté, Saint-Michel, Lorraine (Francis

Russell (ed.), *Christie's Review of the Season* (1992), p.137).

15 McKerrow and Ferguson 1932, no.164.

16 H.43.

17 Riggs 1977, p.334, no.96, fig.145.

18 They are now in the Blue Bed Chamber at Hardwick, where they may have been set up in 1691: the upper entablature is missing, suggesting that the overmantel was reduced to suit the lower ceiling of its new home, see Girouard, op.cit. (at n.11, above), p.1672.

19 The source of the scenes on the table-carpet was identified by Ksynia Marko, at the Textile Conservation Studio, London. The prints are NH, Heemskerck, nos.189–98.

20 Carbrook Hall near Sheffield; I am grateful to David Bostwick for drawing my attention to this overmantel.

21 Margaret Swain has suggested, that the 'sources from which the designs were taken . . . were from the queen's books rather than Bess's, or at least that they came from books with which the queen was familiar' (Swain 1973, p.64); see also three articles by John Nevinson, 'Embroideries at Hardwick Hall', *CL* (29 Nov. 1973); 'An Elizabethan Herbarium: Embroideries by Bess of Hardwick after the woodcuts of Matthioli', *National Trust Yearbook* (1975–6), and 'Embroidered by Queen and Countess', *CL* (22 Jan. 1976). George F. Barwick, *A Book Bound for Mary Queen of Scots* (London, 1901), pp.19–27, gives two lists of books belonging to the Queen: the first, dated 1569, contains no obvious ornament books, but the second – a list of books in Edinburgh Castle delivered by the Earl of Morton to King James VI – includes (besides the popular 'Treatie of the Sacrament by Petir Martir' and 'The Answer to Johnne Calvynnis Epistle') 'The Metamorphosis of Ovid in Italian', which may have been illustrated, 'The Historie of Jasone' – presumably the *Historia Iasonis* illustrated by Leonard Thiry and published between 1540 and 1550 – and 'The Historeis of the Bible in Figures', which must be *The true and lyuely historyke pvrtreatvres of the vvoll Bible* published in Lyons in 1554 with Bernard Salomon's illustrations.

22 Swain 1973, p.63.

23 They are now divided between Oxburgh Hall in Norfolk, the V&A and the Palace of Holyroodhouse in Edinburgh, Swain 1973, p.102.

24 This book was also used in the decoration of a plaster ceiling at Sheffield Manor in the 1570s supplying the motif of a bunch of flowers held in a hand. Later, Paradin's emblem book also seems to have influenced the decoration of the superb contemporary andirons in the High Great Chamber which take the form of caryatid figures supporting a flame, set on pedestals carried on winged sphinxes. The pedestals have a motif of a winged thunderbolt, emblematic of Jupiter and here signifying fire, which derives from fol.130 of Paradin's *Devises Héroïques*, and would have been known to anyone who was familiar with Wollaton, where the same motif was used over the north door.

25 The four survivors are now divided between the hall and the Chapel Landing.

26 For the publishing history of these masks see Byrne 1981, p.37: the suite was copied by an unknown Italian who signed his work IHS and reissued in 1560 with a new titlepage by the French engraver René Boyvin. Perhaps it was

this later set that supplied the source for the embroidery. The masks may also have been used for the decoration of plaster ceilings at one or other of the lost houses the Shrewsburys built, for Floris's masks are a prominent feature of many yeoman farmhouses in north Derbyshire and south Yorkshire – houses whose plasterers had undoubtedly previously been employed at Hardwick itself.

27 Information from Rosalys Coope via David Bostwick.

28 For representations of Roman Charity see, for instance, prints by Hans Sebald Beham (several times), and by an anonymous artist working in the manner of Gaspar Reverdino, but not by many others, *TIB*, 15: 72–5 and *TIB*, 31:2(487).

29 An incomplete suite of prints, lacking no.6, Fortitudo, is in the Museum Boijmans Van Beuningen in Rotterdam, L1965/116A-F (H.IV, nos 32, 33). A third hanging, depicting Hope with Judas, survives in fragmentary state in store at Hardwick. Sardanapalus was mentioned in opposition to a virtue (Prudence) in two fourteenth-century Italian manuscripts (Evans 1931, I, p.141, n.5), named by Boccaccio and described by Filarete in his treatise on architecture (1460) as 'the inventor of the feather bed' (Jack, J. Spector, *Delacroix: The Death of Sardanapalus* (London, 1974), p.50). Spector illustrates (fig.34) the ornament print by Jan Theodor de Bry in which Sardanapalus is depicted (see also Amsterdam 1988, no.47), and his behaviour is the subject of one of a series of four prints dealing with the power of women over men by Raphael Sadeler after J. van Winghe (H.XXI, no.182).

30 German artists were greatly preoccupied with Turkish figures as a result of the Siege of Vienna by the Turks in 1529; see, for instance, the series of woodcuts by Erhard Schoen, B1301.238ff. Enough remains of the third, fragmentary, hanging at Hardwick to show that the figures of Hope and Judas were undoubtedly derived from the same suite of prints by Hans Collaert perhaps after Crispijn van der Broeck.

31 A.H. Malan (ed.), *Famous Homes of Great Britain and Their Stories* (New York and London, 1900), illustration between pp.100 and 101.

32 Is this what the 6th Duke of Devonshire implied in his 1840s handbook to Chatsworth and Hardwick? 'The hangings on the other frames [the Virtues and their Opposites] were in the green room: they appeared to great advantage when relieved from all the frippery with which they had been surrounded by an ignorant hand. To fill the space had been the sole object of the decorator, and half a head appeared on one side of the room, remote from its face and body, and both, being of a man, rose from the petticoat of the cardinal virtue Spes; and these, but detached from each other, you may still see in the small ante-room of the drawing-room and bedchambers.'

33 An item in the list of disputed goods suggests that this may have been amongst furniture 'varnished like brass and other that Cornish and Trumpeter bought in France and cost £100 and above', Henry Kirke, 'An Aristocratic Squabble', *Derbyshire Archaeological Journal*, 32 (1911), see also David Bostwick, 'The French Walnut Furniture at Hardwick Hall', *Furniture History*, XXXI (1995), pp.1–6. The table was described in the 1601 Hardwick inventory as 'drawing table carved and guilt standing uppon sea doges inlayde with

marble stones and wood'. The 6th Duke of Devonshire described it, equally picturesquely, as '. . . a wonderful old table, with sliding tops, in which the travelled curious of former days inserted, as we do now, the bits of marble they may have picked up in their Italian journeys, mounted on chimeras, that is to say, dogs with bosoms and dolphin's tails, with garlands round their necks, and ostrich feathers instead of ears'.

34 The Cavendish, Marian and Shrewsbury hangings in particular answer closely in description to the 'hangings of green velvet, birds and fowls and needlework set upon the velvet' which the Earl claimed in 1586 were made at Sheffield Manor: Kirke, op.cit., pp.19–38. The Earl argued that hangings were 'made by Thomas Lane Ambrose, William Barlow, and Henry Mr Cavendish's man, and had copes of tissue cloth of gold and other things towards the making thereof; meat and drink and wages paid to the embroiderers by the Earl during the working of them . . .' The Countess replied: 'The copes bought by Sir Wm. St Loo. At Chatsworth at the time of the deed of gift. That of the hangings made at Chatsworth some of the Countess grooms women and some boys she kept wrought the most part of them. Never had but one embroiderer at one time that wrought on them. His Lordship never gave the worth of £5 towards the making of them.' Swain 1973, however (pp.102–3) suggests an alternative route by which the Cavendish, Marian and Shrewsbury hangings came to be at Oxburgh.

35 Girouard 1983, p.145.

36 From Serlio (Book IV, fol.61r), the double-scroll pilasters of the chimneypiece in the drawing room (My Ladys Withdrawing Chamber in 1601) – see pp.15–16 for the use of the same woodcut at Baddesley Clinton, Arbury Hall (both Warwickshire), Lower Old Hall, Norland and Wentworth Woodhouse (both Yorkshire); and at Elmore in Gloucestershire; see n.6 on p.303. Serlio's *Libro Estraordinario* may have provided the inspiration for the chimneypieces and overmantels in the gallery, the collaborative work of William Griffin and Thomas Accres. Vredeman's 1577 *Architectura* suggested the overall character of the hall screen (1597), and his 1565 [*Architectura,*] *Das Erst Büch*, pls.I and P, the capitals, metopes, triglyphs and guttae. The same publication provided the source of strapwork decoration in the pilasters of Abraham Smith's hall chimneypiece, while Vredeman's *Pictores, Statuarii . . .* 1563, pl.8, was plundered for details of Thomas Accres's chimneypiece in the High Great Chamber.

37 The classical pilasters that articulated the panelling in the Giants Chamber can still be seen, incorporated into the Mary Queen of Scots Room and the Low Great Chamber of the New Hall, where they must have been taken after the Old Hall fell into disrepair, and probably even before 1764, see Durant and Riden 1984, II, p.liv.

38 See Turner 1927, figs 51–3.

39 William Reason was Bess's receiver of rents, Mark Girouard, *Hardwick Old Hall* (London, 1993).

40 Durant and Riden 1980/84, p.xlix.

41 Veldman 1977, fig.39. All the drawings for the suite are dated 1559.

42 Girouard suggests that the placing of this figure in such a prominent position may allude to the anticipated marriage between Arabella Stuart and Ranuccio Farnese, son of the Duke of Parma,

which was under negotiation in 1591 and 1592; see Girouard op.cit., at n.39, above.

43 By Mark Girouard, following the author's discovery that the Amman woodcut was copied for one of the intarsia panels in the 1570s.

44 Girouard, 'Solomon's Temple in Nottinghamshire', in Girouard 1992, pp.187–96.

45 Most of the masonry at Hardwick was contracted for by John and Christopher Rhodes (Roods in the accounts) who had been the main contractors at Wollaton: besides the lion's share of the external and internal masonry, they carved most of the doorcases and chimneypieces, and were paid in all £890. Individual elements were carved by a number of other masons, Thomas Accres, William Griffin, Henry Nyall, Richard Mallory and Abraham Smith, who was also a plasterer. Most of their work survives intact except for the original overmantels in the Blue Bedchamber and the Withdrawing Chamber: The former disappeared *c*.1691, the latter when the ceiling was lowered before 1764; a list of alterations to the house since it was built is given in Durant and Riden 1980/1984, II, pp.lii, liv and lv.

46 Bostwick 1990, p.77; the soldier to whom he refers is illustrated on p.92 but is mis-captioned as being on the chapel landing.

47 The figure is called Ceres by Girouard 1989 and Bostwick 1990.

48 The date appears on the allegory of Fire, *TIB*, III, 0302.020.

49 Bostwick's identification of Diana herself with the figure of Flora in the titlepage to Gerard's *Herball* (1597) sadly will not do: the pose was quite a common one in sixteenth-century prints and she is much closer to Fides in Hans Collaert's print of Faith, Hope and Charity, after Lambert Lombard, published by Hieronymus Cock in 1558, Riggs, fig.139.

50 In Ovid's *Metamorphoses* Callisto, Diana's favourite nymph, was loved by Zeus and only escaped Diana's retribution by being turned into a bear.

51 Tipping n.d., p.63 lower.

52 From their Scottish provenance, a number have been described as Franco-Scottish, see Nevinson 1940, pp.8–9. Examples include a hanging depicting Lucretia's Banquet, at Compton Verney, which depends upon an engraving by Philips Galle for three of its figures, and a valance showing scenes from the life of Daniel, at Drumlanrig Castle, which derives several of its figures from an engraving after Maarten van Heemskerck; see Swain 1977, pp.343–5.

53 *TIB*, XVI, 377.4.

54 Betty Radice, *Who's Who in the Ancient World* (Harmondsworth, 1980), p.192.

55 Bastelaer 1992, nos.98–108. The print in question is Bastelaer 1992, no.106. Riggs has suggested that the print was engraved not by Frans Huys but by Cornelis Cort, Otto van Simson and Matthias Winner (eds.), *Pieter Bruegel und seine Welt* (Berlin, 1979), p.173.

56 Arnold 1988, pp.77–80; the Hardwick accounts record a payment to Jones in 1601.

57 Foister 1981, p.274: Robert Waryn, a shopkeeper in 1494 . . . had in his parlour: 'iii costryngs [a common type of hanging] of flaunders work paynted with pecocks and flowres', while Richard Bromer, a joiner of London, had in 1490 'iii costrengs stained with the story of danyell'.

58 Cited in Ralph Edwards, *The Dictionary of English Furniture* (London, 1954), II, p.105. The best recent discussions of the use of painted cloths are

59 Watt 1994, p.197.

60 Foister 1981, p.274.

61 It was divided horizontally between 1792 and 1811; the 6th Duke of Devonshire wrote in his Handbook: 'In our youth the pulpit and desk were below, the middle space being open to the lower story [sic]. There must have been great want of offices to make the sacrifice necessary: it was not done in my time, and were I to live here less seldom it should be restored.'

62 MS6, fol.82. I am indebted to David N. Durant for this reference; see also Girouard 1989, p.79, and Kettle 1991, p.10.

63 Veldman 1980, fig.19.

64 TIB, 56.048:1–16, and TIB, 56.049:1–17.

65 Mario Cartaro following Etienne Delaune after Jean Cousin (TIB, 31:17), or Enea Vico after Frans Floris (TIB, 30:13).

66 The painted cloth depicting the Conversion of Saul, for instance, measures 85 × 110¾ inches overall, the pictorial zone occupying 62 × 87 inches.

67 TIB 56.077:3.

68 TIB 56.101:8.

69 Veldman 1986a, pp.82–6, pl.48.

70 Veldman 1986a, no.11.2 (fig.53).

71 For de Vos's suite, Christ, St Paul and the Twelve Apostles, see M.-H. 868–81, and H.XLIV, nos 845–58; the scrolled consoles of the building in the right background appear to have been taken from the frames of the prints which were probably engraved by Johannes Ditmar. Heemskerck's suite is undated but preliminary drawings date from 1565, Veldman 1986a, p.58.

72 For other uses of Galle's prints see pp.115–16.

73 TIB, 5601.016:1.

74 Veldman 1992, pp.227–64: two of the series are illustrated in figs 14–15. See H.XLVI, nos 1257–60 for the whole suite. I have relied heavily on Professor Veldman's article for the information about this suite of prints.

75 H.XLIV, nos 613–20. The prints are undated but Avery 1969, p.12, states that this suite was issued by Crispijn de Passe in 1608, five years after the death of Maarten de Vos and eight years after the Hardwick hangings were painted. This fact suggests that there was an earlier edition which was used by the painter, and Knipping dates the suite c.1600 (Knipping 1974, Plate 316).

76 Durant and Riden 1980/84, p.xxiv.

77 The printed sources are the Huguenot Society of London Publications vols 8 and 10 etc.

78 Philip Heath, in correspondence with the author in 1993.

79 E. Bénézit, Dictionnaire des Peintres, Sculpteurs . . . (Paris, 1948), I, p.363. At this date he was living in the parish of Notre-Dame-de-l'Ecrignole, see E. Giraudet, 'Les artistes tourangeaux', Memoire de la Société Archéologique de Touraine, 33 (1885), p.12; I am indebted to Mme Idelette Ardouin of Tours for this reference and for other information on members of the Baleschoux family.

80 Proceedings of the Huguenot Society of London, LVII. Pierre and Catherine must therefore have arrived in England no later than 1576: if they were Protestants, as seems quite likely, they may have fled as a result of the turmoil that followed the Massacre of St Bartholomew's Eve in Paris in 1572; if they were part of John Balechouse's family they would have arrived before 1570

when he probably painted The Return of Ulysses to Penelope.

81 It is worth mentioning a fourth possibility, that he was another son of Jehan Balechou, born perhaps c.1550, in England twenty years later.

82 I am indebted to Mrs G. Delgueldre for scouring surviving sixteenth-century records in Antwerp in search of Balechoux's name.

83 Charles E. Lart, 'The Huguenot Settlements and Churches in the West of England', Proceedings of the Huguenot Society of London, VII (1903), p.287.

84 Durant and Riden 1980/84, p.xxiii. On 6 November 1591 the joiner was paid for wainscotting a little chamber 'next to John Painter's chamber'; Kettle 1992 is the fullest account of Balechouse's work to date.

85 Girouard 1989, p.88; Kettle 1992, p.11.

86 According to William Senior's survey of 1610 when his name was spelt Ballashawe, Kettle 1992, p.11.

87 Durant 1988, pp.165–77.

88 Barnard and Wace 1928, pp.279–80; they doubt this connection, on the grounds that the most of the replacement arms were actually painted rather than woven; additionally, there was a Mr Sheldon on Bess's staff.

89 Pp.221–34 above.

90 Girouard 1989, p.51.

91 A.H. Malan (ed.), Famous Homes of Great Britain and Their Stories (New York, 1900), opp. p.100.

92 Aston 1993, pp.214–18. I am most grateful to Margaret Aston, Mark Girouard and Alastair Laing for their views on this enigmatic painting, whose commission deserves further investigation.

93 Aston 1993, p.190.

94 Henry Kirke, 'An Aristocratic Squabble', Derbyshire Archaeological Journal, 33 (1911), p.22.

95 Aston 1993, p.26.

96 Aston 1993, fig.56.

97 Thomas 1991, p.166; Aston 1993, pp.74–5; Hill 1994, p.110.

98 It is interesting to note the comment made about The Return of Ulysses to Penelope by the 6th Duke of Devonshire in his 1845 Handbook of Chatsworth and Hardwick: 'The old picture in a black frame was always supposed to represent Mary informed at Fotheringhay of her execution.' If the painting was, as I have surmised, given to the Earl of Shrewsbury by his wife, it is inexplicable how it remained in her possession at Hardwick.

99 For Lucretia (and Susanna) see Veldman 1986b, nos 2–3, pp.113–27.

100 Veldman 1977, p.63.

101 'Ac velut angustas rosa candida pullulat inter Spinas, nec premitur: florent & lilia Vere: Sic iam magnifico vehitur PATIENTIA curru, cui FORTUNA potens, fractis concessit honorem Viribus, & vinclis sequitur constricta, pudore: Hunc SPES alma trahit, volucri STUDIO comitata.' Veldman 1977, caption to fig.39, p.62.

102 Haeger 1986, nos.2–3, pp.128–38.

103 Veldman 1992, pp.227–64.

104 Haeger 1988, p.128.

105 Veldman and de Jonge 1985, pp.178–9.

106 Veldman and de Jonge 1985, p.187.

107 Watt 1994, pp.212–13.

108 Veldman 1977, p.63.

109 Veldman 1977, p.68.

110 Veldman 1980, pp.169–76.

111 Tillyard 1982, pp.68–73.

112 Veldman 1992, pp.237–8.

113 Veldman 1992, p.238; Veldman has also suggested that the prints carry a topical meaning,

being intended to show the Spanish authorities who had recaptured Antwerp in 1585 that de Vos and the publisher Philips Galle were prepared to do their duty as Catholic burghers. If so, this additional function was either unknown to whoever purchased the prints for Bess or considered irrelevant.

114 A.L. Rowse, review of Wallace MacCaffrey, Elizabeth I, in The Times (16 Sept. 1993). Until recently writers have been reticent in expressing opinions about the Queen's personal religious views: Christopher Hibbert, The Virgin Queen: The Personal History of Elizabeth I (New York and London, 1990) is quite clear: 'She warmly approved of a statute passed in her father's time, an Act Abolishing Diversity in Opinions; yet, provided people outwardly conformed to Christian belief and accepted practice, she did not much care what their inner beliefs might be . . . A Protestant at heart, she liked her services, which she attended regularly, to be conducted in English, but she also liked to have crucifixes and candles in her private chapels . . .' (1992 edn, p.89). The fullest discussions of Queen Elizabeth's retention of the cross are to be found in Aston 1988, pp.313–14, and Aston 1993, pp.101–7.

16 SOME CONCLUSIONS

1 Watt 1994, pp.185–6.

2 John Strype, Annals, quoted in Denvir 1988, pp.127–8.

3 Aston 1988, p.313.

4 Aston 1988, p.336.

5 Aston 198, p.294ff.

6 This would have been made for Sir Thomas Tresham of Rushton who was reconciled to the old faith in 1580 by a Jesuit missionary, Robert Parsons. Tresham expressed his religion in the Trinitarian Triangular Lodge and spent in total fifteen years in prison, paying the enormous sum of £7,717. 12s. in fines and penalties; Sir Gyles Isham, Rushton Triangular Lodge, Northamptonshire (London, 1975), pp.5–6.

7 Archer 1990, p.308.

8 W. Prynne, Canterburies Doom (London, 1646), p.59, cited in Archer 1990, pp.314–15.

9 French 1972, pp.113–25. The question of Queen Elizabeth's religious views has been surprisingly little discussed in print until the publication of Patrick Collinson's chapter 'Windows in a Woman's Soul: Questions about the Religion of Queen Elizabeth I', in Collinson 1994. It has too readily been assumed, as by A.F. Pollard, that she was 'sceptical or indifferent', being 'almost as devoid of moral sense as she was of religious temperament' (Collinson 1994, p.87, n.1). This verdict is remarkably similar to that on Bess of Hardwick cited here on p.247.

10 Lionel Cust, 'The Lumley Inventories', Walpole Society, VI (1917–18), pp.15–35, and Mary F.S. Hervey, 'A Lumley Inventory of 1609', ibid., pp.36–50.

11 Halliwell 1854.

12 Leicester kept a 'Christ taken from the Crosse', which Protestants would certainly have considered idolatrous, not at Kenilworth, which the queen visited, but at Wanstead in Essex, otherwise the biblical subjects were mostly drawn from the Old Testament.

13 This would have entailed splitting one scene into two, for Heemskerck's suite has only six plates: *TIB*, 5601.013:1–6, NH, Heemskerck, I, 132–7.

14 Susanna, six plates, H.76–81, 522–7 and 528–33; Prodigal Son, four and six plates, H.50–53 and H.282–7; Tobias, six and ten plates respectively, H.44–9 and H.512–21 (Foister 1981 p.276, has shown that Wassell Wessells – a man probably of Flemish extraction – also had in 1575 'a storie of Tobias' in his parlour); David, H.491–500 and H.501–5; Abraham, four plates, H.16–19; Sampson, six plates, H.224–9; Judith and Holofernes, eight plates, H.272–9; Jacob, in thirteen plates, H.33–45.

15 Recounted by Margaret Jourdain, 'Embroideries in the Possession of St. John's College, Oxford', *Connoisseur* (Jan. 1916), pp.30–31.

16 Paget Toynbee, 'Horace Walpole's Journals of Visits to Country Seats, &c.', *Walpole Society*, XVI (1927–8), pp.9–80 (7 June 1761, p.35). For a modern explanation of the meaning of this portrait, which is at Hatfield House in Hertfordshire, see Yates 1977, pp.216–8.

17 Foister 1981, p.279.

18 Charter of the Painter-Stainers' Company, 1581 (Watt 1994, p.198, citing W.A.D. Englefield, *The History of the Painter-Stainers' Company of London* (London, 1936), p.68).

19 There is a single hanging of the later sixteenth century at Christchurch Mansion, Ipswich; and a set of *c.*1700 at Owlpen Old Manor in Gloucestershire, *CL*, XCVI (25 Aug. 1944), p.329 and CX (9 Nov. 1951), pp.1544–7.

20 There are well-known sets by Hans Burgkmair, Daniel Hopfer, Lucas van Leyden, Cornelis van Oostsanen, the monogrammist MG, Virgil Solis, Maarten van Heemskerck, Nicolaes de Bruyn, Maarten de Vos, Antonio Tempesta – and a less familiar set engraved by Nicolaes de Bruyn and published by Assuwerus van Londerseel (eight prints from this set published are in Antwerp, Stedelijk Prentenkabinet, F.II/B.505–12, inv. nos 6181–8); individual figures also appear in single prints, for instance in a titlepage border by Hans Holbein, Michael Kirmer, Conrad Hillebrand, and Johann Hauer (Holbein, H.31a; Kirmer, Warncke 1979, nos.499–500; Hillebrand, H.1–4; and Hauer, H.3–4).

21 F.W. Reader, 'Tudor Mural Paintings in the Lesser House in Buckinghamshire', *Archaeological Journal*, 89 (1932), p.142.

22 Horst Schroeder, 'The Nine Worthies a Supplement', *Archiv fur das Studium der neueren Sprachen und Literaturen*, 218 (1981), p.336.

23 A broadside ballad of *c.*1626 entitled *A brave warlike song. Containing a brief rehearsall of the deeds of chivalry, performed by the nine worthies of the world, the seaven champions of Christendome, with many other remarkable warriours* contrasts with a woodcut emblem-type book, Richard Lloyd's *A briefe discourse of the . . . actes and conquests of the nine worthies*, 1584; Watt 1994, p.213.

24 Nevinson 1964, p.106.

25 There is no evidence for the use in humbler circumstances of the sets by Nicolaes de Bruyn (most often noted in England as busts in roundels on the plasterwork ceilings of substantial early seventeenth-century houses) or Maarten van Heemskerck (the painted cloths at Hardwick and wallpaintings at North Mymms Park in Hertfordshire). A set, now unidentifiable, inspired figures of the Worthies in niches in the hall at Blickling Hall in Norfolk. James Avis was paid in 1627 'for makinge and finishinge' a statue of Hector, but by November 1765, when the Earl of Buckingham was reluctantly about to destroy them, they were very damaged: 'Some tributory sorrow should however be paid to the nine worthies; but Hector has lost his spear and his nose, David his harp, Godfrey of Boulogne his ears, Alexander the Great his highest shoulder and part of Joshua's belly is fallen in . . . Hector is at all events determined to leave his niche' (Stanley – Millson and Newman 1986, p.10).

26 Watt 1994, pp.202–3.

27 Hartley 1984, p.39.

28 The value of establishing family links has been demonstrated recently for the patronage of carvers and plasterers in Bostwick 1994, pp.24–8; the educational value of attendance at the universities of Oxford and Cambridge, and at the Inns of Court, has been explored amongst families in late Tudor and early Stuart Northumberland, S.J. Watts with Susan Watts, *From Border to Middle Shire Northumberland, 1586–1625* (Leicester, 1975), pp.91–3.

29 Yates 1975, p.XVII.

30 Van Dorsten 1970, p.27.

31 Van Dorsten 1970, p.34. Plantin's active membership of the Family of Love, which was propounded by Max Rooses, *Christophe Plantin, Imprimeur anversois* (Antwerp, 1882), p.75, and followed – somewhat more critically – by Leon Voet (Voet 1969–72, I, p.386), has been doubted more recently by Paul Valkema Blouw, 'Was Plantin a member of the Family of Love? Notes on his dealings with Hendrik Niclaes', *Quaerendo*, 23/1 (Winter 1993), pp.3–23.

32 *A supplication of the Family of Love . . .*, (Cambridge, 1606), cited in Marsh 1994, p.119.

33 After all, something of this kind occurred in music: adherents of the old faith saw the exile of the Israelites in Babylon as an analogy of the plight of Catholics in Elizabethan England, and used the text of Psalm 137 as a gesture of solidarity. In an exchange of eight-part motets on this psalm in 1583–4, Philippo de Monte opened with 'Super flumina Babylonis' and William Byrd responded with 'Quomodo cantabimus'. See A.L. Rowse, *The Elizabethan Renaissance: The Cultural Achievement* (London and Basingstoke, 1972), p.94.

34 Patrick Collinson, 'Windows in a Woman's Soul: Questions about the Religion of Queen Elizabeth I', in Collinson 1994, pp.87–118.

35 Collinson 1988, p.117; for a discussion of this assertion on the evidence of 'cheap print' see Watt 1994, p.134ff.

36 Thomas 1991, p.185.

Bibliography

Airs 1994
   Malcolm Airs (ed.), *The Tudor and Jacobean Great House* (Oxford, 1994)
Alcorn 1993
   Ellenor M. Alcorn, *English Silver in the Museum of Fine Arts, Boston*, I, *Silver before 1697* (Boston, Mass., 1993)
Amsterdam 1986
   J.P. Filedt Kok, W. Halsema Kubes and W. Th. Kloek, *Kunst voor de beeldenstorm* (Amsterdam, 1986)
Amsterdam 1988
   Marijnke de Jong and Irene de Groot, *Ornamentprenten in het Rijksprentenkabinet: I, 15de en 16de Eeuwe* (Amsterdam, 1988)
Amsterdam 1993
   Ger Luijten et al. (eds.), *Dawn of the Golden Age: Northern Netherlandish Art, 1580–1620* (Amsterdam, 1993)
Archer 1976
   Michael Archer, '"Beest, Bird or Flower": Stained Glass at Gorhambury House', *Country Life*, CLIX (3 and 10 June 1976), pp.1451–4, 1562–4
Archer 1990
   Michael Archer, 'Richard Butler, Glass-painter', *Burlington Magazine*, CXXXII (1990), pp.308–15
Arnold 1988
   Janet Arnold, *Queen Elizabeth's Wardrobe Unlock'd* (Leeds, 1988)
Arthur 1995
   Liz Arthur, *Embroidery 1600–1700 at the Burrell Collection* (Glasgow and London, 1995)
Aston 1988
   Margaret Aston, *England's Iconoclasts*, I, *Laws Against Images* (Oxford, 1988)
Aston 1993
   Margaret Aston, *The King's Bedpost: Reformation and Iconography in a Tudor Group Portrait* (Cambridge, 1993)
Auerbach 1954
   Erna Auerbach, *Tudor Artists* (London, 1954)
Auerbach and Adams 1971
   Erna Auerbach and C. Kingsley Adams, *Paintings and Sculpture at Hatfield House* (London, 1971)
Avery 1969
   Charles Avery, *The Rood-Loft from Hertogenbosch* (London, 1969) reprinted from *The Victoria and Albert Museum Yearbook*
Baggs 1969
   A.P. Baggs, 'Sixteenth-Century Terra-Cotta Tombs in East Anglia', *Archaeological Journal*, CXXV (1969), pp.295–301
Bankart 1908
   G.P. Bankart, *The Art of the Plasterer* (London, 1908)
Barnard and Wace 1928
   E.A.B. Barnard and A.J.B. Wace, 'The Sheldon Tapestry Weavers and their Work', *Archaeologia*, LXXVIII (1928), pp.255–314
Bastelaer 1992
   René van Bastelaer, *The Prints of Pieter Bruegel the Elder* (San Francisco, 1992)
Baty 1982
   Mavis Baty, *Oxford Gardens: The University's Influence on Garden History* (Amersham, 1982)
Bayliss 1993
   Jon Bayliss, 'A Dutch Carver: Garrett Hollemans I in England', *Church Monuments*, VIII (1993), pp.45–56
Berliner and Egger 1981
   Rudolf Berliner and Gerhart Egger, *Ornamentale Vorlageblatter des 15. bis 19. Jahrhunderts* (Munich, 1981)
Biddle 1970
   Martin Biddle, 'A Fontainebleau Chimneypiece at Broughton Castle, Oxfordshire', in Howard Colvin and John Harris (eds.), *The Country Seat: Studies in the History of the British Country House* (London, 1970), pp.9–12
Blunt 1969
   Anthony Blunt, 'L'Influence Française sur l'architecture et la sculpture décorative en Angleterre pendant la première moitié du XVIe siècle', *Revue de l'Art*, IV (1969), pp.17–29
Blunt 1980
   Anthony Blunt, *Art and Architecture in France, 1500–1700* (Harmondsworth, 1980 edn)
Bober and Rubinstein 1986
   P.P. Bober and R.O. Rubinstein, *Renaissance Artists and Antique Sculpture* (London, 1986)
Bostwick 1990
   David Bostwick, 'Plaster to Puzzle Over', *Country Life*, CLXXXIV (12 July 1990), pp.90–93; 'Plaster Puzzle Decoded', *Country Life*, CLXXXIV (26 July 1990), pp.76–9
Bostwick 1993
   David Bostwick, 'Decorative Plasterwork of the Yorkshire Region, 1570–1670', unpublished PhD. dissertation, University of Sheffield (1993)
Bostwick 1994
   David Bostwick, 'The Jacobean Plasterwork at Gawthorpe Hall and its Sources', *Apollo*, CXXXIX (May 1994), pp.24–8
Boynton 1971
   Lindsay Boynton (ed.), *The Hardwick Hall Inventories of 1601* (London, 1971)
Brooke 1987
   Xanthe Brooke, 'Design Sources for 17th-Century Pictorial Embroideries', in *'Men, Birds, Beasts and Flowers': An Exhibition of Seventeenth Century Pictorial Needlework* (Bath, 1987)
Busch 1969
   A.F. Busch. *Handbook of Renaissance Ornament* (New York, 1969)
Byrne 1981
   Janet Byrne, *Renaissance Ornament Prints and Drawings* (New York, 1981)
Cabot 1946
   Nancy Graves Cabot, 'Pattern Sources of Scriptural Subjects in Tudor and Stuart Embroideries', *The Bulletin of the Needle and Bobbin Club*, 30, nos 1 and 2 (1946), pp.3–57
Carrick 1989
   Muriel Carrick, *Essex Domestic Wall Paintings* (Colchester, 1989)
Cescinsky and Gribble 1922
   Herbert Cescinsky and Ernest R. Gribble, *Early English Furniture and Woodwork* (London, 1922)
Chaney 1991
   Edward Chaney, 'Henry VIII's Tombs, "Plus catholique que le pape?"', *Apollo*, CXXXIV, no.356 (October 1991), pp.234–8
Chaney and Mack 1990
   Edward Chaney and Peter Mack (eds.), *England and the Continental Renaissance* (London, 1990)
Clair 1960
   Colin Clair, *Christopher Plantin* (London, 1960)
Clark 1966
   Kenneth Clark, *Rembrandt and the Italian Renaissance* (London, 1966)
Clark 1983
   Jane Clark, 'A Set of Tapestries for Leicester House in The Strand', *Burlington Magazine*, CXXV (May 1983), pp.283–4
Clifford Smith 1930
   H. Clifford Smith, *Catalogue of English Furniture and Woodwork*, II, *Late Tudor and Early Stuart* (London, 1930)
Cole 1980
   William Cole, 'Stained Glass after Designs by Maarten van Heemskerck', *Antiquaries Journal*, LX (1980), pp 247–67
Cole 1993
   William Cole, *A Catalogue of Netherlandish and North European Roundels in Britain* (Oxford, 1993)

Collijn 1933
Isak Collijn. *Katalog der Ornamentstichsammlung des Magnus Gabriel De la Gardie in der Kgl. Bibliothek zu Stockholm* (Stockholm and Uppsala, 1933)

Collinson 1988
Patrick Collinson, *The Birthpangs of Protestant England. Religious and Cultural Change in the Sixteenth and Seventeenth Centuries* (Basingstoke and London, 1988)

Collinson 1994
Patrick Collinson, *Elizabethan Essays* (London, 1994)

Colvin 1978
Howard Colvin, *Biographical Dictionary of British Architects, 1600–1840* (2nd edn, London, 1978)

Corbett and Lightbown 1979
Marjorie Corbett and Ronald Lightbown, *The Comely Frontispiece: The Emblematic Titlepage in England, 1550–1660* (London, 1979)

Croft-Murray 1962
Edward Croft-Murray, *Decorative Painting in England, 1537–1837*, I (London, 1962)

Davies 1964
D.W. Davies, *Dutch Influences on English Culture, 1558–1625* (Ithaca, New York, 1964)

Delen 1934–5
A.J.J. Delen, *Histoire de la Graveure dans les anciens Pays-Bas et dans les Provinces Belges des origines jusqu'à la fin du XVIIIe siècle* (Paris, 1934–5)

Denvir 1988
Bernard Denvir (ed.), *From the Middle Ages to the Stuarts: Art, Design and Society before 1689* (London, 1988)

Dickens 1968
A.G. Dickens, *Reformation and Society in Sixteenth-Century Europe* (New York, 1968)

Dickens 1989
A.G. Dickens, *The English Reformation* (London, 1989)

Dinsmoor 1942
W.B. Dinsmoor. 'The Literary Remains of Sebastiano Serlio: I', *Art Bulletin*, XXIV (1942), pp.55–92.

Van Dorsten 1970
J.A. van Dorsten, *The Radical Arts: First Decade of an Elizabethan Renaissance* (Leiden and London, 1970)

Drury 1983
P.J. Drury, '"A Fayre House, Buylt by Sir Thomas Smith": The Development of Hill Hall, Essex, 1557–81', *Journal of the British Archaeological Association*, CXXXVI (1983), pp.98–123.

Durant 1988
David N. Durant, *Bess of Hardwick, Portrait of an Elizabethan Dynast* (London, 1988)

Durant and Riden 1980/84
David N. Durant and Philip Riden (eds.), *The Building of Hardwick Hall* (Chesterfield, 1980 and 1984)

Eisenstein 1993
Elizabeth Eisenstein, *The Printing Press as an Agent of Change: Communications and Cultural Transformations in Early-Modern Europe* (Cambridge, 1993 edn)

Elton 1974
Geoffrey Elton, *England under the Tudors* (London, 1974 edn)

Evans 1931
Joan Evans, *Pattern: A Study of Ornament in Western Europe, 1180–1900* (Oxford, 1931)

Fairclough 1984
Oliver Fairclough, *The Grand Old Mansion: The Holtes and their Successors at Aston Hall, 1618–1864* (Birmingham, 1984)

Farmer 1984
Norman K. Farmer, Jr, *Poets and the Visual Arts in Renaissance England* (Austin, Tex., 1984)

Finsten 1981
Jill Finsten, *Isaac Oliver: Art at the Courts of Elizabeth I and James I* (New York and London, 1981)

Foister 1981
Susan Foister, 'Paintings and Other Works of Art in Sixteenth-Century English inventories', *Burlington Magazine*, CXXIII, no.938 (May 1981), pp.273–82

Ford 1989
Boris Ford (ed.), *The Cambridge Guide to the Arts in Britain*, III, *Renaissance and Reformation* (Cambridge, 1989)

Forman 1971
Benno Forman, 'Continental Furniture Craftsmen in London: 1511–1625', *Furniture History*, VII (1971), pp.94–120

Forssman 1956
Erik Forssman, *Die Saule und Ornament, Studienzum Problem des Manierismus in den norischen Saulenbuchern und Vorlageblattern des 16. und 17. Jahrhunderts* (Stockholm, 1956)

Freedberg 1987
David Freedberg, 'Aertsen, Heemskerck and the crisis of art in the Netherlands', *Bulletin van het Rijksmuseum*, 35, no.3 (1987), pp.224–41

French 1957
Kathleen and Cecil French, 'Devonshire Plasterwork', *Transactions of the Devonshire Association for the Advancement of Science, Literature and Art*, 89 (1957), pp.124–44

French 1972
Peter J. French, *John Dee: The World of an Elizabethan Magus* (London, 1972)

Fuhring 1989
Peter Fuhring, 'Ornament Prints in Amsterdam', *Print Quarterly*, VI, no.3 (September 1989), pp.322–34

Gapper 1990
Claire Gapper, 'Decorative Plasterwork Ceilings in London, c.1540–c.1620', unpublished MA dissertation, University of London (1990)

Van Gelder 1964
H.A. Enno van Gelder, *The Two Reformations in the Sixteenth Century* (The Hague, 1964)

Gent 1981
Lucy Gent, *Picture and Poetry, 1560–1620* (Leamington Spa, 1981)

Gent 1995
Lucy Gent (ed.), *Albion's Classicism: The Visual Arts in Britain, 1550–1660* (New Haven and London, 1995)

Gent and Llewellyn 1990

Lucy Gent and Nigel Llewellyn (eds.), *Renaissance Bodies: The Human Figure in English Culture, c.1540–1660* (London, 1990)

Girouard 1962
Mark Girouard (ed.), 'The Smythson Collection of the Royal Institute of British Architects', *Architectural History*, 5 (1962), pp.23–184

Girouard 1983
Mark Girouard, *Robert Smythson and the English Country House* (New Haven and London, 1983)

Girouard 1985
Mark Girouard, *Cities and People: A Social and Architectural History* (New Haven and London, 1985)

Girouard 1989
Mark Girouard, *Hardwick Hall*, guidebook (London, 1989)

Girouard 1992
Mark Girouard, *Town and Country* (New Haven and London, 1992)

Glanville 1990
Philippa Glanville, *Silver in Tudor and Early Stuart England: A Social History and Catalogue of the National Collection* [at the Victoria and Albert Museum], (London, 1990)

Globe 1985
Alexander Globe, *Peter Stent, London Printseller circa 1642–65* (Vancouver, 1985)

Gotch 1914
J.A. Gotch, *Early Renaissance Architecture in England* (London, 2nd edn 1914)

Gould 1962
Cecil Gould, 'Sebastiano Serlio and Venetian Painting', *Journal of the Warburg and Courtauld Institutes*, XXV (1962), pp.56–64

Hackenbroch 1960a
Yvonne Hackenbroch, *English and other Needlework Tapestries and Textiles in the Irwin Untermyer Collection* (London, 1960)

Hackenbroch 1960b
Yvonne Hackenbroch, 'A Mysterious Monogram', *Metropolitan Museum of Art Bulletin* (Summer 1960), pp.18–24

Hackenbroch 1979
Yvonne Hackenbroch, *Renaissance Jewellery* (Munich, 1979)

Haeger 1986
Barbara Haeger, 'The Prodigal Son in Sixteenth and Seventeenth-century Netherlandish Art: Depictions of the Parable and the Evolution of a Catholic Image', *Simiolus*, 16, nos.2–3 (1986), pp.128–38

Haeger 1988
Barbara Haeger, 'Philips Galle's engravings after Maarten van Heemskerck's *Parable of the Prodigal Son*', *Oud Holland*, 102 (1988), pp.127–40

Hall 1984
James Hall, *Dictionary of Subjects and Symbols in Art* (London, 1984)

Halliwell 1854
J.O. Halliwell, *Ancient Inventories of Furniture, Pictures, Tapestry, Plate, etc. Illustrative of the domestic manner of the English in the sixteenth and seventeenth centuries. Selected from unedited Manuscripts and edited by J.O.H.* (London, 1854)

Harris and Higgott 1989
John Harris and Gordon Higgott, *Inigo Jones: Complete Architectural Drawings* (London, 1989)

Harris, Orgel and Strong 1973
John Harris, Stephen Orgel and Roy Strong, *The King's Arcadia: Inigo Jones and the Stuart Court* (London, 1973)

Hartley 1984
Susan Hartley, 'The Artist Patronage and Influence of Bishop John Cosin, 1595–1672', unpublished BA dissertation, Leeds University (1984)

Hayward 1976
J.F. Hayward, *Virtuoso Goldsmiths and the Triumph of Mannerism, 1540–1620* (London, 1976)

Hearn 1995
Karen Hearn (ed.), *Dynasties: Painting in Tudor and Jacobean England 1530–1630* (London, 1995)

Hedicke 1913
Robert Hedicke, *Cornelis Floris und die Florisdekoration* (Berlin, 1913)

Hernmarkt 1977
Carl Hernmarkt, *The Art of The European Silversmith, 1430–1830* (London and New York, 1977)

Hill 1994
Christopher Hill, *The English Bible and the Seventeenth-Century Revolution* (London, 1994)

Hitchcock 1981
H.R. Hitchcock, *German Renaissance Architecture* (Princeton, 1981)

Hodnett 1971
Edward Hodnett, *Marcus Gheeraerts the Elder of Bruges, London and Antwerp* (Utrecht, 1971)

Howard 1987
Murice Howard, *The Early Tudor Country House: Architecture and Politics, 1490–1550* (London, 1987)

Howard 1990
Maurice Howard, 'Self-Fashioning and the Classical Moment in Mid-Sixteenth-Century English Architecture', in Lucy Gent and Nigel Llewellyn (eds.), *Renaissance Bodies: The Human Figure in English Culture, c.1540–1660* (London, 1990), pp.198–217

Hülsen and Egger 1975
C. Hülsen and H. Egger, *Die römischer Skizzenbücher von Marten van Heemskerck im Königlichen Kupferstichkabinett zu Berlin* (Soest, 1975)

Humphreys 1924
John Humphreys, 'Elizabethan Sheldon Tapestries', *Archaeologia*, LXXIV (1923–4), pp.181–202.

Hutton 1994
Ronald Hutton, *The Rise and Fall of Merry England: The Ritual Year, 1400–1700* (Oxford and New York, 1994)

Imrie 1993
Margaret Imrie, *The Manor Houses of Burton Agnes and their Owners* (Beverley, 1993)

Irmscher 1985/86
Gunther Irmscher, 'Hans Vredeman de Vries als Zeichner', I, *Kunsthistorisches Jahrbuch Graz*, XXI (1985), pp.123–42; idem., II, XXII (1986), pp.79–117

Jervis 1974
Simon Jervis, *Printed Furniture Designs before 1650* (Leeds, 1974)

Jervis 1984
Simon Jervis, *The Penguin Dictionary of Design and Designers* (Harmondsworth, 1984)

Jessen 1920
P. Jessen, *Der Ornamentstich* (Berlin, 1920)

Jourdain 1924
Margaret Jourdain, *English Decoration and Furniture of the Early Renaissance* (London, 1924)

Jourdain 1926
Margaret Jourdain, *English Decorative Plasterwork of the Renaissance* (London, 1926)

Kendrick 1912
A.F. Kendrick, 'The Hatfield Tapestries of the Seasons', *Walpole Society*, II (1912), pp.89–97

Kendrick 1924
A.F. Kendrick, *Victoria and Albert Museum, Department of Textiles, Catalogue of Tapestries* (London, 1924)

Kendrick 1926
A.F. Kendrick, 'Some Barcheston Tapestries', *Walpole Society*, XIV (1925–6), pp.27–42

Kerrich 1829
Thomas Kerrich, *A Catalogue of the Prints which have been Engraved after Martin van Heemskerck* (Cambridge, 1829)

Kettle 1992
Pamela Kettle, *A History of the Hardwick Inn* (Sutton Scarsdale, Derbys., 1992)

Knipping 1939
J.B. Knipping, *De Iconografie van de Contra-Reformatie in de Nederlanden* (Hilversum, 1939)

Koenigsberger, Mosse and Bowler 1989
H.G. Koenigsberger, George L. Mosse and G.Q. Bowler, *Europe in the Sixteenth Century* (London and New York, 1989)

Kuyper 1980
W. Kuyper, *Dutch Classicist Architecture* (Delft, 1980)

Ladd 1978
Frederick J. Ladd, *Architects at Corsham Court* (Bradford-on-Avon, 1978)

Landau and Parshall 1994
David Landau and Peter Parshall, *The Renaissance Print, 1470–1550* (New Haven and London, 1994)

Latham 1980
Robert Latham (gen. ed.), *Catalogue of the Pepys Library at Magdalene College, Cambridge*, III, *Prints and Drawings*, i; *General*, A.W. Aspinal (ed.) (Woodbridge, 1980)

Los Angeles 1994
Henri Zerner et al., *The French Renaissance in Prints from the Bibliothèque Nationale de France* (Grunwald Center for the Graphic Arts, University of California, Los Angeles, 1994)

MaCaffrey 1975
Wallace T. MacCaffrey, *Exeter, 1540–1640* (Cambridge, Mass., and London, 1975)

McKerrow and Ferguson 1932
R.B. McKerrow and F.S. Ferguson, *Titlepage Borders Used in England and Scotland, 1485–1640* (London, 1932)

Mann 1933
J.G. Mann, 'English Church Monuments, 1536–1625', *Walpole Society*, XXI (1932–3), pp.1–22

Marsh 1994
Christopher W. Marsh, *The Family of Love in English Society* (Cambridge, 1994)

Mauquoy-Hendrickx 1978
Marie Mauquoy-Hendrickx, *Les Estampes des Wierix* (Brussels, 1978)

Mercer 1962
Eric Mercer, *English Art, 1553–1625* (Oxford, 1962)

Mielke 1967
Hans Mielke, *Hans Vredeman de Vries* (Berlin, 1967)

Mielke 1975
Hans Mielke, 'Antwerpener Graphik in der 2. Halfte des 16. Jahrhunderts. Der Thesaurus veteris et novi Testamenti des Gerard de Jode (1585) und seiner Kunstler', *Zeitschrift für Kunstgeschichte*, 38 (1975), pp.29–83

Moore 1988
Andrew W. Moore, *Dutch and Flemish Painting in Norfolk* (London, 1988)

Mowl 1993
Timothy Mowl, *Elizabethan and Jacobean Style* (London, 1993)

Moxey 1976
Keith P.F. Moxey, 'The Humanist Market Scenes of Joachim Beuckelaer: Moralizing Exempla or "Slices of Life"', *Jaarboek van het Koninklijk Museum voor Schone Kunsten te Antwerpen* (1976), pp.109–87

Nevinson 1938
John Nevinson, *Catalogue of English Domestic Embroidery of the Sixteenth and Seventeenth Centuries*, Victoria and Albert Museum (London, 1938)

Nevinson 1940
J.L. Nevinson, 'English Domestic Embroidery Patterns of the sixteenth and seventeenth centuries', *Walpole Society*, XXVIII (1939–40), pp.1–13

Nevinson 1950
J.L. Nevinson, 'Fashion Plates and Fashion, 1625–35', *Apollo*, LI (May 1950), pp.138–40

Nevinson 1964
J.L. Nevinson, 'A Show of the Nine Worthies', *Shakespeare Quarterly*, 14 (1964), pp.103–7

Nevinson 1968
J.L. Nevinson, 'The Embroidery Patterns of Thomas Trevelyon', *Walpole Society*, XLI (1966–8), pp.1–38

Nicholl 1993
Charles Nicholl, *The Reckoning: The Murder of Christopher Marlowe* (London, 1993 edn)

Nordenfalk 1985
Carl Nordenfalk, 'The Five Senses in Flemish Art before 1600', *Netherlandish Mannerism, Nationalmusei Skriftserie*, n.s.4 (Stockholm, 1985), pp.135–54

O'Dell-Franke 1977
I. O'Dell-Franke, *Kupferstich und Radierungen aus der Werkstatt des Virgil Solis* (Wiesbaden, 1977)

Oman 1978
Charles Oman, *English Engraved Silver, 1150 to 1900* (London, 1978)

Von der Osten and Vey 1969
Gert von der Osten and Horst Vey, *Painting and Sculpture in Germany and the Netherlands, 1500–1600* (Harmondsworth, 1969)

Oswald 1959
Arthur Oswald, *Country Houses of Dorset* (London, 1959)

Panofsky 1970
Erwin Panofsky, *Meaning in the Visual Arts* (Harmondsworth, 1970)

Parker 1979
Geoffrey Parker, *The Dutch Revolt* (Harmonsdworth, 1979)

Penoyre 1994
John and Jane Penoyre, *Decorative Plasterwork in the Houses of Somerset, 1500–1700* (Taunton, 1994)

Puloy 1983
Monica Puloy, 'Decorative Plasterwork in Hertfordshire', *Hertfordshire Archaeology*, 8 (1983), pp.144–99

Purvis 1935
J.S. Purvis, 'The Use of Continental Woodcuts and Prints by the "Ripon School" of Wood-carvers in the early Sixteenth Century', *Archaeologia*, LXXXV (2nd ser., XXXV, 1935), pp.107–28

Ramsay 1975
G.D. Ramsay, *The City of London in International Politics at the Accession of Elizabeth Tudor* (Manchester, 1975)

Ramsay 1986
G.D. Ramsay, *The Queen's Merchants and the Revolt of the Netherlands*, II (Manchester and Dover, N.H., 1986)

Riggs 1977
Timothy A. Riggs, *Hieronymus Cock (1510–70): Printmaker and Publisher in Antwerp at the Sign of the Four Winds* (New York and London, 1977)

Riggs and Silver 1993
Timothy Riggs and Larry Silver (eds.), *Graven Images: The Rise of Professional Printmakers in Antwerp and Haarlem, 1540–1640* (Evanston, Illinois, 1993)

Roberts 1941
J.F.A. Roberts, 'English Wall Paintings after Italian Engravings', *Burlington Magazine*, LXXVIII (1941), pp.86–92

Rowse 1972
A.L. Rowse, *The Elizabethan Renaissance: The Cultural Achievement* (London, 1972)

Saunders 1979
Eleanor A. Saunders, 'A Commentary on Iconoclasm in Several Print Series by Maarten van Heemsckerck', *Simiolus*, 10 (1978–9), pp.59–83

Saxl and Wittkower 1948
F. Saxl and R. Wittkower, *British Art and the Mediterranean* (London, 1948)

Schele 1965
Sune Schele, *Cornelis Bos: A Study of the Origins of the Netherlands Grotesque* (Stockholm, 1965)

Sellink 1992
M. Sellink, 'Philips Galle als uitgever van prenten aan het eind van de zestiende eeuwe', *De zeventiende eeuw*, 8 (1992), pp.13–26

Sellink 1992a
M. Sellink, '"As a Guide to the Highest Learning": An Antwerp Book Dated 1589', *Simiolus*, 21 (1992), pp.40–53

Sellink 1993
M. Sellink, 'Een teruggevonden *Laetste Oordeel* van Hendrick Goltzius relatie met de Antwerpse uitgever Philips Galle', *Nederlandse Kunsthistorisch Jaarboek*, 42–3 (1991–2), pp.145–58

Simpson 1977
Richard Simpson, 'Sir Thomas Smith and the Wall Paintings at Hill Hall, Essex . . .', *Journal of the British Archaeological Association*, CXXX (1977), pp.1–20

Stanley-Millson and Newman 1986
Caroline Stanley-Millson and John Newman, 'Blickling Hall: The Building of a Jacobean Mansion', *Architectural History*, 29 (1986), pp.1–42

Strong 1960
Roy C. Strong, 'Edward VI and the Pope: A Tudor Anti-papal Allegory and its Setting', *Journal of the Warburg and Courtauld Institutes*, XXIII (1960), pp.311–13

Strong 1967
Roy Strong, *Holbein and Henry VIII* (London, 1967)

Strong 1969a
Roy Strong, *The English Icon. Elizabethan and Jacobean Portraiture* (London, 1969)

Strong 1969b
Roy Strong, *Tudor and Jacobean Portraits*, I (London, 1969)

Strong 1986
Roy Strong, *Henry Prince of Wales and England's Lost Renaissance* (London, 1986)

Summerson 1966
John Summerson, 'The Book of Architecture of John Thorpe in Sir John Soane's Museum', *Walpole Society*, XL (1964–6)

Summerson 1977
John Summerson, *Architecture in Britain, 1530–1830* (Harmondsworth, 1977)

Summerson 1990
John Summerson, 'John Thorpe and the Thorpes of Kingscliffe', *The Unromantic Castle* (London, 1990), pp.17–40

Swain 1973
Margaret Swain, *The Needlework of Mary Queen of Scots* (New York and London, 1973)

Swain 1977
Margaret Swain, 'Engravings and Needlework of the Sixteenth Century', *Burlington Magazine*, CXIX (May 1977), pp.343–4

Swain 1980
Margaret Swain, *Figures on Fabric: Embroidery Design Sources and Their Application* (London, 1980)

Thomas 1991
Keith Thomas, *Religion and the Decline of Magic* (London, 1991 edn)

Thurley 1993
Simon Thurley, *The Royal Palaces of Tudor England* (New Haven and London, 1993)

Tillyard 1982
E.M.W. Tillyard, *The Elizabethan World Picture* (Harmondsworth, 1982 edn)

Tipping n.d.
H. Avray Tipping, *English Homes of the Early Renaissance* (London, n.d.)

Tipping 1927
H. Avray Tipping, *English Homes, Period III, II, Late Tudor and Early Stuart, 1558–1649* (London, 1927)

Tipping 1929
H. Avray Tipping, *English Homes, Period III, I, Late Tudor and Early Stuart, 1558–1649* (London, 1929 edn)

Turner 1927
L. Turner, *Decorative Plasterwork in Great Britain* (London, 1927)

Van den Coelen 1995
Peter van den Coelen, 'Cornelis Bos – where did he go? Some new discoveries and hypotheses about a sixteenth-century engraver and publisher', *Simiolus*, 23 (1995), pp.119–46

Van Uchelen 1987
Ton Croiset van Uchelen, 'The mysterious writing-master Clemens Perret', *Quaerendo*, XVII/1 (Winter 1987), pp.3–44

Veldman 1977
Ilja M. Veldman, *Maarten van Heemskerck and Dutch Humanism in the Sixteenth Century* (Maarssen, 1977)

Veldman 1980
Ilja Veldman, 'Seasons, Planets and Temperaments in the Work of Maarten van Heemskerck: Cosmo-astrological Allegory in Sixteenth-century Netherlandish Prints', *Simiolus*, 11 (1980), pp.149–76

Veldman 1983
Ilja Veldman, 'De macht van de planeten over het mensdorm in prenten naar Maarten de Vos', *Bulletin van het Rijksmuseum*, 31, no.1 (1983), pp.21–53

Veldman 1986a
Ilja Veldman, *Leerijke reeksen van Maarten van Heemskerck* (The Hague, 1986)

Veldman 1986b
Ilja M. Veldman, 'Lessons for Ladies: A Selection of Sixteenth and Seventeenth-century Dutch Prints', *Simiolus*, 16, no.2/3 (1986), pp.113–27

Veldman 1987
Ilja M. Veldman, 'Maarten van Heemskercks visie op het geloof', *Bulletin van het Rijksmuseum*, no.3 (1987), pp.193–210

Veldman 1991
Ilja M. Veldman, 'Philips Galle: een inventieve prentontwerper', *Oud Holland*, 105, no.4 (1991), pp.262–90

Veldman 1992
Ilja M. Veldman, 'Images of Labor and Diligence in Sixteenth-century Netherlandish Prints: The Work Ethic Rooted in Civic Morality or Protestantism?', *Simiolus*, 21 (1992), pp.227–64

Veldman and de Jonge 1985
Ilja M. Veldman and H.D. de Jonge, 'The Sons of Jacob: The Twelve Patriarchs in Sixteenth-century Netherlandish Prints and Popular Literature', *Simiolus*, 15 (1985), pp.176–93

Voet 1969–72
Leon Voet, *The Golden Compasses: A History and Evaluation of the Printing and Publishing Activities of the Officina Plantiniana* (Amsterdam, 1969–72)

Voet 1973
Leon Voet, *Antwerp – The Golden Age: The Rise and Glory of the Metropolis in the Sixteenth Century* (Antwerp, 1973)

Ward-Jackson 1969
Peter Ward-Jackson, *Some Main Streams and Tributaries in European Ornament from 1500 to 1750* (London, 1969)

Wardle 1981
Patricia Wardle, *Victoria and Albert Museum: Guide to English Embroidery* (London, 1981)

Warncke 1979
Carsten-Peter Warncke, *Die ornamentale Groteske in Deutschland, 1500–1650* (Berlin, 1979)

Waterhouse 1983
Ellis Waterhouse, *Painting in Britain, 1530–1830* (Harmondsworth, 1983)

Waterson and Meadows 1990
Edward Waterson and Peter Meadows, *Lost Houses of York and the North Riding* (Thornton-le-Clay, 1990)

Watt 1994
Tessa Watt, *Cheap Print and Popular Piety, 1550–1640* (Cambridge, 1994)

Wayment 1958
H.G. Wayment, 'The Use of Engravings in the Design of the Renaissance Windows of King's College Chapel, Cambridge', *Burlington Magazine*, C (November 1958), pp.378–88

Wayment 1982
H.G. Wayment, 'The Stained Glass of the Chapel of The Vyne and the Chapel of the Holy Ghost, Basingstoke', *Archaeologia*, CVII (1982), pp.141–52

Wells-Cole 1981
Anthony Wells-Cole, 'The Montacute Bed: A Study in Mannerist Decoration', *Furniture History*, XVII (1981), pp.1–19

Wells-Cole 1983
Anthony Wells-Cole, 'Some Design Sources for the Earl of Leicester's Tapestries and other Contemporary Pieces', *Burlington Magazine*, CXXV (May 1983), pp.284–5

Wells-Cole 1990a
Anthony Wells-Cole, 'Oak Furniture in Norfolk, 1530–1640', *Regional Furniture*, IV (1990), pp.1–41

Wells-Cole 1990b
Anthony Wells-Cole, 'Who was Walter Gedde?', *Furniture History*, XXVI (1990), pp.183–90

Wells-Cole 1990c
Anthony Wells-Cole, 'The Elizabethan Sheldon Tapestry Maps', *Burlington Magazine*, CXXXII (June 1990), pp.392–401

White 1982
Adam White, 'Tudor Classicism', *Architectural Review*, CLXXI (June 1982), pp.52–8

White 1992
Adam White, 'England c.1560–c.1660: A Hundred Years of Continental Influence', *Church Monuments*, VII (1992), pp.34–74

Williams 1988
N.J. Williams, *The Maritime Trade of the East Anglian Ports, 1550–90* (Oxford, 1988)

Wilson 1987
Timothy Wilson, *Ceramic Art of the Italian Renaissance* (London, 1987)

Wingfield Digby 1980
G.F. Wingfield Digby, *Victoria and Albert Museum: The Tapestry Collection: Medieval and Renaissance* (London, 1980)

Wittkower 1984
Rudolf Wittkower, *Palladio and English Palladianism* (London, 1984)

Yates 1975
Frances A. Yates, *The Valois Tapestries* (London, 1975)

Yates 1977
Frances A. Yates, *Astraea: The Imperial Theme in the Sixteenth Century* (Harmondsworth, 1977)

Yates 1984
Frances Yates, 'Print Cultures: The Renaissance', *Ideas and Ideals in the North European Renaissance* (London, 1984)

Yates 1986
Frances A. Yates, *The Rosicrucian Enlightenment* (London, 1986 edn)

Zerner 1969
Henri Zerner, *The School of Fontainebleau: Etchings and Engravings* (London 1969)

Zweite 1980
Armin Zweite, *Marten de Vos als Maler* (Berlin, 1980)

Index of Artists, Printmakers and Publishers

Index of Subjects

General Index

Photograph Credits

Cambridge, The Provost and Scholars of King's College: p.2.

National Monuments Record (RCHME) © Crown Copyright: 1, 2, 9, 10, 13 (Photo: Peter Williams), 20, 65, 77, 81, 87, 89, 93, 140, 142, 143, 158, 172 (Photo: Peter Williams, courtesy of Brian Kingham), 209, 241, 242, 265, 266, 280, 306, 319, 325, 327, 328.

Photo: Anthony Wells-Cole: 7, 27, 36, 45, 49, 54, 55, 58, 60, 63, 68, 69, 76, 80, 82, 84, 94, 96, 97, 99, 119, 121, 122, 178, 206, 209, 212, 243, 244, 247, 248, 251, 278, 279, 282, 284, 285, 288, 289, 326, 331, 333, 335, 336, 337, 340, 341, 343, 358, 361, 364, 365, 367, 369, 371, 417, 443, 444, 445, 448, 450, 454, 456.

By Courtesy of the Board of Trustees of the Victoria and Albert Museum: 5, 111, 127, 129, 138, 183, 379, 394, 414.

By Courtesy of the Board of Trustees of the Victoria and Albert Museum (Photo: Anthony Wells-Cole): 16, 19, 24, 31, 33, 43, 46, 48, 53, 70, 72, 73, 74, 75, 78, 79, 107, 109, 112, 116, 118, 120, 123, 124, 197, 201, 203, 219, 229, 231, 234, 235, 236, 237, 246, 274, 275, 329, 330, 339, 341, 343, 363, 370, 373, 377, 380, 387, 407, 408, 415, 420, 433, 462, 464, 466, 475.

By Courtesy of the Board of Trustees of the Victoria and Albert Museum (on loan to Oxburgh Hall, Norfolk) (Photo: Anthony Wells-Cole): 432.

Courtesy the Royal Library – National Library of Sweden: Maps and Prints Department, De la Gardie Collection: 14, 51, 57, 61, 62, 64, 67, 95, 98, 100, 211, 223, 258, 385, 435, 451.

Country Life: 17, 18, 110, 126, 180, 190, 194, 204, 205, 218, 268, 272, 276, 277.

By permission of the British Library: 21, 26, 29, 191, 193, 215, 216, 217, 264, 382, 397, 421, 422, 425.

Norfolk Museums Service: Strangers Hall Museum, Norwich: 22, 23.

The Conway Library, Courtauld Institute of Art (Fred H. Crossley and Maurice H. Ridgway): 25.

Ronald Lee, photo courtesy of The Antique Collector's Club: 32.

The Marquess of Salisbury: 34, 35.

Bibliothèque Nationale de France, Cabinet des Estampes, Paris: 37, 38.

Reproduced by courtesy of the Trustees of the British Museum: 39, 40, 137, 141, 144, 145, 148, 149, 220, 270, 271, 281, 308, 332, 346, 349, 350, 351, 381, 426, 492.

By Courtesy of the National Portrait Gallery, London: 41, 44.

Warburg Institute, London: 42, 161, 249, 261, 286, 287, 290, 291, 292, 296, 298, 299, 301, 304, 338, 347, 368, 372, 383, 400, 442, 455, 458.

Crown Copyright – reproduced by permission of Historic Scotland: 47.

Museum Boijmans Van Beuningen, Rotterdam: 50, 128, 134, 357, 437, 439.

Photo: John Wright: 52.

Devonshire Collection, Chatsworth. Reproduced by permission of the Chatsworth Settlement Trustees: 56, 378.

© Rijksmuseum-Stichting, Amsterdam: 59, 130, 132, 133, 151, 153, 155, 157, 160, 171, 181, 182, 245, 250, 310, 311, 316, 317, 320, 334, 355, 362, 366, 404, 410, 412, 452, 457, 471, 472, 474, 478, 479, 480, 481, 485, 486, 491, 493.

Stedelijk Prentenkabinet, Antwerp: 83, 101, 102, 165, 168, 174, 176, 177, 226, 240, 323, 324, 483, 484.

Stedelijk Bibliotheek, Leeuwarden: 85, 86, 88, 91, 104, 113, 239.

Photo: A.C. Cooper: 90.

Copyright Bibliothèque Royale Albert Ier, Cabinet des Estampes, Brussels: 92, 139, 173, 262, 283, 359, 389, 390, 391, 392, 402, 403.

British Architectural Library, RIBA, London: 103, 195.

The Royal Collection © 1996 Her Majesty The Queen: 105, 108.

Staatliche Museen zu Berlin, Kunstbibliothek: 106, 117, 374.

Courtauld Institute of Art, London: 115.

The National Trust Photographic Library: 125 (photo Nicolette Hallett), 230 (photo: Robert Truman), 233 (photo: Angelo Hornak), 238, 360

(photo: Andrea von Einsiede), 423, 430, 431, 498.

Courtesy of Claire Gapper: 135, 269.

The Museum of London: 136.

By courtesy of P.J.N. Prideaux-Brune Esq.: 146, 147.

Photo: Florence Morris: 150, 152, 154, 156 (courtesy of Colonel Sir Walter Luttrell), 227, 228, 263.

Photo: Douglas Atfield: 162.

Bristol Museums and Art Gallery: 175.

Photo: Jacolyn Wakeford: 185, 192.

Courtesy of John and Jane Penoyre: 188, 260.

The Metropolitan Museum of Art, New York, all rights reserved: 196, 393.

Skokloster Slott, Sweden: 198.

Sir John Soane's Museum, London: 199.

Oscar Johnson: 200.

Reproduced by permission of the Marquess of Bath, Longleat House, Warminster, Wiltshire, Great Britain (Photo: Courtauld Institute of Art): 202, 208.

Photo: John Crook: 210.

Private Collection, photograph Courtauld Institute of Art: 225.

Photo: Robert Thrift: 252, 416, 424, 427 429, 434, 436, 438, 440, 441, 453, 459, 460, 461, 463, 465, 468, 469, 477, 482, 487, 494, 497.

Devon Record Office, Exeter: 253, 254, 255, 256, 257, 259.

Koninklijke Bibliotheek, The Hague: 283, 359.

Graphische Sammlung Albertina, Vienna: 293, 428, 467, 495, 496.

Photo: Richard Littlewood: 294, 295, 297, 300, 302.

Courtesy of Beamish, The North of England Open Air Museum: 305, 307, 309.

Courtesy of the Chaytor Family: 312, 313.

Private Collections: p.vi, 314, 315, 376.